THE PHILOSOPHY OF MORALS & VALUES

Nicola

Nicola

THE PHILOSOPHY OF MORALS & VALUES

Library of Congress Number: 00-193222
ISBN #: Hardcover 0-7388-5441-7
Softcover 0-7388-5442-5

This book was printed in the United States of America.

To order additional copies of this book, contact:
Xlibris Corporation
1-888-7-XLIBRIS
www.Xlibris.com
Orders@Xlibris.com

Dedication

This Book is Dedicated
To
Amy Lynne David Pamela & Beth
My Children
and
Their Children
and
Their Children's Children
ad
Infinitum

Contents For

The Philosophy of Morals & Values

Acknowledgements

Introduction to The Philosophy of Morals and Values

BOOK I. DEFINING PHILOSOPHY: It is a history of man struggling by living philosophically, then his introduction to the myths of gods, and the conflict with philosophy.

BOOK II. METAPHYSICS: We begin with Mythical creation, and the scientific reality of creation. Then we learn of the individual nature of existence.

BOOK III. EPISTEMOLOGY: Here we learn to find the truth in the real world and how our perceptions are motivations to think.

BOOK IV. MORALS: Ethics is dead. The self-evident necessity of the Moral Code, in principle, is Natural Law.

BOOK V. VALUES: The theory of values, the meaning of life, and our own hierarchy of values, become socioeconomic responsibilities for our happiness. We may pursue any value providing we do not infringe upon the lives o thers.

BOOK VI. GOVERNMENT: We have here the history of government from the primitive to the despotism of ruling classes in theocratic, socialistic, and democratic politics. Introducing Promoteanism and the end to the 'party' of party politics – if we are brace enough to live truly free.

BOOK VII. AESTHETICS: There is a conflict between art and aesthetics and how they may not sense the 'sport' of it all.

ACKNOWLEDGEMENTS

The bibliography lists about 95 books that I used for reference, in this work. To all the authors and publishers, who granted me permission to use their material, I thank them all. There are some that I leaned on heavily, quoting much, and other authors, though using few words, were precious. 'I could not have said it better.' The following is to give special thanks to those I quoted a great deal, and whether listed first or last, they are equally important, in this work.

"World Religions" (1984), edited by Geoffery Parrinder, first copyrighted in 1971 is still on the book market. It is an excellent source of the mythology that created religions. I used the book for reference throughout and quoted much of the creation myths in my Book II, Metaphysics. Thanks to The Octopus Publishing Group, Limited, and their division Hamlyn Books, London, England for graciously granting me permission to reprint.

Another informative book I enjoyed as a reference is "The Columbia History of the World." (1988) Edited by John Garraty, and Peter Gay. Each time I picked it up, it spurred my imagination, much like a video documentary it is so well written. I owe thanks to Harper Collins Publishers, Inc.

One of the first books that I purchased about primitives was, "Primitive Societies" (1947), by Robert Lowie, Ph. D. an ethnologist. This is a fascinating account of primitive cultures, their laws, traditions, and clues to their philosophy. Thank you, Liveright Publishing, Corporation.

The novelist and philosopher, Ayn Rand, in her Objectivist movement helped many to put philosophy in perspective. Her writing, is the pen of reason, best recognized for her theory of concepts, in defining, identifying and teaching to find meaning—to go beyond the emotional, subjective, or our perceptions—to think and be objective.

In 1966 she published the "Ayn Rand Introduction to Objectivist Epistemology" which I used as reference in Book III, Epistemology.

"Egypt Before the Pharaohs", (1979 + 1990) by Michael Hoffman, an excellent work that gives life to pre-historic Egypt. Archaeology has devoted much of his attention to the historic Egypt of the pharaohs and pyramid era, 5100 BP to 2000 BP (BP or B.P. Before Present). Hoffman takes us back into pre-pharaoh times, about which there have been many misconceptions as man was first taught religious rule. With a lively text, giving one a feel for a dig, the science, historic substance, and over 400 references, it is a gold mine of the pre-historic tending period. I thank the copyright holder, Alfred A. Knopf, and Random House Inc. and for England, Routledge Publishing, for granting permission to reprint their material.

Special thanks go to my children for their support, and those who had to listen to me expound, on morals and values, when they were growing up. Thanks to my typist, Janet Fonseca, who skillfully deciphered my original hand written manuscript, including many revisions.

Books of all kinds cannot be written without the help of other authors, who labor in solitude and thought, with pencil or pen, typewriter, or word processor. Whether or not they reach conclusions contrary to ours in their analysis, is not the issue. Their knowledge and experience, right or wrong, good or bad set in type, gives us our differing frames of reference, even if it is just 'to know thy enemy.' It is why we don't burn books. They are our thoughtful authors who supply us with food for reason, and in their works earn a measure of immortality, which we cannot deny.

Nicola 2000

INTRODUCTION

It was a long hot summer when Marjorie and Mike strolled through the grass along the hedgerow. It was a repeat of the spring and summer ritual of "taking off" away from her house and people to be together, alone.

It was a time to talk about things, of hopes and dreams. There was a search for shared values the surprise they felt the same way about things. There was also the chemistry of being together, close, the holding of hands, the feel of each other's bodies as they encircled each other's waists, the trembling as they drew together, snuggling as tightly as possible. Each evening they grew closer and more intimate in words and touch until this great need, they knew would have to be acknowledged and satisfied. This evening as they sat together, eyes glazed in awe of each other they knew that the time had come.

"We're not married, you know", she said softly.

He replied, "I know".

She said, "I could get pregnant."

He responded, "I won't get you pregnant." He fiddled around in the grass between her bare thighs, pulled up a blade of grass, then he took her hand and tied the blade of grass around her finger and he said, "You know the words, say them with me."

Together they went on "with this ring I thee wed . . . For richer for poorer in sickness and in health . . . for better or for worse . . . I love you . . ." and there in the tall grasses of the hedgerow the world stopped . . . and in a little while started up again.

She got pregnant.

To the more 'sophisticated' today, this is not a moral question of whether it is right or wrong. It is just a case of human love and they are committing themselves in the consummation of that love. In some areas of the world, she would be ostracized or probably punished physically in some way. It would be appalling in some cultures if she were promised to someone else.

We should not conclude that, 'it is just a case of love' and let it go at that. Nor should we take the view that two people do not have the right to make their own decisions. Neither should they be ostracized nor be 'owned' by another. In this case however, there may be some nagging questions.

To begin, we may ask, 'just how old are these two?' Are they 40 years old, 30, 22, 16, or thirteen? The question begs the question "is this couple responsible?" In some tribes existing today, thirteen might be a responsible age but not in the rest of the world. A case may be made for the 16, 22, 30, or 40 year olds, the key question here as well "do they fully know and understand the consequences of their commitment?" Are they capable and do they fully understand the responsibility that may be the result of their action? Were they taught anything about such responsibilities? What can we say about their commitment? Is this piece of grass and the few words said in passion a valid commitment?

Are these questions for philosophy? Yes. But we would be hard pressed to find a philosopher who has any definitive answers to the questions, or problems we raised. The thesis of this book 'Morals & Values are subjects of Books IV & V that will give us an understanding of the two lovers and provide the answers we all search for in what is right or wrong, and what is good or bad.

This is a book about our lives, our natural environment and human nature that philosophy may answer in the sciences or branches ahead. If we ask a philosopher a question, he may straddle the issue, by giving us a couple of answers recommending none. The problem is yours . . . you decide? Many have been doing this for so long that no one takes them seriously. The average person has little or no knowledge of what philosophy is all about. There have been attempts to bring the science of philosophy to the general reader but they are too few and incomplete. This book will give general readers a general view of philosophy's sciences. When you have read this book you may discover your own philosophy.

Twentieth century philosophers have all but disappeared from everyday life. There are no discourses to help increase man's knowledge, understanding or comment on the joy of reality. They give no direction through modern man's progress and the problems of crime, drugs, racism, war, fluorocarbons, space flight, or of love, family and children. Some universities are planning to do away with philosophy departments' altogether and many are reducing staffs. Most philosophers are out of touch with the real world having no words of wisdom on such things as earth cooling of the 70's or the global warming of the 90's. They are in search of some ultimate truth, which everyone knows is impossible. Philosophers have assigned themselves an academic task, in which people will expect no progress and the philosopher diddles in semantics, of theories about the theoretical and do not seem to address social reality. They seem to convey that there is no truth.

There will be *no* lessons or exercises in logic, syllogisms, math or semantics, but only a few philosophical terms (definitions will be given) not commonly used. We will have discourse about current human needs. We may gain wisdom and a philosophy, perhaps with an understanding of religion's conflict with philosophical thought. The climax or outcome of this experience will take us through an intellectual solution into the mystery or meaning of life in MORALS, VALUES, and GOVERNMENT.

What philosophers forgot is that man is asking for their best assessment or comprehension of reality today, now, in our lifetime. Man is not asking for an omniscient god. Man wants a flesh and blood being who studies reality and understands the principles of how we may live in the material universe. This is the function of the philosopher. It is his or her work. The product produced should be some meaningful answers to the many problems human beings confront in the real world every day.

Greek societies, around 2600 BP, differed from oppressive Egyptian and Mid Eastern religious cultures. The Greeks had little interest in the afterlife. Their gods were celebrated in political festivals but in their private lives they were free to pursue success and happiness.

They were unencumbered by any religious dogma to rule every thought. Greek gods had basic human traits such as strength, beauty, love, courage, and weaknesses.

The Greeks properly identified their gods as mythical beings created by the imagination trying to teach a lesson or moral in a fable. It is understood how in such a culture as in Greece, conscious philosophical thought would emerge. Philosophy (love of wisdom) became at that time a worldly, materialistic thought process. They understood the imaginary mythical nature of the gods, but asked the simple question, "how do we live, the good life, as the primitive existed in the natural world before the invention of the gods? How do we modernize primitive motivations and family life, naturally?" These are the basic questions reasonable people have been asking of philosophers.

In the beginning of this introduction we raised a few questions about the lovers. However, many questions not only need a rather comprehensive answer but convincing, reasoned evidence that show the answer to be the truth. The purpose here is to show us how to find answers for the many questions that plague us. The way we learn the truth is not to find it or discover it some day, but, to observe, read, learn, think and analyze, then make informed reasoned decisions. Below are some of the questions we may be looking for answers to:

Such as, what is the nature of the universe?
What is man's place in the universe?
What should be the nature of government—man versus the state.
How should we vote?
What is 'Individualism' and 'Collectivism?'
What is art and aesthetics?
What is the nature of man's mind—mind over matter?
Do we have innate knowledge, primordial, inherited or
intellect from the gods? Natural gifted ability?
What is moral?—What is right or wrong?
What is virtue and what is evil?

What is the difference between, 'Ideas & Thinking' vs 'Faith & Mysticism?'
Does fate or free will rule our lives?
What are values? What is good and bad?
How do we know what to do in every situation?
What is the meaning of life?
What is it like to have complete freedom?

Until this book there have been five branches of study in philosophy and in this book there will be *six* sciences. The *five* previous branches or sciences (Rand) were, 1., Metaphysics (the nature of existence), 2., Epistemology (the nature of learning), 3., 'Ethics' (the nature of human behavior), 4., Politics (the nature of government), and 5., Aesthetics (the nature of art).

It will become evident that, 3.,)'ethics,' is not a science and is replaced by, 3., Morals (the nature of right and wrong), and 4., Values (the nature of good and bad). Number 5., becomes Government (the nature of governance), and 6., Aesthetics. Morals, Values and Promotean Governance are my contributions to philosophy. Therefore, as you noted in this book's contents, there are seven books, The first, DEFINING PHILOSOPHY, BOOK I, will define philosophy and religious mythology. The following *six* books are philosophy's sciences, METAPHYSICS, EPISTEMOLOGY, MORALS, VALUES, GOVERNMENT, and AESTHETICS.

Defining Philosophy; This book was written so that one may understand the full 'essence' of philosophical thought. Can its basic, real, and invariable nature be explained in a short paragraph, a small sentence, a phrase, or just one word? Was the genetic birth of mankind the birth of a philosophical mammal? Was the birth of philosophy introduced by the first philosophers beginning with Thales of Melitus? Is philosophy religious? In this book we will take a trip in time through human evolution and answer the question "was primitive man philosophical?" We define 'primitive' man existing before 10,000 BP. Thereafter; the primitive was introduced to religious practices, which has spawned huge savage sects, the wars among the hundreds of religions in the world and their conflict with philosophy and peace.

Metaphysics; is the study of the nature of existence, that which is animate and inanimate, i.e. all of that which exists, the material universe. We contrast, 'in the beginning' creation mythology from around the world, with the scientific struggle by scientists on earth to study, experiment and formulate theories to understand our universe, and to answer, 'how did it all really begin?' It is a search for all that is knowable by using our senses and the reasoning process of our mind. It is the study of reality the nature of the universe, its phenomena, all living (organic) things and man's place in nature. As you can see, this is a large area in the study of man. We have in the inanimate area, astronomy, astrophysics, geophysics, geology, meteorology, biology or livingthings.

Metaphysics is the study of the whole material universe, part of which we are made of. Organically, we have biology, physiology, botany, anthropology, paleontology, ethnology, ethnology, ethnography and many more. The philosopher must perceive reality, as such, and endeavors to identify, interpret, and give understanding to the essence of existence. It is another trip through time, the birth and evolution of the universe, and man's struggle to understand existence. We will discover metaphysically, the true essence of existence for human beings, and about our autonomous nature.

Epistemology: is the study of knowledge, how we learn and/or substantiate (prove) that something is true. It is the science of awareness, how we learn: to perceive, reason, and conceptualize. It is an analysis of the nature of the human mind. Where does knowledge come from, how do we learn, or do our senses control what we learn? Does knowledge have to have any basis of fact in reality? What is belief, opinion, ideas, possibility, truth, or certainty? Philosophy, could make its presence felt in society, to be the guiding light of reason, instead it is silent. We learn everything because nature made us equal in that respect. Learning seems to be a child's work and teaching the parent's, but to be aware, is to learn every day of our lives.

'Ethics' *was* the fourth branch of philosophy, the study of social and personal behavior, the goal was that both could be combined in synergistic absolutes (Synergism; joint action, combined cooperation) (Absolute; in this context, right, fully perfect code of 'moral values'). There was never any clear distinction between morals and values, and no absolute rule or principle to combine both is possible. 'Ethics' is dead. Ethical history and the reasons for its demise are covered in BOOK IV, "Morals," and "VALUES," in BOOK V, is its funeral.

Morals; is the study of behavior of human beings as they interact. In every social encounter between friends, lovers, husbands and wives, business and working associates, rulers and countries, or any government and its people, the relationship is subject to moral question. Infringement on the rights of human nature, individualism and man's culture is immoral. The chapter on morals explores the concept of non-infringement in moral behavior and much more. Justification for moral principles in The Moral Code is scientifically proven, or justified by sensual, historical experience and is fact.

Values; is the study of those things in life man seeks for himself. Value, is a relative term that depends on we as individuals, to set a priority on each value in our special hierarchy of values. In values we will explore the full range of values from birth, career, love, and happiness. Although people may make what appears to the overseer subjective choices, are in fact for the person who understands his needs, objective. It is values that give meaning to life, and in its science we may find the experience rewarding and the foundation for our own philosophy and hierarchy of values.

Government; is the study of governance, the law, how man organizes the society in which he lives. It is the means by which he can assure his pursuit of happiness. Philosophy must guide man through the quick sands of theocracy and socialism that inevitably turn out to become totalitarian regimes. Communism is like Anarchy with an absence of a governing body, except that the former is collective in interests, and the latter a society of individual interests. Democratic people believe government should take the role of providing for the economic needs of its citizens. The people in this field are political scientists, politicians, statesmen, socialistic engineers, bureaucrats, the judiciary, lawyers and many others who play a part in the governing of our society. The chapter on 'Morals' will be the foundation upon which all governments will inevitably be founded. A new theory of government is outlined in this book, putting an end to political party ideology. Fact: we will have to control people's moral behavior, but in his pursuit of values man must be free of constraint.

Aesthetics is the study of art and is the last branch of philosophy though many think it should be the first. To create an image of man, his nature, courage and accomplishments, and the future of mankind, aesthetics should represent new goals and foretell the efficacy of human life. The artist is the leader, the example of the ideal, an illustration of beauty, strength, health, love, passion, the proponent of success, and encouragement, through his art. He leads us to what is and should be the right and good in a human's sense of life. To do this the artist becomes an aesthete. But there is controversy on both sides of the artist and the aesthete to be explored, and you will know what to look for to find meaning in art.

The Conflict between religion and philosophy: Most are familiar with the age-old conflict between philosophy and religion. To their discredit both have borrowed each other's concepts. Religions have attempted to borrow the term philosophy to give it 'intellectual' credence and many in philosophy have borrowed ethical altruism as a 'moral' concept. Their opposing views are examined as they apply throughout this book to highlight their glaring differences.

Philosophy came into formal intellectual thought to expressly examine, analyze, learn, reason and explore the world around us and to define human needs and our nature—anything that can be sensed. Theologian's religious concepts are pure abstractions—in the imagination only. There is no sensual basis in reality to identify an imaginary god. A person cannot sense to analyze examine, learn, reason, and explore the deity or its domain. One can only deny his senses and imagine Where the theologian teaches about an unreal spirituality the philosopher deals in material reality. Theologian write and speak of the imagination, myth, dogma, supra "unnatural" beings, or a grownup's imaginary friend. Philosophy deals with scientific reality and how to survive on a real planet, for that is all we can know.

The philosopher attempts to analyze the physical universe, those theories that may have been proven true, and conceptualize to replicate scientific discovery or contemporary invention into survival behavior for our species. The philosophers who argue for some kind of agnosticism have lost their sense of reason as philosophers, and are in reality theologians. There can be no such term, theological philosophy, which is an obvious contradiction. The conflict between religion and philosophy is between the unreal versus the real. In religion, where there is no metaphysics there is no reality, where there is no epistemology there can be no reason, only the word of someone else's fancy in which people have faith. They are opposites both physically and mentally, religion is spiritual not of the senses with no basis for debate in sensual reality, Philosophy is that which can be sensed, the only means by which we can survive. In the books ahead we shall explore both in the context of the sciences or branches of philosophy, i.e., metaphysics, epistemology, morals, values, government, and aesthetics.

It has been established from numerous sources that before 6,000 BP many people were accustomed to burying their dead with memorabilia, those things that they were associated with in life. There was also the respect of friends and relatives who owed the deceased a favor or something, to repay, or donate a token in his memory. 'Egyptian religion can be traced back, in its prehistoric origins to as early as 6,000 BP, when the careful burial of bulls, jackals, and other beasts indicates animal worship.' [53] There is a very strong possibility that it was 'pet devotion.' It was about the time animals were being and were fascinated with the perception of animal devotion with an association from birth that would cause it to be loyal, and have love for its keeper. They buried their pets, much the same as we do. We may experience some animals as being mysterious, such as cats, not in a spiritual sense, but as night prowlers, with cunning we respect or admire.

Pets were revered, loved, and occupied the tombs of the elite but an animal could never compete with the shaman as a god. Pets may compete for evil demon status. Only the witch doctor could be the good demon, or a god. If we understand anything about religious intentions, then we know the pharaoh, king, or pope would never share power with an animal. There was never any animal worship except in the role of demons. The gargoyles, half animal and human figures and the grotesque in ancient tombs, modern temples, churches, and artifacts are meant to be symbols of people's own demonic evil.

Today anthropology placed man's realization of human fertility about 5,000 BP. It is without question man did not know how a child was conceived before that time. In the interest of probability, one might say some realization was occurring between 9,000 and 5,000 BP when strides were being made in understanding seeds and animal husbandry. It was not until 5,000 BP when male deities, who now understood their role in the birthing process, forcefully assigned his role as the most important controlling factor in creation of his kind. His kind, the male head of a family (or a pharaoh) meant his blood, from his wife—they were his children. From 5,000 BP to the present, a woman was relegated (by religious tenets) as the property and possession of the male.

If there had been no religious intervention into people's lives by myth perhaps the light of reason may have prevailed. We may have seen equality in marriage, joint parental responsibility, and the separation of cultural institutions from governance. This was evident during the male and female side by, side, period of rule, sometime before 6,000 BP. It ended with man's realization of his fertility less than 6,000 BP which he turned into a religious advantage for male domination, and allowed his culture to be ruled by the whims of a pharaoh.

What had been maternal lines of inheritance then became paternal, and male children were valued increasingly more than females. Males were to inherit the estate or kingdom, leaving the female ownership of some chattel property, and in some cases perhaps the home, usually not land.

Male dominance meant that his son(s) would inherit the throne of the 'god-king' or pharaoh. The dilemma of male a blood lineage inheritance was that if the god king had no sons it would go to his daughter. This was bad for a pharaoh's ego, since it would break the lineage or, hopelessly dilute the male line, thus ending his blood lineage, and family reign, knowing it was his only claim for immortality. The pharaoh had convinced all that he was a god's representative, godly, and related to the gods through his blood.

To keep the kingship purely paternal and lasting eternally, it was crucial to have boys. The clever strategy, in this issue, was to grant the same rights of inheritance, as a pharaoh had, to the man over his family, thus eliminating any power women had. This would assure support from men to perpetuate the pharaoh's reign and his ruling elite, and men ignobly in practice agreed. But rules of incest applied to the common man, but never, to royalty who wanted to retain means, to guarantee the purity of royal blood, and if the blood lineage were a healthy one with obvious longevity in the family intermarriage would guarantee a lasting dynasty. The pharaoh forbade the common man of falling in love with his family his greater first love would be for gods or the state.

When the pharaoh Menes (5100 BP) conquered all of Egypt the organizing principle was kinship. Their alliances were through marriages. It was the cement that guaranteed family inheritance and created a power elite. By Mene's time, the witch doctors had created a huge mortuary cult. During these times, pharaohs and the elite would devise a code of ethics for their followers—its principle altruism (self-sacrifice) would prevent its people from rebelling against any sacrifice demanded by the elite.

As the Nile valley flooded and receded during the period 9,000 BP to 6,000 BP, groups of people of 25 to 50 settled in areas that produced more and more food as the agricultural technology improved. It is suggested, that since the witch doctors were conning their way to wealth, others would also want to do likewise. Small groups were vulnerable to attacks by marauding tribes.

Raiding obviously motivated the creation of a system of defense. In most cases, the heads of families were the leaders and responsible for defense of the tribe. In many cases, a clan of two or three families headed by brothers or a brother-in-law shared the leadership.

'The village of Omari—yielded remains of more than 100 circular and oval huts.' This area was first occupied around 6,000 BP, and was still occupied in Archaic times (5100-4700 BP). 'The small size of Omari houses and their distinctive separation from one another and the degree to which economic activities were self-contained within ones own yard, suggest a pattern of residence that revolved about the small, nuclear family (father, mother, and offspring). It reflected the basically equalitarian way of life of Predynastic lower Egyptians that set them apart from their more political and status-oriented neighbors to the south.'[54]

Such people as in Omari lived, for more than a thousand years, and 'passed their lives in small towns of domed huts, tended their fields of wheat and barley and bred sheep, goats, cattle, and pigs—in short, lived a life but little changed from that of their predecessors—.' 'Through the centuries these changes that did occur were

RUSS

gradual—almost imperceptible—as new ideas about wealth, power, and the afterlife slowly filtered into their society'.[55]

Systems of defense had to be created for the villages. The leader(s) set the rules and goals of the tribe. In larger tribes, it may have been a council of the heads of families. The largest family (clan) may hold the leadership. In the council, the strongest, bravest, most respected hunter or defender might lead or have had the most influence. This is where the defense was planned, rules formulated, and disputes handled.

However, the chiefs or council members may have found that the shaman, through their wealth and influence, among the people, had become a significant power for the council members to consider. Any tribal leader, who made a new proposal, perhaps felt it prudent to consult with the witch doctor who had a measure of control over peoples minds and behavior. Relationships between the tribal leadership and witch doctor were as varied as there were tribes. It became common, as time went on, that these tribes were ruled by the shared power of both the witch doctor and the leader or chief. As the witch doctor's wealth increased, he needed protection to guarantee the safety of himself and his wealth. If a tribal leader were prone to raiding smaller tribes, for any reason, it would be with the help of the witch doctor, who could deliver the people's support.

Witch doctors did not work alone and needed cohorts. They chose trainees, who may be abnormal, physically (epileptic etc.), socially dysfunctional, or a loner. Far from the tribe, the experienced witch doctor taught the trainee the incantations, 'magic', healing, and the psychology of the trade. He then gave the new shaman sustenance to get started, and the trainee was indebted to his benefactor for life. A person that may lack economic will or responsibility and favors a homosociety, say of men, to join a brotherhood where he will be supported for life, and where his loyalty will lie.

The roots of religion spread and grew from a witch doctor's will to survive at all costs. Since failure was the rule in their 'medicine', then death would be the key to credibility, and the burial would be its vehicle. Memories, dreams and a great sense of loss psychologically needs at least a perception of survival—even if it is just in the imagination. The burial or 'heaven' demonstrates a resemblance of survival for the living. The natural attributes of memory—'seeing' in the mind and 'seeing' in the dreams enabled the witch doctor to create a counterfeit imagining of survival in that what one dreamed etc., was real, that a person's soul existed. The burial transferred the person's personality or soul (mind), to the gods. When the person died, only then did good things happen to him, and he would have eternal life—be immortal.

As tribes invaded and occupied areas new alliances were made for the common defense, witch doctors would introduce their common practices, i.e. the same beliefs in witch doctoring. A large area of villages then would, in effect, begin to be influenced in that version of witchcraft, or by force if necessary.

With this new type of leadership, a combined group of the tribal defenders or the chief's council became the henchmen for the witch doctor who controlled the tribe's wealth. They were paid well for their services, as well as the craftsmen who created 'artifacts' (works of art) coined by Hoffman as 'Powerfacts', which gave the pharaoh prestige, and power. Huge tombs or mastabas were built in which the king would attempt to take his art, possessions and entire fortune with him, to his grave. Henchmen were dispersed throughout the kingdom as systems of gathering wealth were perfected. Collection, storage, and devotion to the pharaoh and the sun god created a strong centralized organization to control people's lives, work and production.

The tombs of the first pharaohs at Abydlos in Egypt were separated from the commoners, contained massive quantities of grave offerings and contained evidence of human sacrifice. Sati was a practice of pharaohs, in early dynasties, whereby his retainers (henchmen) and family, at the time of his internment, in the tomb, would be buried alive with him. It would be their way to thank the gods for the good life their pharaoh gave them, their code of altruism in practice.

Hoffman writes 'To date the most reliable analogies of the

evidence for sati in the royal tombs of Abydos was presented by George Andrew Reisner in 1936, in his definitive book, "The Development of the Tomb Down to the Ascension of Cheops." ' Hoffman, '. . . he systematically evaluated analyzed and critically evaluated the evidence for sati on a tomb by tomb basis." . . . 'The following excerpt, taken from his account of the burial pits of Kerma in Lower Nubia, reads like an archaeological version of Edger Allan Poe:' [56]

> "The location and various attitudes of the bodies show that they must have entered the grave alive on their own feet and taken their positions as they could find place . . . the movements exhibited are largely those of emotion at the prospect of death by burial under earth. The most common thing was for the person to bury the face in the hands. It was also not unusual for one hand to be over the face and the other pressed between the thighs. But most of the better preserved graves presented a case or two of unusual attitudes. In K XX, three bodies have one arm passed around the breast clasping the back of the neck from the opposite side . . . In K X B, the very well preserved body AC has the head bent down into the crook of the elbows in a manner most enlightening as an indication of her state of mind at the moment of being covered. . . . . 'In K 444, the two bodies, G and H, lie with their foreheads pressed against each other as if for comfort. In K 1026, body B has the fingers of the right hand clenched in the strands of the head circlet . . . Another most instructive example is body B in K 1047, a woman lying at the foot of the grave and under a hide; she has turned slightly on her back with the right hand against the right leg and clutches the thorax with the left hand as if in agony. But it is unnecessary to multiply these gruesome evidences any further. No one of normal mentality who will read the detailed evidence in the descriptions will escape the

> conviction that these extra bodies are the remains of persons who died in the places where we found their bones, and who had been in fact buried alive. [57]

The early Pharaohs, or the Archaic Kings, built burial tombs of unusual size and wealth. They contained huge quantities of luxury items, food and evidence of human sacrifice. To quote Hoffman, 'although a tempting comparison the evidence supporting Sati (human sacrifice, Egypt.) in Archaic Egypt is not nearly as clear cut as that from Sumeria and China.' [58] Human sacrifice occurred in public rituals by the thousands in many religions including the Mayas, Aztecs, Sumeria, and in China.

Of course, sacrifice, as a principle, in the extreme, could not work. The most important value, life, is not easily given up. Most people were rounded up and forced to be buried alive or be summarily killed. His retainers were the most vulnerable to the pharaoh's wishes. They would be the first to be sacrificed, to show their gratitude for the good life he had given them, by demonstrating the supreme sacrifice for their gods. Their reluctance, refusal, or avoidance of such ritual was thought would weaken the religion. If only the 'pure innocents' had been sacrificed, they may begin to question their faith. Hoffman, 'Such practices seem to be most typical of early emerging states such as Archaic Egypt, early Dynastic Sumer, and Shang China, but quickly disappear when the elite realize that it is consuming its most useful and skilled henchmen.' [59] The new pharaoh needed the more experienced people to help maintain his empire. But also like incest, their principle of altruism, self-sacrifice very quickly would not apply to the ruling elite.

Egyptian tombs were plundered by ancient robbers some inept scientists, or religious fanatics. Despite that, only a fraction of burials, in general, were unearthed from these distant times (7,000 to 5,100 BP). We can extrapolate from the evidence that it was substantial. Some sites have uncovered 50 to 400 victims and we've uncovered only a small portion of the victims. Human sacrifice was a practice that seems to have become a custom as religious rulers experimented with the limits of power. Sati (human sacrifice) to join the pharaoh on his ride through the sky did not last but a few thousand years in Egypt. By 4,700 BP, the experiment in Egypt ended with the Pharaoh Khasokhemvi and the Second Dynasty.The ultimate test of their code, altruism, under all conditions failed, and as for religious benevolence, it was not of life and happiness, but of death, slavery, and deprivation for the common folk.

Life, was not the only sacrifice the people were to bear, to quote Hoffman. 'Enough was left in the 40 chambers of Ka'a's tomb to indicate that separate rooms were reserved for different types of offerings, for example, wine storage, jars, ivory, grain, oxen, meat and so on. 'The variety of food, drink, weapons tools, furniture, containers, ornaments, and games stored originally in the tombs must have been vast so that it is a small wonder that tomb robbery flourished even at this early date.' [60] Hoffman is being too kind when he calls looting people of their wealth, 'offerings,' it was forced labor and outright confiscation of peoples earnings.

Djer had his Queen interred with him as well as some of his retainers were sacrificed and: 'also from the tomb of Djer came an attractive pin of gold alloy, surmounted by a round head. Small ivory labels were found in most of the tombs and were usually incised with the king's name and provided with a hole for fastening to objects to indicate ownership. Fragments of thousands of finely made stone vases and bowls of alabaster, marble, diorite, slate, schist, breccia, volcanic ash, gray limestone, and even rock crystal attest to the high development of the stonecutter's art and the demand for his products among the prestige conscious ruling elite.

'Even after being despoiled on a number of separate occasions, the tomb of Khasekhemui yielded enough wealth to hint at the vast drain on technology and productivity that the construction and stocking of a royal tomb involved:—a scepter of sard and gold, gold bracelets, copper bowls and ewers, numerous model tools of copper including drill bits and adzes and elegant small white marble vases tightly sealed with golden lids. In all the tombs, Petrie found fragments of finely carved and inlaid wood and ivory artifacts, including bull's-hoof furniture legs and ivory, ebony and horn tubes decorated in favorite geometric designs.' [61]

In Egypt and Mesopotamia between 9,000 and 5,000 BP, the combination of successes in agriculture and animal husbandry created larger villages and towns. Each village, archeologists have found, had central groceries, which is an indication that food was put in control of the 'leaders' and they dispensed the food by whatever rules they had concocted. The witch doctor controlled the food, i.e. the wealth. 'We do not know how far increasing centralization of wealth and power by late pre-dynastic times (ca. 3300-3100 BC) had restricted the protein intake of the average farmer. But this factor had probably become a serious problem by Archaic times (ca. 3100-2700 BC), with the solidification of formal, social and economic classes.' [62]

The farmer's production of food was confiscated and doled out to the people in subsistence quantities. The pharaohs were starving their people, and creating poverty, which is not very different than every country has since governed, creating poverty by taxation.

Fifty one hundred years ago, the formed social 'aristocrats were being buried in bigger tombs and taking as much wealth with them to their graves, were doubtless helping themselves to more and more of the herds and other valuable possessions of their subjects'. [63] Egypt had organized all tribes into two large religious territories, southern and northern or the upper Nile (south) and lower Nile (north). Menes, The Pharaoh King of the lower Nile family, in the first major religious war, conquered the upper Nile. All of Egypt fell under one huge religious sect, increasing the pilfering and excesses of religious power over a huge population.

Menes controlled all wealth and the culture. Grains and goods were kept in granaries, silos, or in locked rooms stored and kept by the pharaoh's henchmen. He owned the land, animals and the people were his flock. That's how the witch doctors and priests became known as the 'father.' He was the head of this huge 'family', and owned them all. It has become the foundation of rule for all theocracies and later the grand design for secular socialism.

RUSS

As the quantities of goods and trade increased, so did methods of keeping track of them, which led to hieroglyphics, numbers, calendars and geometry to help in the building of the pyramids. The Pharaoh now owned all including the tribal chiefs. He was the commander-in-chief and all his efforts were concentrated on maintaining the illusions that be was a god, god-like or chosen by a god to rule over his people. He also had to work at convincing people he had the power of a god. King Djoser about 4,700 BP directed architect Imhotep to build the largest step pyramid tomb ever erected by man, at Saqqara. This began the Pyramid Age.

Pyramids were designed and built using primitive geometry by using a set, square, with the sides of a triangle made of 3, 4, and 5 units. With methods and materials, and the technology available it was impossible to erect a vertical wall straight up for any more than a couple of stories. The stepped or angle wall was their only means of building high structures. The higher the pyramid, the larger the base. However, 2,000 years after, methods were in common use to build vertical high walls, the Egyptians were still using the step pyramid with angled walls. The pyramid was for the Pharaoh, the ultimate 'powerfact.'

L. Sprague de Camp, in his book "The Ancient Engineers", states in all seriousness, 'the pyramids and other Egyptian monuments were not as is often thought built by hordes of slaves.' Then citing other sources, says, 'that 100,000 men working twenty years—two million men—years of labor—is much exaggerated.' But then admits, that to build the great pyramids, the barracks of the builder, his staff, responsible for construction, housed 4,000 men. 'In addition the pharaoh conscripted tens of thousands of peasants to help with the heavy work during the season of the annual flooding of the Nile when the farmer would otherwise have been idle. It was forced labor but the laborers were conscripts, not slaves? [64]

de Camp, on pyramid 'forced labor', 'They were probably paid in food, because money did not exist.' This meant that this poor peasant worked during the growing season to produce the food then was forced to work again for the king in order to earn back a subsistence allowance of food he produced during the growing season! This is not slavery? 'With this exception such slaves as existed (The Egyptians elite kept slaves—captives of the conquering armies) were mostly the house servants of the rich men and officials.' [65] It is obvious that forcing the farmer to work on the pyramids, to suffer whipping and excruciating pain, the slaves were better off than the pharaoh's subjects. Philosophically, its common sense, we just know better, the dictionary tells us a slave is a person who is the property of and wholly subject to another. They were not free men and women to be conscripted. They were slave laborers all of their lives, on the farm and on the tombs in principle and fact.

de Camp, again—On the other hand, forced labor was common. It was the standard method of building roads, canals, temples, and other public works, because tax-gathering machinery was not yet effective enough to make the hiring of voluntary workers practical.' [66] It may be true that they could not begin pyramid building without an efficient taxing system. But, they had one. Evidence shows they had complete inventory of all animals and harvested crops (in the central granaries) as well as anything else of value. They could not persuade a 'voluntary worker' for the low food sustenance allowance. It was not a voluntary choice but slavery ('forced labor,' to quote de Camp).

de Camp, ever loyal to the pharaoh, thinks the 'forced workers' who are not slaves organized themselves in gangs willingly, and loved to work for the Pharaoh. 'They were organized with such heartening names as "Vigorous Gang" and "Enduring Gang".' [67] DeCamp completely misses the irony men can display in what they may call themselves, that can have double meanings. Such names and graffiti were plastered over much of these inner tombs of death. Most of the tombs and pyramids were broken into and its wealth reclaimed likely by the same people who worked on those 'vigorous' and 'enduring' gangs. In some of these tombs, in which they spent years building, they would know precisely how to get in and out with all the time needed to create a plan. The 'heartening' aspect of these capers perhaps was, they were intelligent enough to understand they were being conned, and in effect went along with the charade, while pulling off the ultimate sting and raided the tombs.

What happened to people as they embraced a god? The agricultural payoff primitives sought so hard to achieve was now firmly in control of a Pharaoh. The primitive did not own what he produced, it belonged to the Pharaoh and an invisible god. Sacrifice became the moral ideal. Man's lot was to suffer, reject his natural ambition to profit, and give his sweat and blood for a god. All the wealth he produced was immoral to keep for him self. Man owed that bounty to a god or the pharaoh to build monuments to something no one knew existed. This happened about 7,000 years ago, and most people still, have not caught on to the deception.

In late 1992 or early 1993 the body of a twenty year old female buried near one of the pyramids was discovered. Workers who succumbed during the building of the pyramids, to save time, were buried in the desert near the work site. The skeletal remains showed that the bones of her vertebra were worn down considerably, probably from pulling huge stone blocks over the desert, with her shoulders. This meant that every disc in her vertebra had herniated, and pressed against the column of nerves, grinding down the bones all along her spine. As any neurologist could tell you, this resulted in excruciating pain, when her first disc herniated to the day of her death, then was buried where she died, likely without ritual or recognition.

That story is tragic, and anyone of compassion, must consider the cruelty imposed on these poor people, to satisfy the whim of a pharaoh. But, the real horror of this story is that when the anthropologist at the site, was explaining to the observers, the condition of the crushed vertebra, she gushed, "Isn't it wonderful how these people sacrificed themselves for their pharaoh!" There was no indignation in this woman towards such a ruler who would be so cruel and elitist to enslave his subjects with selfish disregard for human life and freedom. Would this woman surrender her freedom to a totalitarian king?

CHAPTER 8

The Secret Medical Texts

"A History of the Sciences," by Stephen F. Mason is a valuable book with emphasis on historical scientific progress, while reporting on a period's philosophical intellect or theological mythology, chronologically from early Egyptian times. In Babylonia and Egypt, 8,000 to 6,000 BP, he says, 'Whilst the Mesopotamians excelled in the field of astronomy, perhaps because of their preoccupation with astrology, the Egyptians were the more able in the field of medicine.' [68]

Mason is scientific, yet refers to Egyptian with doctors as 'Physicians)' or their secret pseudo-potions as 'medicine.' However, his choice of words does not detract from the truth of what he says:

> '...Egyptian medical papyri go back to 2,000 BC and contain earlier material of the time of Imhotep who was physician and vizer to King Zoser 2980 BC' . . . 'In the medical texts of both the Egyptian and later Mesopotamians the 'demon' theory of disease was prevalent. The illness itself was personified as an evil spirit, which the physician sought to expel from the patient by use of emetics (agents to induce vomiting) and purges or revolting medicines to put the demons to flight.' [69]

Such was the state, the high point, of the art of 'medicine' in Egyptian times. Without any detail, they were vaguely referring to diseases in their texts. After 2600 BP, please note, 'later texts are more magical in character' [70] In the 27th century BP, the Sumerian's unusual lead glaze process was a secret skill.

The reason for secrecy was that most medical 'cures' were frauds, but in their 'treatments' were perceived by the people to be of great knowledge unknown to the common man. Real knowledge such as the lead glaze secret could not be kept from the craft traditions, because it worked and was no longer theoretical, but could be proven by anyone. Much of craft knowledge was passed on orally, such as surgery, which at that time was a separate craft from the pharaoh's 'medicine.'

Egyptian witch doctors and pharaohs had little contact with craft professions, including embalmers. About 1100 BP. The clerical and craftsmen were in conflict at the time. 'The priestly scribes came to depend more and more upon the written word of their predecessors, valuing their texts more highly the older they were.' [71] Yet theology's unscientific strategy survives today. Their secret medical texts, Talmeds, Korans or bibles of theology were their prescriptions for healing or to explain existence, to be kept secret, but never read by the flock, only to be interpreted by a god's shaman. Crafts gave birth to science, reason, logic, and philosophical thought, but they soon became the enemies of theology.

From the beginning of organized rule, secrecy in leadership and the privileged gave them power a sense of mystery, the miraculous and 'their real truth' was kept by the gods. They created the emotional perception that they knew more. The priestly scribes have all since relied on old texts. There are no new texts in religion. Any new works are re-assertions, or new revelations of old ideology. Tradition is encouraged in the written word, in behavior, and in life in general. It is an overt attempt to discourage learning, or search for truth or new ideas, i.e. not to use one's reasoning process. Such a mentality was even more pronounced and evident in the Americas. Following tradition or old knowledge orally, among the tribes, so arrested their progress so that they were two to four thousand years behind the rest of the world in 1492.

In the Old World, there was a greater population and more people likely to 'go against tradition.' There were the Greeks who gave rise to thinking in philosophical terms and became secular in conflict with theology. So fertile was the mind that unlocked the mystery of fertility, that there continued outside the temples of religion a thirst for knowledge, invention, and exploring.

The Pharaohs and priests found that people may not sacrifice life for death, but, could be persuaded to sacrifice living for just a mere existence. As all religions tested the endurance and the length to which they could impose suffering, they found the limits of their power and the limit to which man would sacrifice his wealth.

Cooperation to the primitive was sharing together, the burden of scavenging, foraging, and hunting. Since the clan was a family, mother, father, sisters, brothers, and the elderly it was important to impress on everyone not only to share the work, but also to share the fruits of the labor. This is as a family should be. It has nothing to do with communism, socialism or theocratic sacrifices, but it was loving the people they valued most. United, they would survive, but divided, that would destroy their family, and happiness. Together, there was a measure of safety and a better chance of survival, and happiness, that is still true today.

The male head of a primitive family may have done the most work and defended his clan, but, he slaved willingly for the love of his mate, and a measure of pride with those offspring who were contributing more and more as they grew. However, it was with he and his mate consistent training and reminding the children that a successful family shares everything—work or what is earned, and knowledge. If each member of the family treats everyone else with respect, love and intelligence, then there is a good chance the clan will survive. If people lacked respect, love, and sharing of knowledge, their clan may not survive.

The witch doctor, in order to survive, by charity or 'sharing,' or forcibly confiscating all of man's wealth, expanded the family concept of unity, into a concept to include all. He gave birth to the concept of 'altruism' (self-sacrifice is the unselfish concern for others) for anyone or anything the witch doctor could dream up, especially for himself and his gods. It was sinful (immoral) to need or desire, to want or to possess something, to have ego or self esteem, to be selfish or have pride, to be naked or enjoy the sexual, and man was to reject materialism, his only source of survival.

By a god's principle of altruism, man was no longer sharing with family or one he valued most, but with anyone. It became the community, the village, the town, and especially the huge bureaucracies of government, and religion, all of which was now a man's obligation. The gods superseded the family, sex was evil, the body was a source of shame, the child was born with sin, and our souls corrupt or lost. Proportionate to the amount of suffering and self-sacrifice, became the amount of reward man would earn in heaven. It became the perfect secret scam. The priest, minister, guru, witch doctor, or shaman, never have to keep their promises of rewards from the gods or of heaven's existence, but, man must keep his word, with real material sacrifice—his nature, mind, and wealth. Later, secular politicians adopted those ideas, to worship the state.

This book is an attempt to define our human history in terms of our primitive philosophy. We have inherited a profound legacy out there in the heart of Africa during the Pliocene and Pleistocene epochs. By the time our primate ancestors reached human status 5,000,000 BP, humans were being born in love and care of two parents. From little "Lucy" to the "foot prints' in the ashes of time, we know there was meaning to life, survival, and experiencing human interaction with a realistic view towards nature intellectually.

What this former nomad, fisherman, hunter and trusting ancestor could not understand, including ourselves, is that those who have the most eloquent proposal for us, do not have our well being at heart, but only to control our minds and wealth. The more beautiful the story, the uglier the truth. Our trusting minds cannot understand that people like our selves could be savages. Yet these savages will still cheat, defraud, con, coerce, foster guilt, create war, kill, take people's wealth by the force of the state or god's law, and our allowing it to happen, is savage within itself. The savage was perhaps, created in the tending period. Whatever philosophy he had for 5,000,000 years was gone. He was no longer an individual but part of a huge unnatural collective. The books ahead build a case for a secular society and to defend philosophy.

The philosopher's work is to tell us how to live in our time to teach the truth of things to help make our life here on earth a most pleasant time. From the beginning of our genetic birth to the present, to his credit only the primitive has been philosophically correct, because only he and his clan faced the reality of nature individually, and succeeded. We can, without reservation, give our thanks to "HIM," "THE PRIMITIVE," for creating mankind, US! We will learn how it has played out historically, and how it should conclude ultimately.

BIBLIOGRAPHY: DEFINING PHILOSOPHY

Chapter 1
Ref.
No.

1. "The Random House Dictionary of the English Language" Second Edition Unabridged, New York, NY, 1987: Definition, "philosophy" 1.
2. Binswanger, H. Editor: "The Ayn Rand Lexicon" Publisher, NAL Books, The New American Library, New York, NY 1986: P. 359
3. Leakey, Richard; "The Origin of Humankind" Publisher, Basic Books, Div. of Harper Collins/Publishers, New York, NY, 1994.
4. Dart, Raymond A.; "The Missing Link," Publisher, Time Life Books New York, NY, 1972: (Paraphrased), Pages, 14, 15.
5. Lampton, Christopher; "New Theories on the Origins of the Human Race," Publisher, Franklin Watts Publishers, New York, NY, 1989: Pages, 71-72.
6. IBID, Page, 82.
7. IBID, Pages, 82, 84, 85, (paraphrased).

Chapter 2

8. Lambert, David; "Field Guide to Early Man," Facts on File, Publications, New York, NY, 1987: Pg. 82.
9. IBID, Pg. 70.
10. IBID, Pg. 7.
11. Morgan, Elaine; "The Descent of Women," Stein and Day, Publishers, New York, NY, 1972: Chapter, 'The Ape Remolded.'
12. Lampton, Christopher; "New Theories of Origins of the Human Race," Publisher, Franklin Watts Publishers, New York, NY: 1989: Pages, 114, 115.
13. IBID, Pages, 114, 115.
14. IBID, Pages. 116, 117.
15. IBID, Pages. 116, 117.
16. Leakey, Mary; "Disclosing the Past," Pub. By, Dell Bantam Doubleday, New York, NY, 1984: Page, 184.

Chapter 3

17. Morgan, Elaine; "The Descent of Women," Stein and Day, Publishers, New York, NY, 1972: (Paraphrased).
18. IBID, (paraphrased) 'The Ape Remolded' P. 34—5.
19. IBID, (paraphrased) 'The Ape Remolded' P. 34—55.
20. IBID, (paraphrased) Chapter, 'Aggression,' P. 56—72.

Chapter 4

21. Furneau, Rupert; "Primitive Peoples," David and Charles, Publishers, Devon, England, 1975: Pages. 133, 134.

Chapter 5

22. Ardrey, Robert; "The Hunting Hypothesis," Simon & Schuster, Inc., New York, NY, 1976: Page, 162.
23. IBID, Pages, 162—165.

24. Garraty, John A., and Gay, Peter, editors; "The Columbia history of the World," Harper Collins, Publishers, Inc., New York, NY, 1988: Pg. 45.
25. Ardrey, Robert; "The Hunting Hypothesis," Simon & Schuster, Inc., New York, NY, 1976: Page, 165.
26. Bronowski, Jacob; "The ascent of Man," Little, Brown and Company, Boston, 1974: Page, 54.
27. IBID, Page, 54.
28. IBID, Pages, 54, 56.
29. IBID, Page, 55.

Chapter 6

30. Definition: "wealth" in PHILOSOPHICAL terms is defined as any amount of food, money and things of value that may be used to procure food, in excess of what is needed for subsistence. Anything earned beyond the minimum need to sustain physical life is wealth.

In southern primitive times it was food in *excess* of what was needed on a daily basis for survival. In northern regions that have cold seasons, it would be whatever was in *excess* of food, clothing, and shelter needed for subsistence. Those are wealth values for all organic beings. Life values beyond survival needs if earned is wealth for one's sense of well being on earth, and morally belong to individuals for happiness.

31. Furneau, Rupert; "Primitive Peoples," David and Charles Publishers, Devon, England, 1975: Pg. 48.
32. Issac, Glynn; "Olorgasaile," The University of Chicago Press, Chicaago, ILL. 1977: Pg. 93.
33. Parrinder, Geoffrey Editor; "World Religions," Facts on File Publications, New York, NY, 1984. Copyright holder Octopus Publishing Group Ltd. Hamlyn Books London: Introduction, Page, 13,
34. Hoffman, Michael; "Egypt Before the Pharaohs," Marboro Books, Books, Corp. Dorset Press, New York, NY, 1990,—Copyright

holder, Random House, Inc. NY,—For England Routledge Publishers, London: P. 80, (parentheses mine).

35. IBID, P. 82.
36. IBID, P. 83.
37. IBID, P. 87.
38. IBID, P. 88.
39. Desmond, Kevin; "A Timetable of Inventions and Discoveries," M. Evans & Company, New York, NY, 1986: Pages in chronological order, 22,000 to 7,350 BC.
40. IBID, P. 2400 BC.
41. Stone, Merlin; "When God Was A Woman," Marboro Books, Corp., Dorset Press, New York, NY, 1990: Page, 13.
42. IBID, Page, 3.
43. Chagnon, Napoleon A.; "Yanomamo," 'The Fierce People' second edition, Holt Rinehart & Winston, Inc., New York, NY, 1977: P. 24.
44. Harner, Michael J.; "Jivaro; People of the Waterfalls," Anchor Books/Doubleday, Garden City, New York, 1973: P. 117.

Chapter 7

45. Stone, Merlin; "When God Was A Woman," Marboro Books, Corporation, Dorset Press, New York, NY, 1990: P. 12.
46. Ardrey, Robert; "The Hunting Hypothesis," Simon and Schuster, Inc., New York, NY, 1976: P. 163.
47. Bronowski, Jacob; "The Ascent of Man," Little, Brown & Company, Boston, MA. 1974: Page, 42.
48. Braidwood, Robert; "Prehistoric Men," Scott, Foresman and Company, Glenview, Illinois, 1967: P. 93.
49. James, Edwin Oliver, author; Parrinder, Geoffrey Editor; "World Religions," Facts on File

Publications, New York, NY, 1984. Copyright holder Octopus Publishing Group, Ltd. Hamlyn Books, London: Prehistoric Religion, Page, 23.

50. Lowie, Robert; "Primitive Society," Liveright Publishing, Corporation, New York, NY, 1947: Page, 244.
51. Furneau, Rupert; "Primitive Peoples," David & Charles Publishers, Devon, England, 1975: Page, 24.
52. Hoffman, Michael A.; "Egypt Before the Pharaohs," Marboro Books, Dorset Press, New York, NY, 1990, Copyright holder Random House, Inc., NY; For England, Routledge Publishers, London: Page, 111—113.
53. Griffiths, J. Gwyn, author: Parrinder, Geoffrey Editor; "World Religions," Facts on File Publications, New York, NY, 1984, Copyright holder Octopus Publishing Group, Ltd. Hamlyn Books, London: Ancient Egypt, Page, 137.
54. Hoffman, Michael A.; "Egypt Before the Pharaohs," Marboro Books, Dorset Press, New York, NY, 1990, Copyright holder, Random House, Inc., NY; For England, Routledge Publishers, London: Pages, 194, 195.
55. IBID, P. 200.
56. IBID, P. 277.
57. Reisner, Ph.D., George A.; "Harvard African Studies," Vol. V 'Excavations at Kerma,' Parts I-III, Harvard University Press, Cambridge, MA, 1923: P. 70, 71.
58. Hoffman, Michael A.; "Egypt Before the Pharaohs," Marboro Books, Dorset Press, New York, NY, 1990, Copyright holder, Random House, Inc., NY; For England, Routledge Publishers, London: Page, 277.
59. IBID, Page, 261.
60. IBID, P. 272.
61. IBID, P. 274.
62. IBID, P. 152, (Emphasis mine).
63. IBID, P. 152.
64. de Camp, L. Sprague: "The Ancient Engineers," Ballantine Books, New York, NY, 1988: Pages, 32, 33.
65. IBID, P. 32, 33.
66. IBID, P. 32.

67. IBID, P. 33.

Chapter 8

68. Mason, Stephen F.; "A History of the Sciences," Collier Books, Macmillan Publishing Company, New York, NY, 1962, Copyright holder, Simon & Schuster, Inc., NY: P. 21.
69. IBID, P. 22. (Parenthesis mine).
70. IBID, P. 22.
71. IBID, P. 24.

BOOK II

METAPYSICS

CONTENTS

FOR

METAPHYSICS

Chapter:
1. Creation Mythology 101
2. The Big Bang Theory 115
3. The Magna Cosmos: A Theory 121
4. Geological & Biological Earth 123
5.The Natural Law of Snowflakes 128
6. The Environment 135
7. The Re-Emergence of Philosophy 138
Bibliography 152

CHAPTER 1

Creation Mythology

Metaphysics, is derived from the Greek word *meta*, meaning to go "beyond" or "over" physics. It also is referred to as, "after" physics, the latter term from the Gr. *physiko*, "pertaining to nature" or "physical nature." Aristotle never referred to 'metaphysics,' but a classification of his works by Andronicus of Rhodes at around 2070 BP, was a compilation of his works dealing with the study of nature and natural phenomenon and was given the title 'The Metaphysics.' In the order he compiled Aristotle's manuscripts, called it, what is sometimes referred to as the 'first' philosophy. He was the first philosopher to study nature, such as botany, animals, and taught the methods for scientific inquiry, which became the foundation for science and many of his principles of inquiry are valid today.

Peter A. Angeles, "The Dictionary of Philosophy" defines metaphysics with many variations. But the most appropriate is Angeles' first definition. '1. Metaphysics is the attempt to present a comprehensive, coherent, and consistent account (picture, view) of *reality* (what exists, beings, the universe) as a whole.' [1] Metaphysics is the study of the real world its focus is reality and proven science. The opposite is true for theology they deal in the spiritual, nonexistence, and have faith in their mythology, for which there is no evidence to empirically prove what they believe.

We begin with creation mythology, fictional characters and stories that were handed down until someone lied and said it was a true story. And after many generations being told it was true, people began to accept or had faith in whatever a storyteller told them.

In Metaphysics we will explore our nature, to learn of the past, and find out what happened, "In the Beginning," or if there ever was a beginning and if there, indeed, will ever be an end. To explore the nature of the universe, the solar system, and earth, is to discern the reality of our natural roots. Only then may we fathom the natural world, our own nature as living organisms, and how we should exist. We shall look beyond to learn how to live together in nature, and govern our actions. It is in the nature of our being, our biology and how we learn. What lies 'beyond' that knowledge will become our philosophy.

'In the beginning'—What created the universe? How did it get here? What caused it? How did life begin? Do we know how it will end? Yet, what do our senses tell us? Is the universe is its own creator? We want to know the truth—or do we?

We will begin with some religious accounts of creation lore or what Lloyd M. Graham calls 'kindergarten cosmology.' If we think some of the following is perverted creationism then we must in that light examine our own beliefs. Then we may logically and reasonably accept the truth that *men* create our myths and its spirituality. The term 'theology' is derived from the word 'theory' which ancient intellectual compilers understood was the speculative study of 'divine theories.'

The following myths came from the spirit of men's creativity, for pagan ritual or to deceive, and by no stretch of the imagination can they be defined as real, metaphysical, or called a philosophy.

YANOMAMO Mythology: Creation in the Amazon—In the beginning, the cosmos, earth was formed in four layers 'like inverted platters.' The top layer is no longer inhabited but some things had their origins there in the past such as 'an old woman,' so-called as an abandoned garden or a barren female, a layer with no function. And the next layer, called (hedu), provides the home for souls departed. The spirits of men garden, make witchcraft, hunt, eat, and do everything living people do. Everything on earth is repeated like a mirror on hedu. The underside of this layer is all the sky we can see. And celestial beings are up there and move across it. Man dwells below this level which is a vast jungle, sprinkled with Yanomamo villages.

And the people were created with the earth and there were those that hunted, fished, created plants and objects. 'One of the first beings was called Boreawa, who first had plantains and many other crops and one by one, taken over by others. Another was Iwa, who kept fire in his mouth, and only when they made him laugh did a bird steal it from him and everyone then had fire to cook their meats and insects. Haya and his wife, who hunted together, lived among the first beings and eventually turned into deer.'

'The daughter of Raharariyoma went to fetch water,' and was taken by Omauwa and Yoawa who copulated with her, quenching their desire for sex. 'Omauwa caused her vagina to become a mouth with teeth'. 'Howashiriwa,' another first being, hungry for sex, seduced Raharariyoma, 'and lost his penis; her vagina having bit it off.' Then Omauwa's son became thirsty and began digging a water hole and water gushed out causing a great flood and some of the first beings cut down trees and floated away on logs. Because this was a strange thing to do, they also changed into foreigners speaking in strange tongues. 'This is why foreigners have canoes and cannot be understood.'

The Yanomamo climbed the mountain to escape the flood and the foreigners became their enemies. 'After the flood, there were few very original beings left.' Peri—boriwa (spirit of the Moon), 'had the habit of flying down to earth to eat the soul parts of children,' usually, 'between two slices of cassava bread.' Uhudima and Suhirina became angry. Uhudima tried to shoot him down with arrows many times. 'People say he was a very poor shot.' Then with one arrow, Suhirina shot at Periboriwa and hit him so that his blood spilled on to earth. 'The blood changed into men as it hit the earth, causing a large population to be born.' Most Yanomamo are blood descendants of Perboriwa.

The soul of a Yanomamo is his "will" or "self" (bubii) which goes to hedu, the second layer where departed spirits may hunt, fish and live just as they did on earth. The spirit (soul) travels up and reaches a fork in the trail where the son of Thunder, Wadawadariwa, asks the soul if it had been generous or stingy during its life on earth. 'If it had been stingy, Wadawadariwa directs it on the path to where souls of the stingy Yanomamo burn eternally.' Author N. Chagnon, in questioning these people on this point, found that they just planned to lie to Wadawadaiwa and avoid going to hell (shobariuaka). They had no fear and were convinced they would never be sent there. 'They expect that the Wadawadariwa would send them on to hedu proper.' [2]

The Yanomamo live in a tri country area of Venezuela, Colombia, and Brazil. Note, that there is no supranatural, all knowing, being. They felt assured Wadawadariwa would *not* know they were lying and everyone would go to 'heaven' (hedu proper). They also send malevolent demons against each other and preoccupy themselves with defending themselves from evil spirits. It is interesting that in this story, their 'Heaven' had to be identical to life on earth. It has been suggested that it is a typical myth created by men since Yanomamo men have an easier time, because women do most of the work.

ABORIGINES Mythology: Creation in Australasia—At first 'the earth was uncreated, a bare plain,' without hills, or valleys, trees, or animals and no humans. It then came to pass, 'in the mythical past or the Eternal Dreamtime' that many gods or spirits or 'totemic ancestors emerged from their sleep under the surface of the plain' and gave them form. 'Where they emerged' there came to be sacred features of landscape, rolling hills, of clear pools, 'watering holes, and caves.'

'The supernatural beings were linked with particular animals and plants and so a rainbow snake usually moved about in human form but could, at will, change back into a rainbow snake.' From him, 'the rainbow snakes of his original district are believed to have descended, as well as human beings conceived in that district, which were regarded as reincarnations of this ancestor and of his supernatural children.'

A totem is a representation of an animal from which a clan or tribe believes it is descended from. 'After the process of creation, the supernatural beings either returned to earth or into sacred rocks and trees and went back to eternal sleep.' 'They retained power to send rain, produce plants or animals of their own totems when summoned by the magic rites which human forms recited the secret verses that they themselves sang during the creation process.'[3] (Brown)

ASIAN Mythology: Creation in Asia—Central Asian pastoral tribes such as the Altaians, Tatars, Borjat, and Yakuts, conform to a general pattern. Their sky is, 'referred to as "Sky" but occasionally also as Creator.' Most of the myths of Central Asia and even in Siberia relate how 'in the beginning the world was filled by an immense ocean and how the Sky God obtained, by various means, a small lump of earth from the bottom of that ocean, and out of this created the entire earth which was soon to be inhabited by people and animals:'

'This New World was divided 'into three spheres; 'the upper world or sky, the middle world or the earth and the underworld or hell.' The spheres are divided in numerous divisions such as the skyworld which is, 'subdivided into either seven or nine separate layers. Their supreme being or 'sky', 'is credited with qualities of unlimited authority, creative power, wisdom bordering on omniscience and benevolence.' This celestial god also has an adversary representing evil and darkness, which he keeps from dominating the world. 'According to some myths, 'this adversary succeeds in leading people astray and bringing about a fall similar to that of Adam and Eve.'

The shaman in Asian religion is the great specialist in human souls. 'He acts as healer of the soul; the soul can forsake the body even while the person is alive and while straying,' fall 'prey to demons and sorcerers.' In such case, 'the shaman diagnoses the trouble, goes in search of the patients fugitive soul, captures it, and makes it return to the body' ' . . . for he alone sees a soul.'

'The ecstatic state is considered the religious experience par excellence, and the shaman is the great master of ecstasy.' He can be like the fiery evangelist, control the spirits by dance and song, and strike into the hearts the fear to drive you to a god. 'While the shaman is in a state of ecstasy, his or her own soul can safely abandon the body, roam through distant regions and rise to the sky or penetrate the underworld. The ascent to the sky is enacted in elaborate rites, which include the climbing of a ladder or a pole.' + (Furer-Haimendorf)

JUDEAN Mythology: Creation in Genesis–'In the beginning, God created the heaven and earth. The earth was without form and void and darkness was upon the face of the deep; and the spirit of God was moving over the face of the waters.

'And God said "let there be light." God saw that the light was good; and God separated the light from the darkness. God called the light day and the darkness night. And there was evening and there was morning one day.'

'And God said; "let there be a firmament in the midst of the waters from the waters . . ."

'And God said "let the water under heavens be gathered together into one place, and let the dry land appear.'. .Then God said, "let us make man in our image, after our likeness and let them have dominions over the fish of the sea and over the birds of the air and over every creeping thing that creeps upon the earth . . ."

" . . . And the Lord God planted a garden in Eden, in the east; and there put man whom he had formed. And out of the ground the Lord God made to grow every tree that is pleasant to the sight and good for food, the tree of life in the midst of the garden, and the tree of knowledge of good and evil." . . . And the Lord God commanded man saying "You may freely eat of every tree of the garden, but of the tree of knowledge of good and evil you "shall not eat, for the day that you eat of it you shall die." . . . but for man there was not found a helper fit for him. So the Lord God caused a deep sleep to fall upon the man, and while he slept took one of his ribs and closed up its place with flesh; and the rib which the Lord God had taken from the man he made into a woman and brought her to the man.'

' . . . Therefore a man leaves his mother and father and to his wife and they become one flesh. And the man and his wife were both naked and were not ashamed.'

'And now the serpent was more subtle than any other wild creature that the Lord God had made. He said to the woman 'Did God say, 'you shall eat of any tree of the garden?" And the woman said to the serpent, "We may eat of the fruit of the trees of the garden, but god said, "You shall not eat of the tree in the midst of the garden neither shall you touch it lest you die." But the serpent said to the woman, "you will not die, for God knows that when you eat of it your eyes will be opened and you will be like God, knowing good from evil." So when the woman saw that the tree was good for food, and that it was a delight to the eyes, and the tree was to be desired to make one wise, she took of its fruit and ate; and she also gave some to her husband, and he ate. Then the eyes of both were open and they knew they were naked; and they sewed fig leaves together and made themselves aprons.'

'And they heard the sound of Lord God walking in the gardens . . . the man and his wife hid them selves . . . But the Lord God called . . . Where are you . . . and he said, "I heard the sound of thee in the garden, and I was afraid because I was naked; and I hid myself." He said, "Who told you that you were naked? Have you eaten of the tree of which I commanded you not to eat?" The man said, "The woman whom thou gavest to be with me, she gave me fruit of the tree and I ate." Then the Lord God said to the woman, "What is this that you have done?" The woman said, "The serpent beguiled me, and I ate." The Lord God said to the serpent:'

'Because you have done this cursed are you above all cattle and above all wild animals; upon your belly you shall go, and dust you shall eat all the days of your life." . . . the woman he said, "I will greatly multiply your pain in childbearing; in pain you shall bring forth children, yet your desire shall be for your husband, and he shall *rule* over you." And then to Adam he said "Because you have listened to the voice of your wife, and have eaten of the tree of which I commanded you. 'You shall not eat of it' cursed is the ground because of you; in toil you shall eat of it all the days of your life; thorns and thistles it shall bring forth to you; and you shall eat the plants of field. In the sweat of your face you shall eat bread till you return to the ground for out of it you were taken; you are dust, and to dust you shall return . . ." 'Then the lord God said, "Behold, the man has become one of us, knowing good and evil; . . . '(Bible)

This is Jewish mythology written in 2,400 BP, by writers mythically explaining creation. Every religion adopted ideologies where men were superior to women. If Adam were to go back to the Garden of Eden, he in effect would have to give up knowledge, not eat from the tree of life, and therefore, be mindless, never knowing he existed or was a male or female. However, with no brain, Eve would again be 'beguiled,' not knowing right from wrong, and Adam too, again and again. Was this god fair because they had no knowledge, could not remember, or was ignorant? It is also evident the god they created was not intelligent, but created a man and woman without a mind, so does man follow this example? Will man go to heaven where the tree of knowledge is guarded, and to know nothing about anything, and be unaware? Or, why would a god make billions of people suffer on earth for one mistake made by two ignorant people, Adam and Eve? Is this fair?—Justice?—Benevolent?—Tolerant?—An eye for an eye or an apple for an apple–punish a universe for the mistake of two people??

Creation of Mythology: The New Testament–'The Church, and

Christianity, were all the creation of the Calpurnius Piso family, who were Roman aristocrats. The New Testament and all the characters in it—Jesus, all the Josephs, all the Marys, all the disciples, apostles, Paul and John the Baptist—are all fictional. The Pisos created the story and the characters; they tied the story into a specific time and place in history; and they connected it with some peripheral actual people, such as the Herods, Gamaliel, the Roman procurators, etc. But Jesus and everyone involved with him were created (that is, fictional!) characters.'

In Abelard Reuchlin's "The Authorship of the New Testament," his researched account tells of the fictional authors and their story. In the middle of the first century, Roman aristocracy became concerned with the growing problem of a huge population of Jews living in Italy—over 10% and 20% east of Rome. The religion was growing, creating more proselytes. More than half the Jews lived outside Palestine, marrying, producing converts all over the Roman Empire. But what worried the elite was that the Hebrew ethics and morality were in contradiction to Roman institution of slavery. This was a confrontation to the aristocracy's means of surviving, lifestyle and the way they ruled and controlled the empire. (Reuchlin)

The Romans feared that the Jewish religion would spread through the empire. Religious zealots, who preferred to be governed by the Romans, were in revolt. Something had to be done. Gaius Lucius Culparnius Piso, Seneca's friend and leader of the family, was married to the great granddaughter of Herod the Great. They found the solution in the Jewish holy books, a Jewish Messiah—a New Testament—maybe a rendering of what is Caesar's.

The plot was to pacify the Jews with this new book. The first version of the Gospel of Mark (Ur Marcus), upon encouragement by Seneca, was then written by Piso who was assisted by his wife's relative, Persius the Poet.

Nero, for reasons of his wife's Jewish stance, opposed the idea—foiled a plot for his assassination by Piso and friends, then had Piso, Seneca and friends forced into suicide. Exiled by Nero, Piso's son Arius Calpurnius Piso, was sent to Syria as governor, where he provoked the Jewish revolt in 66 C.E. so he could destroy the temple in Jerusalem. They would not accept his father's story of Mark. He was stopped in the Pass of Beth Horon. (Reuchlin,)

In 70 Piso again attempted to assault the temple in Jerusalem, 'burned it, slaughtered many thousands, sent thousands more into slavery and gladiatorial combat and death.'

'Then, Arius Calpurnius Piso wrote, in sequence, the following:

Gospel of Matthew	70-75 C.E.
Gospel of Mark (the original was lost)	75-80 C.E.
Gospel of Luke (with help of Pliny the younger)	85-90 C.E.'
	(Reuchlin)

The Jewish people did not accept the story. They understood its purpose, the creation of their Messiah, and they refused to join the religion. They reject it to this day. However, the Pisos continued to write and start sects or cults, where they could in the Mid East and Roman Empire. You may wonder why a great Jewish event such as the 'Messiah' or 'Savior' happening, to the Jewish people, never established a following where it was supposed to have occurred. Certainly descendants would have learned of such things, when at least some portion of the Jewish populace would have embraced a 'Messiah,' now you know. Jews did not accept the fiction, because it was a Roman invention, and remains established in Rome where its mythology was created. There are no historical records of such a happening in Palestine.

'The principle authors of the New Testament were Arius Calpurnius Piso (Josephus); his son, Fabius Justus; his granddaughter's husband, Pliny the younger, and his son, Julius.'

"THE CHURCH FATHERS. Between 100 and 105 AD, additional Christian books were already being written—by the same authors who were finishing the New Testament itself. Julius wrote an epistle as Clement of Rome. Pliny wrote a number of epistles as St. Ignatius. Proculus wrote one as Saint Ploycarp." By these writings, the authors were installing themselves in their own time, as legitimate successors of the apostles Peter and Paul who had supposedly written their accounts in the middle of the past century. This facade entitled them, as they now went among their new believers, to be the legitimate propagandizers and interpreters of the Christian writings."

"THE SEPTUAGINT. Father, too, was busy. Piso was rewriting the Greek Septuagint. In his gospels he had strengthened his story by misquoting places from the Hebrew Scriptures. He changed language in Septuagint to make it conform with the New Testament misquotes. That way, there would be an alleged 'correct' translation of the Hebrew Scriptures with which the New Testament quotations agreed." (Reuchlin)

"THE APOCRYPHA. Piso wished to create a strong foundation on which to place the new faith. So between 100 and 115 AD, he recreated the story of the '400 lost years' of Jewish history. He did this by also writing most of the 14 books of the Apocrypha, including Esdras, I Maccabees, Judith, Tobit, Bel and the Dragon. By making Jewish history brave and glorious, the empire's peoples would more readily accept it as their own history and become the new Israel." [5]

Obviously, the Jews (especially their leaders) knew, and 2000 years later are still convinced that the 'Christ' is an Italian invention much like their own mythical 'Moses' in Egypt, and their tall tales of 40 year wanderings in Arab deserts. But to show credibility for the slavery question we must take a reasoned approach mentioned above. We know from experience, that the bible is full of contradictions that we will not pursue, except for one at this point.

In the "Old Testament" Exodus: 21, we find their ruling principles for justice, such as in 21: 23 the rule of "an eye for an eye," is an old reference to reciprocity as being justified. In the "New Testament" Matthew 5:38, "You have heard it said, 'An eye for an eye and a tooth for a tooth.' 5:39, But I say unto you. Do not resist one who is evil. But if anyone strikes you on the cheek, turn to him the other also." But this rule is morally unjust, cruel and unusual punishment for a victim and a *slave* mentality.

The Italian's meaning of slave was to become a member of a family. That is, 'family' means 'slave' in Latin. Also, when the

Romans took people against their will to serve them, and to assuage their servitude to the master, he addressed them as a family member, one of his slaves. And so the state did also, for those who were in state employ also called them slaves. We can replicate this to mean, Christian rule was to forgive the transgressions of the ruling elite against the slaves, as their god commands. It was a means to control the slave, justified by the word of a slave's 'new' god. That is, to forgive us our trespasses as we forgive those who trespass against us. Therefore, the god of Israel who gave the commandments, and the other rules (Exodus 20. to 21) such as he gave Moses to follow on Mt. Sinai, is a much different mythical god than the mythic Christian god. Therefore, the Italian's Jesus cannot be the Jew's Messiah, making Italy's Messiah mythology an inept creation.

When they put the bible together, the old and New Testament do not think they were not aware of its contradictions. What they had was a document that they could argue both sides of any issue, implying righteousness. They never intended to let the flock read or interpret the bible. When they did, it just confused them, and rather than think or reason which they never had to in the past, they left it up to the kings, popes, priests and ministers to define their gods. Gods did not create mankind, only mankind can create gods.

OUT OF AFRICA: It is ironic that out of Africa would *not* come a religious 'truth' that man was created in Africa. We are *all* descendants of an African heritage. We are bleached blacks, born on the savanna five million years ago which *is by far* THE GREATEST STORY EVER TOLD. It is not just a story or myth fixed in content, but historical reality being revealed to us by scientists searching for the answers to our existence—to know where we came from is to foretell where we're going. Every day and every year, there is continued search, research, digging and dredging to unearth a more glorious past than anyone can imagine, shedding new light on the truth of our lives today, or to forecast future possibilities.

Out of Africa came many lovely stories of savage understanding of the world around us. They are myths of the imagination, told by pagan elders to children, and adults, about how we came to be, around the communal fire. As metaphors they were good. Later, the new story teller, shaman or witch doctor who was learning how to control man's mind and wealth, never told them it was a myth or a metaphor, but that he was all-knowing, and speaking the truth. See Jan Knappert in the bibliography "African Mythology," Ref. Nos. 6, and 7. We can easily detect influences of Hebrew and Egyptian religions in their creation myths.

Much of Africa is frozen in time, with little in the way of modern evolution in scientific progress, i.e. to live and prosper in the real world. Knappert is justly enamored with African culture, but, as an anthropologist he observes, 'We cannot create a new philosophy of life for Africans. Much of the good faith has been overgrown by sorcery and witchcraft in the last 100 years, precisely because the old true religions crumbled. Good gave way to evil.' [8]

Monks and priests wrote down thinking no one would ever disprove material existence was created by their god. With such a stupendous idea, one would invent greater and more plausible myths concerning this supragod. According to them, (based on a priestly account of Bishop Ussher), creation of heaven and earth, and man was, carried out by the Trinity on the 26th of October, 4004 BC, at 9 o'clock in the morning. In addition, most suspect the following written by Lloyd M. Graham in his work "Deceptions and Myths of the Bible."

> 'The Bible is not, "the word of God", but stolen from pagan sources. Its Eden, Adam and Eve were taken from The Babylonian account; its Flood or Deluge is but an epitome of some four hundred flood accounts'; . . . 'even the names of Noah's sons are copies, so also Isaac's sacrifice, Solomon's judgment, and Samson's pillar act; its Moses is fashioned after the Syrian Mises; its laws after Hammurabi's code. Its Messiah is derived from the Egyptian Madi, Savior, certain verses are verbatim copies of Egyptian scriptures. Between Jesus and the Egyptian Horus, Gerald Massey found 137 similarities and those

> between Christ and Krishna run into the hundreds' The masses never read these other sources and the churchmen who do keep silent about them.' . . . 'Solomon was not David's son: that Jews were never in bondage in Egypt, nor is Exodus their escape therefrom;' . . . 'Who does not know these things is wholly ignorant of the Bible's true meaning. He is also ignorant of the fact that he has been deceived, [9] Graham reasons, 'We little realize the price we've paid for these deceptions: thousands of years worship (and plundering) instead of welfare, of darkness disease and war, the Crusades, Inquisitions, massacre, prejudice, and bigotry. Even today, the religions founded on it are dividing the races and fomenting war. Because of its diversionary influence, we are thousands of years behind the planetary schedule; our consciousness is wholly inadequate to our place in evolution. It is not qualified for the coming Aquarian Age,' . . . 'it cannot solve the problems of this one. It's time this scriptural tyranny was broken that we may devote our time to man instead of God, to civilizing ourselves instead of saving our souls that were never lost.' [10]

The atheist is a natural human being, existing entirely in the world of nature, living by natures laws, within the confines of reality or what one reasons to be true, with no illusions. Existing in the real world will always be goal. His truth is, what you see is what you get, and what you do not see is nothing. The conflicting issues in religion and philosophy are the unreal versus our science of reality.

CHAPTER 2

The Big Bang Theory

Stephen W. Hawkins author of, "A Brief History of Time", 'in 1981, attended a conference on cosmology organized by the Jesuits in the Vatican. The Catholic Church had made a bad mistake with Galileo when it tried to lay down the law on a question of science, declaring the sun went around the earth. Now centuries later, it had decided to invite a number of experts to advise it on cosmology. At the end of the conference the participants were granted an audience with the Pope. He told us that it was all right to study the evolution of the universe after the Big Bang, but we should not inquire into the Big Bang itself because that was the moment of creation and therefore the work of God.' Hawkins reflects, 'I was glad then that he did not know the subject of the talk I had just given at the conference—the possibility that space time was finite but had no boundary, which means that it had no beginning, moment of creation.' [11]

Consider the impact of the pope's request. It is clear that theology has no creation myth, no Eden, no Adam and Eve, no Moses, no Messiah, no African Mulunga, no Australian totemic supernatural beings, no Yacatecuhtli in Central America, and no reasoned explanation for anything they teach. Mankind may want to answer the question of what caused it. But, there need not be a first cause, only causes and affects within a cosmos, of natural phenomenon, going on forever—forever in the past and forever into the future.

Theologians and their 'pure innocents' are hoping their imaginary heaven will not be shattered. They hope time will stand still within their traditions and ignorance—that is why the Pope said 'look no further.' But the nature of human beings will continue to evolve intellectually searching for an understanding of reality the nature of existence.

Hawkins was working on quantum mechanics and doubted that the universe had a beginning and an end. This work was published in 1988, and since then, other discoveries continue to lend credibility to the Big Bang theory. Factual data continues to support that there is indeed birth, life, and death of the universe, eternally.

There were many theoretical models for the universe before and after 1916, the year Einstein introduced "The General Theory of Relativity." Einstein's theory replaced Newton's theory of gravity, and subsequently, the static universe theory based on the relative stability of our earth, sun, and galaxy (the Milky Way). However, eventual successes in physics and by using the Theory of Relativity, Alexander Friedman in 1922, and Abbe Georges Lemaitre in 1927, independently theorized through Einstein's equations that the universe is expanding. Both men are credited for the Big Bang Theory. [12]

In 1917, Willem de Sitter, a Dutch astronomer, discovered that the universe has the peculiarity that light from a great distance would be blue if traveling towards us and would shift to red when going away from us. This was called the 'red shift' and was observed by astronomers for 10 years. However, no one related the red shift to an expanding universe.

Unaware of the works of Friedman and Lemaitre, Edwin Hubble, in 1929, using a spectrascope with the 100 inch telescope on Mount Wilson, observed the red shift, and from it calculated the speeds and distances that galaxies were moving away from us. This provided empirical evidence (derived from experience or experiment as a natural occurrence in reality), that all matter in the universe was moving farther apart, much like spots on a balloon as it expands. It was theorized that all matter came from a central point, and that if all matter were at one point at some time in the past, then only a large explosion (a big Big Bang) could send all that matter into space, thus creating our universe.

Hawkins 'More surprising was the finding that Hubble published in 1929: even the size of a galaxy's red shift is not random but directly proportional to the galaxy's distance from us. In other words, the farther a galaxy is, the faster it is moving away! That meant that the universe was not static but in fact expanding; and the distance between the galaxies is growing all the time.' [13] There was a moment in time when all the matter in our universe was in one place, compressed by gravity, Joseph Silk, author of, "The Big Bang;" 'The initial instant of time, the *singularity* . . . ' [14] ..'Imagine a moment so early and a density so high that the gravitational stresses were capable of ripping apart the vacuum.' [15]

'Let us now consider an era so early that the entire observable universe was contained within its own Compton wavelength. This is the ultimate limit of our theory of gravity, where uncertainty reigns supreme. At this instant, known as Planck Time, only 10^{-43} second after singularity, all matter we now see in the universe, comprising some millions of galaxies was compressed within a sphere of radius equal to one hundredth of a centimeter, the size of the point of a needle.' [16]

In the early Planck time, this point of a needle attained the incredible temperature of 10^{-32} degrees Kelvin after 10^{-43} second had elapsed since the beginning of the expansion. '..when about 10^{-35} second had elapsed since the beginning of expansion.' . . . 'the temperature had dropped sufficiently that there was no longer enough energy to maintain the perfect symmetry of the early phase. The inflation was over by about 10^{-33} second, by this time, the transition to the new phase of broken symmetry had occurred.' [17]

"One second after the bang, the density had dropped to 10 kilograms per cubic centimeter" . . . "At the Planck time, the density approached 10^{-90} kilograms per cubic centimeter. These physical conditions are so extreme that it seems entirely appropriate to regard the Planck time as the moment of creation of the universe." [18]

'The early universe was uniformly filled with radiation and neutrinos, in which a relatively small number of electrons, protons, and neutrons were interspersed. During the course of the expansion, the radiation cooled and eventually became the relic background radiation that has been measured by radio astronomers.' [19]

This *cosmic microwave background radiation* was another proof helping establish the Big Bang Theory, further overthrowing the 'Steady State Theory.' Arno Penzias and Robert Wilson at Bell Laboratories in New Jersey, with the help of a new radio telescope, found excess noise detecting cosmic microwave background radiation in 1965 and won the Nobel Prize. This provided the evidence proving the early hot phase of the universe. [20]

The following was reported editorially in the Democrat & Chronicle, Rochester, New York on April 28, 1992. The headline: A look at the beginning of time? Wow!

'Berkeley's Astrophysicist George Smart who headed the team of researches using the Cosmic Background Explorer Satellite in April 1992, 'say they have looked at light waves that emanated from that explosion.'

'For the first time the scientists say, they can see irregularities in these light waves—wrinkles that suggest differences in radiation and temperatures.'

'The irregularities, they say, acted like 'seeds' around which matter would condense just as dust particles act as seeds in the condensation of rain drops.'

'Because no one had ever seen those irregularities, which explain the formation of stars, planets and galaxies, the Big Band Theory had come into question in recent years.'

'If Smart and his colleagues are correct, the Big Bang Theory will be much harder to refute.'

But the central question remains; what *caused* the big explosion in the first place? The scientists will continue to investigate; the theologians will say they already know the answer.'

'All of us are awed by the questions, and the possibilities.' [21]

It is precisely this cause of the Big Bang that scientists have attempted to answer, in theory, and with formulas as they gravitate towards their blackboards and computers. From Einstein onward, the question soon became, what would happen if all the detected material in the universe calculated from the gravitational concentration, were drawn together in one huge black hole? In those formulas and calculations, they determined that all material would collapse into unimaginable density into the space of a period on this page, which would cause temperatures to rise millions of degrees, causing a rather, BIG BANG!

The laboratories, observatories, and radio telescopes, and now satellites in outer space are telling us, yes, its what caused the Big Bang. All the material was in one place and reacted, just as scientists theorized it would. We heard and know, all the material in this area of the center of the universe came together, and subsequently when the crunch came it blew! It will take no rocket scientist to reason—"this had to be going on for a very long long time."

The universe is, self-causing material existence of phenomenon or laws of nature that is our reality, going on forever. Much knowledge supports that conclusion, in 1929 Edwin Hubble discovered by observation that wherever you look distant galaxies are moving away from us. [22] If before our time it had also expanded then a contraction of sorts had to take place. Therefore, if all the material in the universe was at one time, calculated by scientists, to be in one place, and infinitesimally small, it was *not* the beginning of *time*, it was the beginning of our *universe, in our time, making our time finite and the cosmos infinite.*

Nature's essential characteristic is change, all inanimate and animate material is in a process of life and death even our universe. Nothing we do on earth will alter evolution. We cannot stop or change what is natural and evolving. We must in all our endeavors obey the laws of nature, and in the end it will randomly claim our beings. We are lucky for the experience, to live and be conscious of the inevitable, an evolutionary end, and a recreation of another universe—a new BIG BANG!

CHAPTER 3

The Magna Cosmos: A Theory

At one time, we believed that the earth was flat and the stars were holes in the sky where the sun showed through at night and that was all there was. Then we believed the earth was round and the center of the universe and we were alone. Next, we reasoned that our solar system was the center of the universe. Later we discovered that we were only part of a great universe and soon learned that we were just an insignificant star system in a huge galaxy called the Milky Way.

Knowledge; is to know, and is truth. That which is not true is not knowledge. Our means of survival in the universe, as it evolves and changes, depends *entirely* on our learning the truth about nature, to accumulate knowledge.

Hawkins explains that if the static state theory had prevailed, then: 'One could account for what was observed equally well on the theory that the universe existed forever or on the theory that it was set in motion at some finite time.' [23] Theology has stated emphatically that there had to be a first cause, and without evidence they claim that cause was a god. The Big Bang Theory with much supporting evidence suggests that our universe has existed forever.

When singularity took place, there followed a moment after singularity means that the entire universe was within that needlepoint of matter. It is where all the laws of nature potentially exist, within that tiny universe being remolded by powerful natural laws of gravity in space. Once the pressure reaches the moment of singularity, a moment, not of time, but, an immediate transition to the next universe, with no interruption in the laws of nature. It did indeed explode, spewing out all the gaseous material and giving birth to galaxies, our own galaxy, solar system, planets, earth, and eventually our own existence, which could only happen in a phenomenal material universe.

There was 'in the beginning' at the moment of singularity where the pressure of gravity and space vacuum was approaching ignition or planck time, the birth of our universe. Then, the moment, before the moment of singularity, was near the end of re-gathering the material of a previous universe. It is self evident that there cannot be a Big Bang without a previously existing universe. Logically then, there may be no first cause for existence.

Today, with some reservations, we believe, ours is the only universe and that it is exploding and imploding in some sort of rhythmic fashion.

We could theorize something else (a Magna Cosmos) taking place, which is mentioned at times in astronomy, and that is, there may be more than one universe—an infinite cosmos with an infinite amount of universes. In the interest of finding how theory, fact and the truth is reasoned, let us exercise our brains, and come up with a theory on how the material in the universe may come together in one place, in order to create another Big Bang.

The universe, from the time of the Big Bang, has been expanding for 15 billion years, give or take a few. The force of the explosion created an outward motion of material that eventually formed into nebula, galaxies, suns, and planets. The universe may continue to expand for billions of years until the initial force of the Big Bang dissipates. Most will be dead planets and suns similar to our moon, all being drawn into huge black holes.

What will draw all the bodies and black holes back to their original point? In all these dead entities, the only attraction would be gravity. Our moon would eventually crash into earth, and the earth would crash into a dead sun and the sun would, we believe, may be sucked into the center of our galaxy, as it becomes a giant black hole. But galaxies or black holes will be very far apart and seem to be systems in themselves. The balloon effect has created great distances between systems. Science has asked, "What will give the push in order for the dead universe to implode?" All bodies are too far apart to have any gravitational affect on each other.

Some scientists reason, because there's nothing left at the center of the explosion, there is no gravitational pull there to pull us back either.

We could reason that like our predecessors (who finally discovered we were not the only planet), and propose that our universe may not be the only universe in space that goes on forever. If the expansion goes on for, say, 50 billion years, it is not very much time in terms of forever. There is the possibility that there are billions of universes out there going on infinitely just like ours and that we may not entirely ever dissipate the force that sent us out in the first place, since empty space has little or no effect on moving bodies. It is gravity that binds the universe together.

Is it not possible then that we would 'run into' these other dead universes? Picture a barrel full of balloons, each a universe in total expansion. Each surface is touching the surface of another balloon. The centers of the empty space furthest from the touching surfaces of the balloons (universes in full expansion) would be an apex where the greatest amount of galaxies and/or black holes would gather. The universes of billions of black holes, these magna cosmos, would begin to collide swallowing each other.

The huge imploding black holes, that were once our galaxies, would be attracting each other as they travel through the increasing density of several huge portions of universes coming together from all directions. Almost like a snowballing effect, the immense black holes, traveling through the cosmic debris, will be gathering material, and building up the pressure of gravity at a new center. With enough material it would create another moment of singularity—then again—a Big Bang! Like Yogi Bera said, "Its déjà vu, all over again."

Everything in all the universes would find no escape from the giant black holes of colliding and crushing of material in space. Almost in unison there would be a rebirth of existence throughout the cosmos. However, in that far off future there may be such beings with an intelligence that may find its means to survive such annihilation.

They just may, in suspended animation, program their means to travel back to the center of where their universe or Big Bang took place and await for billions of years to join the birth of new galaxies and solar systems. Don't you just love a happy ending, or a new beginning?

The above—is it true or not true? We may never know, but that is how theories are created. We have some perception, therefore, we will have to research more, reason, calculate, observe, and finally *SENSE* something, to perceive, identify, quantify and classify our observations to comprehend what is the truth. Our *senses* must answer the question, just as we experienced when we saw the data from that little satellite, which added another empirical fact, background radiation, showing that a Big Bang had most likely occurred and that we live in such a universe.

CHAPTER 4

Geological & Biological Earth

The Big Bang, theoretically, occurred about 15 billion years ago. From Planct time the moment of explosion, to the present, this huge gaseous fireball went out in all directions, coalescing into spiral nebula, galaxies, suns, planets, asteroids, comets, creating new black holes. Our galaxy is about 10 billion years old and about 4.6 billion years ago, spawned our sun and solar system. It is estimated that our sun's life is 10 billion years and will be active for another 5 billion years.

'The mass of gas from which the sun formed slowly rotated, like most gaseous masses in the universe.' ' . . . some of the rotating matter was left behind in a flattened disk around the sun.' ' . . . various elements began to form molecules and other compounds' . . . 'were sticky and coagulated to form small dust like particles later, even larger units. Once a few larger units had been formed, gravity tended to bring in more matter until eventually bodies of planetary mass were formed,' picking up our moon from this debris. 'Meanwhile, the contraction of the sun triggered nuclear reactions.' causing earth to become hot, but had little effect on those far from the sun.' 'Smaller planets closer to the sun, temperature rose enough for the volatile substances like hydrogen and helium to evaporate. Only the solids remained behind and these compacted into the earth and the surrounding planets as they exist today.' 'It is almost certain that comets are made from this material . . . ' 'Most comets remain far from the sun but occasionally one ventures close to it. The sun's heat causes the evaporation . . . giving rise to the spectacular comet tails.' [24]

'In the past the moon must have been very close to earth.' The moon created a gravitational pull on the oceans causing tides and subsequent drag on the earth slowing its rotation. 'In fact, it is probable that the original earth rotated about six times faster than at present, corresponding to a "day" of four (present) hours.' [25]

For the geological evolution of the earth there is another group of scientists, the geologists, meteorologists, seismologists, ecologists, chemists, and others, who probe, dig, listen, travel, experiment, observe, and drill a lot of holes in the earth, to understand the nature of our planet.

The center of the earth contained radioactive material that created a hot interior. As the earth heated up, the center became molten and the rest is semi-molten to rather solid on the surface. The earth probably expanded slightly from the heat, creating fissures or cracks in the earth's outer crust. The heated molten lava spewed out, through the fissures, into space, carrying with it steam, causing huge earthquakes, pushing up of the crust and forming mountains, valleys, plains, and basins, where condensed steam as water collected on the earth's surface, creating lakes, rivers, and oceans.

Volcanic action, lava, and gaseous clouds enveloped the earth, and in time formed an atmosphere. The layering down of lava on the earth's surface gives our geologist the means by which they can determine the age of the earth. The geologist's, ..'golden rule of the bedding of sediments says that the rocks at the bottom are the oldest and those at the top are youngest.' [26]

Scientists, using sophisticated radiocarbon dating methods, geologists can estimate the age of each layer of sediment, and chemists can tell us of the materials that were in the atmosphere at that time. The golden rule of sediment layering the strata can be dated, much like the rings on a tree, and the radiocarbon method of dating creates, 'a double check for both methods.' Scientists have given us a means of comprehensive dating anywhere in the world. [27]

The earth that came into existence 4.6 billion years ago was evolving and by 4.0 billion years ago, within 600 million years, the origins of life were present. Many scientists understood that the atmosphere had erupted from the interior of the earth. The atmosphere was a cauldron of minerals and may have contained hydrogen, carbon dioxide, nitrogen, sulfur dioxide, methane, ammonia, and perhaps there was a buildup of chemical molecules.

Therefore, a buildup of chemical molecules had to begin with those materials on the earth at that time. About 1950, 'Nobel prize-winning scientist, Harold Urey, mentioned this to one of his students, Stanley L. Miller, that this mixture of materials could be duplicated in their laboratory. No sooner said than done: and they set up a container with the right mixture of gases and subjected them to artificial electric sparks to simulate lighting. In a week a little red liquid started to form; analyzed, this was found to contain amino acids, the basic building blocks of organic life. From these sorts of compounds, by whatever method, it is generally believed that life began in shallow pools on the earth's surface, as a so-called organic soup.' [28]

Some reason that life may have begun in ice. Molecules form in the crystalline structure and line up in such a way that may produce life. Leslie Orgel took some of the basic elements, which he was sure was in the atmosphere at that time, in a solution of water and froze it for several days. The frozen solution formed a peak just as you might observe in ice cubes at times, and sure enough, it appeared at the

USS

very top. 'Orgel found that he had formed one of the four basic constituents in the genetic alphabet that directs life. He had made adenine, one of the four bases in DNA.' [29] But there may be another answer to the age-old question, "How did life begin?" and that must be the moral sense of a conscientious scientist, to have an open mind for the truth.

Life may have begun in the Precambrian period from 4.6 billion years ago to 4.0 billion years ago. By 1.5 billion years ago the first primitive life forms in the organic soup came into being. In the Cambrian period 600 million years ago, we see the first shell forming vertebrates. In the Ordovician period, there was an Ice Age in Africa, South America, Africa, Australia, India, and Antarctica. At this time, all continents were contained in one huge land mass called Gonawondaland. During the Triassic period 250 million years ago, an unidentified huge event caused the continents, as we know them today, to begin drifting apart. There have been speculations recently, that movement may have been caused a great meteor, to hit a large continent. Continental plates, such as India's, has crashed into Asia pushing up the great Himalayas mountain range which are still growing in height. Plates are moving, today, at the rate of one (1) inch per year.

'The Jurassic period (180 million years ago) seems to have been a time of world-wide mild climatic conditions, marked by lush vegetation.' 'No ice sheets covered the poles, both of which were situated in the ocean areas (western Pacific and southern Indian Ocean) and thus equable currents prevented any extensive freeze-up.' The equator of the time passed over what is now the southeastern United States and so the climates were either warm and humid or else in the more continental parts, hot and dry.' [30] This was the Age of The Dinosaurs. They were of a wide variety, the smaller evolving eventually, during this fifty million year period, into the first birds.

One hundred and thirty five million years ago, the dinosaurs became extinct, probably by another tremendous meteor crashing into the earth. This was the Cretaceous period in which new organisms appeared and much of Mesozoic life became extinct.

We came to evolve in a period called the Tertiary Period, between five and 65 million years ago. All through this period, worldwide mountain building occurred. This was the age that mammals became abundant and the evolution of grasses took place. In the beginning of this period, there was mild weather and eventually flowering plants and the first primates, our animal descendants, came into being. The forests became lush and for primates that took to the trees, it was a life of plenty. Thirty six million years ago, Dayopithecenes evolved from these first primates, which gave birth to Asutralopithecus. Our genetic birth occurred during the 12 million years drought. Then came the Ice Age, two and a half million years ago. With the water frozen and the oceans at a low level, major deserts grew larger and man entered the Stone Age.

The formation of the earth, geology, and how life emerged, as related here, is a very brief account. Physicists, astrophysicists, geologists, biologists and many scientists have created volumes of knowledge for an understanding of nature. For those with general interest "The Columbia History of the World" edited by Garraty and Gay is a very good source.

It is known that before the eighteenth and nineteenth century man's exposure even to a sporadic scientific view was practically non-existent. More important to man were the mythical creation stories the world had always been here. They imagined, "Is there any reason to think that there has been a history of life other than the cycle of birth, maturation, and death? Have not things remained the same since the time of creation, which Bishop Usher tells us occurred in 4004 BC?" But in these centuries, gradually, 'theory became less and less constrained by scripture and ancient authority and more and more on observation and experimentation.' Life has been going on for, 'Hundreds of thousands or even millions of years; therefore, the earth could not have been created in 4004 BC, as Bishop Ussur had claimed.' [31]

Man came to find, 'nature and nature alone became the guide to natures secrets.' and to uncover them required 'two fundamentals,' 'One was a method, the other a discovery.' [32] Method is man's genius, and discovery may lie at his feet as nature changes. It leaves a record imprinted in time and material on earth for man to recognize. Geologists and paleontologists discover and date by turning over the strata's pages of history for the story of the fossils, to chronicle the changes in sediment, stone, weather, foliage, (much like the rings on a tree for identifying age and weather) the tragedies and successes of mankind's history.

CHAPTER 5

The Natural Law of Snowflakes

Life on earth, as we learned from the preceding chapter, probably began in the shallow parts of primordial slime or 'organic soup' during the Precambrian period, 4.6 billion to 700 million years ago. Fossils from this period are few, but since life was generated out of shallow pools, there may have been simple organic cells developing from amino acids and also base materials of adenine, as well as thymine, quanine and cytosine. These cells were the first building blocks of organic life, each of an individual nature. How did these first cells evolve in nature, 'in the beginning?'

There is the possibility that life did not occur on earth, but was alien, whereby organic material came to earth via meteors or meteorites, of which there were many in pre-Cambrian times. Some believe that life may have been planted here on earth or even colonized by an alien intelligence. Surely, we should ask the same question—how did their organic alien life forms evolve within space on bodies in nature that came into being since the big bang similar to our planet?

Our best estimate shows that experiments lend credence, at this time, that the nature of our planet and its distance from the sun were the generating factors that led to life on earth. The *odds* of other planets similar to our geological past with the incidence of a species of animal that would evolve with intelligence aware of the universe and its own consciousness is rare. It has happened to us and we may postulate that we are highly individual and a unique happening in planetary evolution.

Life did exist from the period of 600 million years to 500 million years ago. There were trilobites (marine anthropod with oval, flattened, hard jointed limbs, 1 inch to 2 feet in length), brachiopods (a mollusk-like marine animal), many invertebrates and a variety of aquatic plants. Algae, fungi, and bacteria evolved as each were creating variations as the genetic pool of life was growing. Life forms were also changing, diversifying, and in each, breeding organic uniqueness.

Five hundred million years ago, in the Ordovician period, marine variations were colonizing along the shores into a changing environment, evolving into the first plants. Life in waters, such as crustaceans lived, died, and created living coral reefs. Chordates appeared which were true vertebrates, spinal, with a sac-like body and lancelets. Club mosses appeared 450 million years ago in the Silurian period together with a greater abundance of land plants and some anthropods (trilobites) were crawling on land.

In the Devonian period, 395 million years ago, we find evidence of many fish, horsetails, ferns, and by 350 million years ago, amphibians and reptiles appeared on the scene. By 280 to 230 million years ago, there were extinction of many species, and fewer amphibians. From 230 to 180 million years ago, forests of conifers and cycads were spreading. Spiral-shaped shells of ammonites were found in fossil records of this period. Reptiles were abundant during this time and we think, gave rise to a large genetic pool to give us 'Jurassic Park' 180 to 135 million years ago. [33]

Physiologically, man came from huge gene pools of organic cells that evolved in Precambrian times.

Physical construction of each cell in the human body contains 46

(23 pair) structures that are called chromosomes. The chromosomes are made of a chemical called deoxyrobonucleic acid referred to as DNA. The ingredients of this chemical is made up of the four basic amino acids arranged in pairs of thymine, cytosine, adenine, and guanine, of which we learned earlier. Each ingredient or unit is made up from these coded instructions called genes that are the same in each one.

There are thousands of genes in every human organic cell, in a spiral which determines the color of our eyes, hair, skin tone, and the entire make up or design of our physical body. The woman's egg cells contain 23 chromosomes and a man's, 23 to make up the 46 for the life of a newborn.

We readily understand that in nature everything in the universe is changing. Everything in space, from the time of the Big Bang, to the present, is evolving, and change in all natural things will go on in the life of the universe. Our genetic codes of our mother and father, has likewise been changing, and what they inherited comes from a long line of changing genes from their mother and father, and so on back to primates, the dinosaur, reptiles, and to single cells in the primordial swamps. By change in the genetic code, we don't refer to the basic thymine, adenine, guanine, and cytosine, but to change in the genetic coded instructions that determine our physical make up. We learned from Sarich and Wilson that we came from a long line of changes or mutations, happening to us predictably. The humanoid species began five million years ago, and mutations occurred throughout history in our lineage to the present. We were surviving on the savanna by the water's edge, with longer arms than we now have, beginning to walk upright well, and naked, losing most of the hair we had twelve million years ago. We were genetically changing and improving our chances for survival.

Each primitive family was coming from a different lineage. Every lineage going off in different directions, joining with others and genetic mutations occurring naturally, so that not any two individuals of the homo species were identical. All inter family mating, which was the rule rather than the exception, which seems to have had no adverse, but beneficial, affects on the individuation of our species to survive. If the family had healthy genes, their isolation as a nuclear family retained and assured passing on survival genes. If a union happened between two from different families (clans) and one was genetically diseased then there offspring would be at risk, with no guarantee for healthy children. Since primitive man did not understand how a woman became with child genetically healthy sisters and brothers or first cousins mating would guarantee survival of the clan.

Children receive half of their genetic codes from each of their parents, of which they may resemble one or both, but with a unique genetic code or DNA different from any human being that was ever born, is alive today, or will be in the future. Identical twins are an exception since they have exactly the same chromosomes and it may be difficult to tell them apart. Though they may have slight differences in their genetic coding within the chromosome genes, their experiences make them usually, socially and intellectually unique.

As scientists decipher the body's complex genetic code, a new gene is being formed every month. Our physiques although similar in shape differ in every aspect, in measurement of every feature of contour of body, bones, and organs. Ayn Rand defined our species as distinguished from all others by our rational faculties and the concept of man or women by their physical characteristics (hair, facial, features, organs, fingerprints—all in common) but with measurements excluded. [34]

We are naturally individual in most respects, in that our immune system rejects all foreign invasions of harmful bacteria or germs. No part of our cell structure, especially organs, can be transplanted into our body without recognition by our own immune system to reject them. All genetic codes are rejected as foreign, even among family members.

Much of our individuality has to do with evolution. We are each another rung on the ladder of an evolving species. We all represent different steps, at this time, in evolution. It is believed that without variety, the species will die. Species of animals may differ in genetic code but mutations seem to be slower over very long periods of time.

The change will be forced only by subtle changes in its environment. It will force them to change ever so slightly in behavior and eventually the genetic code will mutate to change their physique, to accommodate the behavior. But if the environment changes faster than the mutations can accommodate a change by behavior, the change in physique cannot mutate quickly enough and the species becomes extinct. We can see that today as our human population is accelerating and pushing animals into different environments where they are not equipped to cope successfully and are doomed to extinction.

We are fortunate that our primitive ancestors were able to survive the environmental changes by learning to scavenge effectively, on the savanna, by the water's edge or in any environment. They learned when and how to keep on the move rather than wait for environmental correction to suit their needs, survival is an intellectual process.

Through behavior, the primitive accelerated genetic mutation, changing their physique—to develop an effective thumb—walk upright—to make tools and carry things with their arms. Why did our arms get shorter? We need a longer reach at the table. Who knows? Genetic mutations increased our brain case to accommodate increases in the brain (Is that why we get headaches? Is our brain mutating faster than our brain case? Oooh!).

In a large group of people, even in large companies, there can be found a few 'dead wood' who have a tendency to not pull their weight. They could cause a company to lose its competitive advantage. In a tribe, their presence would mean less food for all would reduce the overall energy level of the group. Food gathering, scavenging, and hunting are almost entirely physical activities. Thus, anyone who did not contribute to the food supply was perhaps turned away from the tribe. Just as animals kick out their offspring once they begin to eat as much as their parents, primitive hominids perhaps behaved the same way, in the beginning.

Fewer people in the clan enabled them to hide more effectively from predators and travel more efficiently. A large group would create a strong concentration of humanoid scent that would attract large groups of predators. The strategy, which was forced on them, when the drought forced them out of the trees, was to disperse at the sign of danger and hide. They would form into small family clans forming a smaller target group and could be more flexible when threatened by predators.

As each hominid family, five million years ago began the human saga, they remained separated and as nomads, had a better chance at survival physically and genetically obviously. They remained essentially in this nomadic condition in individual family units until about 50,000 to 35,000 years ago when the small animal population was dwindling. They joined forces with their brother's and sister's families (or they just grew up and remained together and intermarried) to become a larger unit to cooperate in hunting large animals.

Each of those family units were socially different, because other clans were avoided for reasons of security or perhaps because they acted differently. They were alien to them in ways we can't imagine. But they most likely intermingled at times, cautiously, and may have traded things, and socially fell in love with women or men if there were shortage of males or females. We can believe that in their primitive state, had a great reluctance to let someone go with the other family because we know how we feel when someone we love and value leaves. We have to give them that—there had to be a strong bond within a primitive family that had to struggle for their food and existence, in exceptionally hard times, always at risk and very close together.

There can be no doubt that there was an individualism, not only family oriented, but each member, was mentally and physically unique which caused each to perceive and identify things just a little differently than everyone else. It is that sense of difference in their relatives and at the same time familiar and comfortable that caused them to change their hunting strategies and fall in love.

It was mental individualism that led to the creation of stone tools, cutting stones, chopping stones, sharp points, axes, and frond lean-tos. Some time later, they made fish hooks, snares, bows, arrows, and spears. All those tools for acquiring food were not easy to create under the conditions where they lived on the ground, under a tree, or under fronds which eventually leaked as it rained and they got soaking wet for hours, the terrible steam heat, that would turn into a dry burn. It was each thinking just a little differently that spawned new ideas from perhaps the most unlikely members in the family. Someone said to another, "No hit that way—look, try like I do," and it was better.

Today, we live much better, closer together, and it allows us the opportunity, in a civilized way, with less caution, to trade, marry outside the clan. (OH! those in-laws!—they're so different!), and to join socially with those, we value greatly. They're not the same as us, but are somewhat. Most of us understand that this individuality may prevent us from ever knowing the family down the hall. It's not wrong or bad, but good, it strengthens family or our independence and self-actualization—to be on our own. The only way any two people, two families or two nations can live together peaceably, friendly, cooperatively and separately is to *respect* their individuality. That respectful distance that we allow between us, even the closest in the clan, or between you and me, is called autonomy, its natural or in our nature to be as such, to be individual.

Manufacturing engineers know it is impossible to even manufacture, with tools or sophisticated methods, millions of parts and items, identical. Nothing in existence has ever been identical. It is one of the great wonders of reality.

The 'metaphysical natural law of snowflakes' is that like snowflakes, every single thing on earth and in the universe shall by nature be different from everything else. From a grain of sand to a universe, *all* is unique. Nature is in a state of flux; everything that comes in to being exists or lives, changes, and ceases to exist, all in their own unique way. If you think we are each physically one of a kind, just imagine, the infinite diversity of human minds. What we call that "rugged individualism" can be as subtle and delicate as a snowflake. *Individualism is not a theory, nor an abstraction, it is a fact of reality, i.e., that is a universal natural phenomenon and is our nature.* No one has the right to force us into a collective society. It is the most important issue in the universe. Watch the face of a child, or anyone else for that matter, when you call him or her by some other name—they are appalled! It is their sense of identity, their individuality, which we have forgotten and is an affront to their nature.

CHAPTER 6

The Environment

Many scientists seem to agree that the universe is random and as we know in a constant state of change. There is no balance of nature, there never has been or will be. That is like saying the present ecological balance should remain as a perpetual motion machine forever. That cannot happen. We could, at any time, go into another 12,000,000 year of drought or glaciers could cover the earth. The poles could shift as is being predicted by some, so that the North Pole, as calculated may be at Los Angeles (no more heat and smog) at-40 F. some day. There is no *balance* of nature. There is a grand evolution of the universe but nature, the environment, and our lives, i.e. the ecology, depends on the evolutionary exigencies of the universe, the galaxy, the solar system, and our aging earth.

The condition of this planet will depend on our moon, orbit about the sun, sun spots, solar flames, and any debris out there that may run into us in the form of cosmic dust 'alien invasion', or an asteroid collision with the earth. We have as much chance of controlling such events here on earth as we do of preventing our galaxy from being sucked into a black hole. And where we can do something, we do nothing to limit birthing by moral abortion or to encourage scientific genetic research and proper fertilization or pest control to salvage crops.

We can preserve much on earth but preservation of any ecological

USS

balance or living organisms is a waste of human effort. Our efforts should not be directed at a balance preservation per se, but, should be directed at science, reason, research, discovery, experiment and *very limited rule* to solve the problem of feeding the five and a half billions of people we now have on earth. Our problems are still primitive—we must produce food and stop governments from confiscating from those who produce.

Primitive men followed the animals scavenging kills and wandered around the earth in search of better producing forests and savannas. Three hundred thousand years ago they had filled up African continent then proceeded to fill up Asia, Europe and the Americas. When they could not go any further, they stayed in one place to tend and nurture those plants that produced the most food. The human species did not wait for ideal natural conditions to improve the quality and quantity of plants and animals. Nor could he maintain their natural quality forever. But man could bring change and clear a new patch of land or live and farm by a flooding and receding river to grow those plants that produced the most food. Man learned how to control, and follow a herd, began to understand fertility and genetically improved animals, FOR FOOD! We still have to work in order to eat.

With success in agricultural and animal husbandry we occupied lands all over the world and then, with plenty of food, began to 'pack' them in. So successful were the new technologies that the shamans and politicians saw the phenomenon as something that could never run out. There was no limit to how much food an 'ignorant' farmer and herder could produce. The more souls or people the more food and goods to confiscate—tax.

Wealth was being grown out of the earth and witch doctors wanted control of the wealth and minds of the producers. The more people, the greater the wealth for the state ("Have many children!" "Its a 'sin' to abort a pregnancy!" or "Its a god's will!") Then they glorify poverty as an ideal for the common citizen. If they could do that, they would rule and become the (elite) group exercising authority and control over more and more people. That strategy works! They could live well, not have to toil in the fields, pastures, in mines, industrial complexes, manufacturing, or supplying goods and services. Rulers take what we earn, control how we behave, and we let them.

Secular and theocratic political greed wants to replicate every human seed and embryo into a working soul. The lack of a reasoned immigration policy is a government's need to keep expanding their taxpaying power base for wealth and power, which *is raping the environment*. The free market traders, the creators of technology, investing to meet overpopulation needs, are being ostracized blamed by the very people who are creating this inhuman and environmental tragedy.

Today, the world is not quite 'totally occupied' we still have the rain forests and they will soon be cut down. In the next 50 years our world population of 5.5 billion people will have doubled. Not only will the forests come down, but also we will be picking the earth clean of everything organic. Our great grandchildren will become a swarm of locusts scouring the earth clean. Then we'll turn on ourselves like a bucket of maggots, eating ourselves back into a primordial slime, easing back into the rivers and oceans.

It is understood that one may think the above is rather extreme, overstated or 'will never happen.' But, there is cause to be gravely concerned today. We see an exploding population in the Americas and the attack on every piece of land that has the potential for growing. South America, Central America, Africa, and much of Asia, as well, cannot feed its people. Immigration is politically motivated for more earning and taxing power and not tied to working men's economic factors, his needs (employment, wages, etc.).

Our own urban areas are becoming a can of worms, inhabitants killing and butchering each other. The pro-life, pro-choice, and environmental activists should be joining forces because their problems are the same, how to save viable living people and our environment. They should be working together, *their* world as well as ours is at stake.

In Book I, 'Defining Philosophy', we historically, ended in dynastic Egypt. During the 3,000 years of the pyramid building era, the lack of scientific progress, heavy taxation, and its excesses would create weakness. By 2525 BP, the Egyptians had fallen to the onslaught of the Persians. Alexander the Great, in 2332 BP, conquered Egypt and ended Egyptian independence. By 2030 BP, Rome was the victor. The world was experiencing subjectivity in action. There came those who would use force to confiscate any food producing territory. There has been no end to such governments, theocratic and socialistic wars, and taxation to create a poor society. Mankind owes all its environmental problems to such political ideologies. We will explore this tragic turn of events for the primitive and ourselves in Book VI, on 'Government.'

CHAPTER 7

The Re-Emergence of Philosophy

Most of the world 2600 years ago, including Greece, had experienced a diffusion of religious control radiating out from Mesopotamia and Egypt. This new theocratic rule was dispersing throughout the occupied world where success in producing food surpluses was occurring. It would vary in practice, having less of an effect in Greece, where there was no consideration in an afterlife and burial cults were not evident. The Greeks had many gods who took on human qualities in their own image: The God of War, was Mars; of Love, of Eros; Hymen, The God of the Wedding Feast, etc.—you get the idea. The Greeks understood them as myths or poems, but with a message in morals or values, which is why they wrote so many, and so eloquently. More concerned with reality, a few began to look to nature to discover perhaps a better way to live in the real world, to affect a re-emergence of a primitive's method and thought, before theocratic rule.

The Ionians about 2600 BP, were anew kind of thinkers. Thales of Miletus, who is considered to be the first philosopher, was a modern observer of nature who sought to identify its substance and phenomenon. We learn about Thales from early references by Herodotus and Aristotle, but post-Aristotlian historians depended heavily on Aristotle's manuscripts, which was obviously an admirer of Thales' scientific contributions. It has been said that Thales showed remarkable wisdom predicting a solar eclipse on May 28, 2565 BP, during a battle between the Lydeans and the Persians. But it is also believed no facts were known to make such predictions at that time.

As an engineer, Thales redirected the Halys River for King Croesus and his army to pass. He traveled over the known world to Mesopotamia and Egypt. He speculated that the world originated in water, floated on, and was sustained by water. In geometry, he proved the circle was bisected by its diameter and that the angles of an isosceles triangle are equal at its base. He also figured out how to measure the height of the pyramids. In another experiment, he determined the distance of ships at sea. He was a thinker and doer. He was sensing the real world. He was the first in 6,000 years of emotions and fantasies, who was not concerned with the spiritually unreal, myths, intuition, and those who did not look for proof. But it is known most philosophers at that time believed in some kinds of gods. The age of the philosopher was upon us. '. . . in Thales we see clearly the transition from myth to science and philosophy, and he retains his traditional character as initiator of Greek philosophy.' [35]

The philosophers of Greece began to focus their attention to natural elements, and as we noted, Thales had reasoned that all matter primarily came from water, 'The Babylonians and the Egyptians had conceived of water, then air and earth,...' '. . . Anaximander, c. 2611-2547 BP, added a fourth element, that of fire.' [36] He thought that there was a substance, '*urstoff*", that made up these elements.

Anaximenes, c. 2550-2475 BP, chose air as a primary substance. But creation stories of Egyptians and the Babylonians differed markedly from the Miletians who seemed more scientific in their evaluations of nature. [37] Philosophers respected craftsman who worked

USS

in the material, not the imaginary world, for their materialistic sense of life.

Pythagoras was born around 2582 BP, was the first to call himself a 'philosopher' devoting his life to mathematical speculation and theorems. Pythagoras mathematics demonstrated in geometry and its principles in relationship to physical reality. Pathegoras, '..founded a brotherhood devoted to a life of mathematical speculation and religious contemplation.' [38] Later in the 2500 BP, they split into two wings, one theistic and the other scientific.

The early Atomists were Leucippus of Miletus, 2440 BP, and Democritus of Abdera, 2420 BP, believing that everything in nature consisted of atoms that were indivisible. They thought there were many different kinds of atoms of different sizes, shapes, and density. Atoms were believed to exist forever and Mason writes, 'The atomists supposed that life had developed out of the primeval slime, man as well as animals and plants; man was a microcasm of the universe, for he contained every kind of atom.' [39]

The Atomists believed atoms dissipated from the body and taken in by air and when breathing stopped, life ended. Cosmologically, their concept of existence was that everything was operating automatically–*predetermined.* Once it began working, we could do nothing about it. Therefore it was by necessity things were as they were. [40] Miletus was conquered in 2494 BP, perhaps ending the Melisian School of science and philosophy.

The idea that our lives are predetermined has been argued for some time philosophically, but its main objection is that it relieves people of responsibility for their actions. We explore this problem in greater detail ahead, in Book IV, "Morals", in the chapter on 'Determinism'.

Plato, 2428-2348 BP, was born in Athens Greece and thought of generally as a philosopher, but is, in actuality, false. Any references to Plato in this work will refer to him as a theological thinker, reflecting sixteenth century thought when his 'works' were created in Florence. Plato's beliefs and principles were religious and therefore, cannot be called philosophy—he was, perhaps more a theologian than a philosopher. He was a student of Socrates, who also seemed to be a theological orator.

Of all the writings about Plato in antiquity, most were short references by philosophers, historians, and writers. The greatest and most lengthy was by Diogenes Laertius who wrote some time between 1990 BP, and 1500 BP, on the History or Lives of the Philosophers. 'His account of Plato, one of his longest (Book III) clearly shows how superficial and unreliable he was' since the 'work was intended for a woman who was an ardent Platonist.' [41]

"The Riddle of the Early Academy", by Cherniss shows that Plato's 'writings' are highly questionable, but, that the concept of Plato's 'ideas' or ideology—innate knowledge—based on Dioganes Laertius, and other early historians, has been established.

Plato believed that, like animals, we had inborn knowledge, but we have since learned, animals learn much like us. His was a process of anarmesis or the recollection of 'ideas' which the 'soul'(one's mind), knew in a previous life and able to intuit (remember) as such. This Plato called the 'dialectic' (logical argumentation), meaning, not by observation or experimentation. But, to embrace the 'dialectic' as fact is the same as putting forth a theory, without proof of scientific observation and/or experimentation and calling it true. To 'intuit' is to *feel* it is true, but *not to know*. Plato believed that the study of nature such as astronomy was a waste of time.

Cherniss refers to the German views of Professor Jaeger and Howald saying, 'Plato's conception of Reality, he contends, was incompatible with the notion of a systematic unification of all sciences, and still more incompatible with an encyclopedic organization of all subjects for the purpose of teaching or research. In short, Jaeger feels justified in referring to the nature of the Academy from the philosophical attitude of the Platonic dialogues; and it is from these dialogues and from the philosophical interpretations of Aristotle that Howald, too, draws his extreme conclusion that the 'Academy' was a mystic cult and not a school in our sense of the word.' [42]

The Platonic Academy, established in Florence about the sixteenth century, and in order to give it a sense of authenticity and prestige, needed a worthy founder of theistic repute such as Plato. In the "Son of Apollo", Frederick J.E. Woodbridge notes that, 'it seems wholly inconceivable that Plato's writings should come down to us so complete. Nothing in antiquity has ever survived so completely.' [43] The Florentines had created a mythology around a known person in history.

Plato, of course, became the darling of theologians and in their reference to 'the Greatest Philosopher' is understandable for them to create an 'intellectual' perception of their faith, and to trust as knowledge, belief in an imaginary, myth, and their deity's ideology.

Aristotle (2384/3-2322 BP) agreed with Plato on some issues but was cognizant of the ontological (theological speculation) nature of his arguments. Aristotle's right, 'indeed, is more securely based than is Plato's: for in his case' (when researching his authenticity, John H. Randal Jr., author of "Aristotle" continues), 'we actually possess large fragments of his "early writings" as an external point of reference. Aristotle's "intellectual development" is based on actual documentary evidence, which is more than Plato can boast of—. . . .' [44]

Aristotle was born in Stagira in Thrace in northern Greece. An Ionian, he shared interest in the facts of nature that stretched back to Thales. It is reported he went to Athens at eighteen and studied at the 'academy' (gymnasium or grove) with Plato and friends. This is also debated. In all his writings he never mentioned the 'academy', but he did know Plato, and some say he was a Platonist, which is also debatable. Aristotle wrote many dialogues of which we have fragments of eighteen that surpassed in eloquence any of Plato's discourses. About the time of Plato's death, he left Athens and 12 years later, he returned to set up a school called the Lyceum, where he discussed logic, ethics, rhetoric, metaphysics, and engaged in research. Aristotle died in 2322 BP.

What we call, "Metaphysics", also called the 'first philosophy', may be attributed to Aristotle. He is considered the father of science, and proposed that in every science, there had to be a method (Methodos) of study. In the 12 years at Lyceum, he lectured, studied plants, animals, human life, politics, art, and physics. He spoke in terms of "hunting" (searching) "looking for" (discovery) or "examining" (researching). 'In the mornings, we are told, he would lecture on logic and first philosophy, as a methodological training for scientists' . . . 'In the afternoons he would give public lectures on rhetoric, politics, and ethics. All the while he engaged with his students and staff in extensive research.' [45] Although he may have had some Platonic ideas, the objective consistency of his philosophical principles never left him. He did much to establish fundamental scientific methodology of which is still in practice to this day.

Aristarchus of Samos (2310-2230 BP) was the first to work, '"On the Sizes and Distances of the Sun and the Moon," WE also learn, 'According to Archimedes, ... earth rotated on its axis daily . . . around the sun.... once a year, ...planets moving in circular orbits with the sun at its center. ' . . . according to Plutarch, . . . ' '....Cleanthes, said that Aristarchus ought to have been indicted for impiety.' [46] Greek gods had established that the earth was the center of the universe, a tradition since the beginning of religion, for thousands of years. It would take 1800 years to be proved by observation (see Galileo Galilei ahead) and he would be forced under the threat of the rack, to read a recantation of his *observable* discovery and spend the rest of his life (8 years) under house arrest by the church Inquisition.

Eratosthenes of Cyrene, (2284-2192 BP) noted that the sun was overhead at Syene at midday in the summer and at Alexander some seven degrees from the vertical from the shadow that was cast by a rod of a certain height. By his calculations Eratosthenes figured that Alexandria was 5,000 miles from Syene and that the circumference of the earth was 25,000 miles, which is only 50 miles off the known value of the polar diameter.

Greece had emerged from barbarism into the Iron Age civilization, and took to sea-going commerce from the start. 'The Greeks had the travelers feel for space, the source of geometry,'. . . . 'They possessed also the traveler's knowledge of a variety of cultures and traditions, which allowed them to pick out what was valuable from each without rigidly following any particular one.' [47]

The Greeks imported goods from Mesopotamia and Egypt, and

its economic advantages spread through the Near East and China. But, religion was so imprinted on the savage mind that it also carried such ideas through China, the Bearing Strait to the Americas, to Europe, and throughout Africa. Yet the Greeks followed no rigid rule, and their gods represented human values and frailties. Their mythology was like all Egyptian and Mid East religious myths, without foundation in reality or fact, was imaginary and fictitious.

The Greeks listened to or read the poems of Homer and Hesiod. They told tales of fear, love, treachery, superhuman strength and bravery. Myths represented human virtues for the living since they had no concern with an afterlife. Myth to the Greek was artistic and aesthetic.

Greece began to import religious thought, by 2700 BP, through the years to 2000 BP, when religious cults were teaching Greeks about gods, souls, and an afterlife. To emerge was Orphism, which would bring to the Greeks salvation through some imaginary mystical communion with a god.

From year, 2000 BP, onward to 800 BP, there was no advancement in science, technology or philosophical thought (see Grun's "The Timetables of History" at end of this book's Bibliography). A hundred years later, Christianity, another myth, with its mythical being called 'Christ,' created by the Romans around the year 60, when they wrote the book of Mark. They began writing the New Testament that became the official religion by the edict of Theodosius in 620.

The church was eventually the law in decreeing lands for royalty, approving and anointing god kings, and the nepotistical *inheritance* of their 'royal blood' as justification or right to confiscate wealth, to rule over people and control their culture. The church controlled all knowledge. Manuscripts to be published had to meet with approval of the church. This was not unique. Religion, as we learned earlier, maintained its power by teaching, preaching and wrote down what was perceived their 'truth' or the word of a god. They emphasized all knowledge had to be in conformity to their doctrine, decrees, dogma and their utterances that were truths, for it was 'the word of god.' If an idea did not fit within the framework of religious doctrine, and to speak so, was witchcraft or heresy, whereby such people would be brought before the Inquisition.

Knowledge, contrary to the church's interpretation, was to be suppressed and kept secret in order to maintain priestly credibility. Nicolas Copernicus (1473-1543), a Polish astronomer proposed the heliocentric theory of the solar system; the theory put the sun at the center of the solar system. In his mathematical theory the stars remained stationary while the planets went around the sun as well, all orbits being circular. His publication made little impact partly due to his editor, Osiander, who was of the opinion that it was not a new physical account of the heavens, but a simplified mathematical calculation for the cosmos. So highly theoretical was the theory of circular orbits of the sun and planets, as well as the Coperincus conception of the earth moving about the sun, it would have to wait for more empirical observational evidence. The injunction by the church, however, permitted reference to the heliocentric theory simply as a mathematical hypothesis.

Galileo Galilei, (1564-1642) an Italian astronomer and natural philosopher, heard of a two lens system being used in Holland that allowed people to see objects more clearly at a distance. He set out to design and build one and turned it towards the heavens. In 1610, he published his findings that the sun had blemishes and rotated monthly. His new lens system told him the moon was mountainous and Jupiter had four satellites circulating around it. This obviously lent observational, empirical support to Copernicus' heliocentric theory and would disprove the Ptolemaic Theory (earth as the center of the universe).

The Holy Officer censured Galileo in 1616 for his findings. He was forbidden to hold, teach or defend his condemned doctrine. In 1632, he published his 'Dialogue' of the two systems, complying with the injunction by the church concerning the heliocentric theory being only a useful mathematical hypothesis. No one really doubted Galileo's strong evidence that supported Copernican theory. The Inquisition summoned him to Rome in 1632. Arriving in Rome, on February 1633, he was examined on June 21 to determine whether he contravened the decree of 1616. Galileo was under the threat of the rack, a torture mechanism, for heresy. He pleaded his case for the years since 1610 and the year of 1633, citing his observational mathematical calculation and recalculation of the theory. He begged them to understand, "I cannot deny what I see."

Forced to recant his findings, Galileo was sentenced to house arrest for the rest of his life where he went on with his scientific work. 'Only months before his blindness, he described the diurnal libration (real or apparent uscillatory motions) of the moon' . . . 'blind, he developed in theory the application of the pendulum to clock work.' Also a new theory of the earth rotating and moving have been credited to Galileo. In 1638, smuggling out a manuscript, he was able to publish his "Mathematical Discoveries and Demonstrations Concerning Two new Sciences". [48]

'In method he related empirical and formal considerations in such a way that mathematical analysis was appropriate to the problem at hand; experiment and calculations were combined to produce results capable of confirming or discomfirming the theory . . . ' 'Galileo made the distinction between primary and secondary qualities which we associate with the name Locke. The objectivity of the measurable and the subjectivity of the non-measurable, powerfully revived by Galileo, have remained standard and virtually unassailable notions.' [49]

Johannes Kepler (1571-1630), a German astronomer, was the first to publicly support the Copernican theory and reasoned that instead of being circular, orbits of planets were elliptical, with the sun at one focus. This was Kepler's First Law for planetary motions. 'His second law was that, 'planets sweep out equal distances in equal times and thus move more rapidly nearer the sun.' The third law states, 'that the squares of the periods of any two planets are proportional to the cubes of their mean distance from the sun, a period being the time required for a complete trip around the sun.' (Kepler) [50]

Isaac Newton (1642-1727) published 1687 "Principia Mathematica Philosophiae Naturalis" that became the foundation of the theory of mechanics of motion and provided a model for physical inquiry for 200 years. He changed the thinking by demonstrating that terrestrial and celestial motion, conform to the same laws of mechanics.

Newton set the course for scientific inquiry that the laws of nature must be formulated mathematically so other laws of nature could be demonstrated. 'Unlike Rene Descartes (1596-1650), however, he did not think that those principles could be asserted with self-evident certitude; he maintained that they are inductive conclusions drawn from properly analyzed experiments or observations.' [51]

After the Renaissance (1300-1700), there were more advances in chemistry and the life sciences leading to the evolution of commerce, industrial manufacturing and military science. The new scientific inquiry brought universities, for the first time, into the sciences. By the nineteenth century, scientific research was an institutionalized profession. Scientific research though somewhat institutionalized today is carried out in most private companies engaged in commercial farming, manufacturing chemical processing, medicines, and mining. So successful is progress in these areas that today our advanced societies live in relative abundance.

There is not enough space for all the scientific advances in the twentieth century, but, to sum it up, Brownowski states that 'Physics in the Twentieth Century is an immortal work. The human imagination working communally has produced no monuments to equal it, not the pyramids, not the Iliad, not the ballads, not the cathedrals.' [52]

Scientific and industrial accumulation of knowledge in five million years of human history has taken place in a very short time. Man's first recorded advance in science was 2 1/2 million years ago when he made the first stone tools. Their next major advance was with the invention of the spears, bows and arrows and theoretical strategic planning on the walls of caves. Then came the period of settling in the tending period and in a few thousand years, he began to understand agriculture and animal husbandry would be a monumental leap in intellect.

From advances in animal husbandry came knowledge of fertility in humans, animals, as well as in agriculture. The next step was backwards where rulers, secular and religious, were in competition for man's new found wealth. The next great advance in human history was in Greece where man challenged the deity and was ready to return philosophically to nature where man had learned so much.

By the year 70 the New Testament was being written. Rome controlled the world and Israelites were periodically revolting. They were also infusing themselves into the Italian peninsula. By this time, Rome had a Jewish population exceeding 10 percent and a need to counter the Jewish religion. Much that was written in Greece was lost and the new church of Italy became the dominant force throughout the Middle Ages. It was an oppressive era, and people after the plague came to question the power of the church and it's leadership. Thinking apart from church doctrine, man began to reason and we entered a period of enlightenment. A Renaissance of man's mind produced men such as Columbus (1492), Copernicus (1543), Galileo (1632), Newton (1687), and from that came Luther, who began the Reformation in 1517, Darwin (1859), and many others creating the industrial revolution.

From the year 1 up to the year 1300 there was *no scientific advances* whatever in the Christian nations or their territories. Any progress of a scientific nature or economic growth came from the Arabs and Asia. During the Renaissance man's knowledge had doubled from 1300 to 1750. 'A mere 150 years later by the year 1900, he had doubled his knowledge again. The next doubling took only 50 years (1900-50); the next 10 years (1950-60); and man's knowledge has quadrupled during each of the last two decades.' 'There are ' . . . twenty five million patent documents worldwide. . . . ' ' . . . Well over four and a half million of these are official U.S. patents, with a total of over two million for both UK and France, . . . '[53]

It was the primitive mind that survived the savanna, discovered a safety net in the water, and using stones to smash shellfish, perhaps by accident, found a means to fashion stone tools. The Stone Age was born lasting two and a half million years.

As man's brain grew he was able to take on greater challenges in big game hunting. When the herds disappeared he began tending small animals and vegetation. By 7000 BP, farming was successful in Mesopotamia and Egypt but under the control of the pharaoh in Egypt, and also as a theocracy ruled in Mesopotamia. Technological progress would remain virtually static during the pharaoh's period to year 1, with the exception of metals developed in Europe and Asia (copper, Yugoslavia, about 6500 BP.; gold, 5500 BP, Mesopotamia; Bronze, 4800 BP, southwest Asia; iron smelting 3500 BP, by the Hittites in Anatolia.

The progress that was made in Egypt were those things that would aid the pharaoh to enhance the burial cult, temples, statues, powerfacts and anything to increase his prestige and/or control over the masses. The pharaoh wanted larger tombs (pyramids) and as much wealth as humanly possible for the deity in the sun. Hieroglyphics were invented to tell *his* version of *his* glorious life that suited *his* image of great deeds in the name of *his* god(s). The invention of numbers and identifications on granaries, warehouses and vessels were for *his* accounting control over the wealth and to establish *his* ownership. So pervasive was this elitist attitude that the pharaoh, his priests, retainers, and scribes, there came a discord between workers and the clerical elite.[54]

From year 1 to 1750 Desmond tells us our knowledge doubled, however, ninety nine percent of that progress occurred between 1450 to 1750, in about 300 years. For 1450 years there was no progress with the exception of gunpowder invented in 1313 and printing in 1396, a time when theocracies were ruling by brute force. The rise of reason during the Renaissance and the rejection of ecclesiastic principles of supremacy, from 1400 to 1700 were freeing man's mind creating an era of invention, discovery, and industry to feed the worlds growing population. Science and industrialization has always been under attack from theological and secular political ideologists as succumbing to materialism. But if you analyze their theocratic and socialistic ambitions they require as an elite, one can find no justification for their greed for materialism they confiscate for themselves.

What might be interesting, is to explore what would have happened if the period from year 1 to 1450 had not occurred. What if the philosophical era that began in 1600 BP, continued to grow beyond year one, and man had chose philosophically, his natural inclinations, over his fantasy with gods. It is probable that if there had been a Renaissance at the beginning in year 1, (1450 minus the year 2000 would equal = about 550 years), means those people by 1450 BP, would have advanced to where we are today. If we add 1450 years to today's 2000, it would be equivalent to living today in the year 3450!

Also note, if there had been no era of pharaoh's rule of 4000 years, we could be living today in the equivalent of the year 7450 of our future. 'Star Trek' would be our reality today. Graham was right, 'we are behind our planetary schedule', and many of the problems we are suffering today would have been solved thousands of years ago.

It is man's responsibility, in every sense *ours*, we let others lead, while we, ignorant of our own metaphysical nature, followed their spirits and its dishonesty to the brink of depravity, 'man's inhumanity to man.' It may be the reason UFOs do not land here, or have any contact with us. They may think we can not deal with the reality of a natural universe. Theology does not want us to deal with reality, governments think we can not, and we do not know right from wrong, or bad from good.

For those who wish to live a fantasy of a great protector, in the unreal, the spiritual, of heaven and hell, there is room within the philosophy of this book, as a value issue. There is no cause for alarm if one speculates, dreams, wishes, or wants desperately to feel there is something beyond existence—it is imagination or "What if . . ." As sentient metaphysical beings, we can only act on what we can know, to live, survive, be happy, and live as long as possible. We never let what we do *not* know interfere or take precedence over what we *do* know. *In the real world, we must never act on what we do not know.* What we need to know for life on earth, the scientist, philosopher, and all of us must observe and learn how to survive, always remembering we are real natural metaphysical beings, which was how primitives lived and that was the intent of the first philosophers.

Theology is by definition is a theory of GOD, or the "supranatural" ("SUPRA" meaning 'beyond the limits of' or 'outside of') i.e. beyond the limits of nature or outside of metaphysical reality is obvious that it *can not be supernatural.* There is no conceivable scientific means for any natural being to metaphysically verify the existence of anything beyond the limits of natural sensations.

Metaphysically the real world is humanity's home, on a journey through time and space. It is within these natural surroundings, that men and women perceive what is real, and emotionally affected so that we may identify and intimately experience existence consciously. It is mankind, a metaphysical being who has, by his and her tenacity and intelligence exceeded all other entities here on earth. People have taken control of their environment, and have built many cultures by accomplishing this clearly when *acting only on what they know.*

Man is creating a new environment every generation, learning new things and by the end of the 21st century cultures will be unrecognizable to those surviving cryonic suspension hundreds of years from now. It is only we humans (homo sapien sapien sapien) who can contemplate existence, metaphysical reality, and now fully understand, that the universe or nature *is knowable* for us to survive in our time. It is within each man and woman to understand their own needs, their nature, that is, *it is fact that everything and everybody is uniquely individual.* We are each separate beings occupying our own niche in evolution physically (metaphysically), and mentally as we will find next in Book III, "Epistemology." And as human beings we have created our physique metaphysically, by reason of our intelligence epistemologically, have become masters of the world, and *therefore it is fact, that WE are truly the earth's only SUPERNATURAL BEINGS.*

JSS

BIBLIOGRAPHY: METAPHYSICS

Chapter 1
Ref.
No.

1. Peter A. Angeles author: "Dictionary of Philosophy," Published by Harper & Row Publishers, New York, 1981: P. 169, 'Metaphysics.'
2. Chagnon, Napoleon A.: "Yanomamo" 'The Fierce People,' Pub. by, Holt Rinehart and Winston, New York, 1977: P. 44 to 49, (quote, paraphrased).
3. Brown, L. Binet, Author: Parrinder, Geoffery, Editor: "World Religions," Pub. By; Facts onFile Publications, New York, 1971, Copyright holder Octopus Publishing Group, Ltd., Hamlyn Books, London: Early Australasia, Pgs. 57, 58, (quoted and paraphrased).
4. IBID, Author, C. van Furer-Haimendorf: Tribal Religions in Asia, Pgs. 46, 47.
5. Reuchlin, Abelard: "The True Authorship of the New Testament," Published by he Abelard Reuchlin Foundation, Kent, WA, 1986: Pgs., 1 to 5.
6. Knappert, Jan: "African Mythology" (1990—1995), P. 24.
7. IBID, P. 24, 58.
8. IBID, P. 11.
9. Graham, Lloyd M.: "Deceptions and Myths of the Bible," Pub. by, Carol Publishing Group, New York, 1991: P. 5.
10. IBID, P. 5, 6.

Chapter 2

11. Hawkins, Stephen W.: "A Brief History of Time," A Bantam Book, Div. Of Bantam Doubleday Dell Publishing Group, Inc., New York, 1988: P. 116.
12. IBID, Pgs. 40, 41, 116, (Paraphrased).
13. IBID, P. 39.
14. Silk, Joseph: "The Big Bang," Pub. by, W. H. Freeman and Company,New York, 1989: P. 24.
15. IBID, P. 110, 112.
16. IBID, P. 112.
17. IBID, P. 120, 121.
18. IBID, P. 113.
19. IBID, P. 115.
20. IBID, P. 6, 82, 83, (paraphrased).
21. Editorial, Pub. by, The Democrat & Chronicle, Rochester, New York, April 28, 1992: Editorial page.
22. Hawkins, Stephen W.; "A Brief History of Time," A Bantam Book, New York, 1988:
P., 39.

Chapter 3

23. IBID, P. 8.

Chapter 4

24. Garraty, John A. & Gay, Peter, Edtrs.; "The Columbia History of the World," Pub., by, Harper Collins Publishers, Inc., New York, 1988: P. 6.
25. IBID, P. 6.
26. IBID, P. 8.
27. IBID, P. 11.
28. IBID, P. 13.

29. Bronowski, Jacob; "The Ascent of Man", Pub. by, Little, Brown and Co., Boston, 1973: P. 316.

30. Garraty, John A. & Gay, Peter, Edtrs.; "The Columbia History of the World," Pub., by, Harper Collins Publishers, Inc., New York, 1988: P.15,16.

31. IBID, P. 26.

32. IBID, P. 26.

Chapter 5

33. IBID, P. 32, 34, (paraphrased).

34. Rand, Ayn; "Introduction to Objectivist Epistemology," A Mentor Book, New American Library N.Y., 1979: Abstractions from Abstractions, P. 35.

Chapter 6

–0—

Chapter 7

35. Copleston, Frederick S.J.: "A History of Philosophy," Pub. By, Doubleday, Div., Bantam Dell Publishing Group, Inc. New York, 1985: Vol. 1, P. 24

36. Mason, Stephen F.: "A History of the Sciences," Pub. by, Macmillan Publishing Company, A First Collier Book Edition, 1962, Copyright holder Simon & Schuster, Inc., NY: P. 26.

37. IBID, P. 27.

38. IBID, P. 28.

39. IBID, P. 33.

40. IBID, P. 33.

41 Hicks, R. D. MA, English translation: "Diogenes Lataertius, lives of Eminent Philosophers," Pub. by, Harvard University Press, Cambridge, Mass., 1980: Vol. 1, Introduction., XVI, XVII.

42. Cherniss, Harold: "The Riddle of the Academy," Pub by, University of California Press, Berkeley Calif. 1945: P. 62
43. Woodbridge, Frederik J. E.: "The Son of Apollo," Pub. by, Biblo & Tannen Booksellers and Publishers, Inc., New York, 1971: (Paraphrased).
44. Randal Jr, John Herman: "Aristotle," Pub. by, Columbia University Press, New York, 1960: P., 11.
45. IBID, P., 19.
46. Mason, Stephen F.: "A History of the Sciences," Pub. by, Macmillian Publishing Co., A First Collier Book Edition, 1962, Copyright holder Simon & Schuster Inc., NY: P. 52.
47. IBID, P., 25.
48. Reese, William L.: "Dictionary of Philosophy and Religion," Pub. by, Humanities Press, Inc., N.J., 1991: (quoted and Paraphrased) 'Galileo'.
49. IBID, 'Galileo'.
50. IBID, 'Kepler'.
51. Garraty, John A. and Gay, Peter, Edtrs; "Columbia History of the World," Pub., by, Harper Collins, 1988: P. 690
52. Bronowski, Jacob; "The Ascent of Man", Pub. by, Little, Brown and Company, Boston, Mass., 1973: P. 349.
53. Desmond, Kevin; "A Timetable of Inventions and Discoveries," Pub. by, M. Evans & Company, Inc., New York, 1986: Intro.
54. Mason, Stephen F.; "A History of the Sciences," Pub. by, Collier Books, Macmillian Publishing Co., New York 1962, Copyright holder Simon & Schuster, Inc., NY: P. 23.

See, FYI: Grun, Bernard; "The Timetables of History," Pub. by, Simon & Shuster—A Touchstone Book, New York, 1991: Tables from, year, 1 to 1200, column, F. Science & Technology Growth, Universities founded during these times were, in actuality, seminaries, training only men in religious related curriculum for the priesthood.

BOOK III

EPISTEMOLOGY

CONTENTS

FOR

EPISTEMOLOGY

Illustrations:
Chapter 4. Fig. 1. Ape and Evolving Human Brain Sizes

Chapter:
1. Perception 159
2. Identity 162
3. Units 164
4. The Brain 168
5. Meat & Brain Building 172
6. The Tools 182
7. The Senses 186
8. Memory 195
9. Show and Tell 202
10. Innate Knowledge 205
Bibliography 212

CHAPTER 1

Perception

Epistemology is the scientific branch of philosophy that studies *how* we learn or gain knowledge. Epistemology is from the Greek forms, *episteme* knowledge and *logos*, or 'ology,' any science or branch of knowledge, about knowledge and their theories. It is the scientific study of theories on how we learn to find facts—the truth. The basic theory that was outlined in the book introduction is that we perceive, we identify, unitize and classify as a means to reason and use them to create other abstractions or theories. Epistemology answers the questions; How do we learn? How do we know we have learned the truth? What is theory? How do we prove it? What is a concept? These are the questions we will explore in the following chapters.

Rand wrote; 'Since mans knowledge is gained and held in conceptual form, the validity of man's knowledge depends on the validity of concepts. But concepts are abstractions or universals, and everything man perceives is particular, concrete.' [1] A concrete constitutes an actual thing or instance, something real. A particular, a specific place, thing, person, class, etc. Rand quotes Edward C. Moore in the following:

> "All knowledge is in terms of concepts. If these concepts correspond to something that is to be found in reality they are real and man's knowledge has a foundation in fact; if they do not correspond to anything in reality they are not real and man's knowledge is a mere figment of his own imagination." [2]

The conceiving of a child, its birth, and going on to maturity is an evolution of a unique human being. In the womb the senses of the fetus are developing and it is known they can feel and hear. Some believe that they can smell, taste, and see shades of light. Whatever, they sense are isolated sensations. The mothers heartbeat, movement, the sounds she makes, unless sudden, sharp, or loud, the fetus may actually have tuned out. The fetus is unaware, it has no frame of reference no real awareness beyond its comfort and the mild sensations it receives. But they seem to be essentially neural reactions that may cause an awakening, or a physical awareness from time to time. And since the child has no memory its isolated sensations produce no emotional perceptions.

The physical and neural stage of sensations is the development of the individual. The mind is tabula rasa (a blank slate) and the fetus is in a complete physical state of dependence on the mother, as nature intended. The fetus has no need, or stored intelligence (memory) to prioritize any sensations to remember. It seems to be a time of body construction, testing and perfecting the physical, and neural systems. The fetus has no responsibilities, no priorities, and is in a passive state, being fed automatically it has no needs, or frame of reference to apprehend reality.

We become conscious of our responsibilities when they are forced on us by our need to eat, survive, and pursue what we desire. When the child is born it has left the security and comfort of the uterus and becomes physically active, aware of the physical needs the umbilical cord provided and there was no need to 'differentiate and integrate' any relatively mild sensations. Once a child is born he receives a prolonged series of sensations which form percepts, beginning the act of perceiving, a neonatal estimate of reality. Rand, 'Consciousness, as a state of awareness, is not a passive state, but an active process that consists of two essentials: differentiation and integration.' . . . 'A percept is a group of sensations automatically retained and integrated by the brain of a living organism.' [3]

What we sense by seeing, feeling, hearing, tasting, or smelling are the attributes of our physical neural system signaling to the brain which cause us to be conscious of existence or the real world. It is from these sensations that we form our perceptions, or is that which we perceived, and have an estimate of what we have witnessed. And' . . . epistemologically, the base of all man's knowledge is the perceptual stage.' [4] Without that concrete base nothing can be proven true, and can never be knowledge. We can sense and perceive something is real, and we have experienced that something exists. Our senses or conscious experience that correspond to something in reality form our perceptions and are immediate evaluations of what we sensed. But, that is all it is, an estimate of something concrete for study to gain more experience, because we know it is a real thing, and a basis to identify unitize classify, to form a concept or abstraction.

The validity of our senses has been long in question by subjective philosophers and theologians. Some say all is an illusion and with their rhetoric they make it *seem* possible, or perhaps its because they never went beyond their perceptions to identify, unitize or classify to establish fact. Perception is a cognitive emotional response, perhaps unclear or unreliable. There are those who say what we sense is not valid due to perspective, shades of color, shapes or light reflections. This is true at first glance, but there is no reason not to experience it again. Those who deny sensual data as meaningless are saying they are unconscious, or may never understand reality, it is self-contradictory and an oxymoron. They are the subjectivists. It is understood that our sensations form percepts that are self evident, becoming an immediate concept or perception, of which we make an immediate value judgment.

What we perceive may be an immediate emotional or intuitive judgment, relative to or dependent on the condition of awareness, to our expectancy, experience or disinterest. One can *not* rely on perceptual judgments, except in an emergency. This was the problem of primitive survival in The Pliocence epoch, five million years ago, as man emerged on to the savanna. A primitive could no longer rely on his perceptions, to learn by accident, take a guess, or act on the first or just any 'idea' that came into his head, they had to learn to remember similarities and reason—to think. With the day to day emergencies to feed oneself they would perfect their primitive epistemology to form concepts into using more and more memory, experiences, awareness of nature, and create reasoned ideas on how to survive. They had to go beyond their rudimentary animal emotional perceptions to identify and classify, if they were to outwit their predators.

CHAPTER 2

Identity

The primitive is out on the savanna and senses a movement in the grasses. He perceives it to be a four legged animal possibly grazing. At the same time he perceives the best escape route, if he should need to run, he could escape into the bush or to the river easily. Subsequently, the first perception now becomes a second studied look (identity) at the moving animal, and it is a four-legged cat-like animal. The primitive now runs. His perception lead to a second look, to an identification of the animal which 'implied' it was some kind of cat. The cat is fast, and the primitive may not make it to the bush. 'The second and closely allied stage is the awareness of specific, particular things which he can recognize and distinguish from the rest of his perceptual field—which represents the (implicit) concept "*identity*." [5]

The first step was the perception of some entity, and the next was to identify—what is it? This is our natural way of learning, by using our senses, which cognitively makes us aware of the world. It perceptively gives us our first estimation of reality, and our emotional curiosity *may* will us to observe further to identify what we are seeing or run like hell just like animals. If we knew nothing about epistemology and were left free to be ourselves, this may be our method of reasoning and we could survive, that happened millions of years ago. The primitive, at that time, had a smaller brain size than we do, but managed through evolution with many failures, to succeed by observation and identification of the world around him, and is the first step in the reasoning process that must be learned.

We might ask; if it is a natural process to sense, perceive, and identify then why learn what comes naturally? One reason is that we should know what we are doing, by understanding our nature. Another is that *we can be taught to do unnatural things*. We must assure that our children are taught properly according to our nature that is crucial to our survival. The predator or fraud plans that we fail to properly identify, to make decisions, based only on our perceptions. There are those predators who encourage or teach, that we not use our senses, to perceive, just have faith in what they say. They are appealing to our emotions only, as a con artist. The nature of fraud is to take advantage of our emotions, or to give us only a perception of truth.

We must learn how we learn, because frauds do. They know how to affect us emotionally keeping us on an emotional level hoping we never see the light of logic or reason. Rand, we perceive 'that' something exists—to identify is to learn 'what' exists. If we did not follow this method there would be no scientific progress or any need to *study* and get an education. The emphasis on 'feelings,' i.e.

perceiving only, or being taught to follow our heart instead of our head, leads to psychological dysfunction and/or mental retardation. Our senses are automatic but the mind is not. We have to learn how to think. To survive is to learn of 'what,' where, who, how, when and why—to think.

Identity:—To identify something is to recognize as distinct, different or conspicuous, with individual features, similar characteristics or attributes, and in the mind a process of integration of all the constituents and similarities to other things. Such thought creates a new concept or idea, which will implicitly be identified as an entity, new or remembered. We give it a name, perhaps a 'gizmo' if it is different from anything else. We do not stop there, for it may be still theoretical, and subject to further study, needing more supporting facts, to be proved mathematically or other method of analysis. Yet within that process, in each step of conceptualization we must *never* break our link with the reality of what was sensed, our perception of a real thing. When we break with reality, our original perception, it can no longer be knowledge, fact or truth.

CHAPTER 3

Units

In chapter one, as a physical process, our senses open the windows to reality for our brain, and cognitively the cause of consciousness. In this moment we are aware of the whole view before us yet our consciousness is limited since our reasoning process requires us to concentrate on or solve one thing at a time. We are forced to discriminate and may focus on one aspect of the whole that may capture our interest. We have been emotionally affected and we have perceived an entity. This is the nature of learning—human nature. Our distinction, above the animal, is that we have learned to remain focused on to identify our perceptions and with an increased capacity to remember, have by discovery, observation, and experimentation, specifically identified entities from our related experiences in order to survive.

'The third stage consists of grasping relationships among these entities by grasping the similarities and differences of their identities. This requires the transformation of the (implicit) concept "entity" into the (implicit) concept *unit*.' [6] It is a process of 'differentiation and integration' mathematically (four or eight legged) or in form, to identify those with similar characteristics that resemble each other but are measurably different.

'This is the key, the entrance to the conceptual level of man's consciousness. *The ability to regard entities as units is man's distinctive method of cognition*, which other living species are unable to follow. [7]

Chimpanzees and other animals may be taught simple tasks but have no way to understand simple concepts. There is no evidence that they form concepts beyond their very limited identity stage. They do not have the brain capacity. 'In more advanced mammals such as the monkeys, the evolving forebrain has grown relatively bigger,' (than in other mammals). 'In man, the forebrain's enormously expanded cerebrum, the seat of reason, has overgrown and dwarfed the rest of the brain, remodeling much of the skull.' [8] We have the ability of great memory, to reason, and conceptualize because we have a greater *physical brain capacity*. This also means, that every one with a *physically normal healthy brain*, has the means to learn equally as well, as any one else—to identify their perceptions (emotions), unitize, classify to learn and create new concepts or abstractions.

Interrelated with the concept of classification is measurement or the math. How many chimps in the group, how many fingers, toes, legs, horns, or how many acres, velocity, and also weight are in units to form new concepts. 'With the grasp of the (implicit) concept "unit"

JSS

man reaches the conceptual level of cognition, which consists of two interrelated fields: Conceptual and the Mathematical. The process of concept-formation is, in large part, a mathematical process.' [9]

Primitive safety, was a factor in judging the speed of an animal in contrast to his. He learned that a heavy stone, on the end of a longer stick, created more kinetic power to the stone as he threw or swung it in an arc. 'The requirements of a standard of measurement are: that it represent the approximate attribute, that it be easily be perceived by man and that, once chosen, it remain immutable and absolute whenever used.' [10]

Whether it was 'measurement', simple math, geometry, trigonometry or calculus it was ' . . . a process of integrating an unlimited scale of knowledge to man's limited perceptual experience—a process of making the universe knowable . . . '. [11]—Rand pointed out that we can only concentrate on one thing at a time and the process to build a concept, which is tedious, to remain focused one thought at a time, to examine and re-examine, to reason, and judge honestly, to gain knowledge—truth. To think is work and many would rather not, and it is such people who run their whole life on an emotional level, that are the first to need a counselor who may also be 'in touch with only their emotions.'

All knowledge is derived from these three concepts, perception, identity, and units or classifying and from these concepts we create larger abstractions. The primitive's reasoning process logically created his sledge, with a handle out of a hefty branch, the right size, shape, weight of stone and an entity to attach them to one another. Put together, they formed a new concept. If it works or serves as one abstractly conceived, then it is true the sledge works. The method applies in all abstractions, concepts, invention or ideas, whether it is the construction of a skateboard or a 747 jet. The basis for their abstractions is about real entities. It is the same process for theories about morals, politics, values, art and social sciences. However, theological theories, ideas or claims have no epistemological foundation, only imaginative abstract theories. If it cannot be sensed to form a perception of an entity, one cannot set out to form an identity or transform a non-entity into an 'implicit' or 'explicit' concept. In this case it is purely an imaginative abstraction, about which they create an abstraction, to create another abstraction, etc., ad infinitum irrationally. An idea without a basis in sense perception in reality can never be true.

An idea becomes fact or truth when it works, flies, or in practice, the system is fair or just and anyone may perceive it, to know it is real. If it works or found to be so over and over again, it becomes fact, which means something that actually exists in reality, something concrete or true, and it becomes knowledge.

To summarize:

Percept—To sense; is to see, hear, feel, taste, smell something.

Perception—Concept Entity: Immediate emotional evaluation of percepts.

Identity-Concept–Identity: Reasoning and defining composition of emotions.

Unit—Concepts Unit & Class: The mathematical, and classify similar entities.

Abstractions—Concepts from Concepts: Subtract, add, combine, abstractions on the basis of something perceived in reality

These are the terms and steps in how we learn to find the truth or establish facts about the real world and our existence—it is our epistemology—how we learn.

CHAPTER 4

The Brain

This, and the following chapter, 'Meat & Brain Building' are metaphysical, because they deal with the physiology of our being and brain which is a physical organ. In answering the question as to how we learn, unanswered for the reader, may be, how does the brain work, and why does ours function better than any animal? The ancients thought that our emotional and reasoning came from the heart. 'Inscriptions' on the walls of the burial chambers, 'of the King Wenis (4350 BP)' were 'hieroglyphic texts dealing with the king's future life and adducing in the process considerable evidence from theology, ritual and mythology. These writings called "The Pyramid Texts," form the earliest corpus of material relevant to Egyptian religion,' [12]

In Egypt the texts show:

> 'Clearly the heart was regarded as the medium of spiritual understanding; it was not removed like other organs (when being mummified), and a short text on the scarab usually requested the heart not to testify against the dead in the judgment before Orisis.' [13]

The early philosophers Pythagoras and Alemaen in the twenty-sixth century BP theorized, or perceived and were scientifically motivated to discover, that the centers of thought perhaps originated in the brain. Hippocrates by 2305 BP had evidence that placed the centers of sight and hearing, and the entire control of our being in that 'Spherical Body,' our head.

We begin with the physical brain: 'The human brain can store about 2 1/2 million times more information than today's most advanced computer. The human brain can hold some 10 million 'bits' of information and all tucked away in a skull that measures about one twentieth of a cubic foot.' It 'weighs about 3 pounds.' . 'To attempt to equal—let alone surpass—cerebrum humanum would probably require the long term pooling of all available computer scientists, psychologists, linguists and brain surgeons in the USSR, USA, Europe and Japan.' [14]

The human brain is similar to a gorilla's when we are born, but, triples in size within the first year. There is nothing to compare it with, in the animal world. It is said that a child within the first two years of life acquires knowledge that is unequaled (in any two years) for the rest of its life. The child's will to learn is voracious during these early years of growth. And we seem to relegate his brain for too many years of frivolity called childhood. The children who are *loved and encouraged* to learn, what they perceive as 'cool,' in any kind of home school atmosphere are among the happiest.

It is thought that the spinal cord at the base of the brain in our head has gradually become enlarged. It is in the vicinity of our chief sense organs called the medulla, just below the pons, which continues up to include the mid-brain. 'The medulla controls breathing, talking, singing, swallowing, vomiting, blood pressure and even (partially) heart rate. The pons . . . neurally links the cerebral cortex and the cerebellum.' [15]

The mid-brain allows us elementary seeing and the cerebellum coordinates body movements. All this is located at the underside slightly down towards the rear of our brain. Located above and all over these parts are the thalamus and hypothalamus.

'The thalamus processes all senses except smell.' . . . 'the hypothalamus' handles things 'outside conscious awareness: endocrine levels, water balance, sexual rhythms, food intake, and the automatic nervous systems. It also handles mood, motivation states, including anger, placidity, fatigue, and hunger.' [16]

The limbic system above the hypothalamus has connections to both cortical centers in the temporal lobes. Please note; it is the primitive or emotional brain. The higher temporal lobes function as our thought and cognitive learning areas. The two cerebral hemispheres are involved with our highest conceptual and motor functions. They consist of the overlying cerebral cortex; the basal ganglia that together with the cerebellum coordinate all body movement; and three large nuclear groups, the caudate nucleus the putamen and the pallidium.' [17]

The most fascinating part of the brain is the cerebral cortex, described by Jack Fincher, in his book, "The Brain: Mystery of Matter and Mind", in the opening paragraphs on "Man's Temporal Heavens":

> 'Most of what they vie to control originates in the gray matter of the cerebral cortex. Less than a quarter inch thick, it forms a fissured mold snug up against the skull. The cortex measures about two and a half feet square, roughly twice the expanse of this book opened and weighs twenty ounces or so. This "bark" of flesh is composed of six layers of cells meshed in some ten thousand miles of connecting fibers per cubic inch. About ten billion pyramidal, spindle and stellate cells spangle the cortex like twinkling galaxies.' [18]

In this section, neurophysiologist Bert MacLean, when asked, 'Is the brain still evolving—and if so, where? MacLean jested that the vaguely charted prefrontal cortex, realm of planning and foresight, might be a proper area for future evolution.' [19]

Will the brain continue to evolve? The brain has evolved from a smaller spinal medulla; pons, and thalamus into one much larger. However, what increased dramatically during our evolution is the great part of our brain sitting high upon the thalamus, the huge fronted lobe parietal lobe and somewhat the occipital lobe. This large part of the brain increased the large cover of cerebral cortex described above in our 'Temporal Heavens,' the gray matter.

> 'Within man's brain billions upon billions of nerve cells in the human brain make perhaps as many as a quadrillion

> connections. As each nerve finger reaches toward another an earthly spark passes; an electrical and chemical impulse that enables us to think feel, learn, remember, move and sense the world around us. Flashing intricate patterns from one neuron to the next, this electrochemical spark somehow builds awareness (consciousness), giving man power to contemplate his own existence. It is indeed a spark of life.' [20]

This genetic ensemble, the structure, physical, electro-chemical and neural activity increased to accommodate knowledge (memory, etc.). This was due to the many complex problems we had to solve in our changing dangerous environment for the last five million years. Within this structure are the 'sparks of life', our awareness. By using our brain, we developed our reasoning and recall skills, which in turn would improve the possibility of evolutionary mutations that would increase brain size, and our memory. The development in our parietal lobe intensified our sense of feeling that is so important in identifying textures by touch, and improved the pleasure of touching and being touched in sexual foreplay. Biologists have observed adolescent dolphins involve themselves in sex play by swimming very close and touching each other. They also will swim belly to belly, rubbing obviously a sensual learning experience to encourage future coitus in adulthood.

How did our brain expand? Why? What caused our physical brain to grow, increase our memory (subconscious) and evolve to a conscious state capable of contemplation and creativity? Why did it happen to us and not other animals? That is the subject of the next chapter. This chapter and the following are metaphysical, scientifically.

There is evidence that Cro-Magnon came on the scene about 35,000 to 50,000 BP. It is also thought that they may have existed around 120,000 years ago and had a slightly smaller brain size than Neanderthal (Fig 1.) that was obviously more efficient. We are Cro-Magnon (Homo Sapien Sapien) and some would say because of our

ss

present high intelligence we should be called Homo Sapien Sapien Sapien which is certainly undeserved. Does anyone know why?

Fig. 1.
APE AND EVOLVING HUMAN BRAIN SIZES

(M = Million years ago) Brain Size(c.c.)

TIME		SPECIES	LOW	MEAN	HIGH
Present		Baboon	200	–	–
Present		Chimpanzee	320	394	480
3.6	M	Australopithecus Afarensis 'Lucy'	435	508	600
1.7	M	Homo Erectus	775	978	1225
0.10	M	Homo Sapien Neanderthal	1000	1500	2000
0.030	M	Homo Sapien Sapien Cro-Magnon	900	1400	1900

Epistemologically, Cro-Magnon, before 12,000 BP, was perhaps more capable than many people are today. *All* primitives in the world were able to provide for themselves. There was practical teaching of the young to survive. They obviously knew *how* to teach, for they passed on their skills for five million years. Cro-Magnon's survival, like 'Lucy's,' heavily depended on knowledge of the real world or he would starve. It was the gathering of such knowledge, experience, and their memory that created our great brain. They had evolved into fully conscious human beings that would eventually begin to understand their own nature and the meaning of existence, because they were using their great brain that a charitable nature had provided.

CHAPTER 5

Meat & Brain Building

When our Miocene ancestors found themselves on a growing

savanna amidst diminishing forests, they had seen their fruit diet disappearing. True, they did not understand where the fruit went. But they did know that on the ground there was food, insects, some berries, and tiny ants or rodents, but none of this tiny ground food could fill them like a lot of fruit. They could not digest any of the vegetation or their seeds. There was nothing on the savanna that they could stuff themselves with. The only other food was live running animals, flying birds, and in the water fish, crabs, clams, etc.

Hunger is pain, and they probably killed to eat any small animals that were on the ground that could fill them. As the forests dwindled primate became used to a meat diet—it was the only substantial food around. As the forests completely disappeared, the primate found itself the object of the savanna predators, the lions, cheetahs, tigers, and pack animals, such as the hyenas.

The primates that were able to escape into the water for refuge were distinctly meat eaters. Fish is good but no substitute for fruit and now meat for which they had acquired a taste. Relatively small amounts of meat may fill them to supply the energy needed on the savanna.

The small animals disappeared under the onslaught of the savanna predators and our primate ancestors. The grounded primate's need for food led them to scavenging anything on the savanna. Such meat forays, from the water to the savanna, to scavenging a large kill by a predator, became the only source of food with millions of years of drought ahead. Between the safety of the waters and the access to his predator's kills, there was a need to outwit both their predators and the other scavengers.

The primitive's basic diet would be meat. They obviously, knew nothing about vegetation, roots or tubers. Grasses, grains and most of the 'edible' plants could not be eaten and digested until man controlled fire. 'Thus the pattern appears to emerge is that fire is only documented in Africa sites that are older than 10,000 to 20,000 years . . . Negative evidence from very old or unprotected sites has little significance, and we are left in ignorance of the time when fire first came into domestic use in Africa.' [21] It is probable that fire was

JSS

in use during Neanderthal's time, but only sporadic evidence of fire is available around 90,000 BP. However, after 35,000 BP, more sites show fire was used, but there is no evidence Cro-Magnon cooked their meat. Fire was for warmth in the northern regions, or to fend off predators for home base for safety, and actual control perhaps occurred about 20,000 years ago.

Besides meat we ate fruits and nuts, grubs and ants, insects, bird's eggs, small animals, and 'If locusts swarmed, then we joined protein scramble, and when wild honey came into its short season, we reveled in honey and ignored the bee stings as well.' [22] We became carnivorous because other foods were not plentiful. The greater bulk of food lay out on the savanna, felled by predators that could not eat their entire kill. With our tenacity to survive, we carved a niche in the order of the savanna. By *increasing our awareness* we began to exert control of our lives within the forces of nature.

How we began to control our lives was through a process of thought. But what made our brain grow? Did thinking, remembering, perceiving or reasoning cause our brain to expand? Was it nutrition? Robert Ardrey, in his book the "Hunting Hypothesis" builds on his recurring theme, that man's nature was to be a killer, because he ate meat. Few anthropologists subscribe to that notion. For five million years man had the capability to kill small animals such as rodents and rabbits. Larger ones, with advantages in speed or numbers (pack animals), could outwit or defeat man in any confrontation. The primitive did not have spears, bows and arrows, fishhooks, or snaring tools until Cro-Magnon invented them 40,000 years ago During the primitive's entire era of evolving into a human being, a time span of 5,000,000 years, less 40,000, he was *unarmed.*

Most animals not only had speed and/or numbers but sharp claws and fangs including great strength. We were not the 'killers' but the *prey* that out-wits them all by our cunning and ability to seize the opportunity to *scavenge* the predators meat successfully, and in safety, his two priorities. Ardrey found reference to meat eating in a book called "What We Eat Today" (1972), by Professor Michael and Sheilagh Crawford. Their findings show that nutrition specifically, *meat alone*, contributed to the physical expansion and maintenance of our *brain, neural, and vascular, systems.*

Crawford, head of the Department of, Nutritional Biochemistry, at the Nuffield Institute of Comparative Medicine at the Institute of Zoology in London and is holder of a special chair at the University of Nottingham. He has written two books and many papers on nutrition, which are listed in the bibliography. It is understood by most, that nutritionally there are two types of fat. The first one is *saturated* or bad fat gives us love handles, potbellies, thighs, and big butts. Saturated fat is the white and hard substance surrounding red meat and/or marbleized throughout on obese animals. Crawford and his colleagues stress avoidance of these hard saturated fats, but in doing so, to take care and *not* eliminate the second *polyunsaturated fats* in our diet. He says we should not throw out the baby with the bath water. Eliminating meat in one's diet will inevitably cause brain deficiencies, and mental or psychological dysfunction. Children are vulnerable in both schools (brain and mental) in their diet.

Please take note, there are two types of unsaturated fats. These are the structural types or invisible fats, and like all foods, the fatty acids originate in plants, but are of a simple order. The first type is Linoleic; which appears mostly in seeds. The second type is; linolenic; which appears in leafy vegetation or grasses but both are *not* of the long chain variety that we need for our brain, neural and vascular systems. We cannot convert them like the herbivore.

The *unsaturated fats* are very simple structures and *only herbivores* can convert them into *elongated chains of fats* required for human vascular, neural and brain building, and maintenance. *Fish* likewise possess, *long chain fatty acids* needed for our neural systems.

Herbivores ingest seeds and grasses and those linoleic and linolenic nutrients passing through their liver are converted to the longer complex chains. We, in turn, consume meat or fish, further processing those nutrients through our liver, completing the process for brain building. More than *sixty percent* (60%) of our brain and nerve tissue is lipid (unsaturated fats). Approximately 50% of our vascular tissue is likewise lipid. It is these complex fatty chains that are found in meat *not* in the simple vegetable, seed, and nuts acids that we eat. Vegetation supplies some vitamins, but *not* the polyunsaturated fats needed build healthy veins, nerves, and brains.

Protein is important but this singular approach to nutrition is dangerous. 'Animal proteins are better balanced than vegetable.' 'Meat also has a spectrum of structural fats. For example, liver is an excellent food source,' so are . . . kidneys, hearts and brains . . . '...'Cold blooded fish evolved with high proportions of complex polyunsaturates.' ..'Apart from well-known fish delicacies like squid, mussels or oysters are good sources of the marine polyunsaturates. [23] .'Crawford spent five years at Makerere University College in East Africa where he taught at Medical school and carried out research on human nutrition. He has studied simple tribes in Africa, complex experiments in the laboratory and Western civilization. The authors in 1972 concluded that the quality of the food supply that guided and helped sustain our evolution is *in decline* and a slow deterioration has been established for several generations and most likely the cause of most vascular and neural illness. They published that book in 1972.

In 1993 "Nutrition and Neurodevelopmental Disorders" in a paper on 'Nutrition and Health' Vol 9 pp. 81-97,1993, by M.A. Crawford and his Colleagues, Doyle, Leaf, Leighfield, Ghebremeskel and Phylactos are from the Institute of Brain Chemistry and Human Nutrition, Queen Elizabeth Hospital for Children, London. I quote from their abstract:

> 'The most vulnerable period of neural development is during embryonic and fetal growth.
>
> There is now both retrospective and protective evidence that maternal nutrition prior to conception is most important for pregnancy outcome.'
>
> 'Our studies on maternal nutrition in pregnancy again illustrate the relationship of maternal nutrition to birth weight and head circumference.'

> 'Our studies also reveal that premature and intrauterine growth retarded babies were born with defects of the type of essential fatty acids (arachidonic AA, docosahexaenoic DHA acids, i.e. the unsaturated fats we speak of here) *known* to be required for brain development.'[24]

The paper's "Introduction" notes the brain is 60% lipid with, 'high-energy consumption. 'During its most active phase in fetal growth uses as much as 70% of the energy delivered to it by the mother and the neonate still uses 60%.' The fetus does not use but stores the same fats mentioned above that can be used later, after birth. Good nutrition habits before pregnancy is advised. 'According to, W H O, each year some 1.4 million babies are born with or develop severe neurodevelopment disorders with life-long consequences.' Appropriate nutritional intervention may eradicate neural disorders.[25]

'Handicap associated with neuro-developmental disorder is however still a serious problem with a disproportionately high cost to society.' The cost in the UK is estimated at about 2 billion pounds a year. 'The cost excludes mild disabilities and those who lost the opportunity to reach their full genetic potential.' ' . . . there is a close relationship between low birth weight and handicap which includes poor cognitive, ability, mental retardation, poor vision, hearing cerebral palsy, retinopathy, blindness, epilepsy and autism." ' . . . then it is clear that most common disorders of the premature and low birth weight infant are also membrane related: The spectrum includes haemolytic anemia, broncho-pulmonary dysplasia, retinopathy, per-ventricular hemorrhage, cerebral palsy and mental retardation.'[26]

Also, ' . . . the Retina Foundation in Dallas have found babies fed breast milk performed better in visual and stereo acuity tests as well as letter matching and other scores for cognitive function when compared with babies fed formula.' Supplementing babies with DHA resulted in performance closer to that of breast-fed babies. Human milk contains significant amounts of DHA. It has also been observed that babies that died for unexplained reasons had lower levels of

DHA in their cerebral cortex if they had been formula fed as opposed to being fed on their mothers milk. (note; animal or cows milk contains *no* long chain fatty acids AA and DHA)' [27]

Crawford's and Marsh's co-authored the book, 'The Driving Force" (Harper & Row, NY, 1989). David Marsh a writer with a background in agriculture and philosophy makes the work an excellent reference that not only reiterates what is said in the first book "What We Eat Today," but updates everything we've learned here. The book's history of evolution argument, which supports the fatty acid brain concept, describes early lipid development. [28] The long chain fatty acid, and herbivore relationship to vascular and brain development, in human evolution is no longer theory, but proven, and has become fact.

We ate meat because our natural habitat was reduced to a few pockets of forest. There was competition to take over the crowded trees but a bloody carnage or great fight was not in their nature or the organizational skills, to kill their own species. Fighting or killing was not imprinted upon their psyche. They, as a rule, moved away from confrontation, to another source of food, and in so doing many species were forced into extinction. Some did survive, but the key was an individual effort to understand their environment, by observing, by trial and error, and the boldness born of their desperation to eat. It was their sole occupation for *five million years.*

Our primitive ancestors ate meat for five million years until 11,000 to 9,000 BP, when they began to domesticate animals and were learning agricultural concepts. They began eating grains, wheat barley in the Near East around 9,000 years ago and meat would be eaten less. The belly could be filled, by relatively passive means, farming vegetation. This sharp change in diet does not bode well for man.

In 1975 studies of human coprolites, (dessicated or petrified remains of feces), 'started by a Canadian Eric Callen in the 1960's' now *show* us a forensic, record of human diet. Dating the finds and examining them for seeds, roughage, etc. reveals diet in periods of man's development. Neanderthal coprolites' showed *no* plant remains whatsoever. Their age is about fifty thousand years, before the widespread use of controlled fire.' Neither do the few tested that are from a much earlier period. Plant foods were just not practicable for humans before their ability to make fire. [29]

However, meat, by itself would not cause the brain to become enlarged. Nutrition from those fatty acids would allow the brain to grow physiologically. Many animals, predator carnivores like tigers, lions, cheetahs, hyenas, wolves, and others never did increase their brain size proportional to man. They were also on a herbivore meat diet, just like us. There had to be some other reason or a combination of causes (meat + plus +) that caused the brain's genetic code to multiply or increase in size. It could lie somewhere in us, in our behavior. If we do not use something of our physique, it withers in time, even in our lifetime.

Nature, evolutionary development, biologically, is efficient in retaining that which contributes to survival, and will *not* retain that which has no use. If we exercise our muscles, they become larger and improve in quality. The same thing obviously, happens when we think, recall, and reason, we *use* our brain. We increased our subconscious, our memory and reasoning in the higher temporal lobes because we had to remember more to reason with. We were on the savanna, by the shore, hunting in the brush, and learning new ways to survive in different environments. We were mentally active.

When we think of the odd set of environmental and coincidental factors that brought about our evolution, intelligent life is perhaps the rarest of events in the universe.

Our need to survive, remember, reason, and learn new ways to survive forced us to exercise our brain, rather than depending on the environment to supply our food, has caused our brain to grow larger. It is evident the predator has evolved in an environment that provided plenty of weaker and slower animals, for it to prey on in relative safety. Sort of a free lunch with no need to think where its next meal would come from—the herd was in front of him. So too was the scavenger who carved a niche in large packs and could out run the large carnivores. But man was no match for the large or smaller pack predator scavengers. However, the primitive, by intellectually

JSS

using his brain to survive the animal became no match for man. Over a few million years by exercising his brain, hands, and body he genetically improved himself. We seem to be the cause of our evolutionary inheritance, not the environment. We outwitted evolutionary extinction by large ferocious and fast animals that had evolved to kill its prey. We began to control our existence with our minds, and a natural universe gave us a. big brain that we used to perceive, identify and unitize.

Anthropologists such as Desmond Morris has warned that eliminating fats altogether from our diets (going vegetarian) is dangerous. We may not know precisely the causes of neural disability, but common sense tells us that if a large component such as fats is eliminated from one's diet, deficiencies will occur in some way. We also know cells, in our body, are being nourished by what we eat, which in turn enters our blood supply. There is in every cell some unsaturated fat, but there is 50% in our vascular and 60% in our neural and brain systems! Thus, if we eliminate unsaturated fats from our diet, it doesn't take a rocket scientist to understand that we are physically devolving since we are now experiencing increasing neural and brain deterioration.

Sixty years ago, Alzheimer's disease and dementia did not exist, as well as infant death syndrome (the neonate forgets to breathe). Nor did all the psychological disorders such as stress syndromes, and many people take an emotional view rather than a reasoned approach. Much of the psychological is taught, but it shows a lack of identifying our emotions, or applying simple logical reasoning in all aspects of our life and its problems. We don't think or really use our brains, but believe anything that fits our emotional desires is valid without question or reason. We have heard and read all the views on the causes of stress, modern civilization, etc., are they valid?

Unsaturated fats increase the efficiency of synapses junctions from our 'temporal heavens' to the tips of our toes. Fats are the chemistry of life that provide the spark and snap to sharpen our senses and the thinking process. If nothing else think what it does for sex. Crawford and his colleagues have found animals low in unsaturated fats, fail to breed. Those that do, have low birth weight babies and all the attendant neural and vascular problems that may occur. There is considerable evidence that the lack of unsaturated fatty acids causes physical and mental degeneration.

The Tokyo Metropolitan Institute of Gerontology after a sixteen year survey of that country's aging population, has found, according to a July 1993 Wall Street Journal article, that fatty acids are essential and good for you. They gave no definitive explanations as to why. But we know they eat a lot of fish—raw.

The recent 1992 movie "Lorenzo's Oil", a true account about the struggle of an ADL victim, a child, to restore his deteriorating brain with long chain unsaturated fatty acids. They were looking for them in vegetation! It was twenty years after the Crawford's had published their findings.

The "20-20" Program on ABC television network aired a segment on July 9, 1993 about the old people. It seems the University of Georgia's, Gloria Clayton, headed a study on 100 year olds of which there were about 36,000 surviving in this country. The study showed they shared four similar attributes. One, they had a positive attitude and were able to psychologically cope with the personal losses of friends, relatives, spouses, and children. Two, they had some basic interest that kept them mentally active and physically on the move. Third, they consumed more calories than others did. Fourth, they ate more *fat* than most people did.

Meat and brain building gave us a healthy brain, a functional mind to use and perceive, identify, unitize, classify or create wider abstractions, in order to succeed and survive. It is this epistemological reason that I felt it appropriate to include the brain's metaphysical science here, in Book III. Learning is dependent upon meat and fish in our diet. And if we eat meat and fish consistently with some of our other tasty favorites, we still have to think to exercise our brain to perceive, identify, unitize, classify and reason for maintenance and efficient growth and for the future evolution of our species.

CHAPTER 6

The Tools

The human brain we possess today has not, noticeably, increased in EQ since the time of Cro-Magnon (Homo sapiens) thirty thousand years ago, and was slightly smaller than Neanderthal's. Cro-Magnon was learning to use this great brain. Millions of years in the wilds of the forests, seas, and savannas sharpened human senses so their perception and identity of the environment was by far more effective than any animal predator. They likely had avoided them, scavenged, and survived, then learned to hunt them down. Their sharp perceptions and identifying on the savanna and in the water led to classifying their similarities and forming concepts of everything they came in contact with. They possibly understood the limits of animals—when the lion got full and left the carcass to lay down or dose—when the hyenas or others would advance—they were learning what they could do to intercede. They classified those that could be intimidated and those they could not. How large had the pack to be, to give up on chasing them off. Then with a leap in intellect to make tools to successfully scavenge.

The club, made of bone or piece of wood, may have frightened a single hyena. However, the prudent idea would be to get away fast before a pack of hyenas grew significantly. They could not rip the flesh off bones, nor sinews, muscle, and skin that held flesh together. It was difficult to break apart those areas where bones were attached to other bones. If it was a small animal they could carry it off, but if larger, it became a problem to dissect or they had to chew it off with their teeth, perhaps.

The primitive saw the tooth marks of the predator that penetrated and tore open the skin to get at the flesh. Every Stone Age tool kit has a tooth like tool. The idea of the tool was 'if the tiger's tooth can do this I will make a tooth from this stone,' 'I can tear the flesh, or cut too, with sharp edge of stone'—definitely involving abstract thought. In their imagination they saw they might be able to quickly cut away all the flesh before the first hyenas got there.

We can be sure that with every new stone tool there was planning and strategy on how best to use it to strip or cut up a carcass more efficiently, i.e. to get the most meat faster. One primitive would wield a hand ax to chop, another a cleaver to slice though tough hides, one with a tooth like wedge to separate knuckle joints, and another one with a sharp cutting edge tool to slice the flesh. In less than a few minutes or maybe, in some cases, less than a minute, when they could strip the largest and most prized meat sections of a large animal, or a small gazelle completely. Later with sharp stone hand axes they would learn to dismember the large animal entirely, and carry the whole thing off to camp. The tool was an idea, to affect a new strategy, both were theoretical, and would be proved or disproved in their execution on the savanna—in reality.

'Some of the Mousterian tools are so beautifully made that some may have been used primarily in formal rituals.' [30] Those found in Volgu, France were dated to be made about 20,000 years ago. Some were delicately sculpted, out of beautifully colored flint, and called "laurel leaves," because they are so thin and delicate to the point of being able to break them with one's hands, and therefore assumed to be of no practical use. Some people have made a 'leap of faith' jumping to the conclusion, without further analysis that the delicate flint knives were made for symbolic or ceremonial purposes, which is highly erroneous, or inventing reasons, and according to the empirical evidence ca not be true.

Most anthropologists would agree that that no one can determine, from any evidence found at sites, including "Laurel Leaves," or "Venus" figures, scientifically determine the thoughts or rituals of early primitives. What we exhume of human remains and their stone tools from the past are real objects, whether made poorly or skillfully, they were manufactured by the mind and hand of a primitive for the purpose of cutting, chopping, and slicing up of animals to eat. Evidence of animal bones (with cutting marks), human bones (on cite), and stone tools attest only to such activities. Throughout history we have created some very thin bladed knives, very sharp, for specific uses such as cheeses, for spreads, serrated knives for bread, and small thin steak knives. Similar tools we use today may have their roots in the Stone Age.

Delicate tools, such as the "Laurel Leaves", may have been used at the scavenging cite, even though it may break easily if not wielded correctly. They may have been used for extremely quick specialized cutting (such as skinning) at the scavenging cite with a skillful hand. Thicker cutting tools have more resistance to cutting and are slower. For hundreds of thousands of years, using such stone tools may have increased their ability to grip and use even the thinnest tools most effectively. But such a sleek beautiful, thin, fragile, and exquisite tool, of colored flint was made with pride in workmanship, may not have been used at the scavenging site, but kept in camp where they have been usually found, and may have been more personal to them.

When the dismembered carcass was brought into camp, all gathered around as the cutters cut up the chunks of flesh for everyone. Each member of the clan received their portion and sat, squatted or stood to eat it. One method of eating raw meat is to cut it in long strips. The strip of meat, in the left hand, he would put as much of the strip into the right side of his mouth as he would like, holding the meat with his teeth. With the thin blade in his right hand, places the flat of the blade against his cheek bringing it to the meat, slicing close the lips, but away from his face. The thinner and sharper the blade, the safer the operation, since he cannot see where the blade edge is cutting the meat off. With their very delicately made cutting tool, which to them was a beautiful implement, they could very leisurely, cut their meat in fine small pieces to be eaten with less chewing and wear and tear on their aging teeth.

I remember the movie made many years ago in the 30's or 40's of the novel "Nannook of the North" looking for his 'good knife' in his igloo, then using it to cut the seal meat that was held in his teeth. I think, since the thin blades are usually found at camping sites, they were the first such eating implements. I think they were being extremely practical with a 'touch of elegance.' We can be sure they maintained them and kept them sharp which is why they all look as though they were never used, just as we keep sharp steak knives, hunting or fishing knives today and small pen knives for feather pen sharpening in our early writing period.

When discussing workmanship in modern times it has been said; 'When you cease to try and improve your skills, you cease to be good at your job.' It is not surprising when scientists see great strides and improvements in the technology they create. We are witnessing invention, manufacture, quality improvement, technical refinement, increased skill, and the *competition* to make something better, and easier to make and use. There is no empirical evidence in any discovery or scientific evaluation of all excavated cites before 12,000 BP that would establish religious, spiritual, or ritual activity in primitive times, except for evidence after 12,000 BP. What we do know is primitive man was learning to better perceive, conceptualize, and identify and form concepts into wider abstractions and becoming extremely skillful becoming 'good' at feeding himself, and with a little class.

The industrial revolution occurred about the end of the Renaissance, but now we know there was a primitive Renaissance beginning about 2,500,000 years ago. Here was the time of enlightenment, the maturation of a young hominoid still learning how to learn, and with a full blown brain in progress, that ushered in a manufacturing revolution we call the Stone Age. It lasted until about 6,000 years ago when man first learned how to smelt metals.

CHAPTER 7

The Senses

Our senses facilitate, metaphysically, an epistemological awareness of reality. From the moment sensations are received by our body, and then transmitted to the brain. They activate our consciousness called cognition, the act or process of knowing or perception. Our senses are like those electronic receptors of light and sound that turn on our lamps or appliances. When we see, hear, feel, taste, and smell something, each activates an area of our conscious brain. If we receive no sensations at all, our conscious state cannot be activated and we are unconscious, until at least one sense is capable of receiving and transmitting it to the brain. If one or two senses are impaired, we may be limited in the process of cognition, being only somewhat capable of self-direction to take action.

Cognitively aware, initially, we are perceiving, a wide field of view, of which we may focus, be discriminate on a particular entity, for some emotional, intuitively or curious reason, and for the moment form a perception of what it may be. Perceptively we are in a process of learning, charged for the moment with an emotional estimate, at some level of interest or disinterest. It is that which 'catches the eye' or one's 'fancy' that deserves our attention, and gives us the motivation to understand the world or some entity we have perceived with our senses.

Consciousness is the result of our physical neural ability to sense through organic means, which energizes the brain. Cognition happens in the womb. The fetus is at its lowest level of consciousness, which happens possibly after the growing, of muscle, bone, organs, neural receptors of the five senses, and brain physiology is complete. It is the evolution of an individual, physically resulting in consciousness, to potentially evolve into an intelligent individual. But in the fetus state, the neural system is undergoing limited testing, where cognitively the brain is idling, only physically responding for comfort, since there is no need to act in its own interest. His physical evolution in the womb is the only free ride he will ever get in life. The only way one can achieve that in the real world is to soundly sleep, become comatose or die.

Once the child is born a more perceptible phase in the evolution of the consciousness takes place. Within the first year, the brain triples in size and his sensual data increases in a new external reality as his body and senses leave the protective confinement of the womb. His sensual neural system receives increased input from the outside world, louder noises, rough clothing, and hunger pains, which he bitches about most. He can see light reflected off entities, and it will take about two weeks before he can visually focus on particular things. It will be some time before he, with the help of his parents, can sort out these chaotic amplified or confused perceptions. Consciousness from the fetal stage, to the neonate, childhood, and to adult, is a maturation of cognitive abilities based on primal needs—self interest, of which if he is to survive, must be primary.

The quality of sensual input to the brain is dependent on the health of his physical being. Affecting the senses may be genetic, disease, or poor nutrition, from the mother's health before conception, to the care of the child, or growing up to young adult. The sensual input is the given and in a normal, healthy neural system all act in much the same way, even with individuated genetic physiological variations. Nature has provided well for us. We all can see, hear, feel, taste, and smell all things equally as well under similar circumstances. With even missing senses or impairment, we can through heroic effort, overcome the disability, and experience a reality quite similar, at least in some respects as our healthy counterpart.

We can all witness the Grand Canyon or Niagara Falls and perceive the same field of view, or in focusing on particular entities excluding the rest of the field, point it out to someone, and they will be able to see the same thing as we do. We can see the smallest microbe through the microscope in the laboratory, perceive it, and identify a certain attribute. This can be shown and demonstrated to the other scientist, in the laboratory, to identify and classify it, as a particular entity. If this can be described and demonstrated to others then we have proved the theory incorrect or correct. The only way we can prove a theory or pass on knowledge to others is that we can all experience and sense reality equally, and not getting that confused with our emotional response, is objectivity. The discovery is dependent on our senses, and proof depends on the senses of others, to verify and experience that of the discoverer. If everyone can sense it is real objectively then it is true.

'Consciousness, as a state of awareness, is not a passive state..'[31] We are constantly aware of our surroundings, our field of view, and may actively perceiving, identifying, classifying, and evaluating all of our waking hours. It may all become memory or be an integral part of our subconscious as another alternative for some task in the future. It is a mental process of distinguishing differences or synonymous with others to merge into concepts in creating new theories.

We are physically and mentally active all of our conscious hours. Physically our body gets tired and we rest by sitting down, stop what we are doing or lay down, but our senses may continue working. Our senses, their neural systems, eventually become physically fatigued, and they need rest. Then they just shut down, putting us in a state of sleep, until the neural system, like all the rest of the physical complexes are rejuvenated. Then, we slowly awake becoming fully aware again. But why does that dam alarm have to go off before rejuvenation is complete?

Some people may deny that our senses are reliable and that to see one must close their eyes and what they imagine the entity is—is true. As silly as this may sound grown men and women believe or have faith that what one cannot see is real and what we see is unreal. The book, "The Evidence of the Senses" 1988, by David Kelly is a scientific work concerning sense and perception. His basic position is realism. 'It holds that we directly perceive physical objects existing independently of the mind that the senses are an open window on a world that is what it seems.' [32] We look outward to perceive that something real exists and to identify, unitize or classify what exists. Only then may we conceptualize to form abstractions from abstractions all based on our original sensual perceptions.

The positions he argues against are, first, 'Representationalism that denies we can perceive this world directly:' [33] It is the argument that what we sense are distortions, therefore, no need to identify, etc.. If this were true then no science would be possible. 'Even further from realism is the phenomenalist or ideal view which dispenses with the external world altogether.' '. . . only the mind and its images exist. "The world that seems to lie before us is like a land of dreams" is just that—a dream.' [34] How does one learn in a distortion or a dream—by imagining? Imagination or to dream up an idea is a mental process of taking known perceptive experiences of objects in reality and imagining them as a reasoning exercise in one's mind as a new concept, theory or invention, is creativity. It is how theories are born. They too must be proven, by establishing roots (perceptions) in reality, to show so that anyone's senses may verify it is truth. That is scientific method.

The subjectivist writer who denies we can perceive this world directly, in his work, is also, as he admits, a distortion, and since his work has to be *his* distorted perceptions, is therefore, not worth reading or believing. The argument is an ancient one used for the vast ignorant innocents, before scientific proof presented itself, that we could identify, unitize, and create wider abstractions. It has become self evident that we can perceive nature and by patient honest conscientious observation, and experimentation to gain experience and knowledge of what is true or false.

The other is the 'phenomenalists or idealist view', which denies any senses at all; The idealist lives in a fantasy. He creates an idea or image in his mind and that is what he would act on—no need to root the idea in reality. Whatever the idealist's imagination thinks of an entity is what really exists. The 'idea' being, our senses are invalid. Well, we know his are.

Kelly's book is for those philosophers and people who would like to study more about senses and perception. It is an objective view on a realist's theory of perception, citing opposing views. An explanation of all the arguments and his analysis is not necessary here, which would take much space. However, he does show us proof for the validity of the senses.

The primitive had no innate knowledge to start on their learning curve through Miocene and Pleistocene periods. As an animal with barely the functioning brain of chimpanzees, they began with an exceptionally limited memory of how to live in a rain forest. Their existence in the canopy and little forays on the ground gave them a little versatility, but the complexity of the canopy may have accounted for a longer childhood or learning period, than most animals. They could not exist in the trees without learning 'how' from their parents. They learned by seeing—observing—looking long and intently to see how their parents picked fruit, peeled it, balanced on a branch to sleep or have sex, and how fruit smelled that was safe to eat. They had to learn how to swing on the branches leaping to others so as not to or fall and be seriously hurt.

They learned the smells of their group, the feel or smell of rotting fruit, and the taste of that which makes one sick.

The chimp learned by the sound of their voices when shrieking of danger from a predator such as a large snake. The curious young have no instinct or innate knowledge of this danger. They will actually go closer and closer to a snake to observe it as close as possible without any innate idea how fast the snake can strike. Strike it does—and the chimp ends up in the snake's stomach. Those observing the youngster being swallowed whole, begin to understand just how fast that slow crawling snake can be. The next time the screeching alarm is sounded, the snake will be given a wide birth except for the young who has never seen a snake and becomes curious ignoring warning sounds from the group. Likewise, they learn the sounds of members screeching, 'food over here!' and all the familiar sounds of the forest that are not threatening.

Every moving organism on earth lives by one or more of the five senses. Some senses are highly developed depending on its environment, its physiology and what it eats. An eagle sees exceptionally well and if it was short sighted, it could not function, and would die. Some nocturnal animals have exceptional abilities in seeing in the dark, smelling or hearing. If we rendered them deaf or without a nose, they would also perish. Each of the species' young have a learning curve over time, in childhood, to learn the skill in using its senses, which in turn gives cause or motivates its actions to procure food, socialize and have sex.

When the primates were forced out of the trees, what they had learned was obsolete or not of great value. They could use their skills and sense data to pick fruit high in trees, but their senses had to be sharpened to a new degree on the ground. Seeing over the high grasses, the sound of the lions roar or growling was now meaningful; the yapping of the hyena—were they close? It did not matter high in the trees. Now it meant life or death. Smell became important, so they learned. Were they downwind—could they be detected? They became conscious of the acuteness of other animal's senses and in the process sharpening and intensifying sensitivity in their own.

Primates were able to learn about the real world around them through their senses. What were percepts, became perceptions, then formed concepts by identifying, by remembering, analyzing much of what was observed, and conceived new ways to survive. The escape into the waters created new sensations new ideas—there were no precedents, without experience, and with few physical attributes. Nothing except their physiology and senses had prepared them for becoming a hairless naked human being and learning to succeed in a world among predators.

Lucy's senses were all sharpened to some degree but crucial was interpreting what she saw, heard, and smelled. Her hands were no longer callous from swinging on branches. They were softer more sensitive to the touch. She was streamlining after millions of years in the water. Her naked flesh had acquired a soft subcutaneous layer of fat under her skin which made her soft to the touch—far more supple and sensitive to the feeling of hands and bodies than any hairy primate or animal had ever experienced. We learned to appreciate and achieve a sensuality that not only increased our sexual happiness but also guaranteed our genetic heritage with new values.

Out of those primitive years they became confident, learning, and inventing new ways to feed themselves. They began tending, of which there were no precedents, innate knowledge, or even principles that would apply to the new kind of settlements. Then, they learned about fertility, an intellectual feat: by identifying how a seed grew; observing where plants grew best; the questioning why does it need water? Why does it grow here and not there? Why does it grow best in dung? Why does the animal stop giving milk? By answering all these things there was food year around with some to spare. That 'spare' or extra food was wealth.

The witch doctor would create gods and the afterlife. The only means by which the primitive would be willing to sacrifice what he had earned was to ultimately create a god that would receive him in heaven for his labor. But the intellect of the primitive had lived and worked by the logic of experience, with real things, and real results. It was his sensual perceptual mind that sparked study, analysis, and real proof of an entity could not be fooled easily.

The primitive mind was one of exceptional ability to identify the real world, and as such, would demand real proof for any claim or proposition. The witch doctor could not convince the primitive in the real world, for that would require proof. The primitive would have to be led out of the real world, in the hallucinogenic dreamy spirit world of ghosts and gods of the witch doctors imagination. They had to create a mystery of the unknown, unseen—out of the realism of senses where learning was impossible.

To make sure one didn't learn, the witch doctor had to discredit the senses by paralyzing the mind in contradictions. 'It is the spirit, the unseen, that is real!' 'It is the holy spirits that give you a bountiful harvest—not you or your mind' 'You cannot see the gods because you are blind.' 'Reality is what you cannot fathom, see, or comprehend.' 'The gods foretell all that is and happens and your mind is impotent against the omniscience of a god.' 'You are not a living being but a spiritual soul using a physical body.' 'To give way to the material wants in success, happiness, or to the flesh is selfish and evil.' They were invalidating nature's senses that stood between the priests or gods, and man's wealth. And when man believed such things he lost his mind and his wealth because his 'gods' stole his life on earth.

Theology in every part of the world is anti-sensual, anti-knowledge, anti-reason, anti-nature and anti-human. Those who claim a 'religious philosophy' are an obvious contradiction. By their act of 'faith' in the 'spiritual', they are in fact, anti-philosophy, meaning they are anti-metaphysical, anti-epistemology, anti-morals, anti-justice, and anti-values. Religion is not an intellectual journey of discovery nor philosophical, but an immersion in guilt, sacrifice, ignorance, and non-intellectual, a denial of the senses. It is not enlightenment, but was a darkening of the mind of man.

The Greeks, after the world had experienced four to five thousand years of religious slavery at the hands of the Pharaohs and the likes of Mid East and European invaders, began to rethink survival and that it may lay in the discovery of the real world, around 2600 BP. They were reintroducing man's senses to reality and turned the first light on in the human mind that had been out for thousands of years.

The primitive's view was not long range, initially, and any of their investment in time and energy had to produce immediate results or was abandoned. He had to eat today, but the only way to eat was to face the reality of the environment, his natural surroundings. The Greeks would agree, but they had more food than the primitive did. They had some wealth and time to think and become cognizant of the fact that our life on earth just may depend entirely on our ability to apprehend its nature that was obvious to one who worked.

The Greeks were the recipients of a primitive legacy—a wealth of food. They had time to study, experiment and learn about the organic and inorganic nature of our world. They had the luxury of proposing ideas, theories, and arguments about a way of living or how one ought to act. It was an explosion of the intellect to look beyond the immediate and to future possibilities. They looked into the day and night sky. They looked into earth the smallest grains of

ss

sand and to analyze the living things that grew out of it, as well as the living crawling walking creatures on earth.

Thales, Anaximenes, the Atomists, and Aristotle attempted to look to nature for answers. Looking outward towards reality there was logic in nature that one could comprehend. The 'ideas' of Plato produced only the 'idea' but that is all was, not a proven idea—theories without facts—just revelations—a day dreaming of the imagination. But the others, Thales to Aristotle, were the new philosophers who used their senses and examined their perceptions of nature.

Governments and religion could not survive in the light of logic and its people learning the truth. The Dark Ages between year 100 and 1300 religious oppression reigned and philosophy was sinking with inquisitions, censorship, and the suppression of all new knowledge was paramount in theology. War was and is today justified on the basis of those people who worship differently—blatant discrimination. Christians launched their own coercive wars with their crusades during the 11th, 12th, and 13th centuries (300 years!) against Arab religions to claim the 'Holy Land.' Three million Arabs perished including 60,000 of their children. Such discrimination created the seed for Arab vengeance to grow, which seethes to this day.

The Renaissance emerged slowly and by 1400 the light of logic and the quest for new knowledge and the freedom to be creative, and being inventive exploded. This period represented by the likes of Copernicus, Galileo, Newton, and others who were looking outward into nature and the sky to perceive, identify, to discover new concepts for life on earth. It was Galileo that told the Inquisition, "I cannot deny what I see!" At the end of the 16th century and of the Renaissance there was a new era that would usher in, eventually, the industrial revolution and enlightenment.

There is no doubt that our senses, what perceptions we have, or our point of view, may be in fact distorted. The distortion may come from our state of mind, poor observations, faulty memories, poor judgment, or injured senses—impairment. There is also light affecting color or there is distance, position and perspective to consider, but what it seems must be a real entity. Obviously, we can not establish truth on faith or initial perceptions. To be objective, what we have perceived, must be verified, re-experienced over and over before it becomes fact. There are no quick means or short cuts to verifying what we sense and perceive.

For every statement that is made, there are many questions that may be raised. For each succeeding explanation there can be inquiries. And if there seems to be nothing to say, one can always ask, "Why?" or "How did you arrive at that?" There are those six little words that help all who wish to sense and know the reason or the truth, why, where, when, what, who, and how. Our first perceptions of someone we meet may be less than complimentary, but justice demands it is wrong not to examine or get to know him better before making a judgment. Epistemology is, in a sense, making sense out of what you sense. I'm sure someone said that before.

CHAPTER 8

Memory

It is generally understood we have a brain size much larger than what is needed for bodily functions. Animals have brain sizes that manage their bodily functions and senses, with a brain slightly larger to learn needed basics for survival, in abundant environments. Evidence shows that most animals have some reasoning ability and limited memory. It is known that there is functional memory wherever something repetitious is done. That is, one remembers by rote or habit (from memory without thought of meaning) with continual parental conditioning learning methods.

Many animals including Dryopithecines, our ancestor, in the forest canopy and on the ground, probably had limited memory ability. They remembered their harem or mate through sight and possibly smell. They remembered their home base, their young, members in the pack, herd, etc., or the troublesome male. The ground animal remembers where its hole or burrow is. The hyena changes camp, quickly remembering where the new one is, and where the pups are. Most animals have varying brain capacities not tied up entirely in bodily functions, learning everything by rote and perform almost as though they were unconscious decisions, usually explained as instinct (inborn, automatic, or innate). However, we know we cannot make an unconscious mental decision any more than we can make an unconscious physical act. Since it is established we have no innate knowledge, it is obviously true for animals because they make mistakes too.

The early primates and even those we observe today have a social life or culture of which there is behavior that is learned which contributes to the survival of the group. Such primates do have longer childhood and it is from these types of animals that we began our trek through the drought and into our history. It was one of perception, limited memory, and by discrimination in assessing their senses.

Animals may perceive, say, bananas and mangos; but the concept of a mango was one of shape, color, and taste memory. No other differentiation need exist in that limited or narrow environment. There is more evidence that animals learn from their parents, and that instinct is a term, used to explain certain actions that don't *appear* to be learned. But every sentient creature has to learn to survive. If it has senses it has perceptions and how well it identifies those perceptions is crucial to the quality and length of its survival. Nature gave animals and man senses to learn to survive, otherwise it would have implanted knowledge for survival and our senses would be useless. We would have lost our senses since that which evolves is that which is being used.

Those primates that remained in the canopy and never went down on to the ground had less to remember. Those that lived in the canopy and having to drop to the ground for foraging, had more to learn and remember! As the drought came upon them, they found the canopy less and less fruitful and had to scavenge more and more on the ground and learn *new* ways to get something to eat. They had to travel further and eventually found themselves on the savanna where they were inexperienced, having to learn scavenging, and be cautious in such areas to avoid danger.

Each step in the new environment meant a new set of circumstances, something new to remember and a new way to cope. With a limited memory, one might not remember the situation and not react properly and become the meal instead. Those that could remember everything about foraging and surviving on the savanna had a chance.

When the primate dropped to the ground and ventured out on the savanna, it was the capacity for memory and to gain new knowledge that became means to survive outside of his old environment. What knowledge, according to Plato, from past archetypes would help them survive the predators of the African plains? The only primordial archetype that can be found in the real world is in the form of a parent. Humans evolved, growing larger and larger brains to store more and more memories of those things we are taught to survive in the next generation. Yet the primitive was not cognizant of his memory or of reasoning at that time.

Later the primitive would take a new step into the safety of the rivers or ocean meant that all he had learned on the ground and savanna was useless in the streams and at the shores of the sea because they had no memory or experiences of such things. Adding the waters to their memory, was a new means to survive, and meant that there were now other options for gathering food. They were perceiving new entities, fish, crabs, mussels, and the whole ecosystem under the water. They were in the process of perceiving, identifying, differentiating and integrating new concepts into knowledge. They had more to remember on the savanna, around the lakes, rivers, and oceans.

To survive, our brain size had to increase substantially over that which was needed for bodily functions. Any genetic mutation that increased the size of the brain's memory capacity increased the primate's chance of survival. Survival was dependent on the many ways in which the humanoid had to gather food. The bigger the brain meant more memory, and the more ways in which to survive. They would have a better chance to survive and more likely to genetically pass those increasing brain genes on to their children.

Mankind inherits only a *capacity*, a large physical brain to store knowledge. Today, like the primate who dropped to the ground and faced the savanna—man is in the same situation because tomorrow is going to be different—there will be a new society—a new environment—he will need to be taught to use his memory and reason to survive. There will be no precedents for tomorrow; primordial, primitive, the Dark Ages, the Renaissance or today's knowledge will always give way to the new. Like the primitive, we are the new people in a changing new world climbing higher and higher on the evolutionary ladder, whether we like it or not. Some knowledge is passed on to us from the past but it takes a reasoning mind to assess the new environment and apply the applicable knowledge and principles of the ages to modern existence.

The humanoid acquired the ability to forage on the forest floor and on the savanna. The thousands of bits of information he had to remember were still useful but there was a reduction in the food supply and the hominoid had to find new sources on the savanna. There were berries and some plants as well as small animals, insects, and birds, but each one required a hundred ways to acquire on the forest floor but the savanna held real food, lots of meat, and predators. The skills to avoid predators required stealth, sharp sight, the ability to discern movement of grass, the wind direction and hundreds of things to remember (all new). The ocean and waters would require them to double or triple their memory capacity.

Primitives were capable enough to live through a volcanic eruption at Laeotoli (evidenced by Mary Leakey's discovered footprints), in the midst of all types of animals, crisis-crossing the fields of ash fallout. Footprints indicate they walked through in some physical embrace. Whether the physical embrace was for assisting or to hold each other from slipping and falling, or simply an affectionate embrace to be close, is evidence of social bonding. Whether he was protecting or helping the person, or for one's happiness because being close to someone you may conceive as a value, is the result of abstract thought (the reasoning of memory) concretized in a social bond, as they made footprints in the ash at Laetoli.

Animals can perform simple abstractions. Take the chimp who discovered, when frustrated by not being able to reach the ants in the hole, grabbed a stick and jabbed it down the hole to smash the S.O.B. But, the stick went into the hole, the ants attacked it, and in drawing the stick out found the ants clinging to the stick. The chimp promptly wiped them off and ate them. He kept repeating the operation of sticking the stick in the hole and eating the ants. The chimp remembering how he caught the ants taught its young by demonstrating the operation, and they learned by observation and remembered. The young learned by trial and error, to plunge the right size stick or straw into the hole. In gaining experience while doing this operation, it may pick up a stick and may examine it with the idea that it may or may not go into the hole. This is a very simple process of abstraction. But to remember all the steps was great mental step for chimps that still have this skill today. Beyond that, it cannot engage in conceiving more complex attributes of sticks for construction, carving, and certainly not numbers. It is obvious that there was primitive thought processes going on in the animal's brain, it is just that he never had to take Shop: 101, only Ants: 101.

Two and a half million years ago ushered in the Stone Age. Our ancestors were scavenging on a large scale and had to cut up an abandoned carcass quickly and efficiently. Nature did provide them with simple tools such as sticks and bones for clubs and rocks of a shape that one could use for pounding or cracking open clam or crab shells. Something that could penetrate and cut had to be shaped. To look at and feel the stone in order to determine whether it will flake and produce a sharp edge involves concept formation. Such process classifies the stones by their characteristics and attributes that it exhibits, differentiating them from all other stones.

How Stone Age man came to make tools out of stone is up for

grabs, but to reason, there may have been many times he had used a stone to break or smash something such a clam's shell or the bone of an animal. In the course of such need, he perhaps used a relatively less dense stone that broke and produced a sharp edge which may have cut him. That incident may have replicated into the idea to cut meat with the sharp edge of a stone that was broken or flaked easily, a process of classification. Determining that a harder stone could become a cutting tool is creative conceptual thought.

Through experience man created the technique of holding, striking, and knowing how to chip the flaked stone into shape. There are many anthropologists who believe, that such tedious crafting of tools for two and a half million years in the stone age, evolved to sculpt our thumb and fingers into the graceful grasping hands we have today. In addition Stone Age man's brain was becoming considerably larger and capable of storing memories, concepts, experiences and entities that he could recall to re-imagine re-examine, and reason its relationship to his needs. It was necessity, the 'mother of invention,' at that time, as man became very capable of perceiving, identifying, with a growing ability recall, reason and create new concepts.

When Michaelangelo looked and examined a huge piece of marble in Italy, during the Renaissance, in it he could imagine it being carved to represent human perfection, called "David". He and the primitive were employing the same intellectual abstractions. However, Michaelangelo had the benefit of better tools and techniques that had evolved from his Stone Age descendants. The abstraction and its execution were far more complex as well.

The more memory capacity humans had, the more they could remember. The more there is one can remember, the more one has to reflect on and the more one has to make comparisons with. The more we can search our subconscious of what we have learned, and the more creative we become. The more we know and remember, the more we understand. It depends on how much we want to learn in order to survive.

Primitives had the will to live and use whatever capacity the brain had at a given time. They were concentrating or focusing, going through one step at a time to learn. It was thinking and forcing their brain to remember more and more. A genetic mutation that made the brain larger was successful because it had the proper nutritional fats to build a larger neural system. This provided the human brain with more capacity to remember and the continued diet would make healthy its gene mutation process. To cease either activity of eating meat or fish, encouraging people not to learn or to follow one's emotions, will reverse evolution.

The human species, and there may be reason to believe, we have begun, to *devolve*. Our flirtation with vegetarianism, new learning disabilities, and lack of interest or ability to teach children, is factual evidence of physical and mental deterioration. Most of the world's population is illiterate with poor memory retention. Our 'idea' that childhood extend into adulthood is not teaching survival. When the child reaches puberty it must be evident, that he was lovingly taught to learn and work for happiness on earth. And he or she will love you for that.

Many of the world's children are abandoned and starving. They are *not* taught how to survive today in this world of plenty. Few could 'graduate' if they were transported in a time machine, to 'simpler' times to survive the beginnings of agriculture 10,000 years ago. They could not survive 30,000 years ago the beginning of Cro-Magnon's time, 100,000 years ago during Neanderthals time, or 2 1/2 million years ago in the Stone Age. Young adults would be hard pressed to find food for them selves in 'Lucy's' time. But they would find they were among capable, intelligent, independent, individuals with the ability to be totally dependent on themselves for survival. The young modern would find their counterpart with a support group or safety net, found in loving parents teaching them how to survive. They had great trials and tribulations and so do we, but overcoming them gives us all strength in character called confidence.

We are losing our ability, as family units, to teach our children to survive in this world. If we no longer understand the basics in life such as what is required to survive in this generation, then we do not have the common sense of our ancestors, which means 'we've lost it', or we may be 'vegetating', going backwards in evolution. We are failing to use the great memory capacity we inherited from the primitive, forgetting that our children need to learn that only a *loving* family can *provide* and *encourage.*

CHAPTER 9

Show and Tell

In Humphrey's "The Social Function of Intellect," 'chimpanzees, for instance, do not come into the world knowing how to fashion a twig into a probe that can be used to fish termites from their nest; nor are they likely to discover the trick on their own. They learn to fish by *watching* older more experienced members of their group.' [35]

In the late 1950's and early '60's, young manufacturing engineers, and others being groomed for management possibilities, went through seminars that taught, among other supervisory skills, how to teach employees anything such as machine, assembly or office operations, among other tasks. The workshop sessions were called "Show and Tell", reminiscent of school children's class demonstrations of their toys, etc., but with some other distinctions. It worked this way, the employee had to be taught—trained—as quickly and efficiently as possible, to learn, simple machine operations or complex assemblies. By arranging a group of parts to be as assembled, in separate piles the supervisor would go through the sequence, physically assembling, and at the same time explaining verbally the assembly procedure. "Pick up the base (pick up the base and place it) and put it in front of you. Then pick up the part and place it with the protrusion down into the hole in the base. Next, pick up the screw and put it in the threaded hole and with the screw driver drive it in." The 'worker' then sat down and repeated the physical assembly while explaining each step. They learned faster and therefore, training time was saved.

In this workshop, other factory functions, and office operations were taught by this method. Follow up by the supervisor was a must to assure the operation continued to be repeated as taught. It gave supervisors a method that was usually successful. In principle all foremen, and managers of people have to know the work and skills to be good teachers and therefore good supervisors. Supervisor comes from the two words *super advisor.* Some management at one time and some authoritarian supervisors believed that supervision is a disciplinary problem, it is a prison guard mentality that will keep people in fear, but never loyal. Patience, and understanding *individual* abilities, skills, interest, dexterity, or physical limitations will be the trainers responsibility to interpret and help the employee overcome, making teaching efficient.

The chimpanzees, above, learned by showing and we don't know but there might have been some communication like grabbing the young chimp and putting them in a position to see the demonstration. It is not thought that they have a means to explain at the scene or back at home base. Most of animal teaching animal, involves the use of *body language.*

The early hominid's young was carried, or if walking was kept close to the female who traveled with her male to help in the day's search for food. The little 'pesky kid' certainly learned most of his skills by being curious, observing closely or by the parent's 'show.' However, by the time 'Lucy' came on the scene, she had a brain slightly larger than a chimpanzee, with the knowledge gained by her predecessor's means of survival that had brought them through 7 or 8 million years of drought. By taking to the water, learning skills, other than tree dwelling, learned also to scavenge on the savanna, making their lives extremely complex compared to any other animal. Teaching the child had to be more intense than when they were tree dwellers.

It is possible that at that time there was 'show' and, some 'tell' or 'grunt' emphasis, a soft grunt meaning, yes, and a loud one, no. That is not certain, but, by two and a half million years ago, at the beginning of the Stone Age, there may have been some kind of speech necessary for their new Stone Age technology to be past on and taught. The complexity of the manufacture and composition of the materials seems to have had to be explained, but there is little evidence to determine just when the larynx evolved downward in the throat and speech ability came about.

Regardless how complex or scientific a problem entails, a version of show and tell or tell and show is necessary. We can establish tell as being theoretical and show as empirical (real) demonstration. This is what happens in the university classrooms of physics, medicine, biology, geology, and all the other sciences and technologies. We tell them in books, or on black boards, and in lectures. Then we send them into the laboratories, interning in hospitals, and in the field to see by empirical demonstration (experience) the theory in the book, whether it is true or not, or for learning to do tasks right.

In the specialized sciences of physics, astronomy, etc., the same learning processes are involved. The Einsteins or astrophysicists produce the theory in formulas; of the possibilities of a neutrino or quarks and in their way 'tell' us the theory or mathematical formula, that something is or may be so and so. The astronomers, field scientists, university or industry laboratories, and super-colliders 'show' us by empirical evidence that some demonstrable facts support the theory.

Plato thought that all knowledge could be obtained through reason, the dialectic (argumentation) or through his 'idea' drawn from some primordial intuition. He believed that in astronomy one could theorize the nature of the universe by which natural laws would be subordinate to divine principle and that observation of the heavens was a waste of time; he was all 'tell' and no 'show.' Eudoxus of Cnidos (2408-2355 BP) a pupil of Plato, however, held against him and did observe the movements of planets. He understood the nature of discovery and learning by uniting astronomical observation with cosmological speculation and/or theory.

Aristotle, in his early work in zoology, biology and some botany, established field or laboratory inquiry. His student, Theophrastus (2360-2287 BP), who continued Aristotle's work, classified plants in botany as well as studied reproduction and the sexual nature of higher plants. Many of the names of plants he established survive today. Aristotle through his searching for answers as to how nature functioned, created methods for scientific investigation. In our simplified version of show and tell Aristotle was 'show', then with reason to 'tell', who also understood the ontological, speculative, nature of just telling as in Plato's theology. Theology being all "tell" and "no show," is an unscientific approach to discovering truth, facts or proof in divine speculation.

The nature of all science is speculation or theories, involving perceptions, identifications, classifications and units, and from those abstractions we create new science. Some knowledge we discover and others we experiment to find out. Then it must be explained and demonstrated or shown for others to know what we have sensually experienced in reality. It is how we add to our knowledge, to find truth about all things.

CHAPTER 10

Innate Knowledge

Innateness; It means, existing in one from birth; genetic, inborn, gifted, intuitive, inherited, or blessed by the gods. The doctrine of innate knowledge, in theology or philosophy, would imply that one, we need not learn anything, two, nor can one think of any new concepts, and if true, our existence is predetermined by the gods or by our ancestors. Innate knowledge is (ideas, principles, non-sensory conceptions, revelations or sort of intuitive memory from past lives) contained in the mind before birth and it does not exist.

Plato as we learned earlier, thought that through intuition, revelation, or emotionally we could find the truth. Within us, we have knowledge, principles, handed down to us by archetypes of our ancient past–that we inherit knowledge. Not only was it implied but it is also believed that we possess innate attributes in skills and character traits. The way we find this knowledge is to look inward to our imagination or emotions and we would intuitively know.

Aristotle agreed with Plato somewhat, but more in the potential, or propensity sense. We can disagree with this also. We are not born with any potential or propensities. Yet he understood the ontological argument to be speculative. But Aristotle was looking outward observing, and analyzing, classifying and identifying plants and animals establishing the scientific methods to learn the truth. To him theory was speculative and the truth must be found in nature (empirical proof). We learn everything, even what seems internally potential, naturally inclined, or to have a propensity for in ability is usually learned very early in life.

St. Giovanni Fidanza Bonaventure (1217-1274) held most of our ideas come from observation, but his imprinted theology culminates in the mysticism, the belief that certain ideas such as a god were innate.

John Duns Scotus (1266-1308) born in Scotland and a theologian believed in a god and self-knowledge, i.e. since the higher power or intellect is intuitively acknowledged apart from his blank slate. We learn nothing from Bonaventure and Scotus except that they wanted it both ways, learned and innate.

Rene Descartes (1596-1650) held that ideas of the mind were merely incidental, almost non-essential and not spontaneous or natural, but artificial or contrived. 'What one perceived was but a representation'—of what? If mankind since the beginning of time could only perceive a representation, how could he ever identify anything? Descartes was in effect saying he did not know what was real or true, therefore there is no reason to believe his theory is true.

John Locke (1632-1704) made the first reasoned argument against innate ideas. He wrote that, there are no ideas stored in the mind at birth. The child is born *tabula rasa*, its mind a blank slate with no memory or experiences. Locke was somewhat medieval in thought having been influenced religiously, yet in a post Renaissance era he shed the light on the real power of our minds. He believed correctly that sensations and empirical experience was the source of knowledge.

Kant transformed innate ideas into a priori judgments; meaning that propositions can be known to be true, independent of experience. Experience philosophically is empirical information gained by the senses and committed to memory. He was saying that we know without reason unconsciously.

The theories of the innate, special, gifted, or inborn knowledge is such that they have yet to be proven as true. Yet today many still believe in miracles or revelations, and that emotion or intuition is valid knowledge. Many think psychics have innate knowledge of other people or that the clairvoyant has gifted insight of the future and that others by mental telepathy can communicate with other minds by means other than sensory. There is a belief in astrology that innately the stars, and planets affect our lives and behavior. All such "ideas" embrace a mystical element. All claim some unexplained or unproved source and assert innate ability, knowledge, miracles or motivation. More than 80% of the world's population actively engages, truly believing and living throughout their lives embracing one, more, or all of such ideas above. However, considerably less than 10% may be truly secular or philosophical without illusions.

Many people will insist that we inherit, inborn, inherit, blessed by gods, have good genes, or possess some other innate intelligence. Any explanation of why we *learn* everything is objected to, sincerely, since they have been taught all their life that, so and so, is 'gifted,' the religious will refer to it as 'god given', or they 'got that' from their father or mother's genes. A highly developed skill is not credited to the person's long hours of study, contemplation, lessons, practice, or hard work that is motivated by a great interest and to persevere in what they like to do.

The rationalization for innateness is that the person did not *learn or earn* his or her ability. We can only wonder how many people, have been very disappointed, their spirit crushed or even insulted, when told they were 'fortunate' to have such a great talent. He or she, was not given any personal credit for their hard work and dedication, to achieve rational goals.

If the envious do not attack talent, reason or ability they attack one's character. Such people are quick to consider attributes, of motivation, persistence, or will power as innate, one is lucky to have confidence, the will to learn, have strong convictions or 'blessed' with more ambition than most. It is the insistence that our character values are innate and possible to only a few, is a gross disrespect for personal achievement. Ambition in exceptional successes may be scorned. Add?

Parents are given little credit for instilling good character in their children. The state wants to take responsibility and credit as a substitute for the gods. Aside from religious coercion to instill guilt and humbleness, envious people are quick to claim others have innate, special, or inherited knowledge, and character, perhaps to excuse their own lack of character, ambition, ability to focus, perseverance, and/or they may be just mentally lazy, incompetent and lack virtue. We must take care that we are not guilty of supporting the idea that talent, ability, and ambition is not the result of hard work, but being 'lucky ' to receive this free knowledge. It is admitting that there is a pre-destined force in our ability and motivation of which we have no control and therefore fall prey to the idea that we are innately not responsible for our actions and/or intellect. They imply that parents have no effect in a child's scholarship or character of their children.

Some theorists define innate ideas, as the means by which we arrive at, principles of reality, and religious ideas or objects that 'transcends' the sensual. Any principle of reality must be proven to be true for every generation, and to say we have innate knowledge has never been proved to be true. Innate ideas if they actually exist must also be proven, as to their origins, which has not been addressed, nor *how* does one know whether an idea is innate or has been conceived in present experience? Those *who* propose they have innate knowledge seem to have no clue how to prove such things, which may mean they know nothing about innate knowledge.

Tabula rasa (a blank slate) means, nature has provided a virgin brain, where nothing happens until we plant the seeds, of knowledge, interest, the will to learn, and the motivation to survive and experience life. There is no hidden knowledge or direction to give us the right answers, or handing us the principles that will solve the problems of survival. There are no free truths; *we learn everything and* we *pay* for all knowledge with *mental effort. We* have to enter it all onto that blank slate, all by ourselves. Others, especially parents should teach us, but we have to write it down in our brain, to perceive, remember, reason, conclude, and act in our own best interest for survival. Milton Friedman has said, "There is no free lunch." We earn all of our knowledge.

The only innate attributes we have are physical, by inheriting our parent's genes that do not store knowledge. *Genes* only store the blueprints for our *physical body* and *brain's structural organic configuration. They do not store memories, propensities, abilities or ideas and certainly not talent.* The body needs nutrition and so does the brain. The physical healthy brain's structure, mechanics, and electo-synapses, are designed by nature to be turned on by our neural systems, creating an organism that can be conscious of reality, and function by intellect to survive in its environment.

Parents are responsible and morally bound to *teach* their children to function intellectually. Thus, *we* may pass on a legacy of knowledge, in their memories of us, with books, by electronic storage, film, and by our example in forming their character.

Epistemology is the philosophical science researching how we learn, is a natural process or method whereby we may understand reality and the means to survive. If we are taught improperly the process is not logical, and naturally difficult to learn. Parents help children to identify their emotional perceptions by show and tell—

point and read—fingers and count–in every aspect of their lives. Children who are left to 'figure it out'—'they will learn that in school,' or 'in time,' may live their whole life by their perceptions, emotionally never to analyze, identify, unitize, or classify feelings and may become the subjectivists of the future.

We are morally bound to teach our children how to survive, having brought them into this world. To meet this moral obligation, we must teach them the world is metaphysical; what is real and what is not real. In epistemology, we teach them how to find the truth about things by our senses looking outward, perceiving what is real, and inward identifying or classifying to understand wider concepts in reality in order to survive.

How we learn is a method or process (epistemological), but why we learn is psychological. What happens after we experience or perceive something in nature or from our memories in recall? Implicitly we are aware of something unique, beautiful, profound, exciting, or a possible fear of some sort which motivates us to proceed further to identify 'what' or reason to determine some mental or physical action. Such emotional experiences should motivate us to think, to discover if our emotional response is truth or falsehood, good or bad, searching our memories and looking outward to learn why we feel that way. Simply put, it is "following your head instead of your heart," or we become emotional basket cases for psychologists, who will ask us, "How do you *feel* about that?" for hours and hours.

In the first book 'Defining Philosophy' we explored our genetic birth, the savanna caper, and the emergence of civilization and religious control that shed light on our prehistory. Primitive philosophy was defined and how it is in conflict with theology.

The second book 'Metaphysics' emphasized the conflict with theology and philosophy, defined as the unseen or unreal in the former and that which can be sensed or metaphysical reality in the latter. It is self-evident that the non-sensed or nothingness is unknowable, and our science in metaphysical reality, is *knowable*. Now we *know* scientifically, that *we* are metaphysically, *individual*, and it is fact and not an abstraction.

'Epistemology,' this book, we summarize there is no free innate, gifted, a God-given or genetic knowledge, nor the ability of how to learn. Someone has to teach us, or with great effort we may learn to survive on our own. We all learn at different rates, have *variable* perspectives or perceptions emotionally. Even twins may be alike or similar metaphysically but each will sense the world differently, each will have their own experiences, and their own perceptions will give them individual perspectives. Everyone's subconscious memory bank is unlike anyone else's, and what we may recall, decide or prioritize and finally will to action, depends on our unique hierarchy of values, our own value judgment of things, people, and events which has created our epistemological individual minds. *Now we know scientifically that we are epistemologically individual, and that it is in fact the truth and real not an abstraction.*

The parental moral necessity is not only to raise a metaphysically healthy child, but epistemologically, to teach him how to survive in today's world. The child will learn only with patient understanding, love and encouragement, with their parents as an example. It is morally reprehensible that one would have a child and allow others to care and teach him how to survive. If we do not teach them, then someone else will, and the child will belong to them. Perhaps we should suspect that is why they do not turn out as we had planned. Knowing that, it is in the home that is the best school for children.

BIBLIOGRAPHY: EPISTEMOLOGY

Ref.
No.
Chapter 1

1. Rand, Ayn; "Introduction to Epistemology" Published by, The New American Library, a Mentor Book, New York, 1979: Pgs. 1 and 2.
2. Moore, Edward C.; "American Pragmatism, Pierce, James, andDewey", Published by, Columbia University Press, New York, 1961: P. 27.
3. Rand, Ayn; "Introduction to Epistemology", Published by, The New American Library, a Mentor Book, New York, 1979: Pgs. 1 and 2.
4. IBID., P. 5.

Chapter 2

5. IBID., P. 6.

Chapter 3

6. IBID., P. 6 and 7.
7. IBID., P. 7.
8. Lambert, David; "The Field Guide to Early Man", Published by, Facts on File Publications, Inc., New York, 1987: P. 31.
9. Rand, Ayn; "Ayn Rand's Introduction to Epistemology" Pub. by, The New American Library, a Mentor Book, New York, 1979: P. 8.
10. IBID., P. 9.
11. IBID., P. 9.

Chapter 4

12. Griffiths, J. Gwyn Author: Parrinder, Geofgrey; Editor; "World Religions", Pub. by, Facts on File Publications, Inc., New York, 1984 Copyright holder is Octopus Publishing Group Ltd., London, granted permission: Ancient Egypt, P. 136.
13. IBID., P. 144.
14. Desmond, Kevin; A Timetable of Inventions and Discoveries," Published by, M. Evans & Company, Inc., New York, 1986: Introduction.
15. Restak, Richard M., M.D.; "The Mind", Published by, Bantam Book, Div., Bantam, Doubleday, Dell Publishing Group, Inc., New York, 1988: P. 18.
16. IBID., P. 18.
17. IBID., P. 18.
18. Fincher, Jack; "The Brain: Mysteries of Matter and Mind", Published by, U.S. News Books, Washington, DC, 1981: P. 34.
19. IBID., P. 35.
20. IBID., P. 37.

Chapter 5

21. Isaac, Glynn and Barbara; "Olorgesaile", Published by, The University of Chicago Press, Chicago, Ill., 1977: P. 94.
22. Ardrey, Robert; "The Hunting Hypothesis", Published by, Atheneum, New York, 1976: Page, 57.
23. Crawford, Michael & Sheilagh; "What We Eat Today", Pub. by,Neville Spearman, London, UK, 1972: Pgs. 34 and 35.
24. Crawford, Michael; colleagues—Doyle, Leaf, Leighfield, Ghebremeskel and Phylactos; "Nutrition and Neurodevelopment Disorders," Publication, "Nutrition & Health" (1993), by, A. B. Academic Publishers, Oxon, England who granted permission to reprint, 'with compliments,' which I appreciate. Vol. 9, Pgs. 81—97.
25. IBID., Introduction.

26. IBID., Pgs. 82, 83, 85.
27. IBID., Pgs. 92,93(parenthesis mine)
28. Crawford, Michael & David Marsh; "The Driving Force", Pub. by, Harper and Row, New York, 1989: Paraphrased.
29. Ardrey, Robert; "The Hunting Hypothesis", Published by, Atheneum, New York, 1976: Pgs. 57 and 58.

Chapter 6

30. Lampton, Christopher; "New Theories on the Origins of the Human Race", Published by, Franklin Watts, New York, 1989: P. 138.

Chapter 7

31. Rand, Ayn; "Introduction to Epistemology", Published by, The New American Library, a Mentor Book, New York, 1979: P. 5.
32. Kelly, David; "The Evidence of the Senses", Published by, The Louisiana University Press, Baton Rouge, La. 1988: P. 7.
33. IBID., P. 7.
34. IBID., P. 7.

Chapter 8

-0-

Chapter 9

35. Humphrey, ? ; "The Social Function of Intellect",

Chapter 10.

-0-

Suggested reading:

Engelmann, Siegfried and Therese; "Give Your Child a Superior Mind", Simon & Schuster, New York, 1966.
Beck, Joan; "How to Raise a Brighter Child", Published by Trident Press, New York, 1967.

ss

BOOK IV

MORALS

Prologue to Morals

The effectiveness of this Moral Code, the commitment to its intangible principles, becomes a reality or tangible, when it becomes self-evident, in the behavior of everyone, that we all experience freedom from infringement by others.

CONTENTS

MORALS

Prologue to Morals

Chapter:
1. What are Ethics? 221
2. Determinism 230
3. The First Line of Defense is Neural 242
4. Human Nature 245
5. Primitive Moral Reality 248
6. What are Morals? 251
7. The Moral Code 261
8. Defining the Moral Code 265
Bibliography 295

CHAPTER 1

What are Ethics?

In the last three books, Defining Philosophy, Metaphysics, and Epistemology we reviewed primitive history, our evolution as a species and our social and economic progress. We found that once man uncovered the secrets of fertility (7,000 to 10,000 BP), for the first time in history he was producing more than he could consume, i.e. create wealth, the con men and frauds came out of the forests, deserts, and woods, to descend upon man, the creator. In order to get man to give up his wealth willingly the frauds would have to destroy people's moral sense.

Whatever primitive man in his time held in property rights and natural justice, were the targets for destruction. We have yet to recover from that onslaught, most of mankind is completely oblivious to the immoral ethics his leaders have imposed on him. This was no innocent ignorant misunderstanding of natural phenomenon, but intelligent planned criminal acts to separate man from any wealth he created. It was the intent to confuse a primitive, in purely imaginative abstract ideas, such as the ethics of omniscient gods or secular states to create huge gray issues, and to never let reason see the light of day.

It is not because theocratic or secular leaders are so intelligent it is because of people's trust, and not looking beyond to identify their emotions or intuitions. People have handed their brains and earnings over to the worst people on earth, the very best in deception. A bumper sticker,—'EVIL THRIVES' 'when good people do nothing.'

We will answer the question; what are morals? How and what factors determine and necessitates moral behavior? What was moral before 'ethical inventions?' Is it human nature, reality, evolution, and our need for happiness that determines and/or justifies a moral code? Is man justified in seeking his earned values, i.e. success, happiness, and to live a long and healthy life? What are man's rights? We will learn The Moral Code that follows, is known and proven but never concretized as Natural Law.

Much is moral and has been defined, in our justice system. But it needs new direction and the right moral reference from natural law principles, to remove from our legal system, all laws that have been theologically and socialistically motivated. Our purpose is to understand moral abstract principles, and learn, that what we seek to *earn* for ourselves is *justifiably ours,* providing we are not immoral by infringing on other people's natural rights.

Ethics is defined as being a body of moral principles or values that would govern a particular culture. It implies that laws of governance give equal weight to morals and values, or that one's values are moral issues. What led to this state of affairs, and how we solve the problem of what are morals, and values, are subjects we will explore in ethics historically and examine its premises and principles that self-serving rulers created for their benefit? We will properly identify 'ethical theory' then discard it as an indefinable immoral idea. When we have isolated its separate premises, we shall have two disciplines or two branches of philosophy, each a science of its own, 'Morals' in this book, and 'Values,' in Book V, that follows.

Many who pick up this book may be interested in philosophy,

but, I suspect most are curious about morals and values, because people have a sense initially to do what is right and good. However, if one mentions the word 'ethics,' there seems to be total confusion or a pained expression. The 'leaders' of our society have no idea, and our justice system is better than most, but may be confused about what is 'ethically' moral. When confronted with an argument that appears unfair but is the law, most people absolve themselves of the fairness question and hide behind an assertion—'its the law' or its for some perceived 'public good.' Most don't have a clue and throw up their hands and cry, "what can we do? It is the law." We do not know what is right or wrong.

The work of justice is Fairness. The court's other assertion is that, 'we cannot legislate morality,' can only be defined as 'we cannot be fair,' or that 'religious commandments are the only 'moral' laws,' which is contrary to the "First Amendment" (separation of church and state) and unconstitutional. It attests to the dilemma that 'ethics' poses for legislatures, the judicial, and mankind. For justice is fairness or moral rightness. Obviously, the justice system has turned its responsibility for justice over to theology. Note, that in every courtroom the words "In God We Trust" (?) does this mean we trust a god's judgment and not the courts. Is it the truth that the U.S. Judicial is MORALLY invalid or the elimination of the court system the final conclusion for a theocratic or socialistic state?

We ask then: What are ethics? What are morals? What do we mean by values? What is the difference? Why do we need Morals? Do morals change in time, culture or from individual to individual? Or, what is right and wrong? What or who decides that which constitutes a moral code? What is justice? What is 'the Good'? Why be moral?

This Book IV, "Morals", the next Book V, "Values", and Book VI, on "Government" together create a new philosophical social system. It is the only socioeconomic political theory that is moral and leaves man free to seek and keep what he values. Much of what is proposed here is well known or understood, today, to be moral. But 'ethically' the world over, societies have waived moral behavior in favor of some evil end, and this is the fault of their leaders and

JSS

people alike. Take note, this is the last time you will be confused about what is moral. Ask anyone in the world and they do not know what is moral, right or wrong, what are values, good or bad, but you will know after reading Morals, Values, and Government.

"The Encyclopedia of Philosophy," lists "Morals," but then refers the reader to 'Ethics.' And ethics is defined as being 'used in three different three different but related ways: signifying-1., a general pattern or "way of life";-2., a set of rules of conduct or "moral code";-3., an inquiry *about* ways of life and rules of conduct.' [1]

Please note in the above source, that there is no reference to 'morals' as a separate science but included in ethical theory. All three imply they are a combination, as if related, of *moral* and *value* issues. A "way of life", is implies a person's total behavior, towards others, and what he did in his own self interest or what he valued. Number-1. Philosophy or theology has yet to describe a general pattern and-2. There is no moral code or rules of conduct (personal behavior), and-3., an inquiry *about* ways of life seems to be an inquiry of 'a general pattern' or with rules on a person's behavior? It is obfuscating two separate issues both morals and values or their favorite term 'moral values.' What this indicates is that they want to create one rule to govern his public and personal behavior and no such just rule has been found.

Many of the early Greek philosophers such as Socrates, Plato, and Aristotle were concerned with people's "way of life." Socrates was concerned with 'analyzing the meaning of good, right, just and virtuous. He never found his universal 'self evident' code. [2]

Plato's writers created an 'ideal' in spiritual terms, a universal model of what is good, as a standard of moral judgment. Plato's writers did not trust man's senses or judgment, and felt the search for goodness would not be found in sense perception or pleasure. Without sense perception, however, we cannot learn anything, not even a 'self-evident' code.

In Plato's "Republic," Plato was to have written that society be ruled by philosophers or intellectuals with visions, 'of eternal forms.' 'Plato was the fountainhead of religious and idealistic ethics.' [3] He believed in an ascetic existence in which the 'good life' has no relationship with pleasure. Plato's 'good,' is duty and to suffer. He was a theologian, not a philosopher.

Aristotle: The Greek word *Ethics* is from 'Ethos' meaning custom or habit. In the mind of Aristotle, the word meant character and/or disposition. Obviously, it was the whole person, his morals and values. Plato was concerned with an ideology and Aristotle with man's nature both, were concerned with man's way of life.

'Morals' came from the Latin term *Moralis* and was introduced into philosophy by Marcus Tillius Cicero (106-43 BC), a Roman philosopher, who one is best described as believing in moderation. Cicero believed moralis was equivalent to Aristotle's *Ethikes*.

Aristotle speaks of the 'good' in his 'Nicomachean Ethics', and of "virtue" and "perfect virtue," "happy and happiness", or good lives and bad lives. He introduced, in this work a metaphysical analytic approach to terms and how they related to the actual things people talk about or do. It was naturalistic logic about the meanings of terms and how they impact society. He believed, 'good means the achievement of the goals at which human beings naturally aim, the balanced . . . which he gives the name happiness.' [4] Aristotle's ethical philosophy narrowed down to 'the mean', or 'everything' should be done in moderation. How this applies to one who indulges one's self in a mate he/she love's passionately is not clear. How may we lie, steal and kill in moderation? Was he referring morals or values?

Aristippus, (435—356 BC) believed that pleasure, a worldly view, was a component of happiness as opposed to Plato's 'pain' and was called Hedonism. The philosophy embraced the doctrine that pleasure is preferable to pain. The philosophy taught how to avoid pain and how to gain pleasure. As you can see this was contrary to every religious tenet of altruism, asceticism, and feeling guilt, for earthly pleasures. I think Airstrips got a bum rap or bad press, they thought it without moral qualification, but 'his point of view does include a measure of rational control.' [5]

Asceticism is a religious theory that demands an unnatural life. '...the anchorite St. Simeon Stylites tied rope tightly around himself until it ate into his body and his flesh became infested with worms. As the worms fell from his body he replaced them in his putrified flesh, saying,' "Eat what God has given you." [6] Asceticism is self-denial, to suffer living, loving unhappiness, sacrificing one's identity, it is penance for being alive, for being human, and the desire for sex. Asceticism is altruistic, an extreme in self-sacrifice and brought to its logical conclusion, is misery or death. Our ethics has been encouraged over the centuries by rulers to create a set of rules for themselves and another for their subjects. Whenever anyone confronted priests with their contradictions, it becomes a 'god's will.' A socialistic state will answer, 'the state knows best.'

If a human's moral concern is to be for the species and not himself then it is a contradiction and can not be a principle for survival, because logically, to sacrifice himself is to sacrifice the species, not save it. It is why morals and values cannot be synergistic in principle, to serve others and one's self interest at the same time. Ethic's claim is that self-interest is immoral, and that concept in itself is inhumane and immoral. To uphold a principle of altruism, to deny self-interest is self-destructive and contrary to seeking a moral happy life. There is no moral reason to suffer.

No one has separated morals and values, because early religious rulers in Egypt and Mesopotamia were more concerned with what man did *physically* rather than be centrally concerned with moral abstractions. If the ruler could control man's physical behavior he could control his wealth. If they had dealt only in abstract moral principles, such as 'Do not; kill', steal, lie, beat your wife, or even be a success, or to find happiness, they found that there would be no obligatory reason for man to give up his wealth for the ruling elite. But the fraud continues.

In order to justify controlling people's physical labor, which created crops, animal meat, and tools to survive, rules, or 'morals' had to be made, with reasons that supported giving up the right to what a man earned. The early witch doctors created burial cults from primitive ritual and myths of an afterlife existence and of gods in charge of the elements (such as a sun god) that helped produce food.

That food foolishly given to the sun god has replicated into wealth for rulers throughout our history.

The evil fraud was, that man had to give, share, and sacrifice in order to give thanks or earn a right to enter god's paradise, or heaven. The pharaohs, shamans, witch doctors, and the priests who 'knew' the gods personally would be the recipients of wealth for the gods. They would take this wealth to the gods and present it as the people's gift in thanks for the giver of food, wealth, and life. The greater the gift, the greater chance of being looked upon with favor from the gods. Man has had to buy his way to 'heaven' ever since as 'moral' duty. Every ruling system's target *is* man's values, not morals per se. That's why no one on earth knows right from wrong.

People have never been fully convinced that they should give up what they earned. It is considered just, in every living thing that moves, especially in the mind of man, which is why every tomb in Egypt, except one, King Tut's tomb, has been ransacked. Even at the height of pharaoh power they still had to use force to extract more and more labor from man in the fields, and after the harvest men and women were under the whip to again work for food they had grown and harvested, to build the pharaoh's pyramids.

We have learned in Book I, which by 5100 BP the protein intake of the average farmer, was being reduced. There has always been many 'poor innocents' with faith in their 'leaders.' The few people, who were not running on their emotions, reasoned it was a scam, and rightly stole their wealth back from dead pharaohs. In many tombs the pharaoh's bones were strewn about the chamber showing us their anger, or the body was not there, and carried away to show others its destruction. There is also the possibility a new pharaoh may have sacked the tomb of the recently buried king in a race with tomb robbers.

Ethics was invented to serve the pharaoh, and later adopted by all emperors, kings, popes, dictators, and every secular leader who followed because it worked. The early religions, then secular rulers, demanded self-sacrifice (altruism) of subjects, to give up their material gains for gods or the state. People, were poor, and had to share what

ss

was left with any one in need, because rulers took all of man's profit. It was another fraud for the poor innocent to swallow an ethical rule 'it is better to give than receive.' They had invented a gray area for man's mind in their ethics—ethics are obfuscation of the highest order.

All thinkers, through the centuries, fashioned their 'ethics' only on accepted results of society's traditions customs and culture they witnessed, (the symptoms) but never questioned the right or wrong and *not* on the *cause or why*. Sharing with those one valued was replicated to self-sacrifice—altruism, to do something for someone else, anyone, for any perceived 'good' that became an 'ethical ideal. If an individual holds his life, as an ideal or to seek personal values, it is contrary to religious and secular tenets of altruism. It is this perceived psychological guilt the pharaohs fully understood—they knew what they were doing. Therefore, thinkers who attempted to find a *justifiable* rule or principle to include abstract morals and the values men seek for themselves would never succeed. The result of theological 'ethics' is that faith replaces reason and altruism supersedes a life of choice for human values. Philosophical ethical thinkers ineptly adopted the principle 'the end justifies the means'—the state or a god is worth suffering for and if suffering is by force for the ends of state or gods, then such ends justify any means.

So vast is the mass of mankind, the individuality of each person, within cultures, religions, nations, or continents (5.5 billion people), we will, never discover a principle as a guide to both morals, and what people value fairly. This is the ethical dilemma. No one religion can agree with another on the 'moral' 'value' rules their imaginary gods have laid down. Many believe it moral to kill those who have no faith in the god they worship. To kill for such a god one can earn their way to heaven. It is dogmatic faith with no relationship to reality, and therefore, 'moral' principles without reason, because their emphasis is on values, of power over man's mind and wealth.

Philosophy is lost in theological 'ethics', unable to reason or discover a guiding principle, to know what is moral. We don't have to solve the problem of values, per se—people's free will can solve that. The conflict is that religion is not a philosophy, but the absence of any philosophy. Metaphysically, they hold materialism and their bodies in contempt. Epistemologically, they hold reason, knowledge (the search for truth) and the means to learning, impotent, by their act of faith. Philosophy has to 'draw the line in the sand,' there must be a division, not a unified principle of morals and values.

Morals: How people interact with each other are moral issues.

Values: What a person does for himself or to his person is not a moral issue but one of value.

These are the two sciences we will explore, *morals* in this book and *values* in the next.

Ethics is an anachronism, a holdover of the laws of the Pharaohs, and every government in the world since that time. The ethical dilemma, the confusion over morals and values has been the tool of leadership. *They could always argue that any value issue is moral, and any moral issue can become one of value.* Thus, total control over man's values, which are unrelated to morals, has been the strategy for our 'leaders' since recorded history.

As a general moral principle any infringement in the life of a person is immoral. The 'leaders' theologians and socialists refer to values as 'desires' or 'materialism', that something man wants for him self is evil, or immoral or 'unethical.' It is the rule or principle that man must accept, as moral, any infringement upon his person or property that will benefit others and to have no selfish concerns for himself. The ethical 'synergistic' principle of altruism is an immoral concept that is contrary to human nature and used to create guilt in people who will give up their wealth to the church or state.

'Ethics' have given rulers, politicians, and theologians, the tool to control what they covet, and imposed evil standards of values, collectivism and/or altruism, that would be immoral, if not obeyed. 'Ethics' dilutes morality in a vast sea of values, where purposely they have dissolved both into immoral gray issues where right and wrong, and good or bad is unrecognizable.

There can never be a synergistic rule or principle unifying or otherwise to become an absolute for morals and values in 'ethical' theory because to live by such a concept is self-destructive.

ss

Before we can proceed to define a moral code or leave ethics, we have to answer the question, *"Why be moral?" If we are not responsible for our actions,* whether they are theological 'ideas' of predestination or secular philosophical theories of determinism, *then there is no need for morals.*

CHAPTER 2

Determinism

Determinism is the concept, that our actions in some way are predetermined by some factors that are beyond our control. Are people not responsible for their actions? Does nature, the material universe, cause us to act in ways we do not understand, by the movement of tides or the planets? Are we predestined, or controlled by the gods? Are we mentally incompetent or do we know what we're doing? Does antecedent experiences influence a person's actions? All the above questions ask do we possess free will or are we conscious?

There are four philosophical theories and two problematic theological ideas. The philosophical theories are ethical determinism, logical determinism, physical determinism, psychological determinism and biological determinism. In theology, the theory is that a god predetermines will and also it does not.

Ethical determinism states if we know what is right we will only choose what is wrong out of ignorance. Common sense proves that this is not true. Many people today who know better will choose to do something immoral. If they know something is bad for them, like taking drugs, they may still elect to take them.

Logical determinism is fatalism, the theory that fate predetermined our future or that it was our destiny. It is when people look for signs or omens, i.e. foretelling of one's future seemed to come true, and one had no control over coming events. It is the fortune teller or astrologist's con game. Many have refuted this by pointing out that most events fail to occur.

Theological determinism, according to St. Augustine, his god, being omniscient, who created existence, knew everything down to its smallest detail, including all actions by man. Some theologians argue that a god knows what actions we may take in advance, and that we have the will to forgo evil acts. But this cannot be true with an omniscient god. The god either knows all actions in advance, which will occur, which can only be predestined by a god or does not. He can not have it both ways at the same time. Both are problematic because either way disproves the theory of a god who is defined as benevolent, omniscient and omnipotent. First; if man has free will and making choices of good and evil, then such a god created a person who may will to be evil and the acts are unpredictable which disproves the theory of a god's benevolence, and in the latter it is not omniscient. Second; if man has no free will then a god has predestined evil deeds, of pain and suffering, which disproves the theory of a god's benevolence or the power or intelligence to overcome *his* lack of will to stop evil. The dilemma is problematic for theology to argue because logic and reason will show contradictions in their mythology. They prefer to avoid all such discourse.

Physical determinism came as the result of the physical sciences, in that the motions of heavenly bodies, moved by the laws of nature and everything had its cause and effect. Therefore everything in the universe is predictable including human actions. Matter being composed of atoms changed directions caused by being hit by other atoms. 'Material bodies arose from the combination of atoms into groups or clusters and perished as a result of their dispersions.'[7] The atomists thought souls were made up of atoms.

Epicureans took off where the atomists Leucippus and Democritus left off, and to get away from deterministic claims, said atoms took on a spontaneous action swerving from time to time.[8] Hobbes noted that free will or—'liberty is simply the absence of all impediments to

ss

action that they are not contained in the nature an intrinsical quality of the agent.' [9] Hobbes used the analogy of water running freely down hill with the constraint where it can not go up hill or sideways. He concluded any body without constraint, can move freely. He nevertheless believed human behavior to be physically determined and necessitated, yet he concluded that we had free will, that is caused by acts of will.

Do we have free will, or our lives predestined by the material universe? Pierre Simon Marquis De Laplace (1749-1827) a French mathematician, astronomer, and theologian. He, 'expressed his view of determinism with the claim that were there an intelligence with knowledge of the position, direction, and velocity of every particle in the universe, this intelligence would be able to predict by means of a single formula every detail of the total future as well as the total past.' [10] Forerunner to this theory was the early Atomist's hypothesis of atoms by Leucippus and Democritus about 2300 BP, their predictability of all caused actions.

Einstein attempted to come up with such a theoretical formula. Later 'quantum mechanics theory' disproved such formulas. It is where the mechanics of atoms, molecules or other physical systems are subject to the uncertainty principle. That principle shows a quantum leap, or jump, whereby there is an abrupt transition of a system from one of its discrete states to another, as in the fall of an electron, in an atom, to an orbit of lower energy. There is a probability of unpredictability.

There is a probability but not predictability in atom structures. Each field can be regarded as consisting of particles of a particular kind, which *may* be created or annihilated to another form. It has been established scientifically that there is a probability of something happening but not predictable.

If one cannot predict the actions of the smallest particle (quantum or least quantum of evidence) which makes up the universe then we certainly cannot predict the whole or any part of it. We can disperse with the theory, that we could if we had super knowledge, predict the future of our universe, but there is nothing that is predestined or determined in physics. The task of any science is to insure we are cognizant of such factors and chart a course through the exigencies that nature presents to human life.

There is also *psychological determinism* of which there are several theories. 'Descartes's idea of a "free" will, conceived of as a will that is not determined by anything else. It appeared to imply that man's choices are completely random and capricious, utterly mysterious, and inexplicable.' [11]

Hume believed that we are both free, and causally, meaning caused by motive. Just as cause and effect occurs in nature, it does so in people. Given a person's background or deprivation he could not act otherwise. Clarence Darrow saved men from the gallows arguing that they could not help themselves in what they did. Few philosophers think that behavior is caused by unconscious motives, desires, etc. Modern psychiatry holds a similar view that man is controlled by inner neurosis and compulsions over which he has no control man has no knowledge of, and is not morally responsible for his actions—he has no free will—things they cannot prove.

Kant's view was similar in that only what one can will that all others should do under similar circumstances, i.e. the unconditional command of the conscience. Conscience is an emotion—a feeling we may be right or wrong. Like all emotions, it is an immediate impression, feeling or perception of our experience that must be further identified analyzed, and fully understood, that what one felt, may be right or wrong, good or bad. Obviously, Kant's theory is wrong, it is a perceptual/ emotional solution contrary to reason as we learned in epistemology.

John Stuart Mill describes philosophical necessity. 'Correctly conceived, the doctrine called Philosophical Necessity is simply this: that, given the motives which are present to an individuals mind, and given likewise the character and disposition of the individual, the manner in which he will act might be unerringly inferred; that if we knew the person thoroughly, and knew all the inducements which are acting upon him, we could foretell his conduct with as much certainty as we can predict any physical event. [12] 'Necessity' meaning that due to influences in life experiences, we will necessarily act predictably. However, Mill departed from this by arguing that man's amenable character may yield to his will. He seems to want it both ways.

Modern psychiatric theorists are determinists and believe they understand the causal factors in deviant behavior. Antecedent cause theories abound in the profession and many philosophers such as John Hospers, think that behavior is due to neurosis, inner compulsion. 'our very desires, volition, and even deliberations are the product of unconscious forces.' [13] They have no theoretical facts that would identify a 'subconscious force' or how it works. They base their evidence on case histories of irrational behavior of which they do not question the possibility of emotional or intuitive compulsions. Most believe the emotional and intuitive is a rational state.

What the psychological determinists are attempting to do is render the conscious mind subordinate to the subconscious. It is a cynical approach to consciousness and reason, and obviously, with no factual foundation. It is also possible they perpetuate the theory that man is not responsible for his actions because it shakes up every social and legal institution, whereby they may become famous and sell more books. They are the intellectual bottom feeders, creating fright in emotionally ignorant people that will fill up psychologist's waiting rooms.

Determinism, psychologically means because of past experiences (antecedent causes), that one can only act in away that is controlled by unconscious or subconscious forces that are out of control of our will. If we take this view, it is impossible to grow mentally. We would still be in the trees, or never grow up—a child acting on his emotions, never to identify, unitize or classify emotional experiences—to lack reason. We are in an unconscious state of mind acting consciously, is an obvious contradiction. We unconsciously have created a 747.

Antecedent experiences should not affect our lives if we will to remember the past, and reason with those of the present to make a decision. We may even make the wrong, right, childish or no choice at all, but it is all done *consciously*. We may make risky, immediate, intuitive, or emotional choices. We must identify our intuitions or emotions, to overcome the errors that quick decisions invariably cause. To choose and act emotionally with or without reason one has to be conscious. Our primary problem is that we must teach children and unbalanced grownups how to identify and classify their emotions.

The subconscious is the warehouse for our memories. We may have put similar or related memories into concepts, context, or in some priority in our memory. How well we integrate and prioritize those memories depends upon our interest or need to know and remember. This is a reflection of our values, careers, personal relationships and all the things we witness. But every memory is recalled willingly by events, suggestions or new perceptions, which implies re-evaluation for the present time. The unpredictable (or quantum affect) is that we may forget some memories, or ignore some. What is a priority today was not yesterday, and we may not remember.

Nothing in the mind is automatic. Our conscious mind *relearns* everything given the occasion or need. We get up in the morning and relearn to walk to the bathroom and depending upon gender sit down carefully so as not to miss the commode whether sitting or standing. When we shave, or put on makeup it is relearning by remembering, almost automatic, but we may cut ourselves because we've changed the routine or forgot the pimple. We do not drive automatically, but we are skilled. Driving is easy, if the seat and mirrors are adjusted to us physically. Out on the road we are conscious of driving, thinking, listening to music or the morning news. On straight-aways we concentrate on both, not simultaneously, but *intermittently.* Remembering only those things we prioritize, we may remember the fender bender or some one stopped by the highway patrol, and we forget it just as quickly because it is irrelevant to our day's priorities.

We can be conscious or concentrate on only *one* thing at a time (Rand). Therefore, driving walking and all dual actions are *split second concentrations on two things alternating* from one to the other. We do not automate our sub-conscious, but are conscious of those things done skillfully. We relearn quickly. The more it is done, the better we are at the skill. Imprinting and conditioning, if it occurs, is

ss

only a temporary condition—reason or forgetting takes over eventually. *All skill is the ability to precisely remember or to relearn quickly.* The skill or dealing is remembered with such great speed that it looks as though it is automatic, but if he does not concentrate on his actions, he will make a mistake.

Our subconscious stores all our *memories*, consisting of all antecedent experiences, of what we learned. If we could recall *all* of these experiences, in the context of today's experiences, we are still unable to predict the outcome of one's evaluations in terms of *new* experience or occurrences and their effect on the whole. But we do not recall all our experiences—we forget many—many are put into contexts that do not apply today—many are put into poor contexts or incorrect concepts. Therefore we re-evaluate consciously what we do remember and anyone who knew *all* of our past experience could not predict the new evaluation. After all that reasoning, one may decide to act or not to act. Sometimes we know enough not to act—such as smoking or drugs—or to be immoral or to make a good decision, and yet, in many cases, we do act contrary to reason *consciously*, by stealing, lying or go looking for a hooker or gigolo instead our mates. (Try telling your wife or husband that cheating was not your fault, because it was *psychological predetermined or you were unconsciously motivated, or without willpower* of which you had no control.)

The subconscious mind has no ability to integrate, identify, put into contexts, concepts or formulate a course of action on its own—only the conscious mind is able to do that. If the subconscious had such ability, it would establish that we have a sixth sense for automatic reasoning. It would replace conscious reasoning and our ability to decide or will to act. To retrieve and re-evaluate would not occur and the person would in effect have no reason, replacing the conscious act of recall. An action may appear unconscious, but it is a split second emotional, intuitive or perceptive conscious decision, when faced with alternatives. Our character is in a state of evolution during our lifetime as we learn and experience new things, gain knowledge, have new insights, make better decisions and some mistakes. There is no predicting what experiences will consciously motivate us in the future.

Because a person knew only abuse, hitting, deprivation, and poverty will not deny them the ability or the freedom to recall or reason. Nor are those events necessarily remembered. Our nature is, in most cases, to forget or bury bad memories and remember the good. With time, memories fade, and if reminded by events we may elect to ignore the memory or find the memory not as vivid. We each, are evolving beings within our own lifetime, maturing, experiencing, or learning new things, creating new memories, with the old relegated into the archives of our subconscious. They are remembered on a need to know basis.

Therefore, so it is with all people, rather than carrying the burden to re-memorize past abuse, mistakes, failures or divorces we take the easy way out and just forget and live for the present with a goal to the future. An intelligent person will not let the past rule the present. *If the past controls our lives it is a conscious decision.* It is remembering and living in the past, today. Any action a person takes is a conscious one, to claim that it is an unconscious one is a contradiction, and impossible.

John Dewey (1859—1952) was a modern determinist and the most influential philosopher in the socialist movement. His importance in that movement (which is still alive and well) was in his advocacy for social reform through the public schools. In 1904 he was forced to leave the University of Chicago over concerns about his, 'Dewey School,' his 'educational' laboratory. From there he went to Columbia and through the Columbia Teachers College, a training center for teachers, spread his philosophy worldwide. The key concept in Dewey's philosophy is experience. He rejects the idealistic concept of experience in which the real is the nature of thought or that the object of external perception consists of ideas. ?

Dewey embraces three similar erroneous concepts. The first, Dewey assumes that in most of man's life, the nature of thought, reflection and inquiry is conditioned, in the context of *nonreflective'* experience, i.e. we perceive but do not identify, analyze, or reason, i.e. emotional

ss

conditioning. This is somewhat true concerning emotions and intuition. What we fail to integrate in our minds is not knowledge and we can not act upon. Nor does what we don't know, or have not reflected on influence us. If one is so conditioned and running on his emotions, he is mentally incompetent. To see, hear or remember something has no meaning unless it is somewhat identified or defined and committed to memory with *some* reflection and personal priority. When we remember 'nonreflective' (He created another word for emotion; why? *To obfuscate?*) experiences, they are only remembered emotions or perceptions and should be identified, unitized or classified–again, or for the first time if the emotion was or was not analyzed initially.

Dewey's second idea for determinism, is that, 'He insisted that life consists of a series of overlapping inter-penetrating experiences, situations, or contests, each of which has its internal qualitative integrity. The individual experience is the primary unit of life.' [14] He was referring to emotional experiences. We may have individual emotional judgments about many things, but where no *proper identification or classification* is known or taught about the scientific nature of things metaphysically, epistemologically, morally, politically, or socially, individual emotional judgments are not fully experienced. Experiences have no quality unless evaluated, i.e. has a conscious analytical aspect that prioritizes the memory as a viable concept, or one is acting on mental garbage.

Dewey's third idea leads to a determinist view—that he, '..discovered in the new developing human sciences, in especially what he called the anthropological—biological orientation, a more careful, detailed scientific articulation of the organic character of experience.' [15]

Dewey thought, in human development, culture, beliefs, and biological maturity affect experience. Learning is reasonable to the extent that it reflects our developmental habits of intelligence. This belief, without any factual basis, states that we suffer from *biological determinism.* What this meant to Dewey, is that culture beliefs or biological immaturity of the child must be taken into account.

Therefore, in practice, schools became *geared to age*, which we have found is not true.

With parental love and encouragement children may learn and comprehend far earlier than the educational planners thought. The child at two has learned a great deal physically and mentally of the world around him, about entities, behavior, social correctness, colors, numbers, word and sentence concepts. The child has been primed, like a pump, for learning and he wants and needs more, not to be relegated to the carefree playpen of childhood but to be mentally and physically challenged. We know all children do not learn at the same rate but that may be the fault of upbringing and teaching in the home and the schools. He should have fun and relaxation when the parents have theirs—together whenever possible.

Dewey saw the school as an ideal environment to foster *social* reform (note: 'social' reform always means socialistic reform) and is the most important medium for planned technological, economic and political development. Most educators today still believe that children should be 'boxed in' by age and the social planners still push socialization as education's prime objective. Families that relinquish their responsibility to teach their child, find the state will, according to Dewey.

Following Dewey are such 'educators' as J. Piaget author of "The Moral Development of the Child" 1932; L. Kohlberg, "The Development of Children's Orientations Towards a Moral Order—Vita Humana" 1963; J. Loevinger & R. Wessler "Measuring Ego Development;" A.W. KaY. "Moral Development" 1969; and a great number of others including Durkhiem, Goldman, Harding, Erikson, Rich and Devitis. Most of the testing research is not real in terms of scientific methodology. Most is quite amateurish. Lovinger based some of her research and findings on only two children. Others fair no better with samplings from 10 to 30 children adolescents or young adults.

Kolberg eliminated women in his original studies that became the basis for developing his "longitudinal survey of developing modes of moral reasoning," in 1958. There has been no serious scientific study that a good researcher could call valid by the many writers, including Dewey, Piaget and Kolberg. The 'scientific evidence' they pass off usually as 'empirical' is really stretching the truth. Like Dewey, they only *believe* but do not *know* what is biological and/or Freudian psychological determinism. The strategy is to confuse and argue over biological and the psychological by citing Freud and Skinner or the interpretations of the results—not in the methodology or investigations in the nature of learning, i.e. epistemological research. Are we to trust them to teach morals? Who is advertising and promoting this moral mental swill?

The moral development movement uses all the 'pseudo-scientific' buzz words like 'Intuitive-Projective Faith', 'synthetic-conventional,' 'Ninety Hedonestic Orientation', "Principled Orientation,' and a host of others that are designed to convince PTAs, teachers, and school officials of its 'scientific' value.

The movement's strategy, to teach children such 'morals' in public schools. But the more insidious stratagem is to teach young law students. They become lawyers and eventually lawmakers a force to be manipulated by social planners for a socialistic state. People who believe in freedom, free will and the efficacy of the mind will reject their ideas of 'moral maturity,' defined by planners, as 'altruism.'

In his book "Moral Development" A. William Kay states, at least twenty five times, the creed of the pharaohs, 'altruism;' 'that the schools should help to produce civilized people who possess, moral responsibility, altruism, independence, and rationality in a more developed form.' This would be a moral ideal, except that it's nullified by 'altruism.' As a true socialist he advocates, rather than teach math that it should, ' . . . well be spent teaching them to calculate how best to help their neighbours.' [16] So what, if they can not pass the tests, or know how to count or read—by the time children leave school, *they* need help.

F. Nietzsche, on faith and altruism, ' faith from the beginning, is sacrifice: The sacrifice of all freedom, all pride, all self-confidence of spirit; it is at the same time subjection, self derision, and self mutilation.' [17] This is what they are teaching and that is what children will learn to do. This is what is driving our now 10, 12, 13, and 18 year old young adults to drink, smoke, and blow out their brains with drugs. Your child is the product of whose upbringing, or do we believe it is predestination?

Jean-Paul Sartre (1905-1980) a French philosopher, 'Hence there is no limitation placed upon man's freedom, and those who argue for psychological determinism, for example, are simply attempting to escape responsibility for their choices.' [18]

Determinism is a theory, and there is no evidence that we are living unconscious, mindless, and existing in reality without the ability to reason. Yet we all are aware, reading this and may be emotionally affected and can determine why, by reasoning. We are not unconscious and out of control or we would not be conscious of morals and values. We would be subject to whim of any criminal. It would be a state of psychological anarchy.

Ethics intent is to create a synthesis of behavior in morals and the values a person seeks. When an ethicist states, that something is 'ethical' or 'unethical,' they believe all behaviors are subject to the judgment of others. The term's impact on society is intellectual confusion over right or wrong and good or bad. It lacks the personal and social logic of individualism whose expectations for survival is our responsibility. Any standard of value we wish to impose on ourselves is not justified, if the rest of an 'ethical' society disagrees.

In man's social life and in his individual pursuits there can be no 'ethical' synergism, a combined interactive principle governing both morals and values that could be defined as *moral* in his relationship towards others or to include the *values* he seeks for himself. They are two separate elements in human behavior that shapes his character, nor can determinism do that for him because it does not exist—only awareness makes us alive to take action.

Man has come a long way from Egyptian theology, Grecian philosophy, the Inquisition, Reformation, the Magna Carta, the rise of secularism, the American colony's revolution, USA's flirtation with socialism in the 1930s, and today we have our new Republican Theocracy, and Democratic Socialism. Man seems to take two steps forward and one backward throughout history, but we have made no progress. This book gives "Morals" its birth, and the next, "Values" celebrates 'ethics' funeral, because 'ethics' is intellectually dead, but only conscientious freedom-loving people will make sure that 'ethics' is buried.

CHAPTER 3

The First Line of Defense is Neural

Our first line of defense against all competitors is in the mind it is the ability to take mental actions of remembering and reasoning. Every living mobile organism must find, steal or overpower its competitors to eat and survive. All have neural systems evolved over millions of years specifically, to learn to locate and devour prey or vegetation in its immediate environment. Memory and reasoning capacity, for most species, in limited environments, may not change for millions of years. Each generation learns the same skills, in the same manner. If the environment changes they lack the skills to change or explore. They seek to cannibalize everything around them, and the specie is starved into extinction. They lack the full-blown brain capacity of man because it was, environmentally not needed.

Man must also eat to survive—it is that simple. Like all organisms we *mentally* act to learn and decide, and then take some kind of *physical* action primarily in the pursuit of food (survival) like all species. Why are the two actions important? What does it mean morally?

To answer the questions, we have to go back to the Precambrian period. This was the time when the first mobile *primitive animals*, invertebrates (without spines), were moving about and evolving in the primordial waters, pools or muddy ooze about 3 billion years ago, in Precambrian times.

Organisms moving about in primordial swamps were ingesting lipids (fats), which helped create neural membranes or primitive nervous systems. They evolved into organisms that swam, their primitive nervous system was a simplified version of a brain.

Looking at our own brain at its base—or the knob like section that caps our spinal cord, the medulla oblongata, is considered as the evolutionary or primordial core of man's brain. The medulla, in our brain today, is far more complicated and not as primitive in Cambrian times. The medulla of Cambrian times had few simple functions. The lipid fats loaded into their neural systems and membranes caused their synapses to fire as they ran into floating or other objects, and they reacted to avoid being eaten or eat what they bumped into. The organism became a self-actuating neural membrane, likely with a system for sensing or feeling at first, for food. There would develop smell to extend its sensations of things further away from it, and taste to increase its range of awareness to identify the wrong or poisonous food.

With two or three senses increased primitive organism's ability to survive and begin to take another step up the evolutionary ladder. There upon the top of medulla would evolve (the Pons) the central control system that would regulate and control and/or give signals to the organism to move, escape or eat. They were very primitive sentient beings—beings that used their senses to survive. To sense things further in the distance and the need to specifically identify what was food or danger, and eyes slowly evolved and popped out to see. Those with improved genetic functions, the better chance for that species of organisms to feed it self and survive. The simple neural system became a micro sensing brain that created an organism with very limited range of awareness.

As primordial creatures began to gravitate on land not only was it important to feel, taste, smell and see one's prey, but to hear in the distance, around or over sight obstructions on land. It was a refinement of the physical ability to feel vibrations in the water, on land, and an evolving need to feel noise for prey or danger in air.

ss

The lipids available produced brain neural and vascular systems of a variable sort we see in all life that has mobility. The lipid chains of essential fats were of the short variety and served evolving primate species in specialized ways according to the particular environmental niche. Beyond that there was no need, and did not evolve further, in a neural sense.

The human neural system became highly improved over the whole body, making man the most sensuous being on earth. All his senses, the windows to reality, improved his ability to imagine, be creative, and to so enjoy sexual intercourse physically, but to increase its joy with one only as aware and discriminating as themselves, in their values, physically and mentally. Species evolved physically and neural distinctive awareness between creatures of a species causing attraction between particular pairs of organisms.

Any action a species takes to survive is an act of value because it values life. It has no concept of value but will struggle and defend to keep what it has discovered or caught. We abhor witnessing an animal taking or stealing from the one who worked to gain the food. Why is this important? Because, it is in our nature to understand that the one who earns it, has the fair claim. Man's reasoning ability can logically justify, 'earned values are deserved values' or justice. It is a *moral* concept of which every leader has sought to destroy or make man guilty for wanting to keep what he earned.

Actions that impede or takes value from people are acts of value, in the negative sense, or is bad for human survival. Therefore the one who acts in such a manner to steal something of value is bad, wrong, and immoral. It means all acts of value have one goal, to support what one values most—our lives. People may err, make bad choices but they are still acts of value, mentally and physically, even when it is decided to be immoral.

All species, including man, take two actions in their pursuits. The first is neural or mental, to sense, perceive, evaluate, and classify, to make a decision. The second, if willing, to take some kind of physical action. Both, in the pursuit of their survival, are acts of value.

Morally, only man has the mental ability to conceptualize or create moral abstractions. A moral principle is a censorship, but only *mentally* where man deems it necessary *not* to take some kind of physical action that will infringe on another. *Therefore the only moral act a person can take is volitional, a mental act of choice not to take physical actions that infringes on others.* Without a moral code and freedom to earn and keep values, survival of human species is doomed to failure. For humans the neural, or moral and value reasoning is the first line of defense, in the pursuit of values. *Whatever neural and physical actions he takes in pursuit of survival are not moral issues but of values.*

CHAPTER 4

Human Nature

Reality, the universe, the world and the nature of human being's values dictates our moral philosophy. Any code or doctrine that is contrary to reality, life or human nature is unnatural, inhuman, and immoral.

The preceding Books II and III were devoted to our nature metaphysically and epistemologically where we have identified a universal fact of existence that mentally and physically, we are individual and is included here as human nature in fact.

Human nature has been referred to as the original uncivilized man. Once we become humanoid, genetically, we developed a measure of civility that improved until we became savages (religious) about 10,000 years ago. The primitive had human spirit, but the religious and their 'ethic' sought to murder it.

Human nature was thought to be humanoids living in an

uncultured state. Humans lived as primitives in a *primitive culture.* Cultures have changed but human nature did not. We can improve our culture, but only if we understand our nature and nature as a whole.

Human nature has been thought to be a primitive wild being. Wild means living in a state of nature, not tamed or domesticated, barbarous, furious, and of unrestrained violence. We humanoids were primitives living *in* the wild, and we were 'heads up' to the wild animals around us, evolving towards a high degree of social and economic intellect.

Human nature: Our physical characteristics and biological functions of our species usually define human nature. Our nature came about as a result of evolution that has given us improved physical qualities for our body arms, hands, thumbs, legs, uprightness, head, brain, organs, and our neural senses. These are the innate physical characteristics of our beings. Our senses are the only means by which our brain functions and our consciousness becomes differentially aware. It is the source of all our knowledge, and metaphysically, nature's link and support for the epistemological success of our species.

Human nature is defined as the psychological and social qualities that characterizes mankind. The character of human conduct generally is regarded as produced by living in primary groups that *may* influence particular combination of qualities belonging to a person's character. There are also laws and principles believed to be followed naturally and rightly by human beings. We usually understand every person is different and that we must all make our own choices.

Human nature some believe, refers to some undefined innate, inborn, intuitive, and an environmentally behavioral, or out of control species. Our nature is philosophical, having natural human characteristics of individuality metaphysically and epistemologically.

Metaphysically we are a biological self-motivating self-actuating sentient organism freely seeking sustenance for its life much like any other species on earth. All sentient species are physically individuated to a very high degree and also within the species itself.

Epistemologically, as sentient beings, we are aware only through our senses. Since we all receive differing sensations by degree, variety, quantity, and quality throughout all of our lives, there is such a differentiation as to decidedly individuate our character and our values. The cause, for the success of our species, is a natural result of having a large brain, memory capacity, and the ability to reason. It is clear, that we *learn* everything, and can control our existence with will power.

The nature of our emotions and intuitions are synonymous mental processes. Both serve the same purposes, to make judgments, to arrive at quick solutions, where neither takes the time to properly analyze or think before one takes action, or makes a choice. Emotion, is an affective state of consciousness in which joy, sorrow, fear, hate, or the like is experienced as distinguished from cognitive and volitional states of consciousness. Intuition is defined as the direct perception truth, fact, etc.,—independent of any reasoning process or immediate apprehension. Whether one senses something as an emotion, to act joyous or sad, or to act in fear without cognitive reasoning, or if one intuitively senses the truth as acceptable or not true and unacceptable, without any cognitive reasoning are in fact, definable synonymous psychological processes. We are emotionally or intuitively affected in both that excites our intellect 'that ' something exists and only reasoning can tell us 'what.' [10] Emotion or intuition is a natural process of which we must learn to control.

We are conscious in every waking hour of the day, as our mind, until our senses tire, receives from our senses continual data (sights, sounds, smells, etc.) like bytes, of the real world around us. All of that information is received in such quantities that most is immediately lost through the mind's sensual shredder because there is no degree of excitable content, a mental and physical dichotomy for human animation—emotional interest should be motivation to think before acting.

Our nature is such that we have free will with a desire to live. It is reasonable to expect that we would learn principles of morals to protect our life, human nature, individualism, freedom, our pursuit of happiness and all the things we value. That's just human nature, to be motivated with the will to take action for survival.

Our nature as individuals is the result of natural events and how we learn. It is the only way we can survive and live happily in a quantum indeterminate universe.

CHAPTER 5

Primitive Moral Reality

Among the many myths associated with religions is that morals are not possible without a god's commandments. To abandon their rules it is threatened, will create moral chaos. It is feared that without belief in a god, people will be free of moral constraints having no conscience, do as one pleases, would lie, steal, kill, and be sexually deviant with impunity, by having no fear of some eternal judgment.

It must be pointed out that 'conscience' the word or the concept is not the property of theology. Conscience, is emotion; but it is not an innate emotion implanted in man by gods. Therefore, it is not an emotion activated only by religious commands, rules, or tenets of altruism.

Conscience, or to feel guilty is an emotional response or a perception that we may cause something to hurt others in our social or economic life. It is clearly mind perception, like any other, only stronger or more upsetting, because it usually involves the life or well being of another human being. If we are moral, we conscientiously bring to bear all of our memory and reason, to right a wrong, of which we may feel guilty. Conscience was an inhibiting force, in the lives of primitives, millions of years before the witch doctors invented gods, 'ethical' dogma or rules of conduct.

Conscience is an inhibition of our will, which early man learned through experience the concept of justice and fairness. If the primitive felt the pangs of hunger, then he began to understood her plea and she understood his, he fed her and so too her child. They understood the pain of injury and remembered their pain as they witnessed each other's. In this they knew they could not or would not want to be the cause of such things. One's conscience became their rein before attempting to steal or harm, for they knew how they might feel if it were done to them. It was memory, maybe not in the beginning, the brain was small with little capacity, but some social bonds handed down from the trees may have helped conscience to evolve further.

On the savanna and by the water, the primitive learned a different kind of lifestyle. Meat was the only diet available and then fish. The lipids helped the neural system grow and so did memory, new memories and things to learn by trial and error. New concepts of sociability and ways to live and survive alone and together in families or small groups.

For five million years, anthropologists believe that man survived in very small family sized nomadic tribes. There were two reasons for this, food was available, but their only means was to forage and scavenge. One doesn't scavenge and forage in large groups because of scarcity and safety. Every animal except those like rabbits was game, but the larger ones ate you. A large group could be spotted and guaranteed a meal for the predators. A small group could easily hide. And a small group could move to other areas quickly when food became scarce. The freedom to move quickly about to find food and safety were their prime concerns. Large groups would not become common until 35,000 years ago when Cro-Magnon man learned big game hunting.

Within the humanoid species and others, individuation of all life was a natural condition physically. Every other species depending on their level of awareness took on an individual nature in personality and a character. Zoologists are familiar with the peculiar personalities within a species. Families, as well, isolated by necessity, with differing experiences enhanced their cultural uniqueness.

When Cro-Magnon man began to organize into larger clans, for big game hunting, they would have never joined a group unless their autonomy, freedom to gather and scavenge and a fair distribution of the big game kill was protected. Robert H. Lowie in his book, 'Primitive Society' writes, that members of a kill received an amount or the first and choice parts of the animal depending on their contribution to the operation. If some did not make any contribution, in the hunting party, those with larger shares might 'loan' part of their earnings and was expected to have it given back in the future—voluntarily. Socialistic, or communistic principles of sharing would not have worked in these societies, just as it doesn't in ours, for if a man could expect equal distribution, few would take the *risk* in the hunt to earn his share. The hunting strategy would produce little or fail. Then the more ambitious could be free to leave the group and go out on their own. That would be the end of the free lunch.

We see the principles of primitive societies working for the survival of the individual and family. The principle of autonomy or individualism guaranteed privacy, the measure of contribution tied to the reward.

Cro-Magnon primitives now had freedom to pursue cooperative means to gain food and or values with some safety from predators. There was safety in numbers, but their ability to kill large animals was a technological advance, of bow and arrow, spears, and fishhooks, that animals couldn't develop or adopt in their strategy. They were outgunned, so to speak. There was another aspect of safety that a small nomadic family had to resolve and that was that his own kind could be a predator. They no doubt understood that animals steal food from one another and that fear, probably through some experience, that his own kind would act against their interests. There had to be an understanding guaranteeing loyalty of the tribe to the individual that safety from each other was paramount. The tribe would protect each clan from any infringement on property or person.

If there was stealing or killing, it was the person or persons wronged who would reciprocate and if the person or family could not, then the tribe as a whole would. This was the foundation that allowed primitive societies to be successful. It was not because they understood the terms 'rights', but for their nature *there was no other way to live*, separately, or all together in a tribe. It was inherent in their logic and set in their tribal rules the principles of non-infringement, autonomy, safety and reciprocation in kind. It had its roots in practice and their perceptions of human nature, as sentient beings to understand the individual needs, freedom and their safety. In the emotional abstract, born in their conscience, they had theorized a moral code to meet the requirements for living together. Success of the theory made the tribe a reality.

Implied in such societies was the overall principle of ownership that includes two areas. First, the ownership of ones self is autonomy, physically and mentally in whatever individual state that might be. Second, ownership in earned food and property was respected, no one, for any reason, could take it away from them. Whatever a person gathered scavenged or hunted belonged to that person. If they were clever enough to even think of it, it was their 'idea' or property, today it is called patent or incorporeal property rights. (See Lowie's "Primitive Society," his chapter on 'Property') [20]

They found a way to live *together* and be successful. The unnamed principles were, I repeat: Non-infringement, autonomy, safety, property rights, and reciprocity or justice.

CHAPTER 6

What are Morals?

MORALS are concerned with the principles or rules of right conduct, or the distinction between right and wrong. The moralist is

ss

concerned with right principles, that is, in conscience, imposes on every person a physical *censorship* when interacting with others.

A *value* is something of relative worth, merit or importance to people as a means or an end in itself. Value is relative—variable not precise—with a perceptive subjective distinction of being either good or bad. Good and bad are *not* precise terms, rigid, inflexible or perfection but is dependent on those who should decide what is good or bad for them. Value implies a personal estimable worth in human interactions socially and in trade, where each may express their own value judgments. A person's hierarchy of values may be perfect, but for another, bad or not too good. It may appear to be subjective and it may be in many cases, but if one is setting goals for their personal needs and happiness, one must be extremely objective when evaluating one's own nature, in their value choices.

Therefore, *Values* can mean anything to different people. But a *moral* means the same thing to all people, all the time, in all cultures, and every situation involving others. It's not something of value or of some relative worth. They are *absolute moral necessities* to preserve our nature and means for survival, and our species.

The term, *'morals values,'* is an 'ethical' term that implies a moral is subject to someone's evaluation in a culture, depending on the person, group, race, tradition, custom, period, or a value that has some relative worth. The phrasing of the two words is incorrect and immoral.

RIGHT and *WRONG:* Right in moral concepts, is in conformity of fact, reason, truth, standard, and principle or it is correct. Wrong, is semantically it's opposite. We are either right or wrong—it is a black or white analogy, and *there are no gray issues in morals.* We might say, 'But the action was not all wrong.' The question to ask then is, 'what was right about what was said, and what was wrong in the statement?" or "what did the person do right, and what was done wrong?" It is a question of true or false. It has nothing to do with time, places, or things, where morals are concerned. It is a right or wrong issue. They are objective terms not subjective. They are absolute not conditional.

Where Morals Apply:

Morals are only concerned for the relationships of trade and sociability—human interactions—between two or more persons and/or a person's property.

It is, in conscience, *a censorship, 'I will not'* in principle infringe on others. Whatever *values* a person earns, in its broadest sense, to be a success, he has a right to own, and to have happiness, and to live as long as possible. In conscience, *"I will not* infringe on those rights."

Rand: 'The right to life is the source of all rights and the right to property is their only implementation. *Without property rights, no other rights are possible.* Since man has to sustain his life by his own effort, the man who has no right to the product of his effort has no means to sustain his life. The man who produces while others dispose of his product, is a slave.' [21]

A person and their possessions constitute life. Stealing from a person's home when he is not there, is still an issue between two people, the thief and the owner.

A person's life, how he lives, works, and plays are *value* issues for mankind. Therefore, what one does to himself or for himself without interfering in another person's life, is not a moral issue, but one of value. How well one succeeds, depends on how much value he places on himself.

A person who leads a life of values, for his own sake and those obligations that were self imposed, without ever interfering in the lives of others, is a moral person.

Why do morals apply between two or more people? If a person found himself stranded alone on an island, hopefully in the South Seas and not in the arctic, every act taken would be one of value. To build a shelter or windbreak to forage and scavenge for food would be paramount to someone who valued life. If one gave up it implies a lack of values. Specifically, it would depend on how much he valued his life, rescue, or reunion with his family or lover. What he does to survive, in this instance is not a moral issue, but one of value.

If, however, another person were washed up on shore, then both would be confronted with moral issues. There would have to be some

ss

agreement so each would have an equal chance to survive. They might elect to share everything each gathered or foraged, which may not work. They may divide the island, divide its resources, or they might each agree to forage, and scavenge for themselves as best they can. This would require, in each case mentioned some understood rules so that each had a sense of autonomy and equal chance to survive in safety. This in effect, would be their 'Moral Code'.

Right or wrong in morals implies a set of rules for societies to live by. The key word is 'live.' Rules govern behavior to clear the road and allow people to *live* in accordance with their own nature—choose their individual values. A moral code establishes the "law" to "protect" people in their pursuit of goals, i.e. it allows freedom to seek and govern their own cultural hierarchy of values.

Aristotle: 'The just and the unjust always involve more than one person. Further unjust action is voluntary and done by choice and *takes the initiative* (for the man who because he has suffered does the same in return is not thought to act unjustly); but if a man harms himself he suffers and does the same things *at the same time*, no one can commit adultery with his own wife or house breaking on his own home or theft on his own property.' [22]

In principle then, self destructive actions are just and unjust *'at the same time,'* whether it is drunkenness, drugs or suicide, no one can commit a crime against their own person. It is just, for it is their wish or error, and may be unjust to one's being of which they hold no value and is an *amoral* act. However, on the other hand, justice (means fairness) in people's actions is paramount when it involves more than one person.

Time and Culture: When do morals apply? Does time, history, era, epoch, or century have an effect on morals? I need no more than to refer to the two beings that found themselves on an island, or of you and your neighbors in civilization. No matter which religion or government ruled, in a period of time, they all had an arbitrary set of rules and gave the reason for their inconsistency, as being the 'country,' 'times' or 'culture' even to call it 'tradition.' But all people through time were faced with the same problems the two found themselves faced when stranded on an island. The state of their culture would make little difference they still needed autonomy, safety, and an equal opportunity to survive regardless of what era they lived in or on what island. Time, culture, or place has no effect on morals. Morals give us equal opportunity when codified into law.

A culture adopts traditions of myths, legends, and history of their ways of behavior, like song, dance, rituals of birth, love, and marriage but such things, in themselves, are not morals. Morals are necessary principles of behavior among people to protect their autonomy (individualism and freedom), with equal opportunity to earn, in safety, for their survival. Our children will change the culture in their time, however, to survive, our moral code will have to endure in all generations.

Moral principles are rules to protect the evolutionary progress of the human species and each individual there-of, in their lifetime, and does not change for any one, any thing, in any time, place, tradition, culture, or custom on earth.

NECESSITY: It is the concept of life that is primary, which makes the concept of morals a necessity that cannot be otherwise and not just something of value. Philosophically, necessity is the quality of following inevitably from logical, physical or moral laws.

Each one of us is physically and intellectually one of a kind in the universe. It is the truth of what we are and/or our children—what we may be. It is an imposition on our nature and progress, in the evolutionary scheme, to infringe on human evolution. The preservation of human evolutionary life (survival of the individual—our species) is what *necessitates* a moral code.

If we exercise our individual nature in every aspect of our lives, morally, and in the pursuit of values, our species will continue to evolve. *Any moral code must be based on the reality of our metaphysical and epistemological nature to be ourselves.* We are in every sense highly individual and it is necessary that we make our own choices. No one should interfere in that process whether they are a person, majority or minority of people, organizations, and especially ideological governments.

Moral principles are life necessities, which can not be otherwise because the loss and or the quality of life, success, and human happiness are indispensable to every person on earth.

INFRINGEMENT: When a government passes a law to legally take our property (tax income) it does so by force and it is immoral. We have analyzed our nature, reasons and criteria to establish moral principles, and now we will create or recreate from history a moral principle that justifies the above paradigms in chapters five, six and above. In morals, infringement is a breach of one's right to exist in accordance within his or her nature. It is a transgression on a person's life or property with no possibility of escape, ability to know or anticipate. Intrinsic within every principle, in the moral code, is in fact, a self-evident fair claim that non-infringement in the lives of people is just and moral. A right is a fair claim, and the role of justice is fairness in all issues of infringement. *The thing we ought not do, is infringe on the lives of others, which becomes the only constraint we have on our free will.*

Infringement is evident when moral principles are not followed. If one is held at the point of a gun, interference occurs. The person, held against his will, is in a sense imprisoned, and if hurt or robbed, is defined as infringements on the person's freedom, life or property. The responsibility of a government is not to contravene the constraints of morality and is obligated to be consistent, as such, by *not* exceeding that of the individual, but by holding non-infringement as a moral ideal. When a government makes law to provide material values for a segment of society they tax people for some perceived 'good.' The law is an infringement providing no escape for those who would disagree and is immoral.

Governments infringe by law, taxing for 'social' reasons of value, confiscating property, and limiting freedoms contrary to the moral code, as you will see ahead. They are motivated (the government and the segment of society who vote for social infringement) by the theological socialistic ethical concept that values are moral equivalents. Also, by the philosophical 'ethical' utilitarian theory that dictatorial governing makes choices to affect, 'the greatest good for the greatest number,' which is *not a valid moral principle, and immoral.* If a state believes it is good to take by force from the people any value (the means), for some greater good for a greater number (the ends), they live by the principle, *the power of a majority rules the minority.* This ruling concept is what theocratic and totalitarian rulers use to seize land, property, eliminate freedoms, and sacrifice lives for some end—which is defined as some common or subjective good. It means they may 'legally' invalidate any moral principle for the good of the state and that is what they are doing in every country on earth today. The USA is guilty and we are no longer free.

If one person infringes on a right of all individuals, then that person is immoral. If all the people infringe on the right of one individual, then all of those people are immoral.

For each person to reach their own level or hierarchy of values, to interact socially or trade with each other, we need a *consistent* code of morals—a just code of non-infringement that respects *every* person. A moral person is free to seek values and may discriminate for social reasons in their private and intimate lives, i.e. family and friendships, without showing cause. However, within our dealings in our economic life we may only discriminate on the basis that they display psychological instability, lack moral necessities, or in the case of career, lack requirements in ability. In all such discriminatory judgments, for infringement of such rights, they must be provable.

To infringe on the life of a person or persons where there is no knowledge of the deed, is immoral. To take advantage of people's lack of intellect, where they cannot possibly know or understand, is to violate such people for ends, not in their best interest, constitutes infringement by fraud and is immoral. Infringement of this kind takes advantage of people's trust in others. Such is the nature of fraud, lying, fraud against minors, those lacking mental ability, cheating on one's lover where both have sworn fidelity, as well as economic fraudulent schemes.

Humans cannot live completely alone, we *are* 'islands' unto ourselves as individuals, but our hands and minds extended outward as 'causeways' to the islands of humanity. We all need interpersonal relationships whether they are lovers or mates, relatives, friends, mutual partnerships at work, the neighbors or to buy at the corner grocer. Human contact is necessary to attain our goals and everything we value, whatever they may be. We show respect for every human being by honoring the moral code

Within ourselves, this island, we are individual, and our life's foundation can only be built with our own feelings of which we must make sense. There is the time to our selves we must be true and contemplate direction for our lives. We have to take stock of career and the homework it requires in deep thought. Then we have got to take the time to remember the place of family, relatives and friends in one's heart. But then there is the love of one's life that we cannot forget because that's the one that cannot be invaded on this island or break our reveries. We need this island of space and time to solve the problems of self, one's foundation for building a successful life of love and true happiness.

The 'hermit' may prove he needs no one, but in a sense it may be a cop-out. In this group of 'hermits' are the fearfully shy, the self-conscious, introverts, and the lonely. The loner may have experienced discrimination dishonesty; unfairness or they were wronged in some way. Their idea of personal relationships may be far more ideal than we may imagine. They may suddenly go mad, kill or commit suicide, so great is their disappointment in the unfairness of those that they have come in contact with—it is disillusionment. Where one trusts to expect truth they find falsehood; to find acceptance, discrimination; to find friendship, an enemy; to find loyalty, treason; to find fidelity, infidelity; or to find intellect, the irrational.

The hermit, loner or single person may be disillusioned, it is an emotional response to events, and must be identified and dealt with rationally as to the cause, the reasons and a reciprocal response that is just, or to avoid such people. No matter how badly one is treated we all have the freedom to avoid ignore or relocate to a place where we may find different attitudes, life styles, and just maybe, people like ourselves. But perhaps they have done that and are happy and secure. That's what a life of values means, to search for those things that one values—it is a *personal necessity*. It is to know enough to get out of the rain. *The only constraint on our free will is we ought not to infringe on the rights of others, by following the moral code.*

Ahead we will define and establish what principles are indeed moral, but we may have a greater difficulty in separating morals from values. The reason is, we have never thought in terms of two disciplines, one 'moral' and the other 'value.' The 'ethical' idea that morals and values are moral equivalents are imprinted in our literature, in our cultures, and in our language or rhetoric, so that separating the two will be analogous to brain surgery. None of us are impervious to mental imprinting and in this struggle to understand together we shall embark on a quest for knowledge, to shed the old, for—truth.

Our first task is to define and analyze the two terms, morals and values, using the definitions that semanticists or dictionary compilers have logically reasoned to be true. *Morals* pertain to principles of right conduct, when making decisions concerning ones interactions with *others*. Values are those decisions concerning ones *personal* desires needs, career, or happiness are *value issues.*

'MORAL VALUES:' A *moral* pertains to or is concerned with the *principles of right conduct* or habitually acting with respect to right and wrong. In human conduct there are two types of actions, the first is mental, to decide, and the second is acting physically to achieve the goal. Mentally we may make two basic choices, one to be moral and follow the universal moral principle of the code; *I will not* infringe on another—the other is to mentally choose to pursue a value. What makes morals in one respect separate from values, is that if moral principles are followed, *no physical action or conduct is necessary to be moral.* What is obvious, is the only action that one needs to take to be moral, is a mental act of necessity, "I will not infringe." *Therefore, the only valid moral act one can perform is an act of volition, to make a choice, to mentally decide not to physically take action that would infringe on others.* We may also volitionally or mentally choose to seek a value, but we must take some physical

action to achieve the goal (to gain value). Morals do not require we do anything of a physical nature to be moral.

All physical acts are acts of value. Values are things we seek to survive and live happily according to our nature. A moral code protects our right to everything we earn, as long as we do not infringe on the lives of others. When we seek those things we need, desire or we value, we perform, two acts. The *first*, is the *mental act*, to reason and decide? The *second* is to take real *physical action*, guided cognitively, to achieve the goal. Both intentions become 'acts of value,' the mental and physical conduct of someone who is seeking their values. The moral code, is a set of principles for right moral behavior, and our will to embrace the rules to follow as an ideal, so as to be 'a moral person,' are abstractions based on universal moral conduct, "I will not infringe on another person's rights."

The phrase 'moral values' quoted by many to emphasize their 'ethical' morality is in fact a contradiction and grammatically incorrect in their two different meanings, a semantic obfuscation. Philosophically, morals are principles of behavior that necessitates a mental act of censure, *not to take an immoral physical action.* An act of value has two components, a mental act of analysis to decide and will to take physical action to gain something of value. No physical act of value can be a moral principle, and no moral principle can be a physical act of value. Therefore, there can never be any such thing as a 'moral value,' which is every sense an *oxymoron.*

The greatest moral abstraction for us, is that mental act that we perform when we decide that, 'I will be a moral person.' And in every instance that we arrive at another decision, not to do this, or that, is when we are reminded of that silent goal, 'to be moral.' The only time that we may feel the effects of mental actions is when someone says 'good job,' 'I trust you', or in the night, when that special someone says, 'Your so good, I'll love you forever.' Only then is moral theory proved to be true for our selves, and like the primitive, the reciprocity of others will make that abstraction real.

Ahead we will explore more reasons for separating morals and values. This moral philosophy, is a set of principles that states; if one must take some physical action to be moral it is in fact infringing on a person's right to seek values in freedom to survive. A moral person's philosophy is guided by, "The Moral Code," ahead, which is man's only obligation to others, and is therefore free to seek his own values. It is contrary to theocratic and socialistic 'ethics.'

CHAPTER 7

The Moral Code

The Moral Code is natural law. It is an outline of principles or abstractions that identifies man's obligations towards each other. Intrinsic, within each abstraction is a premise that justifies as an absolute necessity, an axiomatic principle, that people *do not* infringe on the lives of others whilst pursuing their values.

The reason that humans respect, honor and follow moral principles is to protect their right to reciprocate in kind, to protect their autonomy and individuality, to be responsible for family and children for their lives and physical beings, the protection of their property, and for honest socioeconomic trade. To be against discrimination, against coercive collective rule, their commitment to obligations involving others, and against claims that one is not responsible for his actions.

The principles of The Moral Code are all *known* abstractions that we can all define as correct or right in moral behavior. The following are the specific principles of basic self evident human moral rights, as we now know them. As self evidence they have been proven to be philosophy's natural law of perfect justice. Chapters 3., 4., 5., 6., and Book V, "Values," is the science of social conduct that has been verified by experience which demonstrates and *justifies* (we know to be right and just) morals and values as separate valid scientific branches of philosophy.

Every moral principle is a commitment of necessity, "I will not" but no commitment is ever without reciprocal expectations. Only when promises are reciprocated will people find the code to be real and no longer an abstraction.

EVERY MORAL PRINCIPLE IS A BASIC HUMAN NECESSITY IN HUMAN SURVIVAL.

THE MORAL CODE (Natural Law)

1. I will not infringe unjustly on the life of any human being or on a person's right who is infringed upon to reciprocate in kind.
2. I will not infringe on the free independent autonomous nature of any human being, to be free and responsible in the pursuit of individual values for survival.
3. I will not dishonor nor abandon my parental responsibilities, but cherish in teaching my children and demonstrating by example, this Moral Code, and give them loving care, whilst providing them with knowledge they will need for survival in their generation.
4. I will not discriminate for or against any human being because of their race, gender, ethnic origin, atheistic or secular reasoning, sexual orientation, religious faith, and mental or physical handicap.
5. I will not deceptively influence, vote, coerce, or forcibly obligate another by law to accept my values or to sacrifice theirs for any reason
6. I will not cause to/or kill, harm, torture, or use physical force against any human being, except in self-defense.
7. I will not steal, cause the destruction of, or vote to take by force of law, the property of another human being.
8. I will not lie, nor conspire to cheat or defraud any human being.

9. I will not claim ignorance of this Moral Code as reason to infringe on the lives or values of others.
10. I will not dishonor or change the obligations of this Moral Code, and honor all other obligations that I have imposed upon myself.

These principles of moral behavior are promises we make to each other, including leaders, "I will not infringe.. " They are not a leader's command a mix of morals and values that point only to "*You* shall not..."—by not including himself.

On morals, what will make one credible, in people's minds, will be self-evident in character attributes when one honors moral necessities, and the results are *twofold*, one, in their actions for their own survival, and two, for others. Expectations for reciprocity is necessary in order to interact with others in both morals, and values.

The Necessary Attributes of a Moral Person

1. For the person who will defend the right to reciprocate in kind when infringed upon, are one, that seeks *justice* for him self and two, for others.
2. The person who claims autonomy, freedom and individuality is one, who seeks *responsibility* for him self and two, for others.
3. The people who will set an example and educate their children are *parents*, and two, anticipate that attribute in others.
4. The person who will not discriminate, for ethnic or other reasons is one that has *integrity*, and two, trusts that in others.
5. The person, who will not influence or vote to coerce others to give up their values, is one who has *confidence* in him self and two, in others.
6. The person, who will not harm others is one, who has *empathy*, *sympathy* and *respect* for him self and two, for other human beings.
7. The person who will not steal is one that has respect for *goals* and *ambition* for him self, and two, respect for the values of others.

ss

8. The people who will not lie are one, those who are *true* to them selves, and two, *truthful* to others.
9. The person, who will not claim ignorance is one, who has *intellect*, and two, presumes that in others.
10. The person who will fulfill his obligations is one, who is *reliable*, and two, relies on others to fulfill theirs.

Mothers and fathers become parents by giving birth to a child. It is born by mutual consent and their responsibility by a commitment of love respect in a social and economic union. No one would believe or accept that is *only* what 'parent' means. They have merely begun a life. In every respect, most agree, it is the fountainhead and origin of physical life and a parent is the source of food, affection, and discipline. To be a parent is to educate, teach, love and with *patience* owe the child the means to survive, and the reasons to be moral. If one believes those are 'society's' or a government's responsibilities, it is an immoral belief, because lovers are responsible for their actions—especially procreation.

People, who attack a principle of the Moral Code, have willed, in reality, to attack them all, and our society as a whole. Immoral people who lack moral necessities, will *forfeit* their rights to freedom moral principles guarantee, nor can they claim any attribute. It is moral people who will search their minds to identify the meaning of their conscience, and in doing so, will never permit themselves into becoming frauds or to suffer moral depravity.

The necessary attributes to be moral, in one's dealings with others are a sense of justice (fairness), responsibility, respect, empathy, confidence and all those above. It is the ultimate gift we give to mankind. It is moral respect for our selves and others.

In philosophy, a universal is a general term or concept or the generic nature that a term signifies. It is an entity that remains unchanged in character in a series of changes or changing relationships. In logic, in a proposition or theory, it is asserted of every member of a class. In the classification of morals, i.e. The

Moral Code asserts within each premise an unchanging character, of non-infringement that is a universal in human morals.

CHAPTER 8

Defining the Moral Code

This Moral Code is an absolute moral necessity (it cannot be otherwise), but the outcry will be that it is selfish—it is. Note who yells the loudest; for it is only the selfish who coerce that we be unselfish. This code, embraced by one, may be embraced by all where we share the same defense, to live productive lives, seek happiness, live long, and prosper. To be selfish or unselfish are not moral issues, but of values. The more value people place upon themselves, the greater their selfishness and goals they struggle to achieve. If people are selfish, they seek the best lives for themselves, and we have an equal opportunity to do the same, providing we do not infringe on others.

This Moral Code is not prefaced with theoretical principles of commandments, by men who created mythical beings to command a fantasy of devotion, not to honor man, but for make-believe mystical gods. This Moral Code promises no miracles, but the Code's principle honors human beings, in their pursuit of values. God's commandments do not offer reciprocity nor justice for human nature. The Moral Code gives man such rights, to be human in nature and to live a life of personal values.

The Moral Code is contrary to altruism's code, of self-sacrifice for others. It is equality, not slavery for human beings in the name of humanity. This is justice, man's code of fairness, and in principle, will guarantee mutual reciprocal conduct in *morals* and in the pursuit of *values*. We, being realists, place varying estimates of value on our self and others. But The Moral Code levels the opportunity to seek our values freely with moral protection.

To defend our moral principles we must mentally and physically take actions and as such, justice will vary. Acts of value are, not precise, inconsistent, and at varying costs. Since we place varying estimates on the value of our lives, property, etc., it will be represented by the values that we invest in reciprocity. Therefore, any action taken in the defense of any principle, in this Moral Code, i.e. to protect one's life, liberty, property, and culture, is an act of value.

Any action taken against the Moral Code is the act of a person without moral necessities, immoral, and forfeits any rights granted by the Moral Code. This is true for *every* moral principle within the code.

Immoral acts, intentionally horrible, will provoke a vengeful emotional response. However, retribution is requital, according to its merits or just deserts, especially for evil. We have elected the courts to intervene, in our behalf, to be our agent of reciprocity. They are removed from the alleged offender and the victim's emotional pain and suffering on a personal basis, that may otherwise cloud judgment. It is a reasoned response, justly administered on behalf of the victim in a court. That is why we have police procedures, the dignity of court, and jury contemplation—on behalf of the accused and the victim. It is a means to help achieve a methodical unemotional reasoned acquittal or retribution. But reciprocity or retribution becomes the defining action of the court to be viable.

Man's need to be free of infringement is just since man like the primitive, lives and survives by *his* values, those that he gains by his mental and physical effort. It follows that what he achieves *justly* belongs to *him*, having the right to protect himself, his gains, and those *he* values, if not peaceably, then violently.

Finally, there is no moral principle that would justify that man does not have an inalienable right to life, liberty, and property—what he values and earns. There is not a moral principle that would justify that he *not* defend his right to reciprocate in kind.

The following definitions for each moral principle are not complete, but cover some popular understanding. Like all law codified from the code there are many contexts, not covered here, due to the lack of space. Much that is written here may be common knowledge to many people. Well, this is also written for the very young reader who may not yet be experienced in legal ideas of rights.

1.—"*I will not* infringe unjustly on the life of any human being, or on a person's right who is infringed upon, to reciprocate in kind."

This is a philosophical absolute moral principle, the first of the Moral Code, and is a moral necessity. Every moral principle that follows the first in the Code, in order to guide people's behavior are moral premises that support this principle. To contravene any principle, in some way infringes, on the lives of others. If such infringement takes place, it is obvious *I will not* infringe on their right to reciprocate in kind.

When infringement takes place in human interactions and where it is without any recourse to such invasions, man becomes a 'sitting duck' so to speak. Therefore it is prudent for all that produce something of value to reason a course of action, to protect their lives and property. That is the essence of reciprocity, without which a Moral Code would not be necessary.

Reciprocity some might say is vengeance and retribution—IT IS. There is not a human being who learns his child is molested or killed, and wants to forgive the killer for his act. Vengeance is emotional! Retribution is reason. However, to temper such emotions courts are created in nations to affect reason and objectivity in determining guilt or innocence and the limits for retribution.

The person who is assaulted, the victim of fraud, or has been robbed at gun point, demands retaliation, the infliction of injury, harm, fine, humiliation or the like—vengeance! Yet our laws are becoming influenced by religious 'ethics' of 'turn the other cheek' 'the forgiveness of the killer by the victim's family?' They seem to go into self-serving extremes, to convince everyone they are 'religiously good'. Such irrational behavior is also reflected in reduced or no sentencing for crimes, the parole system, lack of firm policies and the repeal of the death penalty in many states. Hesitancy to use the death penalty, is largely due to inefficiencies by the justice system or errors in methodology, and the science for examining crimes, that may be prudent, when there is a lack empirical evidence.

There are today, some improvements in forensics, police science, and careful handling of evidence in criminal and biological laboratories, which may give people more confidence to apply the death penalty. However, there are well publicized heinous crimes, serial killers and others where there is *no doubt* empirically, in anyone's mind, the people's, jury, and the court, where the killer should receive capital punishment. Bibles indicate that 'We turn the other cheek' and contradicts itself indicating an 'eye for an eye' demonstrating a confused intellect or reasoning in moral and value issues—perhaps intentionally to obfuscate the issue?

The person who is about to commit a crime weighs the benefits if one can get away with it, as opposed to taking a risk of failure to suffer at the hands of a vengeful society. If a risk is perceived too great or their conscience prevails they may not make the choice. Reciprocity (vengeance and retribution) may never eliminate all crimes, because of free will probability, but we will *deter a much greater percentage,* if we reciprocate.

Aristotle: "Some think that *reciprocity* is without qualification just, as the Pythagoreans said: for they defined justice without qualification as reciprocity. Now 'reciprocity' fits neither distributive nor rectificatory justice—yet people *want* even the justice of Rhadamanthus to mean this:

Should a man suffer what he did, right justice would be done, for in many cases reciprocity and rectificatory justice are not in accord, For it is by proportionate requital that the city holds together. Men seek to return evil for evil—and if they cannot do so, think their position mere slavery—or good for good—and if they cannot do so there is no exchange, but it is by exchange they hold together." [23]

Now "reciprocity" fits neither distributive nor rectificatory justice, according to Aristotle, which alludes to the problem of just or fair distribution or rectifying the wrongs is a problem we still face today.

Rectificatory justice asks; what is fair? If someone destroys people's property, they require an equal amount restored and an amount for personal inconvenience and/or rectifying injury.—How much?—Our judicial wrestles with this problem every day. However, people do want restitution and in courts all over the land make their pleas. In cases of killing and the like, our courts hear the pleas of the victims or their loved ones, for what they consider fair punishment, before sentencing. They have the right to plea, not decide.

The foundation, on which a judicial system will exist is to determine guilt or innocence, but to be a moral force in the lives of citizens, *is in fairness of sentencing the guilty*, in reciprocity or rectifying justice. We demand of our judicial system an element of prudent force balanced with police restraint to protect the innocent and the guilty. The citizen shares the responsibility as a jurist in determining innocence or guilt and in some cases their recommendation of the sentence imposed. If the court and/or jury view the system as having 'a god's judgment,' or in a 'god we trust' and no human reciprocity in defense against further invasion of their own lives and values on earth, then we shall see 'forgiveness' in sentencing and an erosion in moral behavior. The courts as a moral force in society will ultimately become *irrelevant*, including people's rights, safety and their lives.

If a person were found guilty for a criminal act, would it be a just sentence if perpetrator became a sorrowful person? Where 'forgiveness' may be possible if the perpetrator repents, he may not be truly sorry, but only glad he got away with it. Also, to be only sorrowful is not a just sentence, because *we cannot read a mind and will never know* if he is sorry, or not, or it possibly being an act of fraud or lying.

Psychologically, we consider the accused as to what *may* be the cause of his actions but we cannot read his mind and can never know why a person makes an immoral decision and wills to take action. To determine innocence or guilt, given a *physically healthy brain*, a person is to be held responsible for their actions. If the person is found innocent then we rejoice in that a competent able judicial system has served justice and the person is freed into society. If the person is found guilty he should receive a sentence like anyone else according to law.

Reciprocity is risking one's values, life, and property for one's own preservation and for that of others. It protects the innocent. It takes *moral courage* to be on a jury, a witness in court, and tell the truth, bare one's soul, to admit complicity. Likewise, to be an expert, to come forward, to risk credibility, to confess to involvement, or one's ignorance, i.e. to help, free an innocent person, to take part in a reciprocal action, in a public court of law.

To reciprocate in kind in our value hierarchy becomes the means for order in trade and social achievement. They are the goals humans seek,—values given to be reciprocated in kind by value received. 'Confucianism has as one of its major tenets a version of a golden rule that states, "What you do not want done to yourself do not do to others." This belief transferred to western culture as, "Do unto others as you would have them do unto you."' Confucius was not concerned with deities, never mentions a god in his analects. As a philosopher he was concerned with life on earth. Concerning an afterlife, he asked, "while you do not know life, what can you know about death?" Of religion, "If we can not know men, how can we know spirits?" [24]

However, all the above relationships were to be built on reciprocity as expressed in the golden rule. We take a risk in trusting others expecting they will do the same. Our only means to keep risk at a minimum is to take heed in Sun Tzu's words, "To know thy enemy." Although he was speaking of the art of war, all life is competition of some sort, so to, 'know all those you deal with' is good advice to lower risk, in the art of surviving.

If the right to reciprocate in kind is infringed upon it is an immoral act. To decide not to prevent someone from reciprocating in defense of values is a moral mental decision. The only action taken to be moral is a mental one, i.e. to make a decision to influence and command the will not to act. This is true for *EVERY* moral principle.

2.—*"I will not"* infringe on the free and independent autonomous nature of any human being, to be free and responsible in the pursuit of individual values for survival."

Autonomy is a concept derived in English from a Greek term "autovopia," meaning, the having or making one's own laws, specifically to be independent not influenced or controlled by others in matters of opinion, conduct, choice, or actions for oneself. In matters of governments for territorial independence it is the right in governing property and citizens to make their own laws and to administer their own affairs of state. That is, providing they do not infringe on their citizenship.

The concept of an autonomous state is to be morally bound to represent its constituency and can not morally contravene the very nature of its own people. A state must replicate its autonomy and not come into conflict with or to go against, deny or impose any law that would violate, infringe, or transgress the autonomous nature of those they claim to represent. What a state is, is a natural protector of human nature and life. An autonomous nation automatically will morally respect, that each individual is by law free to be independent, be entirely responsible for himself and to earn and govern his own hierarchy of values.

A government's role is to protect man's *autonomy*, not to provide people with values to affect or create for them a false ant-like collective automation, but to leave them free and responsible for themselves. However, a government's responsibility is to protect its people from those who would be immoral, i.e. this Moral Code is their legal responsibility. A government is not above this Moral Code. All values, tangible or intangible, real or abstract, shall become the responsibility of the people, by the people, and for the people. The role of government is to protect people's values, prevent crime against its people, and to prosecute those who do. From the beginning rulers have told people what values are best for them, and they are always wrong.

Autonomy for the individual is claiming independence and freedom, something all people have been struggling for the last 10,000 years. The word freedom and independence, implies 'responsibility' for every value in life we need or want. It is complete responsibility for our lives, being, health, jobs, businesses, and all of our economic and social pursuits. That must be our goal, a moral government with a mandate to protect our freedom in order, to responsibly seek our own values. The government's protection must be real and complete.

Selfishness is a fact of nature where every organism places its prime concern on survival, and *is* human nature. It is a moral right, in order for people to live and acquire the 'good' life for themselves. Selfishness is not a psychological or social dysfunction but a *fact* of biological existence. Human beings usually understand that concept in them selves *and* in others. It is a function of their individualistic nature to survive, to seek a good life for themselves and people they value. Self-interest is an amoral value concept, not moral or immoral, and in practice, a universal good value. For the man who takes care of himself shall never be a burden on others.

Autonomy guarantees equality in the pursuit of values, a natural inalienable right to seek their own goals and happiness. It is the 'I' in individual that is to have recognition and respect. *No one* wants to be an 'us' or 'we', part of a herd, in a coercive collective, or to be just a number. Infringing on the autonomous nature of the individual is wrong and immoral. Each person is metaphysically and epistemologically a highly individuated fact of existence who has every right to live free and autonomous, whilst not infringing or transgressing on the lives of others.

3.—"*I will not* dishonor nor abandon my parental responsibilities, but cherish in teaching my children, and demonstrating by example this Moral Code, and give them loving care, whilst providing them with knowledge they need will for survival in their generation."

Like the couple in the introduction to this book they are equally morally responsible for their actions, and their parents were morally bound to teach them sex and its consequences.

It is within the minds of human beings that moral actions take place. There, in fertile minds thirsting for knowledge, children will be shaping themselves for their future and survival. It is where the first seeds of moral behavior should be planted. In those little minds is where our moral necessities, translates into the necessity to be autonomous and responsible in thought, word and deed. If we do not teach our children, they will never be free or will earn any values for themselves in their lifetime. They will be at the mercy of the social planners as sacrificial lambs for some unknown, unseen, always needy people, who will need our child's earnings.

Our moral duty is—how do we teach our children the Moral Code? I will propose that it is simple, i.e. not difficult—reasonably possible for any parent with a child able to talk. I am also saying sooner, rather than later. In other words, make the mistake they may not be old enough and they just might. Children learn, in the beginning, by perception, and we explain to them what they are seeing. Thereafter, the explanation must always be consistent with their observations. All through their childhood they will listen to what we say and relevant to that, our actions or example we demonstrate, consistently, will impress them even more.

Teaching the Moral Code to children requires us to go beyond the abstract perceptual stage to identify morality relative to their experience, i.e. to be rooted in reality. If we give a child a toy and say it belongs to him and then to tell him it must be shared with others, that ownership comes into question and mom and dad has 'spoken with forked tongues.'

A child that is taught to have unselfish concern for others, may wonder why those 'others' are not unselfish and should give to him, or that why isn't that person doing something for himself? What's in life for me? It's not fair to the child and the child rebels against society and screams for freedom not knowing what the word means. *Words* are a child's first exposure to concepts or abstractions and a moral principle is abstract thought for children, but when demonstrated within their real experiences it becomes grounds that establish the abstraction as fact and to do the *right* things in their interactions with other people. I will not lie, steal, cheat, hurt, be hateful, unkind, wrong are simple moral abstractions for the talking child.

I will take each moral principle and attempt to put it in a child's

ss

perspective or how a *parent* might begin to teach their 2 or 3 year olds. I will only give one or two examples, but parents out there will be far more creative and have many situations and opportunities, as their child becomes aware. The idea here is to show and tell, or tell and show. Explain to them your responsibility so they will know why.

THE FIRST; principle is that of reciprocity. "Who hit you?"—"Jason?"—"Didn't you hit him back?"—"He's too big?"—"Then we'll have to tell his mother—she will punish him!"—"I told you not to bother your sister!" . . . "She doesn't have to play with you" . . . "Go to your room until your ready to tell me she can play by herself if she wants to."—time passes—"What is it dear?"—"That's very good honey now play with your Leggo's."—"Don't bother your brother!"

To tell the child to turn the other cheek will not only destroy him physically but will not be teaching the facts of reality. People in society are punished when infringing on others. In some instances we have to defend ourselves, that *is* reciprocity, the only defense the Moral Code has. As parents you are his judge and court and you practice moral law.

THE SECOND; principle has to do with autonomy—individualism. "He doesn't like Cheerios—he's not like you—he's special in his own way and so are you."—"No honey, just because they like to do that doesn't mean we do."—"Well dear we are all different because they don't do the things we do."—"No sweetheart you do what you like to do."—"Stand on your own two feet."

To tell a child that he or she must be like all the other children is to strip the child of their identity.

THE THIRD; principle, is simply this exercise and parents should remind the child of your responsibilities that may be theirs some day and ask, what would you do if you were me?

THE FOURTH; principle has to do with discrimination, "Just because she's a different color than you doesn't mean she feels different."—"If you were white how would you like it if no one wanted to play with you?" "So long as you're good, and nice to everyone, they'll be nice to you."—"I know they eat squid, but we like frogs legs." "How do you know they all sleep naked?" "I'll bet you would—now get your pajamas on, its going to be cold tonight."

The reward in this principle is that children having little experience accept others without judgment, because they like anyone who responds to them. They must be warned of much older people they do not know.

THE FIFTH; principle has to do with vote or the force in numbers. "You mean to tell me if they all agreed to jump over a cliff you would too?" "Just because your buddies want to do that doesn't mean that he has to." "Why should she do that for you and Jason?" Voting for values is

All people have a hierarchy of values and without realizing it, children also. It is here that we teach children that we all think differently and have different values that we are all entitled to.

THE SIXTH; principle has to do with harming others. "You know better—you shouldn't have hit him."—"Do you like to get hit?"—"I don't care what he said you don't have to play with him" . . . "You're going to have to go to your room, and your father will hear about this."

Physically harming others is serious and both parents should make sure the other knows of the incident and should reiterate their disappointment and anguish. They do not like to see you unhappy with them.

THE SEVENTH; has to do with stealing and respect for other's property. "I don't want you to take the cookies—ask first!"—"That's right, I wouldn't give you any, because they are for dessert sweetheart."—"No you can't just take things that don't belong to you. You don't want someone to take *your* things do you?"—"I feel very bad that you did that."

As said above, it's not the amount or the value of what is stolen or 'taken', it is the deed that is just as wrong.

THE EIGHTH; has to do with lying "I know you're lying and I'm really upset with you now, tell me the truth" . . . "No that's not what happened—go to your room until you're ready to tell me the truth."—Follow through to the through to the end.—"You've been up here a long time, have you thought how you might tell me what went on?"—"No that's not true and not what you told me before."—"I know because Mrs.—saw you and told me over the phone.—Now tell me the truth in your own words"—"That's right—now that wasn't hard was it?"—"You want me to believe you when you say something to me don't you?"—"I'm always honest with you, am I not?" . . . "I would be very troubled and sad if I couldn't believe anything you say."—"Can you say you're sorry?"—"Now for lying to me again you'll have to stay in your room until—" "Dad gets home, etc..—"

Never call a child a name such as a 'liar', 'thief', or that they are 'dishonest.' It should be in terms of your hurt, disappointment, sadness or distress that will appeal to their love of you and want to make you happy with them again.

THE NINTH; principle has to do with not claiming ignorance. "Honey, you should know that you can't do that."—"Please stop and think next time."—"Don't tell me you didn't know" . . . "I know you know better than that."—"You should think before doing something like that again." "I'm very disturbed because we went through that just yesterday" . . . "I know you're sorry, I'm sure you'll think next time but you'll have to stay in your—bah, bah, blah."

Asking the child 'what do you think?' before giving him or her an answer, encourages reasoning, and if they are somewhat correct, your praise will lift their self-esteem. Likewise, if the answer is incorrect your giving them clues to the answer will encourage dialogue, an activity that also builds self-esteem in the child.

THE TENTH; principle has to do with obligations. "When I asked you to do that you said 'yes' now I expect you to do that."—"You made a promise and you should keep it." "It's your turn to take out the garbage we all have to help around here." . . . "Mummy has her job and daddy has his and you have yours."—"You said you would do that and now your not keeping your word."

Self-imposed obligations socially, are giving our word and what makes us a credible human being. Since our first obligation is to follow moral principles it is necessary to teach moral behavior in preparation for the child's introduction into society, in kindergarten or home schooling.

If one brings a child into the world we are obligated to provide for the child's physical needs. We must also care for the child mentally, specifically, two distinct disciplines, to teach morals so as not to be a threat to society, and teach them your values, to provide the education for him to survive on earth. Every aspect of morals, their values and education are the socioeconomic responsibilities of the parents, not society or a government. By not providing for a child's survival in later life, parents are committing a most grievous fraud upon the child. If we are not following parental moral responsibilities in this principle, we are infringing upon our own children's lives, and immoral.

4.—*'I will not* discriminate for or against any human being because of their race, gender, ethnic origin, atheistic reasoning, secular intellect, sexual orientation, religious faith, mental or physical handicap,

Discrimination is prejudice that is two sided. The first is positive or people that will favor a person, i.e. be *for* one. That is, a person may get the job, or be accepted in a certain group or institution, company, etc., because of one's race, or national ancestral origins. The other is negative or that one will *not* be favored over the other, i.e. *against*. It is agreed both are immoral. There are similarities in human nature and our values, but it is the differences in each that makes us individuals which is natural and necessary to fall in love.

Racism and discrimination are beliefs, that there are inherent differences in the human race, where they may believe one is less human and one group or person is far superior to others. It deprives others of their potential and is a waste of human resources. These are the seeds of collectivism will lead to socialism or a theocracy that will inevitably lead to killing and war. It may be secular, racist or religious but one immoral group will usually claim dominance over the others and that will mean conflict.

To follow this principle, to not discriminate, one need take no physical actions. Although no outward action, physically, may be detected except in speech discrimination resembles a lie or fraud in its mental and physical ramifications and is a wrong, bad, and immoral act of value. It infringes on the action of the victim to take part in his own survival, i.e. freedom and pursuit of his values. Such discrimination may prevent employment of productive ability, trade of material value, personal association and social discourse. The law in the USA in discrimination issues is seems correct and fair in its reciprocal actions to fine perpetrators, and reinstate or make restitution to victims, of discrimination.

Since many people may not, for various reasons, say hire a percentage of a race, as reflected in society, no law is just in setting such quotas. It in effect relieves the justice system of the responsibility and burden to prove discrimination or racist intent, and set the proper examples for the nation.

The first laws or commandments in most religions establish in their code 'there shall be no other gods.' They assert that their gods are supreme over all others, written or implied, each is prejudicial, and discriminates against all other gods. Such a god's law creates the seeds of religious collectivism as found in their theology and theocracies. These are values of very active imaginations, and not moral necessities, but in our *social* private lives we may discriminate, and need not associate with anyone we choose, even frivolously.

The principle, 'I will not discriminate' also applies to distinction between atheistic reasoning that does not have any belief in a god, and the secular intellect in all of us who may or may not believe in a deity. Therefore, government honors separation of discriminating gods from the people's government that is our moral right in constitutional freedom of religion as a value issue. Since it is impossible to ever agree on one imaginary god, the alternative of hatred and war make it necessary to take an extreme to hide or privatize away from everyone, and all institutions, one's particular god and keep such thoughts within our own imaginations.

The values that make up and/or are included within a person's character may be bad for some and therefore we *may discriminate* in such ways as *not to socialize* or avoid such people, that is not infringing on other people's lives. It is immoral, when the person is discriminated against in the *economic* sector, and is based solely on factors of birth or accident, the cause of which the individual has no control. We know when we are discriminating or infringing on his need to work for his survival and hurting him, and his family in the process. If we do not know, then such ignorance or lack of reason is dangerous to peace, friendship, love and happiness for everyone.

5.—"*I will not* deceptively influence, vote, coerce, or forcibly obligate another, by law, to accept my values or to sacrifice theirs for any reason.'

This principle concerns our politics, the right and wrong of how to govern our selves. This Moral Code establishes that we have the right to govern our own values and no majority, by vote, can supersede that right.

The two major types of government institutions have been religious and secular. Beginning with the Pharaohs, the Popes, Ghandi, Khoumeni and others establish religious states and rule by commandments of their particular gods. Secular governments are the likes of Alexander, Ceasar, Napoleon, Stalin, and Hitler and Cuba's Castro. All royalists shared power with their churches or lords in their religious state and those kingdoms are theocracies. Like all such rulers, the church will guarantee the king and his descendants by inheritance the ownership of the land, people, and power over their morals and values because that is their ideology. Secularly, it would be a dictator's ideology, and in democratic governments, a political party's ideology, *a variant of socialism.*

Socialistic and theocratic governments always ruled until the Magna Carta, and the New World revolution that established the USA. Many secular leaders came to understand the deceptive nature of religious rule and that its ideology offered no hope for happiness, except when one died.

Secular leaders, in their own time and 'ethics', promised the people a utopia in their children's lifetime, and even in five years but never materialized and the people never caught on. Our constitutional government gave us the right to vote for or against political leaders and their policies. It is the 'vote' that comes into question in morals. Is it a just means to govern? If we mean govern, to make laws, run institutions and create a legal environment for a society to live in freedom and peace, then we must vote for people or politicians who we believe will shape that society. But there is no guarantee that the people will vote for freedom, but may vote to empower the state to dictate our values, in effect, surrendering our cultural and economic independence.

When we vote, we do it in two ways. One is that we vote for a *person* who will promote, vote for us in a congress, the type of government, and laws we want. Two is we vote *directly* (by *referendums*), for laws that will shape the type of government and laws that we want. Politicians prefer the first and do not like the second option.

Voting implies an agreement between two or more people that whatever the outcome (vote), everyone will abide by the results. Voting between two people doesn't make sense, since if they both agree to do something then there is no problem for each of them. But if each votes differently there is a stalemate unless they toss a coin agreeing to follow the one who guesses the correct outcome of the call 'heads or tails' or among three odd man out (lost). The agreement is simple and considered fair to each, there is no doubt they both agree and can live with the outcome.

The coin toss is a one shot or one time deal. It's not going to last forever or in every instance this issue is raised. A vote then is a prior agreement to accept the outcome, similar to a coin toss.

A vote becomes a better means to settle a choice (rather than toss a coin) between three or more people since it's not left to chance but to actual personal evaluations, of that which is being proposed. Here, like the two above, everyone knows each other and the outcome intimately agreed upon.

In a family, however, of three or more people, mom, dad, and one, two, or three children votes may be taken for going to the beach or mountain, but not usually in the economic reality of the group. Mother and father make decisions on most matters and usually by arguing, not tossing a coin. Each abides by the results of the argument and presentation of facts, and can live with the outcome even if it is a compromise. Here, too, it is not final, and may be changed at any time they decide, that it is no longer in their best interests.

In a tribe, a group of families or a small town where everyone seems to know everyone, may all agree to put something up for vote and agree to the outcome. However, family 'X,' in this case, doesn't think this should be voted on and is fearful of the outcome. The people may attempt to make concessions to the family or adjust the proposition to minimize the affect. In other cases the loss may be 'made up' in some way. However, if family 'X' disagrees to vote, and the town uses that family's tax dollars to implement some project, it is an infringement on the family and immoral.

It is obvious that the vote may be able to work in small groups, but in a larger one there is hardly any justice for the minority. Whatever the majority decides, the minority must live with. The issue in a large society cannot be adjusted, bent or varied to satisfy everyone who objects and votes 'no.' Voting in large groups is the rule of the many over the few. Individual freedom under such a system becomes irrelevant and a breakdown of society will ensue. And it's not the vote that creates problems, but obviously, the context of what was voted for. Many do not consider that voting is unfair to the minority, but are more concerned with what's being voted on, for themselves, i.e. *their values* (fair for only them).

The question then is "what do we vote for?" Well, it becomes obvious from this principle we should not vote to force others to accept our values or to give up theirs. *What* a moral society may vote on are *moral issues.* They do not vote away moral principles but vote to uphold morality and fairness. It is voting for people who have moral integrity, as opposed to the group whose candidate has *claimed* to have more moral integrity, which should be the necessary issues for vote. Our right to vote for *judges* is in one way, a perfect example, of voting for moral character. We vote for those people who are proponents of or will preserve our freedom, and not infringe on our socioeconomic values to provide for others or build 'pyramids' for government.

The 'ethical' principle that seems to have created the vote as the greatest thing since the pharaoh, was the 'idea' that man cannot live on earth without expecting infringement, and that he *may* benefit ultimately from any infringement. Man's psyche has always been imprinted to expect, that whatever he had, could be judged by a god, leader, or *majority* as to what was 'good' for all whether the minority liked it or not—thus man has lost his property rights since the pharaoh. The vote by majority rule only increased the number of a minority's rulers.

For the first time in history, the voter, a majority in the community, would share power with a political leader and decide a minority's values. It had never been considered that half of the people would be infringed on with each vote. The concept of individual rights in a republic or democracy was intended to protect the minority, but the opposite happened, by invoking a rule of the majority *over peoples values,* they gave up property rights to the majority, an error that must be corrected because it is immoral.

Perhaps it was Jeremy Bentham (1748-1832) whose utilitarian principle was that society should aim for the 'greatest good for the greatest number.' It was based on the psychology of the pleasure—pain principle, the masters of human motivation. Man will do well and avoid pain, i.e. in politics will seek the common good and avoid the bad. What was never resolved, even with Bentham, was the consideration of man's personal motivation when contrary to the community. A synergistic moral and value absolute principle evaded them and as we know from voting experience the happiness for the greatest number does not work at all for a minority.

Whether or not the vote was created, in politics, as a result of Bentham's 'principle' is questionable. It is not unreasonable to say that such thinking was a strong influence as it permeated the political life of English utilitarianism and politics in general. Perhaps political survival was at stake in those times and sharing some of their power was better than none. It gave the people, specifically, the majority the right to vote for *any* issue that was deemed a 'pleasure' regardless how 'painful' for the minority. The result has been that each group of citizens has their own 'idea' or *ideology* of how the rest of society should live, hence, the idea for ideological political parties. We are in a voting war and to the victor, 'legally,' go the spoils. We today did not agree to such voting rules, nor did generations before us have a right to surrender our personal living standards and culture, giving up our values to the state and a greedy majority, which is immoral.

The concept of *what* we vote for is the issue; are we voting for freedom of *all or for our selves only and what we value?* To vote with the concept in mind, that the majority rules the *values* of all, is *wrong and immoral.* Today's voter has inherited an immoral legal system and has every right to revolt and amend the constitution.

Whether we want to believe it or not the congress *knows* the concept of majority rule over people's value choices was not what the planners of the constitution wanted. Only Alexander Hamiltion wanted a theocracy—a king. The rest, without doubt, wanted an elected president and a congress that would protect their property rights, not provide human values. Yet they too did not fathom the distinction between "morals" and "values" but came very close. If their 'ethics' had not existed, majority rule would be limited to moral issues today. The fight to ratify the constitution became one over property rights or a democracy. Property was not secure if the vote of the people could 'legally' vote away a man's property rights. The vote was the underlying problem and still is today. [25]

Any action taken to defend this moral principle is one of value to uphold, maintain, and give stability to this Moral Code. Reciprocal action must be taken by *voting peaceably, protesting, or armed revolution* in civil war to change law of the land to reflect moral principles. People must change the constitution of their country, to eliminate forever government's involvement legally, in people's socioeconomic values. It is the voter who let the barbarians enter the gates of our free nation, and it is only the voter, 'the moral mob' who can push them out. See Government, Book VI, a moral state.

SS

6.—"*I will not* cause to/or kill, harm, torture or use physical force against any human being, except in self-defense."

No person should be forced to do anything against his will. No one should be tortured or terrorized nor to be a slave to anyone. People have the right, but it is not a *moral* obligation to protect others who are unable to protect themselves, it is an issue of values.

No one has the right to kill another human except in self-defense that includes war if one is invaded. Nor do we have the right to help *cause* the death of another human being—it is the same as killing. Cause in the popular sense, is to hire an agent to kill or to cause by reckless behavior such as driving while intoxicated, drugged, or excessive speed in a heavily populated city or suburban area, or to be an accessory in the killing of a person. When two or more criminals are involved in a crime where a person is killed by one, the others have helped cause the death and are accessories and culpable—blameworthy and may receive equal punishment.

There has been a movement to legalize being an accessory to assist in the death of a person. This practice is called 'euthanasia' or 'mercy killing.' It is the act of putting to death someone who is suffering from pain or incurable condition. Some believe in the means, assisting in mercy killing, and the end, is the 'good death.' This is the doctrine of utilitarianism (utility value) whereby the rightness or wrongs of an action (the means) is determined by its ends of goodness or badness. It is another instance of 'ethical' confusion. Good and bad in values are variable, depending on personal preference, in a culture, time or place, is related to value issues and subjective. It can not be moral, in principle, as some one else's right to cause or assist in the killing of a person, even if he believes the end may be good. In this case 'the end does not justify the means.'

Advocates of euthanasia, such as Jack Kavorkian want to change the meaning to 'assisted suicide' to depict a voluntary action and nullify 'killing' in mercy killings. His definition of 'medicide,' "Medicide is euthanasia performed by a professional medical person—a doctor, nurse technician, paramedic, or nurse anesthetist, for example. Euthanasia is humane, merciful death performed by anybody." In one sentence he gave anyone the right to kill another—mercifully? [26] Here, there are no just means to prosecute questionable deaths by anybody. "No . . . Medicine should be absolutely separate from the law, politics, religion and the judiciary." [27]

It is moral legal common sense that a criminal assisting in a death is an accessory to a killing, even given the consent of the victim that is not the issue. Any one wishing to die has that right, and is an inalienable right, as in the right to life. An inalienable right to die is a non-transferable right, not transferable to others to assist someone, intent on dying. Living or dying is a value choice and if we believe in autonomy or individualism then we know a person is responsible in the execution of their own hierarchy of values—they, not others, must act in their own interest. There can be no moral necessity or right to help kill another human being. With freedom comes the responsibility for one's own life, and death.

Abortion is where we have two very lively issues in ongoing argument as to whether or not abortion of a fetus is moral or immoral. The 'Right to Life' proponents are arguing that it is immoral to abort a fetus once the female and male sperm enjoin in her body. They claim this constitutes a human life or that at the moment of conception it is defined as 'life' and has the right to exist. Hence, the slogan 'The Right to Life.' *Life*, in this context is *human life*, and *life* in the human context or just the term *life* is also a generic term. If we had a female egg or male's sperm or we found human brain cells, blood, or organs, all being alive is also human life. However, all such human life is defined as *potential life* whether separately or enjoined until it becomes a physically and mentally viable human being with the potential for learning to survive. Birth control is a human right, a *value* issue for *potential* life. *Viable* human life has a *moral* right to exist. Abortion, is a scientific problem both in the timing and safety of taking such an action. Science has solved the problems of safety despite protestations to the contrary. Governments, legislators and finally the judiciary should look to science to solve the problems of legal *timing* for abortion.

7.—"*I will not* steal, cause the destruction of or take by "law" the property of another human being."

No person shall steal another human's possessions. All people have a right to their earned material gains. Whether they are rich or poor, a company, corporation or an individual, each has a right to profit and keep their earnings. No one has the right to commit arson, deface or destroy another person's property. Rand, "Without property rights no other rights are possible." [28]

Taking a person's property or earnings at the point of a gun is the *same* as taking it by 'vote' or 'law' or 'legal taxation' and they are all immoral. One can hear the outcry—'How will the government operate?' They will not, to the large extent they have created, but morally better than one can imagine. We will explore this concept in 'Government Book VI.'

One might argue that stealing a penny as opposed to stealing $100,000.00 makes a difference in the criminal prosecution of the two cases. No jail for stealing a penny and 2–5 years for one hundred thousand dollars, if convicted. The impact in value whether small or large on the victim is still immoral. It is still a question of right or wrong. The value of what they steal does not make it less wrong. *Value* allows us to fairly (justifiably), reciprocate in kind.

8.—"*I will not* lie nor conspire to cheat or defraud any human being.'

To lie in a court of law, under oath, is punishable and one may receive a prison sentence. The lie in court may cause a guilty person to go free or an innocent person to go to jail in both cases one has infringed on the lives of others and is immoral.

However, all lying is not punishable by prison terms. Yet there is much lying that is done by persons who are trusted and honored. But if we go through life distrusting all people in word (lying or fraud etc.), human interaction would be terribly limited in socioeconomic areas of our lives. Distrusting is the same as making one guilty until proven innocent. Most people, however, do honor people's integrity until they are proven dishonest. Proven dishonest, their reputation may be irreparable. The time, effort and trust the person has invested in the relationship are wasted and no longer viable. The reciprocal action one may take is to tell others and discredit the liar, or cease the relationship. His punishment is loss of credibility, honor, respectability and trust among his peers. If it was a con or fraud and a loss to someone, there should be legal punishment.

The little white lie, if undetected, leads to greater ones. It is 'insignificant', therefore easily forgivable, since its effect is thought to be of no consequence. However, even if the little white lie coming from a child, in the context of a youngster's mind with little experience, takes on immense proportions. In an older adult, it may be insignificant. Yet the perceived white lie shows a lack of self-esteem, and the inability to frame the truth. It is also disrespectful and insensitive to the person to whom the little white lie is told. One must be prepared to tell the truth, by planning for its effect, or damage control. Many liars are mentally lazy, in some respects lacking the reasoning to put the truth in the best perspective. For most it is easier to lie than explain the truth

The lie becomes the most evil of immoral deeds when falsely promising that some perceived good may be accomplished, providing you pay up. If the end (some perceived good) justifies the means (lying), then one is permitted to lie, i.e. be immoral in order to accomplish some 'idea.' It requires little replicating in subjective minds to accept such an immoral concept and rationalize that any immoral act be justified for any perceived 'good.' It is the principle foundation of theocratic and socialistic dictatorships.

Intellectual fraud, academic or economic, is almost uncontested in the world today. Fraud is committed on the people as a matter of right by governmental leaders and especially theological institutions. They all possess free will and are subject to the same temptations or pressures to become rich, famous or gain power. There is the potential for evil amongst us all, rich, poor, intellectual, and 'leaders.' Most can 'get away with it' since we are vulnerable, falling for every con game in town, because we seem to lack the ability to search for the truth, and we run on our emotions, not reasoning or questioning relentlessly—Why? What? Who? When? Where? How?

The reason we present such an easy target is that we are taught at an early age to 'believe.' To believe is to have confidence in perceived 'truth' or rely on a person's word, a sound byte, printed or otherwise without proof, so we have 'faith' in what was proposed without question. That is why the message is short and repetitive. With a minimum of words, analysis or emphasis on one's 'idea' most likely will be accepted as representing the truth. Thinking that it agrees with what one may have *guessed*, the whole 'ball of wax' will be swallowed without any contemplation, analysis or critique.

One may say, 'the intellectuals are the smartest, most educated or experts'—shouldn't we believe what they tell us? The secret to help end dishonesty, and what the perpetrators of fraud understand perfectly, is that many people are mentally lazy—they will believe and not try to understand, but will have faith that what they hear or read is true. The *total* responsibility to completely understand is ours to teach children the truth, and to watch, listen, and analyze critically, this is tedious reasoning.

Lying in print, on TV or other media is rampant. We teach children that Santa is real and later *they* find out he is not. Children are not usually disappointed it is a lie, only that it is okay to lie under certain conditions. What these conditions are, is not hard to understand, 'The end (my happiness) justifies any means.' If he has an imaginary friend, parents worry over his sanity, but if he grows up to have a god as an imaginary friend, his parents think he is sane. His whole life becomes a contradiction. Then he gets drunk and beats his wife.

Children also learn how mom and dad are able to lie effectively. What they learn, at an early age, "They can't read my mind." The seed is planted and the parents continue to fertilize it with irrational explanations of supernatural beings and stories of mythical beings that rise from the dead, far beyond what the real world demonstrates to him or her. They are told things 'for their own good', or 'what they don't know won't hurt them.' They hear their parents lie on the phone and to relatives face to face.

Armed with lying 'knowledge,' children learn how to look sincere, use the right body language, and speak decisively so as to make their lies to friends or family believable. The child's mind integrates all that is available in his or her environment quickly and at an earlier age than what one may think. Loving mom and dad, big sister or brother, as they usually do, children try to emulate them, by loving to do what they do—even better.

By the time the child is grown, they accept without emotion no moral necessity to be honest. Cheating to get 'good' marks or getting away with something is the rule of the day, which may lead them to do things they can easily hide from those at home. The technique and permission has been provided and granted from the home. Now grown, they can accept the fact our greatest leaders, educators, and bureaucrats will speak to the public one way and privately another, and or in politics honesty is not the best policy.

Our political system, which should be our moral foundation, is totally dishonest. Tax money is now called 'contribution to investment' or 'capital for investment' but in reality, just spent. Many guess, there is a deception, but are so conditioned to such lies they even admire their cleverness. They actually believe that the political system has to operate that way. It is expected that leaders will not keep their promises. Also, if they have cheated the public, their intimate mate, less than patriotic, or did not act in an exemplary manner in their life, we are not concerned. 'Hey, what's a little cheating,' 'so he took a little,' 'it's just a little lie,' which means we have no idea of the corruption or the messages we are instilling in our children and the destruction of our nation.

In this period of time we are lying our way out of freedom into moral chaos—socialism. An immoral society is created by an evil government. The deceit and deception leads to a system of lies—i.e. the lie tells us we are free, when in fact, the laws of the land completely control almost every aspect of our lives. The only thing we are being freed from is responsibility, our wealth, and any moral necessities.

The little white lie we permitted is the cancer that invades our Moral Code. It is not socialized medicine but "comprehensive coverage for everyone", a deceit. They say, 'we are far from being a socialistic state', but a socialist Fascism reigns. They lie to us and we lie to ourselves 'we're still free.' Social planners tell us what we want to hear, to create a new artful culture and we vote to coerce other people to accept our values. With their help we have no Moral Code, or the freedom to choose our own values, but we hear a lot of lies telling us we are an honorable moral nation. We have to believe the lies and have faith in their truth or we might have to do something.

Confronted with overwhelming evidence that there was no proof or reason for the resurrection, so Christian theologians proclaimed, the irrational had replaced the rational. A century after Paul, the church father—Tertullian (150-225) pitted his 'intellect' against truth: "And the Son of God died; it is by all means to be believed, because it is absurd. And He was buried and rose again; the fact is certain because it is impossible." [29] It was an attack on simple logic, but dishonest Tertullian knew the people were *not* thinking at all, and full of trust and faith for any contradiction he could create—even the most ridiculous.

When someone is lying it requires more physical effort than telling the truth. It is this fact that helps uncover lies they try to cover up. However, before one tells a lie, it requires inventing a story or statement and in telling it, increases emotional and physical strain on the liar. The liar has further problems in remembering the lie, to be able to repeat it without mistakes. It requires special attention on body language and facial expressions.

We must follow the Moral Code, however, during criminal actions, in principle, one may lie as a reciprocal action to defend oneself, since the offender has forfeited his moral necessities. Lying to a criminal during wrongful acts is self-defense. Hiding a Jew in Nazi Germany was coming to the aid of a defenseless person, and was an act of value, one person valuing another and acting for defense for some perceived moral code.

9.—"*I will not* claim ignorance of this Moral Code as reason to infringe on the lives or values of others.'

Justice demands that it is unfair to expose society to moral mental incompetence or psychological instability. The recent wave of protests over criminals who prey on the young and their demands of 'lockup for life' are morally justified. If moral concepts have no meaning to a criminal, society has the right to protect itself. If they have an animal mentality or lie to commit such a fraud they deserve man's retribution.

The psychiatric, psychoanalytic, and psychological techniques are in their infancy scientifically. They have a long way to go before they will be able to scientifically identify or reasonably show proof of their theories or the efficacy of their solutions to mental deviant behavior in humans. Their science is still in the perceptual stage in evaluation of what is deviant behavior, its cause or how it is to be treated. The root of psychology's science remains that of Freud, Dewey, and Kolberg practicing an unproved psychological determinism. Their technique is to dredge up forgotten memories and tell their patients, 'that's what's affecting your behavior!' The patient is left off the hook, he or she is not responsible, for their feelings, but someone or something else is, in their unconscious mind.

In the interest of justice, the judicial system should be asking for more than a psychologist's guess, of a problematic criminal's motive or lack of, in deviant actions. In scientific research, a theory or experimentation must be tested exhaustively with every known possible factor included. The experiment should be identified as a success or failure. Good scientific results are considered successful if a couple of points from one hundred percent.

Psychologists will never be able to determine guilt or ignorance, since it is impossible to read a person's mind. If empirical evidence is conclusive then the person must be held mentally responsible.

We would not trust a plane, car or heart operation that worked occasionally. Yet in psychology, behavioral or psychotherapy ignores the many failures and points to *any* single success as proof their theory has merit. In a court, it may be phrased, "although it does not happen all the time, our experience is that we can sometime treat this successfully."(?) The courts should promptly disallow any evidence

ss

that cannot be proven beyond a reasonable doubt. This immature theoretical science has no place in a court of law. Psychological 'innocence' is a psychological learning dysfunction or a fraud, neither of which can be proven and is good reason for incarceration. It will have to show the court, in some future decade, the kind of empirical proof like police investigation, forensic, and DNA sciences have to demonstrate in a court of law.

This moral principle requires, as a necessity, that one must know right from wrong at an early age if they value order and safety. It's not something, as Kolberg would have one believe, can not be learned until one is thirty years old or has no meaning at three, four or five. We must teach such rules as soon as the child understands *words*. The younger the child the more likely a lasting psychological impression or imprinting, because later in life will be too late.

It is a feat of simple intelligence to learn how to live among our selves. Even animals have the simple ability by which they interact within their species. There is no evidence that they accept ignorance or an excuse for whatever their code might be. An animal does not have the brain capacity to learn *our* Moral Code or conceive of the concept. We can not have an agreement with animals, so they become value issues. That's why we keep them in zoos or train them as pets.

If a person claims they are not responsible for an immoral act, they did so on the grounds that they are mentally incapable of understanding or learning. If the brain is physically damaged, it may be true that they can not understand or ever learn. The person requires close lifetime supervision. The person who pleads temporary insanity in a fit of passion or other circumstance is obviously a loose cannon in society, and like the wild animal scenario we cannot free them into the community. Psychiatry cannot, today, guarantee that the person, under similar circumstances (or others), would not repeat the act and he should be zooed (new word) for life. Whether it is full time insanity, or part time insanity, there is an obvious risk to our society.

10.—"*I will not* dishonor or change the obligations of this Moral Code, and honor all other obligations that I have imposed upon myself.'

There are two ways in which obligations are adopted in one's life. The first is that which is imposed on us by others and the second those that are self-imposed. Living intimately, as in family and/or pursuing goals, among those in society, we experience both. First, when we adopt obligations not to infringe on others, that is the Moral Code. Second, those obligations we impose upon ourselves for our individual needs, goals, and pursuits are initially for our survival and to pursue values to increase our quality of life and are all self-imposed obligatory value issues.

It was theorized earlier that we have only *one* obligation, that others for reasons of autonomy have placed on each of us to follow the Moral Code. That is, that we may do nothing physically, but, psychologically reason that any moral obligation or agreement will be reciprocated by others *leaving every one free* to take responsibility for their own hierarchy of values upon themselves. We are only obligated to mentally reason as codified in the Moral Code, not to infringe upon those who likewise honor that code. There is nothing else one has to do mentally or physically, to be moral.

All other obligations are individual choices of value. Should one place no value on him self, he may commit suicide, or lay down and die. He may take drugs, alcohol, eat poorly, beg for money, live in a cardboard box or be homeless ('no one can commit a crime against one's self'—Aristotle). It is an amoral issue, of values. There is no reason to 'help' unless it is someone you value, only then it may be a prudent act of value (you know and value the person). It is the extent of people's obligations that makes it evident how much value they place on them selves. If they place no value on themselves, to reciprocate in kind, we can only agree.

Being obligated to ones' self, to survive, demands social and economic contributions and the reciprocity of others to live up to their agreements. When in the course of pursuit and success in one's goals we wish to obligate ourselves in an intimate personal relationship with another, we by fiat (sanction) impose many demands on our selves. Those obligations not only involve our personal, social, and economic commitments, but also, our deepest emotions, sense of life, and freedom.

To take a mate, is to enter into a personal intimate relationship with another, who is in every sense also, an evolving *individual.* They are two different beings in the evolution of a species, who are metaphysical organisms, possessing distinct epistemological and psychological experiences. A whole range of obligations become evident, too many to classify, but the obligation to compromise becomes the key to making this intangible personal value love, real and enduring. Love is being in love with the idea of being *with* him/her. To cheat on him or her is being a traitor to one's own ideals and to murder hers'/ his.

When both people discover they have an enduring relationship they may elect to have children and this becomes a *dual obligation.* It is no longer a compromise of values that is primary but a dual moral obligation to love, teach, and prepare another human being to exist on earth. Just as all individual obligations are one's personal responsibility now becomes a dual moral responsibility to share their morals, values, social and economic, with tenderness, patience, time, consideration, and love for a little human being they created.

The promise: I will' be moral and 'I will' take action to reciprocate and defend The Moral Code for any infringement against mankind for it is the only defense we have. It is the promise, that 'I will swear' to fulfill, honoring all obligations for myself and for those I value, whether it is by contract, promise, hand shake, or a kiss.

BIBLIOGRAPHY: MORALS

Ref.
No.
Chapter 1

1. Abelson, Raziel and Kai Nielsen, Contributing authors: "The Encyclopedia of Philosophy," Published by, Macmillian Publishing Company, Inc., and The Free Press, New York, 1972: Vol. 3, P. 81-82.
2. IBID, P. 83.
3. IBID, P. 84.
4. IBID, P. 85.
5. Reese, William L.: "Dictionary of Philosophy and Religion;" Published by, The Humanities Press, New Jersey, 1980: 'Aristippus,' P. 27.
6. Wellman, Carl, Contributing Author: "The Encyclopedia of Philosophy," Pub. By, Macmillian Publishing Company, Inc. and The Free Press, NY., 1972: Vol. 1, 'Asceticism,' P. 17.

Chapter 2

7. Taylor, Richard, Contributing Author: "The Encyclopedia of Philosophy," Pub. Macmillian Co., Inc. and The Free Press, New York, 1972: Vol. 2, P. 364.
8. IBID, P. 364.
9. IBID, P. 364.
10. Reese, William L.: "Dictionary of Philosophy and Religion," Pub. By, The Humanities Press, Inc., Atlantic Highlands, New Jersey, 1991: 'Determinism' P. 127.

11. Taylor, Richard, Contributing author: "The Encyclopedia of Philosophy," Pub. Macmillian and Co., Inc. and The Free Press, New York, 1972: Vol. 2, P. 366.
12. Mill, John Stuart: "The Logic of the Sciences" Pub. by, Open Court Publishing Company, LaSalle, Ill., 1990: P. 23.
13. Taylor, Richard, Contributing author: "The Encyclopedia of Philosophy," Pub., Macmillian Company, Inc. and The Free Press, New York, 1972: Vol. 2, P. 368.
14. Berstien, Richard J., Contributing author: "The Encyclopedia of Philosophy," Pub. Macmillian Company, Inc., and The Free Press, New York, 1972: Vol. 2, 'Dewey', P. 381
15. IBID, Vol. 2, 'Dewey' P. 381.

Books: Referred to only in name, and/or paraphrased.
Piaget, J.: "The Moral Development of the Child" 1932:
Kohlberg, L.: "The Development of Children's Orientations Towards a Moral Order–Vita
Humana" 1963:
Loevinger, J., and R. Wessler: "Measuring Ego Development" Authors mentioned in text:
surname only: Devitis, Durkhiem, Erikson, Goldman, Harding and Rich.

16. Kay, A. William; "Moral Development" Published by, Schococken Books, Inc., New York, 1971: P. 16.
17. Commins, Saxe, and Robert N. Linscott, editors: "The World's Great Thinkers," Pub. By, Random House, Inc., New York, 1947: Vol. 'Man & Spirit' Friedrich Nietzsche, P.494.
18. Reese, William L.: "Dictionary of Philosophy and Religion" Pub. By, The Humanities Press, New Jersey, 1980: Jean-Paul Sartre, P. 509.

Chapter 3

-0-

Chapter 4

19. Rand, Ayn: "Introduction to Epistemology" Published by, A Mentor Book, The New American Library, New York, 1979: P. 6, ('that' + 'what')

Chapter 5

20. Lowie, Robert H.: "Primitive Society" Published by, Liveright Publishing Corp., New York 1947: See chapter, 'Property.'

Chapter 6

21. Rand, Ayn, Author: "The Virture of Selfishness," A Signet Book, Published by, The New American Library," New York, 1964: P. 94, (emphasis mine).
22. McKeon, Richard, editor; "Introduction to Aristotle" Published by, The University Chicago, Press, Chicago, Ill., 1973: P. 460.

Chapter 7

-0-

Chapter 8

23. IBIB., P. 445, 446.
24. Wilson, Epiphanius, A.M.: "The Wisdom of Confucius" Published by, Wings Books, Avenel, New Jersey, 1995: Pges., ix and 3.
25. Rodell, Fred, (1907—): "55 MEN" 'The Story of the Constitution,' Based on the day-to-day notes of James Madison; Pub. by, Stackpole Books, Harrisburg, PA, 1986: P., 60, 189 and 199, (paraphrased).
26. Kurtz, Paul—editor for: "Free Inquiry" Interview with, Jack Kevorkian, Fall Issue, 1991: Vol. 11,—No. 4, P. 16.
27. IBID, P. 17.

ss

28. Rand, Ayn: "The Virtue of Selfishness" Published by, A Signet Book from The New American Library, New York, 1964: P. 94.
29. Barret, William: "Irrational Man" Published by, Doubleday Anchor Books for Doubleday & Company, Inc., New York, 1962: Pges., 94, 95.

BOOK V

VALUES

JSS

CONTENTS

FOR

VALUES

Illustrations:
Chapter 2. Fig. 1. A Person & Nation's Hierarchy of Morals & Values
Chapter 4. Fig. 2. The Scale of Good & Bad
Fig. 3. Good & Bad Intangible Values

Chapter:
1. Values and the Moral Factor 303
2. Our Hierarchy of Values 307
3. Tangible and Intangible Values 310
4. The Nature of Good and Bad 313
5. Character Values 320
6. The Character of Giving 324
7. Values of Tradition, Culture & Custom 327
8. The Reality 331
9. The Meaning of Life 337
10. SUCCESS 343
Sufficient Success:
Suggestions for Success:
The Foundation—Success:
11. Human Happiness 351
The Birth of Personal Intimate Human Happiness:
Learning to Love or Perish:
Family Relations:
Friendship:
Personal Intimate Human Happiness:
Animal Sex:

11. Human Happiness (CONTINUED)
Things that Help in Orienting Heterosexuality:
The Moral Factor:
Our Human Responsibilities:
12. Long Life 370
What to Live For:
Is That All There Is?
A Contemporary View:
Bibliography 384

CHAPTER 1

Values and the Moral Factor

Values are things people seek that are of relative worth, merit, or importance. It is an estimate of any abstract durable quality that is desirable as a means or end within itself, such as education, success, good character, health, happiness, our lives or the earth. A thing of value may be wealth, possessions, cleanliness, stylish dress, or a place to live. All values are things we must *earn*.

The nature of values is either good or bad which requires personal judgment when they become necessary in our hierarchy of values. How do we know they are good or bad for us? What is the nature of good and evil? What are the character of giving, volunteering, and helping others? What are values of tradition, culture and customs? What is the parent's role in teaching values? What were primitive values?

What do we mean by life? What is success? What is happiness? How may we live long and what is the greatest danger to our personal intimate human happiness? What is the meaning of life? It is within values where we find meaning in our lives, the Moral Code defends our lives and choices, in whatever we value. When you finish this book on values you will never be in doubt again about what is *moral* and what are *values*.

We established in Book IV, "Morals," that our only obligation to others is to honor, The Moral Code, as an absolute necessity (it cannot be otherwise), if we value our lives. The Code promises us no freedom from want, no guarantee of success, provides nothing of value, only mental effort. It provides us an opportunity to mentally and physically gain values, become someone of worth, and we may earn the ultimate in rewards on earth, in our pursuit of happiness. When we defend, The Moral Code, it will guarantee us relative safety and autonomy as we seek to gain *our* values.

One's life, in all eternity, is but a moment in time. Of the trillions and trillions of years in the eternity that came before us, and into the trillions and trillions of years we will finally pass into, means we have but a moment, an infinitesimal sum-in-time, of perhaps, less than 100 years of life. The fact that we exist, overcoming all odds makes it the most valuable cosmic possession we will ever own. If we trust another with our lives we are in fact, giving up our most valuable right to life for someone else. But not to make the most of our experience in reality is to waste a fortune, our lives.

The Moral Code is, naturally, the control in our cosmic life. If we decide that no one shall rule or infringe on our lives, and claim autonomy, we gain, at that moment, all the personal values we can name here. We have become individuals, with authority to pursue our own unique hierarchy of values.

The values people discover by taking command of their lives and begin to reach goals, get educated, create options, set objectives, pursue a career and gain self esteem soon find they can think, reason, make choices, and be successful. Given the responsibility, people find they are capable. Surely, there are anxious times in everyone's life. At least, we do not worry about saber-toothed-tigers or having to outrun a cheetah. But, we too have danger, a different kind than our primitive ancestors, they managed theirs and with confidence, we can manage ours. If we can't, we are human failures.

Some people may say they have it worse now than the primitive and we could beg to differ. However, it *may seem* tougher, in some respects. The primitive had only three careers to choose from to get food, to hunt, scavenge, or gather, and they worked part time in all three in order to make ends meet. We have a great variety of career values to choose from. It's in the hundreds. Well, some say, *that's* a tough problem, because there are so many choices to make, deciding what job they like, getting an education, or the changing economy. Know thyself—it is your life, for others it is a lazy excuse for not thinking or taking advantage of opportunities. If we want to be autonomous, be a unique individual, and be free, we have to assume responsibility for the ultimate value, our own life. *If we do not claim autonomy for our selves it will be at the mercy of other peoples predilections.* It is giving or throwing away our most valuable cosmic possession.

A person who is pursuing goals, seeking values, is successful and happy, whilst not interfering in the lives of others, is leading a moral life. All physical and mental actions in the pursuit of values are acts of value. Morals require only mental reasoning. The pursuit of values is both, mental reasoning and physical action. There is no *moral necessity or natural obligation to physically act to provide value for others.* Giving is an issue of values, whereby one may recognize a reciprocal value in others.

Values are the result of will. "I will" in our Moral Code establishes what ought to be the first obligation in the mind of every human. It is not a guarantee of a successful life, but only that one is free of infringement from others in the pursuit of one's values. It is a person's honorable promise to mankind, in order to necessitate reciprocal agreements in morals and values that is basic to human survival, to claim autonomy, and strive not to become a burden on others, is a moral obligation.

In moral behavior, only mental action is required, but, to gain any value, mental and physical action is necessary. Nathaniel

Brandon; '*Value* and *action* imply and necessitate each other: It is in the nature of value that action is required to achieve and/or maintain it; it is in the nature of a consciously initiated action that its motive and purpose is the achievement and/or maintenance of a value.' [1] It is reason and will that motivates action to gain values, whether they are tangible or intangible.

The difficulty with this radical change, from theological, political 'liberal,' 'progressive,' socialistic 'ethics,' is that man has been socially engineered (conditioned) to *do* something for others (people, rulers or a god) to be moral, but inherent justice makes this philosophically in reality immoral. *In principle the 'ethical effect is the more we provide tangible values for others the less likely they will seek values for them selves, or in character they may become dependent and we are encouraging irresponsibility.* The result of this theocratic socialistic communistic socialization has been to undermine the second principle of the Moral Code, destroying the foundation of human nature, autonomy, responsibility, individualism, and independence whereby we become less human. In principle, when we use *force* or by law provide values for others it is immoral.

Eliminating the altruistic principle will encourage and build, those valued character traits we all want desperately in people that will build their self-esteem. *The principle to make autonomy real, is the less values we provide for others, the more likely they will seek to gain values for them selves, in character they become independent and responsible for their own needs.* The effect, morally, is that it will build more personal character, the intangible values of ambition, pride, perseverance, confidence, ability, and a measure of intellect. Had the pharaoh never existed there would have been no necessity to create the principle of altruism to guarantee that the poor distribute what was left of food after the pharaoh's seizure of peoples wealth.

A moral decision is one where no physical action is required, only the mental act of deciding—not to take physical action. A value decision is when one mentally decides to take some physical action (an act of value) for him self and others, or to infringe on someone's rights. An immoral act is not a moral act, and therefore, becomes an act of value that is wrong, bad and immoral.

The issue of morals is *"I will not"* infringe on people's right to survive physically, mentally, and materially (his property). A moral mental act cannot be a physical act of value. It is a contradiction, they do not mean the same thing nor are they synonymous, and since morality in an extreme is *right* and objective, values by their nature can never be right, but in their extreme may be by some subjective standard *good*. It follows then, that there is no such thing as a 'moral value,' because it is impossible. *Nor does the sciences of morals and values supercede each other as to any priority, but are dependent as equal in necessity for our species to survive and evolve.*

CHAPTER 2

Our Hierarchy of Values

In any hierarchy of values, human nature and the understanding of reality will motivate priorities. Human nature specifically dictates the need for safety, food and freedom to pursue such values, to find happiness and live a long healthy life. The tragedy of our species is that no distinction between morals and values was ever proposed that morally recognized human nature or reality. They were lost in 'ideas' of the imagination—the unreal, nor did they address basic human needs for survival or human happiness. What they proposed was sacrifice, asceticism, humility and to have faith, not to think, reason or question. In faith, one need only to give up all values in anticipation for an ethereal survival beyond the grave, of which they have no evidence, and a hierarchy of hope an end.

'Ethics' in "The Encyclopedia of Philosophy," Max Scheler

argued for a hierarchy open to our intuition, (???). 'In the hierarchy of values phenomenonologically given to man, we have at the top'

'Religious values' (faith, sacrifice and hope),'cultural values' (customs and traditions),' aesthetics' (Pure abstractions), 'Speculative' ('Ideas' of emotion and intuition), 'Scientific' (for scientific sake,), 'Political' (collectivism or redistribution), and finally material values, (useful things that satisfy needs, desires, etc.). [2].

This general hierarchy would be the state dictating the culture of a nation and totalitarian.

Each person creates their own hierarchy of values changing as they evolve. A hierarchy for nations and its people must be for the protection of everyone's autonomy to seek knowledge about the real world or live by whatever they fancy. Culture, traditions and customs will never be static, and are the responsibilities of the people who change in each generation.

There is also great danger in being speculative concerning human survival. 'Speculative,' is reserved for individual risk taking. Leaders should not take social risks on our behalf such as Dewey's experiment with children, or the family, or redistribution experiments in taxation, in our economy, health, or any value that is considered immoral in the Moral Code. State speculation in the socioeconomic fabric of society is a long-term risk and always regressive, since culturally, changes evolve within each individual.

Science is in the domain of human success, not speculation by government to discover knowledge for its own sake. For the state it creates a power base for politicians (like the space program) and is a tremendous drain on the economy and job creation. There is very little benefit to man's survival except for those who make enormous wages in useless research programs. The space program is being designed by government to establish 'legal' control of earth orbits, the moon and space flight. It is science for science's sake, with no survival benefits for the citizens who pay for them. It is for the same reasons and results when the pharaohs built pyramids, statues, temples, and cities.

Governments, theocracies and secular, throughout history created their own ruling hierarchy of values to increase and perpetuate power over our minds and wealth. We have never been free from the politics of confiscation. Please note that it is evident by above list that human needs and/or material values lie at the very bottom of the 'ethical' hierarchy. IT IS UNJUST THAT OUR NEEDS TO SURVIVE COME LAST!

A personal hierarchy must first include the primary necessary moral principles, then, people's values for personal survival and to seek human happiness. Specifically:

Fig. 1.
A PERSON & NATION'S HIERARCHY OF MORALS & VALUES

The Moral Code	(Necessary Principles of Behavior)
Governance	(Governments, to protect man's autonomy, safety.)
Values:	(An autonomous hierarchy, our own)
Success	(Our personal survival)
Human Happiness	(Our pursuit)
Long life	(Our Physical and mental well being)

First, within our hierarchy, our primary obligation is to follow the Moral Code, without which, our hierarchy of values is not possible (Fig. 1.). Our second or next value issue is our safety, how we should be governed as an autonomous independent individual in our lifetime or that of our children and our children's children, ad infinitum. A governing ideal, is a proper system of government that is an inclusive moral force, to promote freedom for people to pursue human socioeconomic values for success and happiness safely. *The people's hierarchy is national neutrality, a codification of The Moral Code that includes all ideologies, if such a government is to be 'for the people.'*

We know everything in the universe is of value, of some relative worth, real, and identifiable, varying in the minds of each of us. There is no standard of value in our hierarchy, except one standard in principle, our Moral Code and a moral government. To be moral is to live by necessary principles of non-infringement a *standard* of human behavior, without which a "good" life of values is not possible. To follow the Code implies one's life *is* a person's prime concern and

ss

it is evident in order to live one must seek the means to survive. Beyond our moral necessities, the choices, or hierarchies of 'what' he values for 'himself' or with 'whom,' if consensual, are not issues for others to provide or judge

CHAPTER 3

Tangible and Intangible Values

There are two types of values, *tangible* and *intangible.* The first is something real that is experienced by the senses. The second is an abstraction or concept, a mental image or idea (theory). Tangible values are real things, like the universe and everything identifiable or proven to exist within it. There are galaxies, solar systems, and planets. Our planet earth and all organic and inorganic entities we can identify and have *proved* to exist (like germs) are tangibles. Known phenomena, such as gravity, electricity, radio or sound waves, heat and cold, molecules, atoms, neutrons, and electrons, are tangibles. More personal, are the things we earn or own, buy or sell to exist, such as food, clothing, shelter, and those things we find comfort, pleasure, and convenience, in order to justify the effort existence demands on our nature. It is tangible, if it is possible to identify an entity by explanation and anyone's sense experience.

Intangible values, are those things that cannot be sensed, unreal or identified, as tangible. They are abstractions, like integrity, self-esteem, intelligence, dependability, virtue, independence, honesty, or loving, courageous, and others. Any hypothesis, speculation, principle, conjecture, or theories are abstractions, all intangible until proven real or tangible by reason of one's senses, its roots based in reality. A contract or a promise is an intangible, until fulfilled; only then will it prove or we will sense it to be a tangible value. What we imagine we would like to be, or what it would be like to own a thing, are also abstractions or intangibles.

To want to own a tangible value (a real thing) is, in the mind, an abstraction or theoretical, since it is not really possessed. How one will procure it, in order to own it, is likewise an abstraction. The whole abstraction is made real by acquiring ability, for what imagines is needed to live the good life. Therefore one's entire life or the idea of what we would like to become, is at first theoretical. As we go through life we earn (learn) to gain ability and use the skills to earn the components that will contribute to the life we choreographed for ourselves. We must *earn* real things, by tangible means, in order to make abstract intangibles real.

The nature of intangibles is that they exist in someone's mind and may have initiated actions to prove such an abstraction is true or exists. Character intangible values, such as honesty, ambition, dependability, etc. are not unlike those for gaining tangible values, except they are never real things but are made evident by real behavior which we identify as right or good—wrong or bad behaviors. A thief is not a thief until proven, nor is a craftsman one until something of value is built. A man is considered honest if he returns a wallet with hundreds of dollars to its owner. The person who is working every day earns character values by being reliable or dependable.

We can become ambitious, mentally, if we desire to achieve or gain some goal or end. But, it is not evident that we are ambitious until we are mentally and physically acting in achieving such ends.

If we want to gain dependability we can only gain it by being dependable (not just thinking or saying we are), so that others may judge that one is dependable by action, i.e. identifiable by empirical tangible actions.

Dependability or ambition are theoretical or abstractions. What we may perceive as dependability or ambition must be identified by such actions that are continually evident over a period of time or *consistently*.

Integrity is an intangible value considered of the greatest worth. To have integrity is to adhere to moral principles while seeking the best values for one's own good, and, in so doing honors mankind. A wholeness attribute such as integrity may be honored when one achieves tangible goals honestly and with perseverance *consistently*.

Intangible values are acquired, not unlike a theory to be proved, by the facts of one's real actions that can be identified over and over until there is no doubt about their being real—empirical evidence of action and accomplishment that is evident or identifiable.

Individualism was thought to be a concept or an abstraction, a theory. It has been socially perceived that all humans were not different from one another. All the people in the world consciously or inadvertently have experienced differences in every human being they have interacted with. We have scientifically proven humans are physically (fingerprints, immune system rejection of organs, physical features, genetic, DNA, etc.) individual in Books II and intellectually unique in Book III. Individuality, one might say, is not so—people like to live in groups that—may be true, but only because we like the variability of human nature and which is inherent in all that exists. Individualism is no longer a concept but a fact of reality and no longer a theory. By experience it becomes, early in life, as real and substantive when referred to in identifying another person or our selves. Our individualism is a tangible value. Not unlike The Moral Code, one's nature and personal understanding of reality will necessitate our *individual* hierarchy of intangible and tangible values.

To gain an intangible value, one must earn a real or tangible value, only then will the intangible value become evident, identifiable, and real.

CHAPTER 4

The Nature of Good and Bad

Good and bad are related to the goodness and badness of the motives and ends of actions. The goodness and badness of all actions or goals are, *imprecise* or *variable by their nature in values.* Where the nature of right and wrong are precise and invariable in moral principles. The spectrum of good or bad is incrementally infinite, as is our individuality, and therefore, may have the appearance of being subjective. It may be truly subjective however, but requires a high degree of objectivity when determining our personal needs as we each search for our own 'good' in values. Good and bad may be applied to personal issues-what people value for them selves, which are not moral necessities. It is a question of choosing good or bad values—what one prefers may be good for him—but bad for another and vice versa. Being conscious of The Moral Code, to achieve one's goals is not done at the expense of others. We make *right* choices morally and make *good* choices in values. This is virtue or leading a good life and in terms of human worth to others—"a good person."

A person who acts and disregards or is contrary to a principle of the Moral Code will in fact, if successful, reduces value in some one's life. An immoral decision becomes a value issue, it cannot be an 'immoral moral' issue. It is an immoral value decision, wrong, or bad, is the act's motivation. Any act of value, *in its physical implementation as in the nature of values that cannot precisely achieve what was envisioned will make it a variable, imprecise act of value.* Once a crime is executed physically it becomes a negative act of value, or bad. An act of value may also be immoral by violating moral principles, or wrong. Therefore, an immoral act of value is bad, wrong and immoral

If in the course of working with another, one steals his money—one is acting physically—an act of value—stealing something of value. It was a *wrong* and *immoral* act of value, and *bad* for the victim. The crook did not make that silent moral decision, "I will not steal." *An immoral act of value is bad wrong, and immoral, but a bad act is not immoral if one chooses a bad value for himself, without infringing on the lives of others.* He is a victim of his own action(s).

Good and bad values, philosophically, have been referred to or known as the 'pleasure—pain principle', where incrementally an increase in pleasure is desirable, being good, or a plus, and an increase in pain, undesirable, negative and bad or minus. We may scale any value, tangible, intangible, any human attribute or material end judged on a base line of positive above or negative below, represented as follows:

Fig. 2.
THE SCALE OF GOOD & BAD VALUES

```
 Pleasure          Good
                             Good
 Positive (+) Value                       Good
-Joe -------Base Line                                      Good          +
-Jane--------------------------------------------------------------------
-Jack-------Base Line       Bad                                          -
 Negative (-) Value                 Bad
                                            Bad
 Pain                                               Bad
```

Fig. 2. is used to illustrate that if we owned a car when it was new, it would be at its highest 'Good' and continue to lose value during its lifetime (base line) of wear and tear. It will no longer be good, if it was no longer reliable. Once it attains a negative value it is considered a bad automobile.

We may have a 'good' career in terms of personal experiences or in times when it was in great demand down to when we 'burned out' or the career skill was no longer needed in the economy.

A person who is dependable currently is very dependable but progressively may become less and less dependable with time, until one can't count on him/her at all. At this point their value has dropped below to the negative area.

Now that would be all well and fine until we throw in the variable factors. The progressive downward trend makes sense as long as we can determine where the base line for positive and negative begins. To be realistic, there is no real base line because it varies. The base line varies mainly for these reasons, of people, time, place, culture, and scientific progress.

What we do is name the base line, say, person (Joe, Jack, Jane etc.). For most people the base line for dependability would differ, some being impatient, deciding the person is not dependable after one or two disappointments. Another may be patient allowing more infractions before considering that the person was bad. The same thing can be said for the car that would be bad for the computer operator, but that would change in the hands of an auto mechanic.

Time—by designating the base line 1850, a buggy whip maker would be considered a good career—but not good anymore by 1950, except for the Amish.

Place—a refrigerator may be of little use to an Eskimo in Alaska, but a fat burning heater good.

Culture—people living on South Sea Islands don't live in cities with skyscrapers, because of limited values. A car would be a bad investment, a boat on the other hand—a good one.

Scientific progress is obvious—obsolescence—of no value. New useful discoveries are of great value, or the new, if of no use, a bad investment of resources in research, etc..

However, as we've seen above, the greatest arbitrator of what's good or bad is people. Depending on their intellect, creativity, circumstance and preference, whether they are intangible, human (personal) or material, what it ultimately comes down to are objective personal judgments concerning what is good for them. Also, judgment in intangible values may appear to be arbitrary, because it is difficult to be objective. We'll list a few below.

SS

Fig. 3.
GOOD & BAD INTANGIBLE VALUES

Intangible Values Above the Positive Good	Intangible Values Below the Negative Bad
Intellect	Ignorant
Ambition	Lazy
Perseverance	Inconsistency
Confidence	Terror
Independent	Dependent
Virtue	Evil
Successful	Failure

Fig. 3.: The positive intangible values are good attitudes for one to strive for, but whether others can correctly judge character attributes in a person may be doubtful due to human emotional involvement. Approaching the good or the bad is blurred, and a gray area of judgment, people refer to in values.

If we chart character attributes from plus—minus, or, good—bad, base line, every person may make a different judgment according to their sense or estimate of value. Influencing people would be emotional involvement, time, place, culture, and or the technical state of a society.

How a person feels about human values or those people who are close to us may also be judged as plus or minus—good or bad. Intimate human values: mother, father, sister, brother, grandmother, grandfather, relatives, friends, lover, mate, husband, wife, children, and neighbors are all valued on the scale, like others mentioned above.

When identifying character values of family members, such as caring, kind, etc. may make judgments about our kin that may differ considerably. Because a mother is called a 'mother' does not automatically lift that person to the highest level of goodness. There are, however, in most, much appreciation for the pain caused her in birthing and the loving attention they received in early childhood. It could also be said that many do not give enough credit to mothers for their unconditional love when making their rating. It is the emotional factor that may cloud objective judgments.

Some may rate too high because of blood ties. Reason in these instances should consider everything in their context, times, places, situations and weighted to measure the impact on ones own values. As human beings, we will find the greatest happiness within our own values and that is human nature, including our view of reality that will determine our hierarchy of values. The people who may have a similar hierarchy as our own, we will approve of, and gravitate towards them to become friends, traders or lovers.

A non-value or negative values are judged to be of no value or bad to some degree. There are two types, those we gain through no intended acts of our own and those we acquire by errors in judgment.

The first, are accidents, being accused wrongly, and acts of nature; Earthquakes, disease, premature death, devaluation of career due to changes in skill requirements because of time, place, culture or scientific progress, and immoral acts committed by someone against us.

The second; are those acquired by our own deliberate acts, immoral acts, errors in judgment, lack of education, reason or character, that may cause us to lose careers, fortunes, friends, lovers and even our lives.

We lose, in every sense, positive values, when we violate the principles of the Moral Code. Whatever one gains in wrongful values is usually only temporary and if caught becomes a non-value if it causes reciprocal action. If it becomes a jail term it is as bad as it can get, except for the death penalty. The jail term is without any personal value of freedom or pursuit, only sustenance, and a minimum of human needs. Likewise, one's social relationships are without value since prisoners usually may have no respect for moral principles and a trade of any kind of worthwhile value is virtually non-existent.

There are values being traded for value in the economic spheres of human interaction. However, if one has nothing, then no transaction can take place. There has always been a certain minority of people who will *not* want to expend effort to serve, produce or grow something of value. The scam for this non-productive person is to get someone to trade his or her something for his 'nothing.' There is the con game, fraud or implied service or goods that are not in a contract, advertisement, or in the context of what they say.

Values, in human terms, implies our own self worth, a code of self imposed hierarchy of values, or an obligation to claim autonomy, individuality and responsibility. The effort we make in meeting those obligations depends on how much we value ourselves. The more we value our life, the greater our effort, the more obligations, and the more specific our goals. To sacrifice our values for others means we have no values left, the result is we are broke socially and economically.

Values of a material or tangible nature include food, furniture, shelter, cars, trucks, boats, VCR's, TV's, RV's, Vans, and others, including body decorations. Since the beginning primitives sought material things. In the canopy, there was territory to defend food to gather and the harem. Our ancestors, on the ground, needed far more material things, such as tools, to help gather, hunt and scavenge for food.

Time, place, culture, invention and personal choice would determine what was valued. Primitives observed their natural world very carefully and knew its limits as well as its beauty. It would be vulgar or snobbish of us if we thought the sunsets, the colors of the flowers, breath taking views, a colorful smooth stone or pretty shell at the waters edge went unnoticed. They might pick them up hold them—show them—then keep them as treasure—a marvel of nature—just the way we feel. Plants, clay, seeds and bark gave them colorful paint for their body, hair and tools. Body decorations were to carry the clay color of a sunset, the memory of a lovely beach and waters, the beauty of the earth, the colors of trees plants and flowers—they loved where they were, their lives, and they wrapped their natural world around themselves. Primitives appreciated the wonders of nature's variety—nothing was identical. Color, the beauty and the oddity or singularity of natural things, peaked primitive curiosity creating a multitude of values.

Sometime in this period of human evolution, that special stone, shell, or eagle feather being different from all others became identified with its owner. It was his or her special stone and could be recognized if stolen, lost or loaned. Thus, if something could be identified with its owner, who discovered the item, it belonged to him. This was no different, in concept, than he who earned scavenging rights for discovering the carcass, or in the hunt, the one who killed the beast and the one who spotted the animal. A colored stone or shell that was owned by the person who discovered it and was considered a fair claim. Those who could be identified or associated with anything found or made, established ownership, implying, something of value.

What one made or created out of the nature's materials became identified with its owner. So were mixtures or recipes of dyes or paints for their bodies. The way they made a tool or necklace. The way one wrapped a spear or arrow was not copied, infringed on nor was a song or special dance and costume. Copyright rules of non-infringement, moral abstractions, have their roots all the way back in time among primitive value systems.

Primitives shared their material wealth with those they valued and there were loans to others, however there is no evidence that they had to share indiscriminately with anyone who voiced a need. There is more real evidence of their pride and fairness where they wouldn't think asking for something they did not earn or belonged to them. If this is true, then envy was not the rule to condemn the ambitious, but was motivation to work. It was sort of, 'Do their own thing' or, 'Do it their way,' or *earn his way*, and they made progress by competition, and human values, creating the human race. It is because they silently said, "I will not . . ."—there was no other way to survive.

In most primitive societies they did not share as in communism and when they did it was never complete materially. A great amount of individualism always existed especially in tribal societies. If a primitive knew the person, who was a good scavenger and hunter, but down on his luck, he would feel bound to help a kindred spirit. Thoughtfully, the recipient felt bound to repay or reciprocate the act with one of his. The ownership of the food one ate was never in question. It was fair (just) trade that a value would be repaid with an equal value, it was still his food or tool and should be returned in the same manner and condition it was loaned. 'The one who makes the loan under the circumstances does not feel justified in asking a return of the article and waits for it to be given back voluntarily.' [3] He may feel that he should not have to ask for its return, i.e. the recipient should know better. This is value's fair principle, to reciprocate in kind, implied in nature in a primitive's time, behaving naturally, and it was *good* then and still is today.

CHAPTER 5

Character Values

We are all characters! But to say someone has character means only that they are an individual, possessing attributes, some physical, how and what the person thinks—a unique personality. It is philosophically, our essence, personality or what makes us individuals. When we say the person has character, we are saying they have an individualistic nature that displays a temperament or disposition, which includes being kind, mean, evil, responsible, courageous, generous, thoughtful, sensitive, or eccentric. Those and many others are attributes of a person's character, but the quality of each individual varies infinitely. Character is the result of self-determination, for all the values we seek, there is within our nature an indeterminism, a natural need for challenge, a sense of freedom, spontaneity, or a variable individual independent will, to change and shape our existence. It creates a quantum effect within our epistemological nature. Watch the children in public trying to shake themselves loose from their mother's grip.

How do we gain those character values that are spoken of so eloquently by our 'leaders?' If tangible values or goals make intangible values possible—how so? One might ask; what comes first the chicken or the egg? Does the tangible have to come first? If the intangible is the cause, doesn't it have to be present first? Is it latent? How so? Is one born with intangible values of perseverance, inventiveness, endurance, or courage? Or is it *all a learning process* for the child with good character, taught by moral parents with good examples of human values?

There has been much discussion in the media about values by self-serving politicians, trying to get elected, by touting a standard or hierarchy of values that everyone should possess and that he will provide. In essence, leaders should encourage good character, but cannot enforce it by law. If things of value are *provided* for people then will they ever gain such character values of independence, ambition, creativity, or be responsible for their own lives? The state and federal governments cannot be 'parenting adults' providing their values through legislation, with the expectation voters will retain or gain such values as autonomy, ambition, individualism, responsibility, or any character value. Character, is created by parents who teach their children morals and values because a person will need food and some other things *very much* to survive and find happiness. His character is his safety net.

Primitive succeeded under much more trying times than we can imagine. To earn values of character requires the implementation of mental and physical effort on the behalf of the recipient for some tangible value. If they have not earned anything of tangible value, they have not earned the essential values that build human character.

To interfere in the process of evolution has always been the ambition of religion and governments, to make us docile like cattle, or regiment us like ants. It is the tangible or intangible human values rulers can never standardize. If they did, it would only serve to reverse what took evolution and an evolving human character, five million years to create. To try to change human characteristic behavior is to make us less human and it will destroy human nature.

All of nature is in a process of evolution, but it is slow and does not change much in millions of years. Even with our intelligence to help affect evolutionary change to our being was unusual will, drive and perseverance. The character of human nature will not change in a million years.

We have general human values:
We will still be evolving within an evolutionary process:
We will still inherit our parent's genes.
We will still be seeking an autonomous existence.
We will still go through a childhood of learning.
We will still love sex at any age.
We will still reach puberty sooner rather than later.
We will still have to seek a means to work for survival.
We will still fall in love.
We will still seek a mate for love, sex, and human happiness.
We will still have families, and may have children and grandchildren.
We will all die, but may want to live as long as possible.

There may be more, the problem of value here is how can we teach our children character values so they can make the most of their evolutionary nature in their lifetime.

Man does not invent these values in life, they are value stages in living our lives that in the overall scheme of life on earth we will experience most of them in some way. What we do, is invent new ways to live through these human values. General human values are consistent, but they may vary in quality and priority within our hierarchy. Therefore, we have no way to invent such human values. As we evolve, new human values may become evident, but in a process of evolution, not by theocratic or socialistic engineering.

How we add quality to values depends on being taught, or learning (self-taught). In this process, our character develops first, as a *moral* necessity and gives rise to qualities of moral courage to say "I will not," taking responsibility for our selves, to be autonomous, stand for justice, have respect and empathy for others, be honest, and will keep his word. It is taught, learned, and by examples parents demonstrate when such issues concern The Moral Code and our values.

To experience freedom, we become individuals, autonomous, able to self govern with resolve, be responsible, have ambition, use discretion, and with drive or a will of our own. To achieve these important values, we must be self-motivated, self disciplined, and in our choices we create a reasoned hierarchy of values. Such values are what form the character of those who love freedom.

To be free, is to set goals, gain values, with the will to reason, intellectually use logic, to have courage in ventures with great risk of savings, true grit, creativity, talent or specialized ability, tenderness, sensitivity, understanding, and good judgment, are all the characteristics of a *thinking* person of values? They are not latent, innate, or inborn, because everything in a brain is learned. These are the abstract intangible values that form human personal character.

A child should be taught to look forward with expectations to earned values. It means we do not provide every need and want a child expresses or anticipates. We do not teach a child they deserve everything by the fact they were born and cute. Otherwise, it may be imprinted upon them to believe they have a right to life, liberty and happiness without effort. Yet the child today may manage to fail, after cheating through school, living off mom and dad, working in dead end jobs, or perhaps killing time in college and graduate schools, in majors not related to the real socioeconomic world. If we can teach them how to fail, we can teach the child, with love, how to succeed.

The spoiled children will be the ones who complain of meaningless work, capitalist pigs, that the government should solve their social, economic and health problems. Their expectations will be that others should provide economic stability, raise their offspring, teach them 'ethics' and are raised to believe that those are their 'rights.' Character begins in childhood and is the parent's responsibility not societies'.

A child will not appreciate the value of a dollar unless he has to work for it. We've heard that many times and it is still true. They may learn later, if not trained while young. Untrained, it is a struggle, but if he is born with parents of moral character, they will teach the child how to survive, while growing up. Childhood is the time for teaching, to delay the process to when he is older, and forced into the world, is cruel and unusual punishment, and immoral. Young, the child is at an impressionable age, and he is all fired up, curious and questioning—teach—answer him—he loves you and is ready to absorb your every word. The development of character begins at home as early as possible. Parents should be cognizant every step of the way, of the child's character they see evolving, and to intervene by teaching with love, understanding, encouragement and training to correct bad character traits.

CHAPTER 6

The Character of Giving

One has to be selfish before one can be generous. To be a success one has to have a personal motivation to want to gain food clothing and shelter for his existence. A person has to be selfish to want the best education, work 'hard and smart' to advance in one's career. He is in search of values for himself, to gain those intangible values of studiousness, ambition, perseverance, courage, endurance, to take risks, and an attitude if one doesn't succeed, to 'try, try, and try again'. But one's hierarchy of values is not procured automatically, it is by reasoned analysis or why and how one *ought* to achieve those goals. It is *good* to want the best for one's self and it may be *good* to give or volunteer, but these are not moral issues.

The questions to ask; 'What are the goals we promised or obligated ourselves to gain?' Are we selfish enough to succeed and gain that noble intangible value to be generous? Once we gain wealth, then is it imperative to examine and re-examine for the right reason, to whom, what, when, why and how we may give to others?

> About twenty three hundred and thirty five years ago Aristotle wrote:' . . . for he will give to the right people, the right amounts and at the right time, with all the other qualifications that accompany right giving;' and further on he said. 'And he will refrain from giving to anybody and everybody, that he may have something to give to the right people, at the right time, where it is noble to do so.'
>
> (Nicomachean Ethics) [4]

Circumspect giving or generosity must be distinguished from altruism. Giving or being generous in practice is usually reserved for those people or causes we personally value. But altruism means the principle or practice of unselfish concern for or devotion to the welfare of others (opposed to egoism). Egoism, is self-centered or selfishness (opposed to altruism). The issue is whether people consider another person's life more valuable than their own, and if they choose altruism, to sacrifice their lives for others even if it means everything they earn, its their value choice. Not to give, giving and altruism are values, *not* moral issues. If altruism became a moral issue we would be *morally bound by law*, to be royalists or socialists and give up *all* of our personal and property rights for others.

To refer to the variable scale in Chapter 4. on 'The Nature of Good and Bad', giving to those we value is good, if it does not subtract (go below the negative line). Indiscriminate generosity will endanger our own well being and the well being of our loved ones. Therefore, as a value issue (if we value our life and loved ones), generosity, may be a good characteristic, but only for those causes we understand or whom we value and know personally, tempered with prudence.

Being overly or indiscriminately generous may cause us to give to the undeserved thus encouraging poor intangible character values of those who are recipients of our generosity. On the good-bad scale, it becomes bad for both giver and receivers. Therefore, the less given may be best or the greater good for the giver, to preserve earned values for future prudent generosity. Also, the less given to the receiver may be better for their greater good, by our prudent generosity which will be as such, to encourage needy attributes in the receiver to encourage a self sustaining character. It follows, as a value, *giving can be bad or good* subjectively, and can not be a moral principle.

Altruism, i.e. self-sacrifice, in values, destroys a person's hierarchy placing his life in a non-value or negative position on the scale of good and bad. It is indiscriminate, lacking reason or evaluation of the impact on the recipient, impeding his need to gain tangible and intangible values to build good character. To teach children or adults that a god expects sacrifice, the unselfish concern for others in order to be *moral*, is immoral.

To love one another is, in a sense, making value judgments in one's life, a contemplation of character or collateral value based on experience. We will seek those, whose values are similar to our own in any social and economic trading. If someone insists we should love *everyone*, it is an impossibility to make value judgments for all people. It is proposed that we love everyone unconditionally and there is no need for judging or to have character values. In such an altruistic state of affairs there are no value issues and we may suspend all moral and value judgments to sacrifice the self to anyone without any concern for ourselves, even theirs. We can respect all people, but we may love those we know and value highly personally.

In practice, altruism means we are not to reason or judge on the basis of good character or those with poor or no character attributes, in morals or values. We must not identify the person's character or their intent or make any comparison to our selves. Then anyone is considered unconditionally without any distinction between good and bad, and right or wrong is just not fair, it is unjust. Altruism, practiced faithfully to its logical conclusion destroys morals and values in the giver and the receiver, leaving us without an identity, or the means to survive. However, the philanthropy of people to help or give to others while maintaining their own wealth or lives is opposed to altruism, since self preservation and self interest prevails for the self first.

We are told that we should *love* everyone unconditionally, and is of great value in creating good character. Love in fact, becomes very cheap, worthless and of no value. If the failure to achieve good character values is of no consequence in judging a person's character or being worthy of love, then there is no need or incentive to acquire personal values. That 'idea' of 'to love one another' indiscriminately *given*, may not create motivation in others to gain values. To love everyone is a theocratic socialistic collective totalitarian concept, created by pharaohs. It is a behavioral altruistic ideal, where one's reason and judgment is sacrificed to the whole or collective, for the destruction of individualism and infer human values are evil. It is a means of brainwashing, to persuade people to give up on themselves, their identity, their minds and wealth, to live, work and die without thinking or to use judgment, is planned ignorance. It is has become an immoral principle of governing by the ruling elite in every country on earth today.

We should not give up on ourselves nor on others, and we do that by not wasting what we value, by volunteering or giving prudently to the right people, for the right reason, the right amounts, at the right time. It is with responsibility to reason what the effect or results of our good or bad giving will cause. But we certainly can give indiscriminately if we wish at times, to those we have won and love.

CHAPTER 7

Values of Tradition, Culture & Custom

Tradition is the handing down of statements, beliefs, legends, practices or long established ways of thinking or habits passed on from generation to generation. In tradition, we find all the myths and legends of a society creating practices, ceremonies and rituals. The legends, myths and folklore are repeated over and over from birth to death and from one generation to another. Traditions become our culture, conventional, and may be formalized into beliefs or having faith that the myths are true. In society they may even be accepted as fact by many and its commandments are social norms and faithfully followed. It becomes cultural in practice, and such customs may come under social pressure by a majority to become law, and are usually unjust.

The young are taught to conform, believe and practice the traditional customs of their culture. To vary from culture is thought to be a rejection of ones roots or ethnic origins. But these are only values, some useful, some false, and some value the rejection of anything new or better a society is exposed to. Motivation to conform in a culture gives us a sense of belonging, comfort, and safety, with no need to reason or act differently, inventively or search to discover something new. Not all is such, but much is of that nature.

Changes in traditions, culture, and customs, i.e. our behavior, depends in all their complexities, on technology, or the economy and locality. We see traditions change in our own society, with no similarity to each other today, or any relation to the past, with the exception of moral principles we have defined in Book IV, Morals.

In all societies we see changes due to new technology or in economic activity. Thus our value system is in a constant change and may be rejected by our offspring for many reasons. The more advanced societies that are melting pots of traditions, cultures, and customs blend into something new, better and courageous. We are like the primitive who left the dwindling or overcrowded hunting ground and went over the mountain and into another valley. It was a new experience where they created a new culture, which was based, somewhat on environment, and new economic values.

Every tradition people learn from their parents will soon give way to their own idea of what they want. We cannot, with any accuracy, predict what our children will become or accept as their roots. Like the primitive and our western folk not long ago, will forgo custom and tradition to strike out to the city, another country or one hundred miles away in an exciting search for their own values, culture, and traditions. For parents there is the wonder of what their children will finally create as their culture, i.e. 'what have we wrought?' Our evolving computer generation today is empirical evidence of this truth.

Children see the world in a different perspective than their parents just as parents have lived in a different world. So each generation finds the world changing, in environment and knowledge. Old knowledge becomes obsolete and of no practical use. The only true wisdom we pass on to children is the Moral Code and our family love by teaching them how to survive in new society. Their genetic inheritance will mean nothing if they cannot find happiness, to create their own traditions, cultures, and the customs that may change. But the principles and codified laws based on The Moral Code will remain unchangeable.

There is a theocratic or socialistic plan, for governing as Dewey envisioned, where the state molds the child to be a servant of a god or government. This century re-embraced that concept, which never understood the plan. It was to create a collective society, an abstraction not cognizant of evolution, nature or of being human. Russia in this century tried to arrest evolution, tradition and culture but failed. America wishes to speed up evolution like the pharaohs building great cities to show progress, but we may also fail.

In order for we humans to expect respect, love, honor, friendship, cooperation, or any tangible or intangible value must be earned by action, to such a degree that others may see a reflection or perception of their own values. It means we are not a classless society, but implies an infinite differentiation of classes, i.e. values. Karl Marx and Frederick Engels, called for revolutionary action to achieve classless socialism. Theologians also, want to create a self-sacrificing world, devoid of materialistic values, a *culture* with no value placed on the individual, his ego, or self worth. The secular social planners, borrowing their 'ethics' from theocracies, wishes to place all value in the hands of the state, or where the right of the individual is deferred to majority will. It is this mental state that creates the idea individual human life is of no value. All such cultures, traditions, and customs in such societies glaringly demonstrate the absence of values, which achieves a classless and valueless world for themselves. We should never let that happen because it is inhuman, immoral, and of no value. What we want for our children is morals and values with our idea of class or values. Each clan or family is a culture or class within itself.

Values created the humanoid species. We spent five million years, without governing institutions, evolving to seek our own hierarchy of values. High in the rain forest, there was no need to search for food, for there was abundance. Nature, however, is in a state of evolution and soon changes, forcing all living things to seek new values, in different ways, or perish as victims of their environment. The primitive with the use of his mind and free, succeeded in overcoming the animal traditions and customs of environmental dependency.

Man, in his primitive wisdom, learned how to think and reason, in order to create new values to survive, and exercised, to a great degree, control over his environment. His basic human morals and values of birth, puberty, loving, mating, teaching, safety, autonomy, and his responsibility towards the obligations that the primitive initiated, never changed.

In our wisdom, what we must give a child, are the necessary principles of the Moral Code, and our values. The most important value is our love for them, which is our emotional motivation to teach them the technology of our time, not unlike our forbears out on the savanna. Also, we practice with them, our traditions, culture, and customs, exposing them to our individuality, which may earn for us a measure of immortality in the child we leave behind. Within their lifetime they shall evolve, discarding that which is irrelevant and retaining ours that is good for their progress in gaining success and human values. They will create for themselves a new culture that will serve them and their children, to make a new traditional beginning. This is the philosophy of the changing values in our traditions, cultures, and customs.

CHAPTER 8

The Reality

The reality of primitive success was that he met all of his self-imposed obligations, and the pursuit of goals was not much different in principle as our own, even in his period of evolving new values. We will take another look back on the primitive, to perhaps gain some insight into their values, and maybe better understand our own.

When I began writing this book, the current theory was that a great drought lasting 12 million years had occurred devastating forests, a habitat for primates. Scientists have now discovered, in 1994, that in the African rift valleys, there seems to be no evidence of a 12 million year drought occurring, and that vegetation or forests existed along with the savannas, much as it is today. OOPS! The idea that mammals were forced out on to the savanna by a drought and the subsequent lack of food may not be true. I will not change what was written earlier in Book I, because of having to go back and rewrite it but that also it illustrates the reality of changes that occur in theories, as new facts are uncovered in all the sciences. However, the only way to get our ancestors to walk upright was to get them out of the trees. Then in theory, it is very plausible that with the fact that 'life flourishes amid plenty' and in the trees food was plentiful for monkeys, whereby they *multiplied.* They had no birth control because they didn't know what caused it. A scarcity of food could occur during the period of an increase in population. The outcome would be the same, many would be forced out down onto the savanna, and out of all the species that were grounded, only the genetic line Homo survived, by the aquatic escape route theory which still maintains its validity.

The theory will continue to change or be reinforced by new facts. But what is certain, we did survive and sound evidence proves from a chimp-like species. We learned to walk upright, leaving our hands free whereby we developed improved dexterously efficient fingers, thumb, and hand. Also we lost most of our hair in the water, learned to make tools, and much later we would hunt large animals. Such change was the root of man's evolving values. Variability created new perceptions that motivated reason, to set new goals for success.

Paleoanthropology is the science or study of the origins of our anscestors, and one thing they seem to agree on is, 'A moment's reflection will show that variability is a necessity for all life.' They cite two reasons, 'There is always a certain amount of selection pressure within a species for self improvement' and 'no environment is static.' . . . 'Primitives illustrate, very well, these two competing forces in evolution; the tendency toward change and the tendency toward stability.' [5] And this fact of variability is another proof of the individual nature within all species.

The tendency to be more intelligent or stronger to overcome the variability in nature is our problem of survival. The tendency towards stability is found in fossils identified as Australopithicus Robustus and Boise who evolved with Homo Habilis and then became extinct. Its heavy square jaw and oversized grinding teeth were that of a vegetarian, unlike that of smaller teeth and rounded jaw of a carnivore, such as Africanus (Lucy). Robustus fits the model for stability, chewing on foliage, leading a sedentary existence, yet it soon became extinct. There is no guarantee that such stability, dependent on environmental factors alone, will cause a species to evolve or not. Yet humans made that breach in nature to take control of his survival in any environment.

Intelligence in our case had evolved to overcome any environment and any weakness in our genetic makeup. Scientists say we still carry a number of non-adaptive traits in our genes, i.e. useless physically. We were forced to change faster than our genetic code could react. We may be genetically a little unstable, but with a brain far more evolved and efficient than animals. We can achieve stability, but only by *thinking* to make those intangible values of learning, education, ambition, skill, courage, reason, perseverance, creativity, and dependability real. They imply reason, purpose, and will power.

If stability is unchangeable then gaining character values of learning, and using our heads is our only refuge for stability.

In the beginning, high in the canopy of the rain forest, food was not a chimp's prime objective. A dominant male ruled a harem of females, his primary goal was sex. With his great build and large incisors, his *work* was to dominate the females, to keep them in line and defended them against all males. This left him free to mount any female, in estrus, mounting her from the rear, impersonally staring off into space, unconcerned for her, enjoying his sexual pleasure over and over. She succumbed to him and any others she could sneak away with. But, forced onto the savanna, these values would change. They would discover new ones and their variability would be infinite. But, what really happened was the 'Free Lunch' and 'Free Sex' was gone forever, the 'party' was over for the new evolving hominoid.

The will to live was primary. The male, forced down on the savanna in strange and dangerous territory, was running for his life and so was she. If they were scavenging for food in an area, they left at the first sign of predators. To hell with the carcass—RUN! Even if she was in heat they ran. Their lives were their first important value, food a very close second. So it is with all creatures large and small.

Safety became of great importance and the search since food which was not readily available became the first order of business, to forage in the bush, scavenge any carcass on the savanna, and hunt for little edible creatures. His great desire for sensual pleasure was not at all diminished. However, now he had to earn his food and sex. She traded herself and her help for his food and protection. Being smaller than the predators, he was unable to physically protect her, but he could feed her or help her hide and feed the child. She would not let go of the child, and he perhaps sensed he could not separate them, and could not eat the child, abandon the brat or throw him to the lions. Even in times of scarcity or the most dangerous of encounters—she would die defending her child. If he wanted sex the child was without question in the bargain—sound familiar! He was learning family values, millions of years before they knew how children were conceived.

As we learned earlier from Elaine Morgan's "The Descent of Women," they found safety in the water, rivers, lakes, and oceans, learned to stand erect, lost most of their hair, and she safely discovered a new source of food—fish. Perhaps life by the water's edge became bearable, then even pleasant as they were standing more and more, face-to-face in the water, communicating, and trading value for value, fish for meat, or food for sex, they were partners in survival.

We do not know how they thought, how they communicated, but we may reason that, from an animal existence in a jungle of plenty that required little effort to eat and unlimited sex, to one of scarcity, it would illicit changes in how these two new priorities would be met. From an almost irresponsible lifestyle to one that required the utmost in care in safety, feeding oneself and sexual happiness, a new set of values emerged for the primitive. They were making personal judgments of each other, their needs eventually, and beside their great sexual motivation, was their judgment of each other and their partnership. She knew his need for sexual favors, and her help in his hunt for food, but her judgment of him as a partner was a new value. It would be measured in his joyous value of her, by his willing to feed her and her child with respect, kindness, and generosity—human values.

Our little primate ancestor's values were changing, creating the means by which we would live on earth. Having only the skill to feed a mate, the only one he could afford with a couple of children, a huge capacity for sex, and to keep it all together, he learned to be generous, kind and perhaps thoughtful of her needs and her children's. In this way, she would be receptive to him and as she gave into him, he became grateful, tender, gentle and learned affection. She in turn would reject cruelty, roughness, and any physical harm since she could easily leave him anytime he was out scavenging, and find another mate. He would be left alone with no one to greet him and no one to share his desires. He would never see her again. This single source of sexual pleasure became his ultimate value. But only now it was a family, a new value he would call his own, as would they all, to be together as one clan against the world, a culture within themselves.

It all added up to a new value, a bonding together of love that was creating a couple's own culture.

The primitive would assure herself of a mate who would 'do good for her,' (the Yanomamo's expression for love) and she would no doubt learn similar values. Also, as he scavenged, foraged, and hunted, she would help him plan, scout, advise, be his lookout, assist in the strategy of a small kill, and help scavenge an abandoned carcass. When not tied down with tending a child, she foraged and helped contribute to the food gathering, not unlike the family of today who work together.

Children were nursed, loved, and taught to do what their parents did. They learned how to forage, scavenge, and hunt as well as to be cautious and run fast as hell. When the child became nine or ten years old, he was self sufficient, could outrun his mother or father and by the time he was twelve or thirteen, he was capable of mating and taking care of a mate. About the age of fourteen the primitive had a mate and a child and one or both of his parents were dead. In childhood, they learned the complexities of nature, animals, birds, fish, and the particular territories they roamed in. The closer to their parents the better they learned. One cannot imagine such a relationship without their newfound value—love. In the beginning, they were together almost, every hour of the day, for their entire life. Parting or a death had to be an incomprehensible heart-wrenching tragedy.

As this new family took hold they too would have learned the values of their parents. The child learned how to survive, to scavenge, with his father, forage likely with her mother and hunt down small animals in a cooperate effort with their parents. Children learned about sex watching their father and mother together in loving embrace. The child likely sexually experimented with a brother, sister or cousin, and took one as a mate—nature's reward. They accepted the challenges, by reasoning, cooperating, discovering, and learning about new territories. They respected one another, were self reliant, confident, objective, responsible, sentimental perhaps and much more. As they settled down each night among the trees at a river's edge, in the bush at the rim of the savanna, or at the ocean shore in a cave of a cliff, they huddled close together. They were relatively safe, confident, pleased, holding each other, being affectionate, a little teasing and tenderness, then may have succumbed to their ultimate human desires. We can believe something like remembering earlier, about those footprints, in the lava bed at Laotoli, made 3.8 *million* years ago.

To forage, scavenge, and hunt was a primitive's 'work,' and if they brought back meat to a camp or ate out on the savanna living as such, day to day, week to week, month to month, with some reflection, they may have felt they were a success. We have no idea as to whether such a concept of 'success' was evident but when they came back to camp with the hind end of a zebra, there were smiles, compliments, and a measure of self esteem in their hearts. All they knew was that they were happy, felt good and secure in the knowledge that they could feed themselves. They could show tangible results of their ability to provide for their survival, and that is success.

If we try to list all the attributes or intangible values they possessed at that time, the list is long, including courage, stamina, persistence, and a host of others, and sometimes they were scared as hell. The clan or family would feel a sense of independence and confidence that they could survive and were successful. When they arrived in an area where they found that the foraging, scavenging, and hunting was good, it was not looked upon with a sense of burden or 'work.' It was with excitement, an *opportunity* to feed them selves. The Yanomamo tribes have no word for 'work'! The essence or impact of their philosophy of values is a *revelation.* It reveals that our greatest cosmic possession, life, is not a question of burdensome 'work' to preserve it, but an 'opportunity' to enjoy existing and earning it. We still have a choice, to live or not to live. If life is too much trouble, we don't have to complain or suffer, just die. If we love life only a little, then we just have to *earn* a little joy.

Some may say, that it is proposed here that we go back to live like a primitive. If they mean back to the jungle to forage, scavenge, and hunt, we all know that is not possible. We must, however, embrace with all of our mental acumen to capture those primitive intangible values that created their greatest tangible success, *us*, and behave as such towards our own *opportunity* to live.

CHAPTER 9

The Meaning of Life

The promise earlier was that I would answer, the ancient question, "What is the meaning of Life?" There have been clues in every book in this volume.

Values are what give meaning to life. However, there can be little meaning in a world where the socioeconomic lives of the citizen are being confiscated by our fellow man coveting our minds and wealth. They commit every crime The Moral Code forbids, with religious wars (not *ethnic*) that are ripping apart any moral fabric that has survived the twentieth century.

Values are what give personal meaning to life on earth, providing one does not infringe on the lives of others. Therefore this discourse on 'the meaning of life' implies a moral society. The reason no one has been able to explain the meaning of life, is because since the beginning of organized societies, the theocratic or secular state has implied the meaning of life is far greater or deeper in purpose than we mortals can ever fathom. They also lead man to believe a state's meaning or purpose was beyond comprehension and any infringement on man or property was a duty that man must trust as just. They taught that in order to gain any meaning we must suffer and sacrifice our selves to a god or state and we will find meaning in some undefined heaven or future. So rulers have made sure we would suffer persuading us to look forward to finding the meaning of life, in death.

'What is the meaning of Life?' is a question asked of man. Many of us may also ask, 'What is the intent or aim (goal) of my life?' 'What must *I* accomplish?' 'What does life demand of me?' or 'Why am I here?'

We were born in a vast universe and we are living reasoning beings with the will to live. If it is our will to live, the Moral Code will protect our life and we are free to value those things that make us happy. That is the natural process of cosmic existence, to be born as a "star", spinning through life, giving birth to "celestial bodies" shining brightly to bring warmth, happiness, and, finally, dying in a super nova's blinding flash. What is left is cosmic dust to join somewhere, in a great black hole, in time, into an unknown form, the entire process proceeding unimpeded to recreation. But that is not an answer, it's too abstract and not *personally* meaningful, yet perhaps true.

Some believe that the only meaning in life is to devote one's life to a god and its heaven. Its because our death is but a transition to a heaven where we will exist eternally. Pascal's was willing to concede in his wager that he would gamble on the possibility for eternal life. If one goes to gamble in a casino or the tract *somebody may win.* We witness some winners meaning a lot to many, in casinos, but we can not find or know of any winners in a god's heaven that will give meaning to life or death. In the true sense for the gambler it is not a gamble because no one ever saw one win. Pascal lost his money every time and he deserved to lose, because he could *not* see and reason that the game is permanently fixed to lose. So its not a gamble but a fraud.

"Why am I here?" There are only two ultimate reasons, to live and to inevitably die. We do not know of anything before we came on earth and will know nothing about where we are going when we die. What will give meaning to our life then, *depends on learning how to live on earth—now—happily, during this infinitesimal lifetime we have in eternity.* We have been given a *natural opportunity* to exist for a moment in time—it is not a test, it is a fact of existence that we all experience life with our senses and death is its opposite.

We have let our imagination and ego run wild to think we are not part of nature's life and death process, but that human beings are a higher form of consciousness that may transcend a final black hole. But our counterparts of a future universe will be given the same conscious opportunity to be born evolve and learn of the wonders of cosmic existence and sex too–and death.

Paul Radin's book: "Primitive Religion," his imagination runs wild too, but *he did rightly identify primitive values*: he wrote, 'His mentality was still overwhelmingly dominated by definitely animal characteristics although the life-values themselves–the desire for success, for happiness, and for long life—were naturally already present.' [6] .("for success, for happiness, and for long life")

Radin did not know he had found the basis for goals and motivation for all life, even the animals, insects, birds, and those that live in the sea, all seek such meaning in life. For humans it lacks one qualification for happiness. *Success, happiness, and long life,* in the context of this book, are in their broadest meaning.

Success, the choices for success are endless, infinite in quantity and quality with man's creativity that increases his options in each generation, is what gives meaning or the purpose and means to *survive* for all people. Success means one's own measure of survival.

Happiness and happy are also variable in value, a problem in defining the 'good' or the 'ultimate good.' Some say happiness is found in 'success,' an exciting career, promotion, or being famous, gives us self-esteem making us happy. 'Living long' or good health in well being, makes us happy. But, what about 'happiness' it is a separate value in and of itself? It is the key to values on earth.

Of happiness, Aristotle wrote; 'Happiness then is the best, noblest and most pleasant thing in the world and these attributes are not severed as in the inscription at Delos-

Most noble is that which is justest, and best is health;

But pleasantest is it to win what we love.'

Aristotle understood happiness to be an activity of the mind, the essence of man, a mental state, ' . . . and of states of mind we call those which merit praise virtues.' '.In many actions we use friends and riches or political power as instruments; and there are some things the lack of which takes the lustre from happiness . . . ; for the man who is very ugly . . . ill-born or solitary .. had thoroughly bad children or friends; or had lost good children or friends by death.' [7] Aristotle's 'happiness' implies *human* relationships.

Therefore, 'success' is being *happy* with material survival and 'long life' as being *happy* for a lengthy time on earth, but then, 'happiness' cannot be for just material gain, time or longevity. Ultimate 'Happiness' then can only be for sharing both success and long life with another *human being–'winning "who" we love,'* and this is the highest good or the pleasantest value that exists! So we qualify happiness and call it "*human* happiness." And like success, it is *our individual* measure of *human happiness.*

Long life, the older we grow the more valuable our life becomes. Had one known the value of this gem we would not have abused what we now find frail and vulnerable. The physicians advise, the younger we begin to take care of ourselves the older we will become.

Therefore, the meaning of life is simply, *success, human happiness and long life.* In 'ethics' there are few references to 'a goodly' wife as a lover, good sex, love or devotion to a human being, as virtuous or 'ultimate happiness.' Some philosophers and all theologians take an unreal illogical 'high moral ground,' avoiding intellectual reference to, and/or denouncing any personal intimacy as happiness. 'The joys of the flesh' being obscene and not happiness, is found in many references. The human nuclear family is in many respects personal and intimate intellectually, yet each is bound to the autonomous nature of The Moral Code. In this book, the *ultimate* in human happiness includes intellectual friendships, being in love with one's mate, parenting and to experience "the joys of the flesh" with her/him, are all factors that encompass *personal human happiness.* And with one's mate, being helplessly in love is *personal intimate human happiness.* On love, love is when you are happiest because you are with the person you love. Therefore, no one can make another person happy except by being them self. If you don't understand that you will never find human happiness.

To answer all of the questions above, we begin with, 'What is the meaning of life?' we may establish that it is personal, or 'What is the meaning of *my* life?' *Life* is a very broad term but in this context it means, my life, leaving the only term left to define, *meaning*. To define meaning is to ask, 'what is the purpose, aim, end, or the consequence of my life?' The purpose is to define an *identity*, individuality or specific hierarchy of values for success, and to seek as a need for some natural reward. our measure of *human happiness*. How much value do we place on for ourselves will depend upon how much effort we are willing to exert mentally and physically, is what will give meaning for those ends or values of *success, human happiness and long life*.

There are questions that beg for a separate answer, such as 'What must I accomplish?' or 'What does existence demand of me?', is in order. It may mean "Should I do something to save mankind or the world?' 'What deeds must I accomplish?' 'Should I volunteer, be a martyr, sacrifice for some cause?' Or, 'Must I do something for my fellow man, community or country?' If one's work or career propels him/ her into such areas where there are opportunities to do some good, or right a wrong for mankind, it is the good or right thing to do. But beware of volunteering to serve for some 'good' or giving to support to questionable causes or that which may be fraudulently immoral. We may do anything, if we have the means and *good reason* in our values for doing so. But our first duty is to our own values for survival or success and a moral duty to those we may obligate our selves and love intimately. Others come last. There is an old saying, "There is only family—then there is everyone else." That is justified because you are being morally selfish.

The last question is, 'Why am I here?' Some say it is because mom or dad had a gleam in their eye. For much of the world that is true, there are also reasons of error, the lack of freedom to abort morally, others have no freedom or availability to contraceptives, and many are ignorant, negligent, or inexperienced in the sex act. We would like to believe most are here because two people loved each other dearly. One could be on earth for any reason. But we are a phenomenon of existence in a natural universe with a right to exist

ss

within nature's universe as any other natural entity. The only thing we know about the reason we are here, is the proof we were created naturally in reality, and any other reason is purely imagination, speculation, or just may be unnatural. Therefore, we are only aware of this self-evident fact of reality, that we are obviously a natural occurrence. To be unnatural in a natural existence is to be a dysfunctional human being. Our reason for living is to learn to exist naturally, seeking success, human happiness, and to live as long as possible. Everyone with a functioning brain has the same opportunity and we owe others nothing, except to honor The Moral Code.

The child that is born in a loving home, fed and clothed well, and has all the things children love to play and learn with is happy. Life each day is filled with surprises and more of the good things, great food and the love of his parents. Life every day has great meaning, for he is surviving in happiness and a glorious life that has no apparent end. He has never asked, 'What in the hell am I doing here?' but 'Hey! I'm happy is there more?' Then he finds he must grow up, everything that has meaning is changing he must exert mental and physical effort, i.e. earn all those things he took for granted. Whether from a poor or wealthy home his hierarchy of values has new meaning in his life when he has to earn them. It is a parent's moral duty to prepare the child for life.

A meaningful life means that a person's goals are values that mean something (in pride, in victory, or survival) to him personally in his judgment of self-satisfaction and/or happiness. Life means that it can only have meaning for a person who strives for success to achieve his hierarchy of values and there can be no conflict of interest with society, because he is not infringing on the freedom of others.

What we earn, depends upon how meaningful we want life to be. Life has no other meaning, since life is what we make it. We are each responsible for a meaningful career, place to work, or a niche in our socioeconomic society. We are each responsible for meaningful promotion, advancements, recognition, or a profit in our businesses. We are each responsible for meaningful personal friendships and economic relationships. We are each responsible for our personal intimate human relationship with another person, equally, to be meaningful. It all means that *we* are responsible for a meaningful success, meaningful human happiness, and a meaningful long life.

The meaning of life is to seek our values, the tangible and the intangible, within the three general values mentioned where the variability is endless, in quantity and quality. The intent is to live, if we choose, but there is no need feel guilty to accomplish great deeds, do only those things that will make us happy. Our only purpose in life is to take care of our selves, honoring our self-imposed obligations to our loved ones, and only then we may give *prudently* to other people and things we may value. The ultimate contribution we may volunteer to all of mankind is to respect people by following The Moral Code. No one in the world should expect any more from us than that, and if they do, they are *immoral* with evil intent. Every physically normal person has the potential and the same opportunity to learn adding meaning to their lives, and find happiness.

Our individual hierarchy of values in *success, human happiness and long life, is the meaning of life.* We all strive for them in our own way, in every era that man has or will ever exist. To achieve them has meaning for every person *alive* on earth. The only certainty is that success, human happiness and long life ends some day.

CHAPTER 10

SUCCESS

Success may be defined as a favorable or prosperous termination of attempts or endeavors—in other words, the desired result was achieved. For you it is, *your desired results*, meaning *your measure of success.* In primitive terms, one's success was defined as providing enough food to keep him self alive. Today we also wish to survive, but we also want to profit for our 'mental well being', to relax and relieve the stress of responsibilities. But we do not think of our mental well being, only that we remain focused on our goal, studying and working for our dreams.

To succeed we are trying to survive, make enough money, bring home the bacon, pay the rent, buy a small TV, get by, to exist, and so we can relax for a few hours and rest. The next day—up and at it again. There is the constant repetition of day after day, paycheck after paycheck, the work goes on and the activities become routine, habitual, predictable, accompanied by a feeling of security that things are normal and not changing. The result, without realizing it, there is a sense of mental well being. Like our ancestors, we feel good about bringing home that hind end of a zebra safely.

Then one day the company is in trouble and we're home, without a job, we are very insecure, unsure, or uneasy about future prospects. In despair, with feelings of inadequacy, or blame it on everything but ourselves, and are left with two choices. Continue blaming, or we should move on, get up go out and try to salvage something of our well being. Our mental well being is, knowing we can survive, if we think.

Our little primate ancestor was challenged when the food ran out in his area, he got up moved on into new territory that was unfamiliar, and with trepidation, they took root anew. That is the first step in success, a moral principle, to claim autonomy, individuality and responsibility for ones own physical and mental well being, then take the second step, reasoned action towards some goal. The primitive was a self-motivating, self-actuating, physiological organism that had to eat to live, and his primary objective was to forage, scavenge or hunt for food. That was primary, people who now live in colder climates need shelter and clothing as well. If a person can earn enough to feed, clothe and provide shelter for himself, they will be the essentials needed for success to survive in the minds of most. If he is a moral person, and can care for himself, he will not be a burden on others, which is his or her ultimate contribution to mankind.

The essentials above, however, may not be sufficient for most people who choose to set different standards for success. Food is the most important and one is forced to give it priority but we may have as many ideas about what is success as there are people on earth. *We each will measure our own success depending on the values we obligate our selves to achieve.* If the child says he would like to be a fireman or a doctor, we may say one is possible, the other probable. But both are possible by setting goals, good learning attitudes and perseverance, and either success is achievable because we are all *equally* endowed epistemologically if we have a physically healthy brain. Yet one job will pay more than the other, have more responsibility, etc., whichever is chosen as a goal, it is the individual who will judge his measure of success.

Success depends on our rational will. To be successful in one's life depends upon our reasoning process. First, it means a rational prioritized hierarchy of values that become our goals. It will be a choice of what we want to work at, the best education for the money available, and such goals as to where we want to live, and what kind of social life one looks forward to. It is a rational assessment of ourselves, thoroughly examined needs, desires, and an imaginative or abstract view of what we would like our future to be. Then we go for it. It is up to us to perceive and identify the ends and the means to make that distant abstraction a reality. No one else can do that for us.

A necessity in human relationships simplified generally is the Golden Rule, by Confucius such as "What you do not want done to yourself do not do to others." or also, "Treat me the way you like to be treated." The implication of 'treat' is, 'with respect' as one human to another. The short or colloquial saying is "One hand washes the other" suggests reciprocity. If some one we value needs help to succeed we may assist, but with the expectation, it would be reciprocated.

Reciprocity is a necessity in defending the Moral Code but in 'Values' it is always a choice. Whether or not one reciprocates in kind to the kindness, trade or close relationships with others is a good or bad issue in one's hierarchy of values. In trading values it may appear that what one paid for the item was not worth price. Therefore, reciprocity, although required in trade to be good for both, may vary in the outcome. But, reciprocity must be to their mutual satisfaction in free trade to be moral, and rational to be successful for both.

Sufficient Success: The minimum requirements of food, clothing, and shelter, is not sufficient success for most people. We may want to be a good plumber, appliance technician, reporter, nurse, doctor, writer, artist, or find a good job in communication or industry. Whatever work is desired, as a goal, one wishes to create a measure of *profit* from that endeavor. We don't want just an existence or subsistence but some comforts, an better apartment or home of one's own, a car, a van, or nice clothes, TV, all the furniture and comforts of living 'good.' We want vacations, eat out, go out to the theater and live the good life. *We all want profit.* In its broadest terms this may be the 'success' we all strive to earn, and it is what the good 'life' means *to us*, or is 'the good.' And a company that makes a profit after the necessary expenses, means job security, and is a 'good' company. If it can not make a profit it can not create jobs.

Beyond all those things above we may want, fame, to be a rock star or sportsman, inventor, to head a large company or to be a great leader. Whatever we want to be, is *our* dream, (or the 'American Dream' which means we need some kind of profit for our effort!), even if we would love to follow in our parent's footsteps. What ever we choose should be, foremost, is our own idea of success, and what we *like* to do. Someone once said success is a journey not a goal, it is both if the work is fun and what we gain we think is good for us.

Many people have to compromise along the way, or one's career may take surprising turns (being at the right or wrong place at the time), but in each case, one takes the opportunities and/or change in the spirit of always doing one's best. Many people do not reach their standard for success and may still be happy and live comfortably. Others may think 'if only'—'It's the system' 'could have tried harder,' 'taken a chance,' 'been ruthless,' 'another job,' or changed with the times. These are unimportant. Success is working at what you want to do and no one really cares to reach the goal in his lifetime, in something he enjoys and finds a challenge in his career, because we never want such a life to end. The goal is also the journey. The Yanomamo's 'heaven' was doing what he loved to do on earth, hunting, growing, and living with his family. An effort is not work if its something a person enjoys doing, and living a life with a loving family is being a success and earning happiness.

What is the most important thing in the world? As a physiological organism without food, we could not exist. FOOD, is the single most important thing to sustain our existence. Without food we wouldn't be functional live human beings and that is why success (to earn food) is foremost in motivational values because the goal to procure food is primary to existence. It's what motivated our primate relatives and we have seemed to forget is that food primarily induces an organism's will to survive.

Within most successful societies, good business practices have created an agricultural and distribution system for food that has increased the quantity and availability almost anywhere in the world. This highly honed technology works so well we hardly notice its existence. The huge food store is there and all we need to do is go buy it. There is no need for primitive endurance and patience to find it, nor the need to face the tremendous struggle to scavenge or kill for it. So great is the economy food created it may be but a fraction of what we might earn. The importance of eating is lost in our endeavor of how to spend all the money after expenses of home, clothing, cable, and oh yeah!—food. For many, the *variable* expense is the food budget, usually settling for cheap, junk, or non-nutritional food such as grains and sugared up carbohydrates, just to fill up. And they spend their profit on foolish things, ending up with poor health (a short life) and little to show for their efforts.

The downside of this 'plenty of food' is, being a relatively smaller portion of our effort and/or earnings, it's assigned a lesser value. Ask anyone what is the most important thing in the world? If you say 'food'—they are appalled—'no! Not really!' And they are not convinced easily, just as you may not be—at this time. Give it time, by the end of the next chapter on "Government," you should be convinced. To continue, the downside is we value food less in our hierarchy of values. It's positioned lower than at the beginning or near the end of the savanna caper when food was critical. Now, food is hardly a consideration, in advanced societies, yet, seventy to eighty percent of the world population goes to sleep hungry with nothing else to think about, except for tomorrow—'what will I eat?'

The upside of our plenty and efficiency in producing food is that we may now contemplate pleasant work, do those things we like, or have a propensity for. Since food takes little of our earnings, we need not work as long, and use the extra time to pursue things that make us happy. To some, the pursuit becomes one of increasing their fortunes, creating, inventing new businesses, for others its the arts, painting, music, antiques, acting, fame, fortune, rest and recreation. And these things make us happy—very happy—we may even call it to some degree, 'happiness.' That is as it should be.

Suggestions for Success: To be a success in anything one wants to do, the following are a few suggestions and not inclusive but may be helpful. There are countless 'Success!' self-help books on the market and they are helpful but will not guarantee success. Many successful people know that you have to *want* to reach some goal very much, and if you are not actually *working* to *remain focused* towards your goal, then you do not have the will to reach your goal, and may not deserve success in that endeavor.

Never expect help because most will have to be accomplished by your own effort. But, you can find help, only if its information, people love to see ambition, and are willing to talk about what they know. All you need to do is *ask* them—like a lady or a gentleman—respectfully. Find a mentor who is knowledgeable in your field, and make a friend for life. Most important is to remain *focused* in your daily work, and always on your career goals while listening to others. To focus and continue to learn is the hallmark of most success.

Always have two career alternatives, a fall back position, or two options perhaps related to what you like to do. The primitive had four, scavenging, hunting, fishing, and foraging—he was never out of work or opportunities.

Do the *best job* you can even if you hate it, it is practicing, and only quit when you have another job, but leave with a 'good taste in your mouth.' Don't *ever* 'burn your bridges' behind you.

In every situation be as proper as you know how—being a gentleman or lady—confidant always. Being cool under fire, will be noted by the 'generals.'

Be loyal to your employer or company on and off the job. If you can't be, have the 'guts' to leave gracefully, so the next person can. Don't bite the hand that is feeding you, animals do that.

Read, "How to Win Friends and Influence People" by Dale Carnegie, it is invaluable no matter what your work or social life. It teaches you how to act and take charge or control of your life by not having to react to people and events, but to act correctly and humanely towards all people you like, and dislike.

Always try to do better or improve your work, skill, technique and quality. Someone once said, "*When you cease trying to improve, you cease to be good.*"

Expect to work *all* of your life, never to really retire, so choose that which may please you most especially in retirement.

No one will hold it against you though, if you play the lottery.

There are others you may have learned to be worthy.

The Foundation—Success: Of life's values, our personal success, is the foundation upon which the rest of our life and happiness is built. If we can feed, clothe, and provide shelter from heat and cold, and with a profit, called savings then we are a success. It is success that builds self-esteem. Who we are, (our identity), what we accomplish (in our career), and how we are judged by our peers, feeds our ego. We feel good about ourselves—we feel proud—we like living—we love life. It is the foundation for our happiness that has *meaning* for the rest of our lives. If you want to feel worthless there are many that will help separate you from your wealth.

The measure of success that we intend to achieve depends entirely upon our effort mentally and physically to gain values that will give meaning to our lives. There are people who give up on *effort* to be a success, may lie, steal or kill for their food because they lack purpose, career goals, moral intentions and self-esteem. They are headed for self-destruction at the hands of their peers. They will not gain those intangible values of ambition independence, honesty or integrity. They cannot be proud among their peers—but be denied the company of honest men, perhaps jailed, without values, and human happiness

The rich child may be at a disadvantage since he may be spoiled and may never understand the struggle for success and fail. The poor man's child may be at a disadvantage since they have little access to money for higher education. The poor child, however, may understand better the struggle and may be better prepared for or can recognize the signs of failure and with such insights avoid it and deal with setbacks successfully.

The rich man's child, however, may understand the opportunity wealth affords them. He may not understand struggle or failure but may overcome it through diligence, scholarship and failures along the way. Wealth could also give the young a false sense of security that may disappear with guidance by good parenting or learning on the rocky road to personal success.

It is difficult to say with certainty, which has the better advantage the rich or poor child for success. Each have disadvantages learning to cope with their lives. To have rich parents can help tremendously if they are wise in the child's upbringing. The poor child likewise, needs a loving parent who will teach morals, values, encourage education and struggle to help their child in his dreams which may level somewhat his chances for success.

At some point all children will be out in society. What they do with their lives as adults, becomes their responsibility and challenge. About seventy percent of all new millionaires have earned that distinction in this generation. If someone could take a poll, we may be surprised to learn how many came from poor or very modest means or how many came from rich parents.

Success for the young is their first real challenge. They may aspire to greatness, as a novelist, actor, sportsman, inventor, scientist, artist, architect, entrepreneur, or president of something. Their ambition, study and reasoning, hard work, long hours, and perseverance, evolve into characters of dependability, responsibility, honesty, and integrity. Their success is the only way they can make those intangible character values real. It is that reality that brings a sense of accomplishment, pride, and satisfaction to find they have ability that gives meaning to their success.

However, theology and sociology condemns all 'worldly' values today, the intangible values of the *self*—ambition, pride, etc., and tangible *materialistic* earnings, which can only be made real by character values of successful men and women. Success then is immoral in the 'ethics' of theocratic or socialistic states with their envious and faithful followers. Yet they will tax, to starve us with just enough to live and work another day, because we are so evil or selfish and do not deserve a profit, but to which they are 'ethically' or 'legally' entitled.

It is from a foundation of seeking goals, the love of our own life that we can appreciate or recognize someone that loves life as we do. Success is the first step that gives meaning to our life. However, a person's success will give him/her a measure of self-esteem, satisfaction, and bring them much *personal* happiness, which is what makes life individually meaningful. But, success alone can not give or buy them their ultimate reward, *human happiness.*

CHAPTER 11

Human Happiness

We are human primates with roots *millions* of years old. The transition from the wild into a humanoid species five million years ago was that of a highly evolved social and sexual primate. We elevated both through our evolution by becoming a naked being, without fur, highly sensual, and developed a lipid brain and neural system with the ability to remember and reason, which increased our social need for sharing our life with someone. Specifically, it is one who shares our values, understands our nature, and reflects the essence of our own efforts or character.

We know that needs desires, and the pursuit of human happiness is not without cost. Everything of value has a price in both mental and physical effort. Each person, in a relationship, must achieve his own measure of success in one's life work, before taking on the obligations in the pursuit of human happiness. It follows that such effort is commitment, or simply put, a promise to each other across the breakfast or dinner table, but better still face-to-face on pillows—heads and body upon the down and fluff in personal intimate human happiness. The rest of the world will know their commitment by public promise in wedding and through their loyalty to each other for the rest of their lives.

'Theodorus, held that happiness should be an enduring emotion of joy rather than momentary pleasures.' Then there is the 'idea' that all pleasure should be balanced by pain, which is a religious concept—to be punished for having pleasure.

What is human happiness? What is personal human happiness? What is personal intimate human happiness? In general we may call all values, human values or all happiness, human happiness. In this book 'human happiness' is familiarity with our species, from friends, relatives, children or a personal lover in sexual intimacy. Things can make can make us happy or pleased with ourselves but human happiness is the interaction with the people who we value. When we wish to express our personal preferences in human sexual intimate relationships they may become close in intimacy with our own. It is in this context that personal intimate human happiness finds its meaning in life for all people. It is taught to our children, by close family members as a mother and father, intimately guiding their children to help the child identify emotions. Teaching sex and tenderness is a parent's moral decision from a child's age two to puberty, and beyond to teach its responsibilities.

All people are to each of us, part of the greater family—the human species. Although there is no need to *love* all people we can respect that most share basic values of life, success, human happiness, and to live a long healthful life. Whatever they 'believe' in Buddhism, Hinduism, Catholicism, Protestantism, Islam Judaism or whether they are communists, socialists, fascists, or live in limited freedom, all colors may want the basic values we seek. How each of us may earn and keep them for as long as we live is the issue of value. Although not all people share the values we do individually, we respect that each has his or her personal cause, but there is also a free press and a need for discussion and critique for all lifestyles especially in religion and governance. It is the only means to bring reason into the light of day for any of life 's values.

We should love the idea that all people share a metaphysical and epistemological common bond. It is with that respect, in our pursuits, that we treat all individuals justly, then discrimination and crimes against humanity should die, and human happiness will be free to flourish.

The Birth of Personal Intimate Human Happiness: Sex occurred, before cultures, customs, traditions, and civilizations. Five million years ago, a primitive culture of small nomadic families had begun. They gave birth to evolving traditions and customs that would change with their technology. Once animal husbandry and agricultural sciences became practical and successful, a pseudo cultural traditional civilization came into being. This false culture came about when people accepted a purely theoretical 'idea' that supranatural beings controlled existence and had rules of behavior.

To go back in time, before any culture, before we were primitives but animals in the trees, our primate cousins only knew the physical thrill of mating, not the consequences of perpetuating the species. Food or success in feeding oneself occupied little time or effort. They lived in clans with the male dominating a harem. With little to do, they were drawn together, played, teased, and doted on one another. Males dominated, females and offspring groomed each other and they became, in a sense, family oriented. Whether due to drought or overpopulation, many were forced on to the savanna where they had to run for their lives and work to survive. Everyone was out for them selves. A male lost his harem, but, if he was kind and generous with food, a female might take time out of her hunt for his gift and allow him to sexually mount her.

However, no matter how he got his food, the female was doing the same and had no time to fool around. More effort on his part could slow her down with a gift of food—for sex. Rape might have been common, but she was fast, and could escape or put up such a ruckus he retreated, to look for a more agreeable female. She had other priorities, or more likely nursing or caring for a baby. Those that escaped to the water's edge had some measure of safety, a source of food or a place where camp was near animal watering holes. They had a home base, safety, and a food source.

In the trees the male had a harem with at least one in any given time, in estrus. Now on the ground he only had one female who was not likely to be in heat or receptive. With one he had to make do in grooming, play, and in his great need, groped, held and cuddled for some sensual contact, it was perhaps, the forerunner of our foreplay. With the loss of hair, their sense of touch was heightened making full body contact, face to face union extremely pleasurable. Facing each other, they could view, play and pleasure each other. Recognition of values, beauty and reasoning with each other became factors in what we now call sexual intercourse that implies communication, not just a sexual act.

Erogenous zones were discovered by play and after many thousands of generations, the vagina came forward just slightly to accommodate his entry. Her breasts became more as an udder perhaps for reasons of the larger quantities of milk that was required as the species became larger in height and weight. Breast evolution reasons are still theoretical. So did her offspring's brain gain size causing greater pain at birth. Our hands developed more nerve endings for our sense of feeling, used in tool making especially to feel her/him. Estrus was shortened and year round, receptivity was a reality. Humans became the most sensual beings on earth.

Learning to Love or Perish: *Sex is a learned action in every way* even for our primate cousins and all sentient beings, humans may metaphysically perceive each other as aesthetically sensual beings first and cognitively or epistemologically second. It is because an expanded memory increased learning skills, in perception—identity—classification,—units, the math, her measurements or his?.

Five million years ago, our humanoid lineage was established with no guarantee of survival. The chimpanzee, of all the primates, is closest to us possessing 99 percent of DNA identical to humans. It may have taken only one percent of the genetic code to create the human species. We may guess that one percent may include the genes of our brain, specifically the cerebellum, memory or perhaps reasoning. The rest of the genetic code, would from that time onward, be somewhat controlled by the brain. We would learn to memorize and reason new skills, social behaviors, and inadvertently force the body to adapt.

With our capacity for memory and reasoning ability, we became a truly self motivating, self activating, but a reasoning organism capable of comprehending our own existence. We evolved with the ability to adapt to any environment before it could affect any change on our genetic code. That code is contingent upon our specie's reason and or motivation. When we take into account our intellectual will, it is truly 'mind over matter.'

The genetic code is subject to control by human learning and action, it's not the other way around. The genetic code controls our physiological attributes which serve the needs we've deemed necessary to our survival for the last five million years. For the proponents of instinct, intuition, and innate knowledge, we *may* have had these *learned* attributes some millions of years *before* our genetic birth five million years ago. But our savanna caper demanded that we learn to survive and learn entirely new socioeconomic behaviors.

It was learn or perish. If we had any instincts when we dropped out of the trees, they would be useless on the ground. Our genetic code was obsolete and we had to learn everything. Our hands, legs, and body had to stretch its limits to meet demands in scavenging, escaping, hiding, and later hunting. But it was a slow process taking millions of years to change our genetics.

The primitive had to *relearn* sexual behavior. Increased memory capacity helped to store the many events in their lives together. They would learn new social behaviors as their memory and reasoning increased. Sex was the motivation but reasoning perfected a new approach to the opposite sex that created more stable, loyal, loving and extended families. That was the nature of primitive sexual intellect that eventually was able to master the world. Our technical and scientific ability was crucial to this process, but it could only succeed with the family as an equal consideration before advancing. That had to be the custom or tradition of our culture, love of ourselves and our family, or we would have perished.

Family Relations: They say, 'we can choose our friends but are stuck with our relatives.' If children are accepted by relatives, outside the family unit, with affection, respect, and just a little generosity, that will be the cement that ties children to their relatives. The child will reciprocate and the bond will be lasting. As the child grows older, respect and interest in what they like to do will keep them loyal to the relatives by their continuing communication, visitation, and interest. It is a two way street and the social trading of value for value received. It is the effort of maintaining friendships with people who may reflect your parent's values and therefore nearer to yours. The blood or genetic tie will be the frosting on the cake,—but 'The frosting alone does not a cake make.'

Our great memory capacity gave man an advantage over all other animals and with more to remember an increase in reasoning ability was enough to survive on the savanna. But without the drive to love and support one female and her offspring there would not be any necessity to survive. One could not exist without the other. *The nuclear family became a necessity and will always be necessary for human existence and progress.*

The footsteps in the ashes of Laetoli *may* be for the romantics, the irrefutable evidence of love and the nuclear family or clan that occupied the earth. The Stone Age technology was merely an expansion of the extended clan or family of aunts and uncles in cooperative efforts. Each newly invented stone tool in the hands of a skilled specialist helped to increase the production of meat in their scavenging efforts on the savanna. In such a society human love was to flourish.

Neanderthal may have increased production and could care for, in some instances older or crippled people in an extended family structure, perhaps including grandparents—they were surviving longer. But Neanderthal was also practicing cannibalism—was he eating his own family or his competition for scavenging rights in an area of dwindling resources? We do not know.

We know Cro-Magnon's extended family could not, by itself, succeed in big game hunting without many young full grown physically strong and agile skilled hunting specialists. They were like the sportsman of today with an age limit on performance within a short life of less than thirty or forty years when they may have been effective in such a physical ordeal to kill an animal larger than themselves. It meant extended clans would not have enough members that would meet the physical requirements. By joining forces with other extended clans created what we call a tribe.

The agricultural period began as a result of large animals becoming scarce which brought about more cooperation between clans and neighboring blood lines. So great was production of foodstuffs there came a struggle for many who vied for control over the agricultural communities. Key to this was family settlements, their need for stability, and to bury their loved ones nearby or store the bones in their homes. Witch doctors, the 'healers' in the Hilly Flanks in Iraq, Mesopotamia and Egypt began campaigns of conquest to control the producers. Many religious wars slew many bloodlines and families became but slaves serving witch doctors or pharaohs, kings, popes and dictators, with a process of elimination for the unbelievers.

Many families have been torn apart forcing the young to give their lives for their rulers. Yet of all the inhumane wars, and the guilt put upon man for what is only human nature, he has always been drawn home to create his family. Today we live in a mobile economy and still have kings, dictators and another evil, the rule by majority to control and regulate our socioeconomic lives. This has split the extended clans that follow companies that uproot to find fair regulations and taxation. Yet the nuclear family adapts and endures.

Today, great organizations such as NOW, may be favoring the liberal cause in a socialistic agenda to have government sponsored day care for our family's children supported by democrats in the USA. Many may want to create a society where the government will be responsible from the cradle to the grave in a communistic or collective of uniformed children who are taught and regimented for a socialistic state.

The family has weathered the theocratic and socialistic attempts at suppressing the autonomy of mankind. They have especially attacked our individuality, independent thought, and responsibility for our children to create some unnatural 'ant' like society. But our nature is as such to make our life a personal ideal in morality and the best in those things we value. Each of us, in material things wants something similar, but different from all others because of our physical and mental nature. It is not that one 'wants to keep up with the Jones's' but to naturally 'want something different we think better than the Jones's' and that is what helps to create our diverse economy that is necessary for family cultures, and people's happiness.

It is in the nature of human life to want an ideal in his love life. He/she needs his idea of a beautiful person, to find their idealistic metaphysical example. All want a person who ideally thinks like they do, understands their sense of being, needs, and their personal intimate thoughts—a sharing of human values. It is the foundation of family and humanity.

We all want a life with some sense of immortality. When young we may be full of life with ambition, curiosity, courage to risk a search for the best for ourselves and we seem to think we will live forever. Yet we evolve during our lifetime to want ideals in our marriages, children and in our old age. There is no happy death, only to die with a sense of values we created for ourselves and those we leave alive.

Regardless of how our life ends, we have accomplished a great search for our ideals in what we valued, but if it was for something some one else valued and not our own, we die human failures. The evil state cannot socialize love or the nuclear family. To attempt to do so is against human nature, immoral, and an infringement on our right to exist autonomously. They may by force fracture the extended family, but we will always create the nuclear family and experience human happiness for our selves and our children. It is much like the primitive of 3 to 5 million years ago which has remained alive and well to the present, and so it will be for the next 5 million years. And it will be because we sought the "good," for ourselves, our children and in them, our values achieve mortal reality.

To understand nuclear family cohesion today, we need only observe that there is not a child, orphan, or adult who is *separated* from their genetic nuclear or extended clan, which does not have a burning curiosity and desire to search for their roots. Many search much of their life for a blood mother, father or siblings and engage in a sentimental journey to make themselves real. Today many are researching their family genealogy, and communication is so improved that they are able to search all over the world. They can trace their roots or bloodlines back hundreds of years.

With the resources we have available today for family historians I can not think of a better way to bring a fractured extended family closer together. There are countless clans writing their own life stories in books of descendants with other members of their extended family for their children and future generations. It will give them another measure of earned immortality.

For those who think they inherited a bad family then *you* begin to make your clan worthy of approval by salvaging and cultivating the old and new roots by setting down your life with your relatives. You may find that there are relatives worthy of your approval. You will also find it will become a labor of love and another way to document human happiness—yours. Our family relatives are like metaphysical and epistemological umbilical cords connecting the great clan to each other.

ss

Friendship: Friendship is a reflection of values we find in others. A friendship is a sociable relationship. It may be a friend in childhood, as one to play with, as a neighbor or in school. This may last into adulthood. Friendships in this respect will be a settled attachment to each other's differences if they do not interfere with each other's priorities in their primary hierarchy of values. They know each other well and the friendship implies equality, psychologically, to some degree, and intellectually to a great degree. There may be little aesthetic attraction except that of familiarity and understanding of each other's psyche and intellect, a reflection of their own values in most things. It is a reciprocal respect for each other, or a mutual understanding. Such deep friendships may begin and develop at any time in one's lifetime. We may have at any one time a few good loyal friendships and they are a source of human happiness.

Friendliness, being friendly, or having many friends is on a lower scale of mutual respect and understanding. That is, we do not know or understand them to any great degree. This is not by intention, but by circumstance and length of time that we are socially attached. It may be because of one's work relationship, distance, occasional social functions, or people we know in the city, town or neighborhood only where one lives.

Therefore friends we may have assumed by our observation and their friendly attitude towards us that they basically have similar values of ambition, honesty, goals and an intelligence which causes us to reciprocate in friendly respect. It begins by being cordial, then being genial and in time, if reciprocated—being friendly—may become friendship. They may even share some of their most intimate thoughts. Friendliness also gives us a sense of community well being.

Children make friends easily. They do not have the experience to make sound judgments and they will accept almost any request by the new friend until there is a conflict concerning what their minds at that time value, "I want that!" "That is mine!" or "I want to go on the swing!" If one becomes too dominant, the other may go home and there will be no one to play with. Children do this unabashed, unrestrained, without regard, due to inexperience. This should be the testing ground where the sexes begin to understand the reality of their individuality and preferences in values. It is how they find *friends*, and *lovers*. A girl's best friend should be a boy and a boy's best friend, a girl, as soon as possible in childhood. We should not create homosocial societies for our children, one for boys and one for girls. Such *isolation* of the sexes early in childhood (age one to puberty) is how and when they *learn* to become homosexually oriented and create adult homosocial cultures. There is not space to explore this subject sufficiently, but isolation is the problem.

When friendships occur, sometime later in life, they may be attracted aesthetically first, then proceed to understand the psychological, social, and intellectual character of this aesthetically attractive human being. Once the elements of friendship fall into place with their own values, they fall in love, and make a pledge of their undying loyalty. Beyond that, if a wedding takes place, the couple may or may not choose to 'raise a family.' But in a friendship, or to be just friendly may have only one component and that is cognitive; intellectually, sociable or economic, i. e. epistemologically socioeconomic, not sexual.

A Sensual Union

To share the window to the world,
Is to sense the breadth and beauty of open doors.
To bare and share the body, and one's mind,
Is to be with one in essence, the mirror of yours.

Personal Intimate Human Happiness: A sensual 'falling in love' requires two components, aesthetic and cognitive, or in philosophy it is metaphysical and epistemological. Which comes first may not be important, however, naturally for the most part, similar to the primitive, the aesthetic or physical sensual attraction usually comes first. There are instances he/she may drawn to their intellect, discovering later, an aesthetic appeal is evident, naturally.

However, in most social instances physical attraction will be the first step, but, for the union to be lasting, there must be a deep conditional friendship component of social and intellectual intimacy—shared morals and values. This love affair may evolve into very personal intimate human happiness, lasting a lifetime, if they share intellectually, moral necessities, intangible character and tangible material values.

In the book on 'Morals', we found that reproduction is *not* a moral necessity. Religious dogma may impose guilt that becomes a dilemma for some married and single people. However, biologically women may sense time passing them by with no chance to have children. The married couple debates, some may feel with religious imprinting that sex is for reproduction only, others with a natural sense of their love's immortality. We are free from age one to adulthood to have consensual sex whether one is married or single, to have a child or not. It is with a sense of moral responsibility in honoring any obligation that may be *caused* by consensual sex, such as causing pregnancy or debt, and the example of the couple in the introduction.

Pure sex is a physical act where one perceives the opposite gender as sensually desirable and they decide to get to *know* each other, i.e. identify their values to determine if they are relative to theirs. After their first perceptions, impressions or observations aesthetically, the person seems to represent values they admire. There is a perceived attraction and an imagining that since he/she fulfills all of one's aesthetic values it is assumed all others may be so replicated. If one's emotions, imagination or fantasy dominates, i.e. believes or may have faith, they rule. Once they assume they have similar values, they go from hand holding to hugging, kissing, feeling, massaging, and stroking each other until they enter into genital union. Believe me, as you know, it usually does not happen that fast, unless both needs a one night stand badly, which this is, a purely spontaneous emotional act—without full reasoning or is just consensual sex.

When there is reason, cognitively identifying each lover's values, courting may begin, usually by holding hands. This is a sensual encounter of the simplest sort. It may be the beginning of personal intimate human happiness with the opposite sex and performing a friendship in public. They hold hands to be discretely intimate, each wants to feel the other's hand or their hand feeling his. We can't do that simultaneously, but intermittently or we alternate our consciousness to feel our hand touching theirs' and they touching ours. Two sets of communications occur between our nerve cells, or neurons, as our synapses sends the message to the brain where we have to sort out, 'do I want to feel her hand or do I want to feel her feeling mine'? Am I feeling him, or being felt, both ideas are exciting—'he's letting me feel his hand and he's really got a grip on mine!' Both conscious evaluations communicate acceptance of each other. After marriage it seems to signify ownership and happiness still evident.

Hand holding is allowing one to feel and be felt, alternating back and forth exciting us terribly, the hands becoming sweaty, almost as if both are in heat. All touch has two sensual messages mentally, to feel and be felt and is experienced intermittently.

Lovers go from hand holding, and proceed to place the hand on a their arm, around the waist or shoulder, even through clothes, this is viewed as a personally intimate privilege. One feels the body contour, movement, and body to body is closeness. As this continues to undressing the unclothed shape of the body increases the excitement as the eyes are privileged to see and be seen. These are signs of encouragement the taste of the mouth, the smell of the body and full body contact receiving and being received sensually. A fitful and fluctuating of one's consciousness feeling and being felt off and on, recurrent, the synapses of all nerve endings signaling to the brain sporadically faster and faster, creating a spasmodic muscle convulsion. When each can not tell where one leaves off or the other begins with their whole being exploding into a neural orgasm. Lovingly, a stage of physical euphoria, ecstasy and mental titillation, which is the feast of sex, the delight of the body and the bond of lovers have been reached.

The above is 'Sexual Personal Intimate Human Happiness.' But for the greater part of their life will be intellectual, as they continue to experience sexual personal intimate human happiness again and again. When their shared intimacy is strong their union may evolve to where they may want their love to last forever, an intimate immortality, to have children replicating into genetic intellectual moral and value symbols of their love. Intimate love and its result is the motivation for all human success. There can be no doubt that the ultimate happiness is 'to win *who* we love,' a mate, children, our family.

Love is emotion, but identified, it is a metaphysical, epistemological, moral and value judgment all wrapped up into one. In our successes we may achieve great fortune, stature, or receive great accolades as to our worth for mankind, but none will mean much to our self-esteem and happiness as that which another human being can bring into our life and bed. We may conquer the world in our endeavors, but the victory is hollow if one cannot share it with another mind and body in the still of the night or in the light of day. Alone we are a part of humanity, but together physically and cognitively, in a sensual sentient union, *we are* the human species.

Sex without love is animal sex
Love without sex is theist deceit
Love and sex is, Personal Intimate Human Happiness

Animal Sex: We send the wrong message, when in documenting animal behavior, we report that males are fighting over the 'privilege' to 'sire' the next generation. By the act, what is said may be correct, but not properly explained, in reality. Children (and some grown ups) watching such programs are under the impression that the animal is fighting to make the female pregnant with his seed, when in fact, he is fighting for the exclusive rights for the *pleasure* of sex (the orgasm)—nothing more!

The result of a bull's sex act is that the cow gets pregnant. She has no idea, that the bull caused it, and neither does he have a clue. She succumbs to him because he may have fought off all others winning the right to have sex with her. She submits, out of fear, resignation or because she is always being serviced by the old goat. But females are known to favor other males who hang around the fringes of the herd.

They may be from other herds, smaller, weaker, having no aggressive qualities, yet allows him to mount her. There is no evidence of purpose or natural inclination to genetically improve any species between males and females in the whole animal kingdom or any sentient being, only humans are the exception. Blood lineage for animals are meaningless. This was the extent of *our* knowledge for *five million years*.

It was not until we understood animal husbandry or agricultural technology of seeding and fertilization that we came to understand the roll of male semen in female impregnation. That understanding came about around 3,000 BC, a mere five thousand years ago a second in time for any improvement in our five million years history of genetic evolution. We can not cite one genetic change with the full knowledge of fertility, resulting only in improving somewhat, our biological health, repairing injury and extending life spans. We have through history improved agricultural and animal genetics beginning in the tending period about 12,000 years ago in everything we eat today.

Our present knowledge of fertilization, birthing, and the physiology of sex are now much greater. However, our philosophy of dealing with our nature and of reality seems to have diminished considerably. Unfortunately, where we excelled in science, technology, and crafts, we also destroyed our social values in the belief an invisible and undetectable force controlled and/or perpetuated our existence. We knew there were unseen forces, but at that time did not fully know that they might be detectable. Later we understood the undetected the unexplained events of births, etc., or there were simple explanations for seeds that needed fertilization, also there were radio waves, electrical impulses, or atomic energy. Yet many still attribute discoveries to invisible forces, and they teach, such forces require us to act on what we don't know and to reject what we do. Much of our social behavior is guided by belief in invisible deities, causing discrimination and wars all over the world.

Religious influence on laws degrade women, creating abuse, male dominance, preventing divorce, nudity, and abortion, by overburdening poor families who can least afford another child. In their zeal, to isolate the sexes, limit sex for procreation, or to prevent natural intimate sexual happiness, *they have driven sex underground*, creating unnatural sexual frustration, pornography, rage, serial rape or murder, homosexuality, masochism, and sadism, as religious prohibition of sexual pleasure is being imprinted upon societies. Today many people have an unhealthy pornographic animal sex mentality, unaware of human nature, the nature of sex, and the need for wholesome sexual relationships or personal intimate human happiness. It is not theocratic or socialistic 'leaders,' *but_only we the people* who have the ability to be responsible for our lives when left free. Free we will act like the primitives we are, basically moral, and verily I say, in values, only we can understand our own nature, "to know what is *good* for us."

The parent sets the moral example to demonstrate and make real what is taught. When answering any sexual questions its foolish to be embarrassed (your the mature grownup here). The parent is not a parent and should be morally ashamed if the child at any age has to ask, 'what is doing "it?" Morally, the parent's obligation in teaching sexual behavior must be within the complete understanding of the Moral Code. That is, to specifically, respect the child's autonomy as a potentially self regulating, self motivating, and independent individual as a child and as an adult some day.

The child's sexual education is the parents moral obligation, primarily for his/her life and her/his decisions, in the future, once the full impact of what they have learned becomes reasoning tools in shaping their lives. The moral obligation, in principle, is the parents to educate, to be involved *intellectually* intimate in the child's personal intimate human happiness, but *not to participate physically or otherwise in any kind of sexual partnership*. Parents teach and allow sociosexual associations, role-playing and experimentation, to create the roots of his/her own affections with one's age-mates or peers. Adults, parents and the like, would be immoral by committing a most grievous fraud on the child's lack of maturity and his inability to make knowledgeable decisions, to engage with a child in physical sexual activity. Every primitive society understands such actions as immoral. It would not be a lesson, but a crime and punishable in a court of law. Present law is quite specific and moral in this respect.

Our Human Responsibilities for Happiness: Total happiness requires, in the natural order of reality, that it be earned. Therefore, any aspect of happiness must be identified as to its cost and responsibility. The home is where cultures, customs and traditions should be born, not in the impersonal institutions of state or theology. It is the family who intimately deals with life, birth, and death. Every family is a culture within itself, the result of two individuals with a lifestyle unique among all others. Just go next door and there is another culture with its own customs and creating new traditions. We are the ones responsible for our families, and we are our own cultural leaders. Teaching our children is being responsible, and how we earn their love and respect.

It is in the home where we train and encourage the children, establish their personality, and prepare them for success. Also, by defining their success and personal intimate human happiness, will give momentum to their physical and mental well being to live as long as possible. That is the essence, spirit, or philosophy of a clan. It will not be some social engineered institution of government or religion that will lead us into the 21st century. We cannot trust our leadership to others we must lead because we are the brains that creates our socioeconomic cultures. The attempt to socialize will lead to disaster as it did to Fascist Italy, Nazi Germany, Japan, and the *socialism* of Russia, China and their followers. We must be prepared to be autonomously responsible for every choice we make in our morals, and values.

To be human is to be your self. To be a human family is to be included in the intimacy of one's blood relatives closely tied to each other, much, to the exclusion of the rest of the world. The family must be prepared to shape their own destiny and especially their children's, as a moral necessity.

Therefore, if a married couple believes children would interfere in their home and careers, there is no moral necessity to have a child, so please do not have any children out of some perceived biological or theological guilt.

If a couple or one of them doesn't want to be bothered by flailing, crying, nagging, stinky-poo babies, or surly teenagers then never have children.

If a couple or one of them doesn't like to teach or having to repeat them selves over and over and over and over and over, just don't have children.

If a couple or one of them lacks patience and understanding to choose what may seem an impossible task in cost—they should not have children.

If you or your spouse or both want to work and put the child in 'daycare' (a human zoo or kennel), please, do not have children, its immoral.

If a couple or one of them would not want to educate a child in their home, if they had to—they definitely should not have children.

If a couple or one of them thinks the public state run schools should teach the social sciences, behavior, be counselor to your child and a then let them educate the child please—*do not have children—they will not be yours anyway.*

If a couple or one of them thinks private or public state run schools should teach sex, anatomy or about homosexuality—do *not* have children.

If a couple or one of them does not want to be creative in teaching their children about careers, hard work and the earned value of human happiness—they should not have children.

If a couple or one of them does not want to justifiably and sincerely praise what their child does right or help them overcome what they lack—please do not have children.

If a person does not want to do these things (and there are others you can surmise) then let's do the world a favor and don't have children. Not to have a child is not a moral issue, having one *is*. Initially, it certainly may be a value issue to have a child for reasons of immortality or to represent the love you have for each other. It may require only 20 percent of your lifetime, unless you have a lot of children. But unlike many of the values one desires, having children is *morally* taking on the responsibility of other human beings so that they may survive in our 'civilized jungle,' and that is your moral responsibility.

Having a child is a serious moral decision because there is the risk of destroying a child physically, mentally, sexually and his needs for survival. The greatest danger we face is turning the child over to state run schools, that they are entrenched bureaucracies who want to socialize future citizens for the state, and create a set of altruistic values that will serve the state bureaucrat, not you, the family, or the child.

"Jeez!" you might say, given all of that, one is obligated to do above "who in the hell would ever want a child?"

You don't owe children, specifically, a lifetime of economic security, personal intimate human happiness, or long life—only 'a taste.' Your love, security, and your interest in their learning to earn so they may want to survive, will give them the potential for success, to earn their own happiness, and a long life. This is not a secret—tell them and show them that, that is what will give meaning to their life. Your love, devotion and interest in them, will be their taste of happiness. Also, I did not give any parameters socially, or any obligations in any real time frame. I did not say you had to be rich or poor, just be human brave and happy with the idea you are human and alive and *you have to love children*. It is happiness, for the rest of your life that you live for. When you think like that, you may find more reasons to create your own nuclear family with children.

As a parent one has to be sure of moral convictions, then take on the task to raise and teach children, using one's best judgment. If we want freedom and independence as individuals, we need the Moral Code. If one wants a measure of 'success' it takes hard work, perseverance and some risk, striving to earn something of value. A measure of 'happiness' depends on learning morals and social values from parents. But we all have a brain and may learn and earn the "good" after one leaves home and parental care. There comes a time when they are to be aware of responsibility for their lives—*at puberty,* because he is no longer a child.

However, if we want to enter the new millennium confident and happy, with family and our individualism intact, we must leave the trees for the new savanna. We take the risk to gain a better future and remind legislators of the separation of church and state. The new human, you, must be willing to take responsibility, be of the type to go to the brink, live on the edge, be a part of an avant garde that will lead, instead of following some 'leader,' into a brave new world. Only then, will you have *earned* nature's greatest reward and find meaning in your life, because you can have success, human happiness, and long life without guilt. "It doesn't get any better than that."

CHAPTER 12

Long Life

Life, all would agree, is our greatest value. Each birthday is personal empirical evidence that we've received one more year of life. The year ahead is the opportunity to live one more day or years, depending on our physical well being, accident, or psychologically our will to live. Despite the inevitability of life and its end, we can do something about the quality of our life, and how long, which is incumbent on the value we place on living. Above we created a moral foundation for as long as possible. Our philosophy has taken care of the psychological will to live and accident is the quantum effect we cannot predict the probability of happening to us. What is left is to physically live as long as possible. You are the judge of its quality, physically. The earlier in life you take care of your self physically, the longer you can live.

To want a long life is a value judgment to survive, which creates the necessity for The Moral Code, without which, our walk on earth would be in jeopardy every step through what might be a short life indeed. It is in our will to live that creates the need to be a success in our work. The code is what sustains our ability to add to the quality of life, earn human happiness, and which may add immeasurably to our time on earth.

When we reach old age, we may place a higher priority on living long. Perceived are those who suffer to 'hang on,' but for them, life is good and worth such effort. To be healthy, it is advertised, to 'get a good night's rest, eat right and exercise.' Also, to eat the right food such as high protein, unsaturated fats in meat and fish, for our body and brain. Also, to eat grains, fruits, vegetables, olive oil, nuts and drink in moderation will keep one healthy. When the doctor told the complaining elderly patient, "Sir, I can't make you a young man!" to which the elder replied, "Doctor, I'm not asking you to make me younger, please, I'm only asking you to make me older!"

Vitamins, colloidal minerals and amino acids are good food supplements since none of us eat right everyday. Days or weeks may go by in our work and social life, when it is difficult to maintain a good diet to live long. Such supplements are 'prudent guarantees.' Another wise effort among the young and many older people who regularly attend health and exercise spas for physically monitored exercise may be 'doing the body good' contributing to the quality and a longer healthier life. The young suffer the 'pain gain' because the good life is, feeling physically strong and looking sexy, in order to metaphysically attract a mate, not to exercise with, but for love and another kind of exertion. The young should begin early with good health checks, eating to live, supplements, and exercise, because they will pass an age when it is too late. The sooner you begin, the longer you will live.

We are subject to accidents by vehicles, and those of nature, but also to be in an undesirable or unfortunate place at the wrong time, when criminal actions or violent events take place where we have no control. Murder and mayhem as well as reckless behavior such as driving while drunk may shorten what may be one's own and that of other's long life. We need not belabor these points of helping preserve our life they are clear-cut. We should heed being in danger, avoid careless behavior and lead a moral life. There is the possibility of an unfortunate coincident.

It has long been felt that many people will live longer lives by reason of sheer will. The will to live, according to physicians and mental care specialists have found this to be true. Doctors, nurses, and psychiatrists find their jobs much easier with a person who has a positive view of life and nurses seem to know those who have the will to recover quickly. Therefore, in cases of 'will' it appears that we can do something about how long we live. What precedes will is reason, its motivation, to be a success, of good character, to enjoy one's material gains, to win who we love, and live a long life mentally aware and physically fit.

The brain in order to be physically fit must be fed (unsaturated fats) and our mind must be mentally active just as the body must be exercised throughout our lifetime. Reaching old age, we need the mental activity of a motivating career or a profound interest in something we sincerely believe worthwhile. It may be different in nature than one's life work, but one that stimulates some mental activity where we continue to learn and animate ourselves creatively, is to reason beyond physical needs.

For some people who marry and have children, they take on the obligations of parenthood and the full weight of responsibility for another human being. They must nurture, love, encourage, educate, keep physically fit, and worry about the child's well being every day of its young life. It is their moral duty to bring up healthy moral educated children. It is the ultimate in volunteerism, the result of which in old age they will feel great pride, be loved and still involved with their family—to watch their garden grow.

The obligation to have children in theology is contrary to volunteering. Theologically, a couple has no choice whether or not to have children, or how many. Devout religious people should not prevent pregnancy, and once it is conceived must raise their children within some religious value system. This is strategy to perpetuate the increase of souls (donors) in every competing religion. In this respect, theology attests that lover's lives together should be another crapshoot. The burden of responsibility is not being governed by their ability to earn, i.e., the value they may receive for the work they love to do, but, contingent on the religion's need to compete for 'souls.' This causes the growth of poverty and the idea that one does not or cannot control one's life. The burden and uncertainty placed on people's lives with the least resources to provide for their family becomes obvious, it is not voluntary.

Thus, with the full weight of unwanted children, the specter of failure and poverty, becomes the cause of much rage, abuse, divorce, and abandonment of families. The full burden is assumed, under involuntary conditions, which has been the rule in the past and still is in many countries, and normal for many families. It is no wonder they can't wait for the last child to leave home, or kick him out. Work under these conditions is a panic—take any job—do anything for a buck—grin and bear it—suffer under inept supervision—don't dream—get drunk—escape! Many collapse into retirement and do not want to *hear* the words 'think' or 'work'—just relax, have fun, drink, and die. "Hey, when your time's up—you go." or "There has to be to be something else." Their lives are over, and retirement under those conditions does not last long.

People who have never worked, stole, lied, cheated, killed or lived an immoral life, and poor values, need only accept that he believes in a god, and he will have earned his way to heaven with a free ride through eternity. These are theocratic values and moral justice.

In this book we've learned that one's highest priority is life and that success was paramount to the quality of life envisioned for ourselves. Having achieved the goal of success that was set, there was pride, and self-esteem in achieving personal happiness. The expectation was to work until the day of death, if physically possible. In success one may have never married but was content with one's own life, progress, and friends. The same is true for people who take a mate, live and love attending to each other all their lives, never having children, it was their choice, their happiness and they are *not* immoral. The issue is what they *value* in their life.

Whatever the quality of life one expects to achieve, and does, may be a formula for long life as a personal choice and responsibility. There are no standards or formulas for achieving life's meaningful values for all individuals, the only guidance being, 'know yourself,' be yourself, and live for your values. It is selfish and unselfish at the same time, without which man cannot achieve 'the good.' One wants to be successful to selfishly strive for the best, and to find human happiness and to share it unselfishly with the one he selfishly values most.

What to Live For: We live to survive, to be a success and to experience reality, our existence, for love and the children we may create. Perhaps the thing we may love most about life is our mate, children, the remembrance real friendships and the good times. That is the driving desire of those who value their lives dearly. It is a person's need to love and be loved that creates the motive for one to be a success, to take on great obligations, and experience the full range of joyous emotional commitment to their family, relatives and friends.

Success, our initial abstraction, once achieved, will make it real or what we want to be as an individual, which will make us happy. The ultimate experience is personal intimate human happiness, another person. To be real it must be experienced cognitively and physically in sexual consummation, the act of bringing that love to a state of perfection, a fulfillment of theoretical life goals we wanted to create. The life process of love and affection, if we so desire, will give birth to a son or daughter that of our flesh, a combined genetic duplicate, a copy or clone that represents each other's love for each other and their commitment, devotion and loyalty to their family.

The child becomes us in miniature, and we enjoy in them another abstraction, a loving person, successful, and with personal human happiness. We love to nurture, teach and guide them through all their large and small exigencies to bring that abstraction into reality. Then we wait in anticipation of our dreams we have of them—what will they become? Will they have our values? What will be their success? Who will they fall in love with? Will they find complete happiness? Will they have children? Will their children achieve success? What will they look like? How will all their children find happiness *and* their children's children, etc., etc.? How long do we want to live, to experience what we have created?

We may have no choice as to how long we exist, since we live in a time that old age is a physical condition we haven't found a remedy for. However, in time, each of us will experience a longer life, of our predecessors. Our descendants may be able to witness all their great, great, great, great, great grandchildren. Living longer presents new problems whether we have been alone, lost our mate or still living together. Each phase in our life, birth, puberty, career, marriage, children or divorce requires new thinking—life is not static—it evolves so that our future is no longer like the past. To live long requires the same attitude of ambition, goal setting, and decisions about the rest of our aging lives. All those values we applied to the earlier phases of our careers must be re-enacted in the light of new challenges.

The aging challenge isn't long life. That is only a result because one had a reason to live. It's another success, a goal, to do what you always wanted to do. To be sure it must be within your physical and mental capability. It was mentioned in Book III, Epistemology, that in a recent study by the University of Georgia who studied people over 100 years old, it was found that they had a profound interest in something. Most of them lost loved ones, their spouses, and even their children, but all was not lost to them. Tragic as it was, there was life, interest, challenge and work to do to find out something, accomplish or help their friends and relatives in some way. Also, just as there is pride in saying, 'That's my great-great-grandmother' and surely there is a proud sense of life in saying, 'that is my great-great-great-grandchild!' Long life is not just to exist for 100 years but to experience life's values and to again achieve personal goals of success and human happiness.

We die reaching for the stars only to become one of them. From where we came is just the same as to where one goes, nobody knows. However, the younger have a chance to push that window of opportunity open, farther and farther, to 120, 150, 200, 500, or 1,000 years. Some scientists believe the body's cells may some day be rejuvenated indefinitely. The work on genetic and molecular biology will in future discoveries, *may* prevent disease and old age problems. If we are to have faith, it is in the efficacy of the human mind to push back that time when we go, where, we don't know, but many imagine a fantasy—heaven. Science gives the perception that we will go where we came from, back to unconscious inert molecules to be scattered, never to be so uniquely enjoined together ever again. For conscious beings, existence depends on the substances and laws of nature, but substance does not depend on consciousness.

Life, i.e. consciousness through evolution has endowed us with an immense capacity for intellectual growth, even those we might believe to be inferior. We all have the intellect to experience reality, the beauty of a blade of grass, the rolling hills and forests, amid the patchwork quilts of the earth—evidence of man. We witness the mighty oceans, the undersea worlds, as well as the wonder about the existence of the stars, and galaxies. We love all the living creatures that move about in animal and fish societies, struggling to exist in a food chain, which preserve their own kind at the expense of others. They will serve our needs since our intellect finds they are crucial to our own existence. It's life and death for all, fish and fowl, man and woman, the ignorant and the intellect.

Most of all we love and respect our own kind. Our intellect reasons that mercy is paramount in dealing with animal kingdom, as they are the means to human survival. Psychologically we replicate sympathy from beings like us to all life, even though no such sympathy exists for mankind in other species that exist. We learned to love mentally and physically. We are changing the world and our socioeconomic cultures in ways evolutionary forces could never accomplish. We enjoy existence on our own terms, we can own its land, transform nature, and create unimaginable entities that give us comfort and the means to extend life as we know it. But for all life and the material universe, evidence demonstrates that life and death of all creations go on forever. But, in this world we created, due entirely to our learning to love on a savanna millions of years ago, we believe we're indispensable and somehow will live in some unimaginable form forever. We believe we are an elite, or egotistically the aristocracy of all living things in life, but it is because we love being conscious of life, we love nature, we love reality, we are in love with ourselves and we love to love so very very much.

We will not have the luxury of a window to the future. If we want that we must take a time machine into the future. Only science and technology may make such a machine, but I think not. If we think we can gain immortality by just dying we are living in a fantasy. If we want to acquire immortality we have to 'earn' it, the 'old fashioned way', with our minds, science, and effort. The science is born and you have to do the work.

Cryonics is the deep freezing of human bodies at death for preservation and possible revival in the future. It raises the possibility that one may be thawed out or defrosted in some giant microwave oven at some future date when science can extend life. Such a future time when old age would be cured and one would have a new vigorous body. Genetics may make immune systems capable of resisting all diseases. You would be able to meet your descendants hundreds of years from now. The possibility of endless life, and everlasting youth, sounds like a heaven, but the only heaven we may experience is the one we will earn.

Robert C.W. Ettinger's book "The Prospect of Immortality" (1966) on freezing, '*The fact*: At very low temperatures it is possible, *right now*, to preserve dead people with essentially no deterioration, indefinitely.' [8] There are a great many explanations in the book. The science is 'cryonics' and since that publication many people have been preserved. They may be revived in the years ahead when the technology advances for reliable rejuvenation to be perfected. There is not the space to give a proper review of the book and I leave it up to you to read and judge for yourself. There is the possibility for a great adventure into the future. If you don't like it when you get there, you can always die. It is the only chance you have 'to go where no man has gone before.' I hope to see you there and have a long life!

Is That All There Is?—"I believe there is something more to life than just being born, living, and dying. There just *has* to be something else." We have all heard this at one time or other. The reasons to want immortality are many.

The first historical reason is theological—what we have heard or been taught ritually, by magic, miracles, and fraud for the last 5,000 years. People believe that at death they will still retain their consciousness and be judged as to whether they will go to heaven or hell. The burial cults of the early witch doctors invented immortality to reward men for their sacrifice to the gods and representatives on earth. That's what people have done for thousands of years—they've sacrificed their wealth to build monuments, temples, cathedrals and created elitist institutions. All they have to do is give their wealth to buy and pray for a glorious ride into eternity. Its sort of a prepay as you go plan, before you get what was promised. The same kind of plan in socialistic Russia where one paid for an automobile before you got it perhaps *years* later and if the wheels were stolen in shipping, you had to pay for new ones before getting the car. So when some one dies, put a *lot* of money in the casket.

People have sacrificed wealth and joy for asceticism, humility and suffered wrath for being human. Is it no wonder when faced with death men and women cry out—'there just *has* to be something else!' It is our fault if we cannot die completely happy. Nature doesn't have to do anything. It's forces and substances will continue their life and death cycles forever, independent of biological consciousness. Our life is but moment of time and an infinitesimal material part of that process and that is why it is so valuable and difficult to let go.

The second historical reason is that we don't believe in our own science and logic that tells us death is real, and that we don't exist as a conscious being once we are dead, but decay and turn into that 'star stuff' we are made of. We can not believe we never existed before and we will not exist afterwards, physically or consciously, illogically we just *imagine we have a second consciousness, a soul, and we will be conscious forever.*

Nature is relentless, it is re-creative, existing for a time, then all its substance and force dies in a large black hole, imploding, only to explode again, which again allows organisms or sentient beings to come to life, grow, evolve and die. Consciousness depends on that reality not upon what we imagine, hope, wish, or even by the plea, "There *has* to be something else." Scientifically there is no evidence or proof of immortality, reincarnation, or that everlasting life exists. One can imagine, hypothesize, listen to a priest swinging a smoking ball, or a shaman in contortions, or incantations, hope, wish, want, need, feel, or have an 'idea' of our own, but, that's all it is—imagination. To want, imagine, have faith, hope, or to *believe* is not proof or scientific truth of their theology.

The third historical reason is wanting, wishing, to be immortal, because *life is good.* Life is wondrously worth living. If we have half-a-brain we can have a very successful life that will give us pride, confidence, have love, children and challenges, things to witness, travel, enjoy one's land, be friendly and have friends. A half-a-brain can have it all. Just *work* at what you like. Only then is life of great value when one can seek success, love and sex, or is it sex and love—it doesn't matter so long as it's *both.* We witness the changing culture, scientific progress, new products that add to our comfort, we understand something of existence, the universe, evolution and we have so much to take part in, to learn, ponder, or enjoy, a lifetime is too short. So we make the most of it, do the very best we can but just hope, wish, 'pray' and think that it should never end. This can't be all there is, because life is too valuable to waste on death. Immortality, a little white lie we tell ourselves will suffice for now. We go on living in the meantime, perhaps go to sleep and die, and *never* wake up again, because the universe is life and death random—uncertain—a natural entity.

The fourth historical reason we want to be immortal is that we cannot accept, psychologically, that *our* unique life will end. Our odds of being born or surviving in the womb in an ejaculate is

100,000,000 to 600,000,000 to one. We've lived through childhood, fearless and would walk off a cliff or into a pool if not restrained. Until our terrible twos, we believed ourselves to be the center of the universe. Everyone dotes on us, saves us from falling down the stairs and caters to our every need or whimper. We are important and invincible. By the time we get into the terrible twos, this seems to wither away and we are left much more on our own. We are no longer the center of the universe and we are devastated and mad, but get over it, and find as we learn to talk, a new world is to be explored. We are fearless, courageous, raise hell, and take risks because we are intrepid.

We are undaunted and risk taking is not all that bad. When we get older we take, somewhat, a risk that this or that career will give us a good life. We take a risk in love, coming to understand her/him; we have *faith* in their fidelity. We are confident we can raise good children and have faith in their mother/father to help. We have taken a risk, have done our best for our children, by example, to turn out well, a balance of risk and reason.

However, as in all relationships with lovers, children, friends, relations, bosses, and all people we deal with, we arm ourselves with knowledge of them to make good judgments and keep the risk of faith in them at a minimum. This is proper since we may witness the real results of our faith in them was correct or not. We have *proof* of our faith, one way or the other. If we are to have some faith, it may be better in someone real. Faith in a god can never be proven, but faith or taking a risk in people can. But of heaven, gods, or the hereafter, we know *nothing*, yet put all our faith and fearlessness in the idea 'we will survive'—after death, which is not being truthful to our selves, even in an imaginary conclusion, because it is contrary to what we naturally witness.

The fifth historical cause that we want immortality is *time*. It just is not fair that would be awarded so little, infinitesimal, or unbelievably minute time on earth. It is stupidly inconceivable that we are here, in a moment of time, and that's the end? We just don't believe it regardless of the evidence—there's got to be something else and we leave it at that. So we live our life as though it will go on forever and that this time is but an interim whether we're 14, 20, 30, 40, 50, or 60 and beyond. We *procrastinate and waste time*. It will be done—someday, (take a course, fix that, see aunt Mary, tell mom and dad I love them, solve that problem, go into business, etc.) manana, tomorrow, later, next semester, year, or some undefined future. The tragic comedy is that some of us often think we might get 'lucky' and really make it, with out effort, by fortunate coincidence or circumstance—or win the lottery.

Some of us think time is on our side to control, but the clock is running and we only get older; we may never finish what we should have started nor did the things we dreamed of doing. It may be we haven't the life we imagined long ago, and that all we have wanted in our lifetime, somewhere, sometime or somehow in heaven we will get a second chance an imaginary place where anything might be possible. So we bet on unlimited time, living in dreams we have eternity, and time goes by, until surprise! The time for us ends. But we think we are immortal and will live forever and there is plenty of time to do all those things—when we are dead.

The best thing to do is have no expectations, if we led a good life and never harmed anyone with intent, what is the best thing that can happen when we die? We will not wake up.

A Contemporary View: Paul Davies' book, "The Last Three Minutes" is a realistic view of the fate of the universe eventually the sun will burn to a crisp. Another scenario is that we will be hit, by earth destroying meteor, traveling at 40,000 miles an hour and that is not speculating. All fossil fuels will run out, minerals, soil erosion, and the sun will die. We will run out of everything, nothing lasts forever in form, even us.

Davies' concern touches upon what so many scientists and anthropologists calculate that, 'the earth's population: it cannot go on growing indefinitely.' [9] Adding to this dreadful gloomy picture Davies notes; 'that Bertrand Russell, in a fit of depression over the consequences of the second law of thermodynamics.' (A German physicist in 1856 proved, heat flows to cool and calculations show the universe is dying, i.e. the stars—suns will eventually, over billions of years will loose their energy), 'wrote in anguished terms about the futility of human existence given the fact that the solar system is doomed. Russell clearly felt that the apparently inevitable demise of our habitat somehow rendered human life pointless or even farcical.' Davies; 'It is not the actual duration of time that counts but the idea that sooner or later the universe will become uninhabitable; this idea makes some people feel that our existence is pointless' [10]

However, Davies is clear that, 'the important issue is surely not whether our species as such is immortal, but whether our *descendants* can survive. And our descendants are unlikely to be human beings.' It was mentioned earlier, we have choreographed our own evolution,—Davies; 'We may soon be able to design human beings with prescribed attributes and physical characteristics by direct genetic manipulation.' [11] This work has only just begun, which is being hampered politically and theologically.

It has been said that we were successful in going to the moon in the sixties, because we *had* the necessary technology. The only pay back on that adventure was a few moon rocks of which only 10 percent were ever examined the rest lie in vaults for 'posterity,' which means the government doesn't know what to do with them. Yet we are afraid to genetically improve our health on earth, while government is trying to live in space which there is no benefit mankind on earth today. We might as well be building pyramids, which in reality government is motivated for the same reasons, for power over our minds and wealth

The time we have on earth is ours. We need not worry about our sun running out of heat or space travel. Our problem is to live as long as possible to help create the best kind of world for our children; to pass on knowledge for our children's survival for their immediate future. That is how we on earth and each succeeding generation will exist. It will be by what we pass on. If we take the view that life is futile, ridiculous, fruitless, pointless, or a farce, then that will be our philosophy. But, if we want our lives to be meaningful, then we must earn values of success, human happiness, health, and hand that legacy over to our children. We have learned of the great struggle of our ancestors, admiring their sense of life, under primitive conditions that we can only imagine. Our science discovered that they indeed existed and have made them real for us. We know in a very real sense, we are their immortal legacy.

We want to live as long as possible to witness and be assured of the passing of our knowledge and any meaningful culture to our children. If we do that, we earn contentment in that whatever they encounter in the future, we will have done our utmost to help. To lead a meaningful life is to pass on the good we created for ourselves. And if we do that, we will have peace of mind, and will not fear that super nova's blinding flash, as our consciousness enters into its own black hole.

If we want immortality, we have to *earn* it, the civilized way, by following The Moral Code and seeking our own values, and what we accomplish, in our careers, personal lives, and with our children will be our measure of immortality. Some may do what people think are great things, in the physical sciences, philosophy, metaphysics supporting scientific progress, epistemology, learning, morals justice for all, values, freedom, government, codification of The Moral Code, aesthetics meaningful humane artistic expression, and as such to be remembered in the history of mankind. There will be many or relatively few, but that will only be another measure of immortality. Those who are dishonest or evil have no sense of immortality are without conscience—where only the immediate is important. Some believe we deserve immortality, with a deep down suspicion in our psyche that we dare not face, that is, we who are fortunate to experience life must do something more than exist for ourselves. It is undeserved guilt, for the only obligation in existence for an intelligent human being is to Honor The Moral Code, i.e. we do not infringe on other people's lives, and by that act earned or justified a great measure of immortality as a moral example.

What does our life *mean?* This infinitesimal time in eternity belongs to no one, but our selves. If we live by other people's values, 'ideas', 'visions' or 'imaginings,' then our lives belong to the minds or meanings of others. Only then we will find there is no meaning we can call our own, and life for us will be meaningless, a victim of fraud. It is what we do for our selves, family, and children that will give meaning to life. Live by THE MORAL CODE, *respect* others, but leave us alone to earn what we value and whom we love, so that we may not become a burden on others. We applaud that for some, it will be to accomplish a great work in research, invention, or in the arts, but not all may aspire to exceed in ambition above all others. Yet most of us wish to live, work, love, and play, to enjoy a long life in peace, knowing that we lived it morally and created our own personal life of VALUES. That is the meaning of life, to experience SUCCESS, HUMAN HAPPINESS, and to LIVE LONG as possible, anything else is pure fantasy.

BIBLIOGRAPHY: VALUES

Ref.
No.
Chapter 1

1. Brandon, Nathanial: "The Psychology of Self Esteem," Los Angeles, CA: Nash Publishing Corporation, 1969: P. 24. (My special thanks to Nathanial Brandon for permission to use this material.)

Chapter 2

2. Nielsen, Kai, Contributing author; "The Encyclopedia of Philosophy," Pub. By, Collier Macmillan Publishers, New York, 1972: 'Twentieth-Century Ethics,' 'The History of Ethics,' Vol. 3; P. 103 (first 6 parenthesis listed, mine.).

Chapter 3

-0-

Chapter 4

3. Lowie, Robert, Ph.D.: "Primitive Society," Published by, Liveright Publishing Corporation, New York, 1947: CH. IX, 'Property', 208-9 quoted and paraphrased.

Chapter 5

-0-

Chapter 6

4. McKeon, Richard: "Introduction to Aristotle," Second Edition, Pub. By, The University Press, Chicago, Illinois, 1973: Nicomachean Ethics, P. 413.

Chapter 7

-0-

Chapter 8

5. Edey, Maitland A.; "The Missing Link," 'The Emergence of Man,' Pub. By, Time-Life Books, New York, 1972: P. 37-8.

Chapter 9

6. Radin, Paul: "Primitive Religion," Published by, The Viking Press, New York, 1937: P. 6 (emphasis, mine).
7. McKeon, Richard: "Introduction to Aristotle", Published by, The University of Chicago Press, Chicago, 1973: P. 359-60.

ss

Chapter 10

-0-

Chapter 11

-0-

Chapter 12

8. Ettinger, Robert, C. W.: "The Prospect of Immortality," Pub. By, A. Macfadden-Bartell Books Garden City, New York, 1966: P. 15.
9. Davies, Paul: "The Last Three Minutes," New York: Basic Books, Div., Harper-Collins Publishers, Inc., 1994: P. 101.
10. IBID: P. 102-103.
11. IBID: P. 103.

BOOK VI

GOVERNMENT

CONTENTS

GOVERNMENT

Illustrations:
Chapter 3. Fig. 1. Collectivism & Individualism
Fig. 2. The Right and the Left
Fig. 3. The Totalitarian State
Fig. 4. States of Fascism

Chapter:
1. Primitive Government 389
2. Cro-Magnon Government 394
3. Rulers and Systems of Governments 400
4. The Magna Carta & The Colonists 417
5. Natural Law 428
6. Economics 437
7. PROMOTEANISM 454
8. The Promotean System of Government 462
9. The United Nations 476
10. The Party is Over 478
11. Privatization 481
12. The Promotean Vision 486
Glossary 493
Bibliography 496

CHAPTER 1

Primitive Government

There is only one question we need ask of governance, what is the proper role of government? The answer could take volumes, but it can be stated simply, in three words, "To be moral."

It has been established and self-evident The Moral Code defines the philosophy of our morals and values. The justification for moral principles is to protect human life and the free pursuit of values (survival). No person, institution, or government has a moral right to infringe upon the autonomy, independence individuality, the responsibility, or the freedom of people, to seek their values and evolve freely. When a state, infringes on socioeconomic values of the people who naturally hold such rights, ruled by a person or a citizen by vote, they are immoral.

The inevitable result of a reasoning moral people will conclude, that the only type of government which can logically survive a hundred millennium is Promotean, that must uphold a morality of natural law, by codifying The Moral Code as shown in Book IV. In principle, why and how we should change present governments, are the subjects of this book.

Philosophically, ruling has been usually referred to as the 'science of politics.' But, the context of what politician implies an artful or shrewd, crafty, a wheeler and dealer, has a seamy connotation in the conduct of politicians, in conducting the affairs of the government. I am sure it is more appropriate to be "The Science of *Government*," the name and subject of this book.

We will be exploring the science of government, known principles, and natural law. We will begin with our historical roots, attempt to determine what principles of government made possible the laws we have today. Why and how we may by our vote, simply and peaceably change the present unprincipled tangible value oriented or ideological theory of 'politics' we have today, that will inevitably destroy any nation.

For five million years, the most stable and lasting collective unit was the family. On the average it consisted of a mother, father and two or three children. She nursed a child for three years, so that if she was nursing one, the elder child was perhaps three or four years old and the oldest of the three seven or eight. The three or four year old was very likely physically well coordinated and could run fast. This child probably carried things, acted as lookout and helped hold the baby if the mother was busy. Perhaps an eight or nine year old was almost self sufficient, taking part in hunting small animals, carrying or helping in scavenging meat.

A clan consisted of the couple's mother, father and perhaps a brother with his mate. The structure of the family was sort of a loose voluntary union. The adult male without the burden of attachment to a child was free to roam the savanna for food. He could leave the family and strike out on his own, but then he gave up his sex with her. She likewise could disappear if he wasn't there often enough and generous, or was cruel and she would go out on her own. Then she would take up with another male, and this one would give anything for his own female. Such a voluntary union reached equilibrium quickly since each had valuable contributions for success and a happy union.

Neither the male nor female was in a superior position so that there was no ruler per se. The male may have initiated the move to new territory or act as defense and doing most of the scavenging. But she was a partner also, minding or leaving the child with an older one to help with scavenging or hunting an animal. If love and sex was good for both, there was no need for a ruler among or over them, *their only restraint was a natural unspoken Moral Code*, 'do not hurt.'

Once a cooperative effort reached a level of respect and appreciation, they could proceed in achieving success in confidence and harmony. This was the ideal marriage or union between men, women, and children each depending on the other to contribute in succeeding to survive against the world. We can appreciate there were problems, compromise, tragedy and unhappiness at times.

A family's goals are different from political goals, but *when they want to be ruled politically* the family will be destroyed and socialism, or a theocracy will become the sole organization of man. To many, this may sound 'ideal' with no obligation to a person, family, or children. A state of communal sex without 'obligation' would exist. Everyone is responsible to work to fill the pot and receives according to need. It is the 'ideal' of collective politics, except for human nature. Where everyone is responsible no single person feels very responsible, and eventually everyone becomes irresponsible, and with such a mob eventually, the 'pot' becomes empty (Note, the perfect example, USSR,).

The rest of the world is headed towards socialistic or fascist rule and there are many totalitarian theocracies that own their people and property in the world. In the USA, people have a false sense of political intent and/or reality. The more that they ask of government the more collective they become, creeping inevitably towards totalitarianism. Yet they still can not believe that it can happen here. Voters now accept the idea the state should provide for their well being will succumb to totalitarianism voluntarily in the next decade and it may be permanent. The pharaoh lasted for 4,000 years and the popes 1,000. Asia and most of the world today live under totalitarian monarchies and socialistic states ever since the pharaohs. We are burying ourselves unwittingly in Fascism marching into the jaws of socialism. And we will be ruled to suffer poverty for many a millennium.

All political systems in vogue or that ever were in recorded history has been collective to a great degree. The attraction for people to come together for 'common' goals is the siren song for collectivism. They attract the politically religiously naive with the idea that politics or government has common goals or values of the family as its political agenda. However, politically, collectively 'common' goals, ideals, the good, and any ideology, is being extremely hypothetical in the broadest widest meaning of the term 'common' (or public good, etc.). Yes, as individuals, we have common goals such as success, happiness, and long life. We also have broad goals of work, play and health. But the individual nature of our species is that we all have a different idea of how, what, quantitatively, and qualitatively that is incrementally infinite, in achieving similar goals. A collective political goal is to bureaucratically destroy individualism by standardizing human behavior, and to eliminate incrementally infinite human values, our social and material values.

Five million years on the savanna the family unit had a common goal to feed itself, success. Each humanoid evolved as a pure individual genetically and mentally, each evolving in a changing world, where over the hill lay another environment, subtly different. The individual nature of the primitive could create new goals and means of survival within evolving environments. Mankind was evolving epistemologically learning how to survive in any environment, and metaphysically, evolving to support the variable intellect of a new species that came into existence by learning. That is the nature of successful evolution and resides in the nature of man. The broadest or narrowest collective goals can only be set, between two consenting individuals—and their family. To increase that collective unit to include others will cause chaos, by individuals asserting their ideas of *how* to achieve and *what* to achieve, which is why it *ends up to be totalitarian, their individuality becomes burdensome in a collective theocratic or socialistic society.* We see this ///, happen even *within* a family as children grow older and begin to create their own hierarchy of values and want freedom from parental rule.

Therefore, given a political system *we may all vote* and agree to live in a socialistic collective, but, when the succeeding generation is born and raised, ruling will have to be at the point of a gun. It is not fair or just to live under totalitarian oppression which is not of his making. In 1913 the amendment to the constitution was passed for pay role deduction of income tax. Even Milton Friedman has regretted making that suggestion. We should not have to live by the archaic rules of our ancestors. Each child is born Petula Rasa with more of a possibility of hating his upbringing, being treated as an orphan or cattle with a revolutionary fervor to break free because he is alive and wants to discover, create, witness the world, to be alive mentally. He has begun to identify all of his perceptions; he is human and like all animals should be free. In his collective this is treason, and may be executed. If that is so then we who vote for government to control medicine, and their socialistic programs is treason towards our own children. We may breed a child of resignation, lethargy, acquiescence, an abdication of reason to think, dare, challenge, to dream or take a risk—invent. But we will have robbed them of their nature to be free and motivated by his dreams, i.e. responsibility as woman or man. The human spirit cannot manifest itself, as his nature requires. Then in such a state people will starve physically and intellectually, then we will have another upheaval peaceably, or war. We have personally witnessed this happen in Soviet Russia and all over the world today.

Revolutions in history has awakened the individual spirit, but only to find that the struggle was for another collective, or one more or less oppressive, with a different name. It has become another king, queen, emperor, dictator, democracy or republic, and the result, a new collective.

There are many questions we must answer, what is the proper

role of the government? How did it begin? How did it evolve? What is freedom? What are the limits of freedom? How do we achieve freedom and what kind of government is the most moral? We will begin with history, to understand the roots of the philosophy or theology of government, and to propose an end to the madness in political ideology. Do we want a *moral secular society*?

The family is not a traditional government. Many believe that it is an authoritative organization with the role as head or dictator or a combined command of husband and wife. It is neither; to be sure they are lovers and an efficient economic unit making most decisions—'two can live as cheaply as one' and perhaps can afford a third. The nuclear family is a moral voluntary primitive autonomous, ideological, loving, teaching and cooperative learning unit. A government's role, morally, is to guarantee human autonomy, to encourage the nuclear family to evolve naturally.

CHAPTER 2

Cro-Magnon Government

We have examined the family—the largest collective body of humans for five million years. It was a time when the human body was changing, their brains were enlarging, becoming ever more capable of reasoning with a greater memory. They were becoming more diverse in their thinking, invention, and in the way they were handling their lives. The little clan, consisting of the father, mother, and two or three children, the oldest being twelve or thirteen, perhaps was sexually active with a sibling or cousin. His or her, father and mother were probably about twenty four which was old by primitive standards, or one of them might well be dead. The young couple may have stayed with the family to help the mother or father to cope with feeding the young.

As the new family took on remnants of the old, it was creating its own children, and possibly, left the family or remained close by as an extended family clan. This may have happened, more and more, two or three hundred thousand years ago, during the increasing productive years of the Stone Age. They were being more creative, improving tools that were very effective in cutting, and getting food quicker and safer to home base. But if the savanna or area they were in, had been incapable of supporting so many people, then scarcity would become evident, and the newly formed families moved on. They would not kill or steal from their own family for territory, and so created an exodus out of Africa to occupy the world.

As the pouring out of Africa continued, about 35,000 years ago Cro-Magnon, our contemporary in many respects, would begin to change the course of human history. Inventing spears, fishhooks, bows and arrows man was now prepared to kill larger, faster, and more dangerous animals than himself. Larger groups of people were needed to accomplish big game hunting. A larger clan or extended family was ideal since all were family members. However, if one or two of the hunting males met an accident or died in the hunting attack, other people were needed to fill in the gaps.

To fill in the gaps, other clans, non-related, would have to be recruited. The only way a non-clan member would join a tribe of unrelated clans would be—very cautiously. He did not expect to receive the personal love experienced among clan relatives, but as a separate family expected *respect*—that his love of his family would be equal in importance to them as they would their own. Only then would they join the tribe in the hunt. How much negotiation concerning equal rights was actually communicated between them and how it became a common understanding is unknown. Perhaps, there was no need, because the only logical behavior was that it be mutual—it was inconceivable to live otherwise.

The tribal leader, the eldest or the most skillful male was looked to for planning, directing, and leading the hunters to the kill. To maintain respect he/she had to be extremely fair in the distribution of the kill to those who contributed the most to the action in bringing down the animal. Those who took no action received little or perhaps none, but may have received a portion from someone as a loan. As a planner of the hunt, the leading organizer may have been the most experienced, with ideas, showing respect for suggestions and wishes of others.

Tribal disputes had to be settled fairly, with mixed clans, perhaps taking care not to favor one clan or relative over another. The leader was the planner of the hunt or in engagements to defend the tribe. And if he 'did good' at all times, when he died, they dressed him up in his finest gear, his tools, all those things he valued, and they buried him with honor. In his place would follow who ever was considered a great clever hunter, fair minded, and a defender of all. How they chose is unknown but it is possible, they agreed perhaps, by some kind of vote.

The common ground that enabled families to come together, and taken for granted or communicated, was that all the people depended upon their leader to maintain respect for all clans and individuals. Each family or person was an autonomous unit and was not to be infringed upon. They were all protected from harm, from outside, and within. Whatever a man woman or child earned was theirs. It was their sense of personal and property rights.

By 15,000 BC large game animals were becoming scarce and drawings identifying hunted animals and its strategy that were sketched on stone walls was no longer needed. Tribes either followed some herds or settled in areas to tend plants and trees. They weren't always successful in farming because in most cases the soil became depleted and they had to move on. But along rivers such as the Tigress, Euphrates, and the Nile periodic fertile silt flooding replenished the fields annually, allowing permanent settlements to flourish, where they eventually developed agriculture and animal husbandry, which seemed to spread rapidly.

In time Cro-Magnon tribes developed animal grazing land and crop rights, i.e. property rights. Robert Lowie's, "Primitive Society", clearly shows that primitive communism did occur in specialized or particular instances but in very limited groups, and never completely or total in any society.

Lowie, '..Man, will consistently embrace the hypothesis that the property sense so highly developed with us was wholly or largely wanting in primitive society, that it must have evolved from its direct antithesis, communism in goods of every kind. This assumption is demonstrably false.' [1] Lowie shows, where some tribes may have shared food and tools, but was highly individualistic, respecting the earned property rights of an adult or child. Other groups such as joint ownership, often interpreted as communistic, was usually between partners or two brothers not unlike our own joint partner or ownership laws. In other cases they may have shared pastoral lands but had strict vegetation tending or growing rights. Poaching by anyone in their gardens, orchards or herds were mercilessly killed.

Chattel or movable property was clear; Lowie, 'complete individualism' and it included the women and children. Incorporeal rights 'reduces the dogma of a universal primitive communism to a manifest absurdity.' [2] Songs sung at gatherings, regardless of its popularity, no one dare, sing but the composer. Chants, a magic ritual or herbal formula to exorcise evil spirits by a Koryak woman, is hers only, and may be sold. Among the Kai poets were absolute owners of their compositions and could *sell* their rights.

Inheritance rights are so universal in all tribes, following either the matrilineal and patrilineal lineage that it is hard to find tribes without complex heritage laws. Now all these laws did not happen immediately, but evolved as a natural manifestation of their sense of freedom to own and since he had earned it was his to give away, preferably to those he valued and loved. He was becoming civilized. As we socialistically remove such rights we become more savage. Mankind lived for five million years in abject poverty, now in the agricultural paradigm he was creating prosperity reasoning that by earning his wealth he was moral and *his need for success was right and just.*

Primitive settlements prospered and a witch doctor's services became more and more expensive. He was soon the wealthiest in the tribe. The chief or head warrior like his people was probably also indebted. In some settlements its possible the chief and his warriors militarily, by force, controlled the Shaman from taking too much wealth from the people. But it seems the pharaohs or witch doctors had their way in Mid East and Egypt starting sometime in 8,000 BP. Where there was wealth, the fraudulent schemes began to multiply and spread rapidly in intensity and territorially like a cancer, which we never cured.

With the advent of farming came a profound personal change in the lives and love of their family. That change would be the love and care of their dead, and burial in order to be permanently near. Neanderthals occasionally buried their dead, but Cro-Magnon with a larger tribe was perhaps, inclined to stay in one place. But if the herd or game moved out or migrated, the transhumance of people in these times is well known. There were more burials and some were elaborate showing great love and care for their dead relatives, friends, and perhaps tribal leaders.

Agriculture resulted in settled villages and permanent shelters. In the chapter 'The Time of Settlement', in the book, "The Early History of the Near East, 9,000 to 2,000 BC," by Hans J. Nissen. 'At this site there were also numerous multiple burials mostly a collection of human bones buried inside the houses underneath benches for sitting or sleeping on, after the dead had presumably been left exposed for some period.' [3] Usually in burials of this sort, they buried the bones of dead ones on top of others with little in the way of grave goods, such as food, stone tools, or beads. It seems they were feeling, 'you need nothing, you are home, and we still love you and need something of you close to us always.'

When burials became fashion to build a separate room or tomb, outside or underground, say on 'boot hill,' when leaving them out there all alone with nothing seemed cruel and insensitive. They wanted to do something for their loving relative. They covered them with ochre to keep them *warm* as they did in life. Religious fanatics see red ochre as a primitive's means to represent blood, which only a savage mind could create such a horrible concept—his loved one covered in *blood?* Friends may have paid their debts, or gifts with cowrie shells. Their family dressed them in their finest wear and jewelry to indicate they would always remember them as they were in life and left them food to make them feel at home and loved dearly.

Once the primitive bought the shaman's idea that the dead lived, sort of, in dreams, the unconscious was conscious, the blind could see, the deaf could hear, and they became mentally incompetent to reject most of the obvious contradictions. The primitive did not 'buy it' for reason, but only, for what he felt emotionally, or what he wanted to hear. The shaman taught them that they would never die, and any attempt at reason or common sense by the primitive was challenged, to have faith, not think or reason, or for what does not make sense is sensible. The man who does not question or think is easily ruled. It is possible that there were religious rites beginning about 8,000 BP, which occurred, as the development of agriculture and animal husbandry became a source of wealth for witch doctors to exploit.

The religionist identifies almost every act especially in the execution of artifacts, beautifully decorated jardinieres, carved tools and art and artifacts of great beauty as having a spiritual (religious) motivation. People make things because they can think in the abstract or have imagination. They think it possible, due to their knowledge, and they can learn how to create new things. Robert Lowie, in "Primitive Religion," makes this observation; 'yet closer attention to the usage's of savage life demonstrates beyond the possibility of doubt that in grappling with the problems of every day life primitive man often employs precisely the same psychological processes of association, observation, and inference as our own farmers, engineers or craftsmen.' [4]

Man can think and create in his work, and is so motivated, but he became savage and inept, socially and in governance, following greedy leaders, unsuspecting of their motives, much like ourselves today. Perhaps, early Cro-Magnon experienced trust, that all were honorable men among men who could not in conscience betray his compatriot or fellow human being. Man has suffered the tragedy of our specie's betrayal, perhaps in self-defense the primitive turned savage, lost his land and was taxed one hundred percent of everything he earned, becoming the property of the pharaoh. He no longer could love his wife and family first, only the pharaoh, and his adult imaginary friend became primary in all things.

We know that Egypt and Mesopotamia around 7,000 BP, were evolving into successful agricultural societies, and the witch doctors were giving birth to burial cults of unimaginable proportions. They would destroy the tribal leader to make him their military commanders and by force, created large empires, which became the foundation for the *savage politics,* we have in the twenty-first century. We enter this millennium, by being the most ignoble species on earth, perhaps in the universe, because for the last 10,000 years, we should have known better.

CHAPTER 3

Rulers and Systems of Governments

Savage rulers use savage politics, to create savage governments and only a savage people will let them. We are at the mercy of rulers or do we as a majority join them to vote for ourselves and not for freedom?

The first rulers in history were Cro-Magnon, a clan or tribal chief in primitive times. As the first true secular ruler who, before any mysticism was introduced, guided, promoted, and was the planner for the welfare of the tribe. He was the original head of the family and then the leader of the extended family or clan. Later Cro-Magnon man as we learned, was helping to combine families into tribes, to create a new technology that succeeded in big game hunting, and perhaps functioning as a mentor and respected as a fair mediator in disputes.

The next ruler was the pharaoh witch doctor or medicine man, who came into being after 10,000 BP. He succeeded through fakery and greed to wrestle leadership from the tribal chief who became subordinated to the witch doctor, pharaoh, as a henchman, or his military commander. The tribal chief or military commander, if powerful enough, could be anointed, making him a true representative of a god, a pharaoh, and later in Asia an emperor, king, or an apostolic pope of the holy see. It gave a 'holy' king complete theocratic jurisdiction, over a country and its citizens (serfs). He *owned* all the land, the economy, the people and controlled their culture (their minds).

The king is not alone, his partners in crime are the lords and barons who control large land tracts under the domain of the king in the name of some god. "His Majesty's" law is the law of a god and to go against the king is to go against their god. His lords rule with the king also as a power of their god and addressed as "My Lord." The lords duty towards the king's for his benevolence, allowing them to rule over his land, are required to supply the fighting force in defense of the king and his realm. In Egypt's time of the pharaohs the first crack appeared in pharaoh rule and changed the idea of gods.

In Egypt the military, through the pharaoh's enrichment by confiscating the wealth of African nations by warfare, also became a great force in society. When the Eighteenth Dynasty became extinct, three military generals took over the throne in succession. One threw out the Egyptian priests from the temples picking replacements from his army thus taking over the greatest source of wealth in the economy. In principle the secular government used the same methods, organizations and idea of loyalty to the god in the devotion to the state and dictator. This gave rise to military rulers such as Alexander the Great, Caesar, Octarian, Augustus, Gengiis Khan, and Attilla the Hun.

The dictator if secular, will embrace some form of socialism or fascism, and may rule with religions in his nation, as was the case

JSS

with Nazi Germany. But Hitler understood and used theocratic methods. "Ominous Parallels," by Leonard Peikoff, 'Hitler—admired the church. He admired not its teaching but their methods, "its knowledge of human nature" its hierarchical organization, its discipline, "its uncommonly clever tactics". One of its cleverest tactics, he believed, is its unyielding dogmatism.' [5] Using Peikoff's appropriate reference:

> Herman Rausching author of "The Voice of Destruction:" "I have followed (the church)" Hitler told Rauschning: "In giving our party program the character of unalterable finality, like the creed, the church has never allowed the creed to be interfered with. It is fifteen hundred years since it was formulated, but every suggestion for its amendment, every logical criticism or attack on it, has been rejected. The church has realized that anything and everything can be built up on a document of that sort, no matter how contradictory or irreconcilable with it. The faithful will swallow it whole, so long as logical reasoning is never allowed to be brought to bear on it." [6]

Peikoff—'Seventeen centuries earlier, Tertullian, one of the church fathers, had explained that religion by it's nature requires the subversion of reason, the belief in the irrational *because* it is irrational. He had delivered a ringing anti reason manifesto, declaring in regard to the dogma of a god's self sacrifice on the cross: "It is believable, because it is absurd; it is certain, because it is impossible."' [7] As such, it is intellectually dishonest and embraced by savages.

Socialists are vulnerable to the pressures of ambition to control, and like the religious ruler's attempt to perpetrate their power they build monuments, expand the power city, art projects, NASA space, statues, libraries, parks, stadiums, and free medical care, all to immortalize then selves with power using the people's wealth. We can see it is the 'pharaoh' all over again. Totalitarian secular/religious governing in a culture means walking a fine line at times. When it happens the leader soon learns the Machivellian 'ethic' must apply in order to maintain his power.

Specifically; Niccolo Machiavelli, in his advice to rulers in "The Prince and the Discourses":

> 'Know, then, are two methods of fighting, the one by law, the other the other by force: the first method is that of men, the second of beasts; but as the first method is often insufficient, one must have recourse to the second.' . . . 'But it is necessary to be able to disguise this character well,' . . . 'and men are so simple and so ready to obey present necessities, that one who deceives will always find those who allow themselves to be deceived.' . . . 'It is not, therefore, necessary for a prince to have all the above named, qualities but it is necessary to seem to have them. I would even be so bold to say that to possess them and always to observe them is dangerous, but to appear to possess them is useful. Thus it is well to seem merciful, faithful, humane, sincere, religious and also to be so; but you must have the mind so disposed that when it is needful to be otherwise you may be able to change to the opposite qualities. And it must be understood that a prince, and especially a new prince, cannot observe all those things which are considered good in men, being often obliged, in order to maintain the state, to act against faith, against charity, against humanity, and against religion. And, therefore, he must have a mind disposed to adapt itself according to the wind, and as the variations of fortune dictate, and, as I said before, not deviate from what is good, if possible, but be able to do evil if constrained.' [8]

Surely, since Machiavelli wrote 'The Prince' in 1513, rulers who aspire to power, raw or cooked, have read it, understood, and practice the principles he set forth. Once control is achieved of a nation, whether by force, coup, or influence of the vote of one group over the other, a political elite is created. When a ruler gains power—the power to tax and spend is theirs. But it is the 'poor innocent' who truly believes in the king's god and every word becomes sacred in his benevolence. And his counterpart the 'poor innocent' who truly believes the socialist leaders will create a perfect utopia. The 'poor innocent' becomes the first victim to feel the wrath of a kingdom or state because if it is not perfect, he will be the first to critique and first to die. However, if such is spotted early enough, he may never get a chance to complain.

An example of a 'poor innocent' may be Margaret Thatcher, former Prime Minister of England. She appeared to most of us, as a no nonsense secular leader who favored a free state, which to many, is in direct opposition to the tenets of most religions. But Thatcher in a speech at Hillsdale College, in March 1995, was totally, a religious commitment. She quoted John Adams, our second president who may have been a pure innocent, who said in 1789, 'Our constitution was designed only for a moral and religious people. It is wholly inadequate for the government of any other.' [9] She implies, constitutionally, only the religious are moral and those who do not totally accept its religious doctrines are immoral, by quoting Adams. Note that England is a theocracy, and has a queen. However, Thatcher did not do her homework.

In 1789 there were still states that had yet to ratify the constitution and Adams may have been attempting to sell it (in 1789) with a religious spin. But the people were extremely disappointed that the framers rejected a specific 'Bill of Rights.' Thomas Jefferson who was in France was also shocked that the Constitution did not contain a Bill of Rights. Under voter pressure, the first congress, later, drew up a Bill of Rights in 1789 that became law in 1791. What framers thought was not important the American people did,—so far as the people were concerned, was their highest priority, because in the very first amendment,—Rodell, 'In one sentence, it guaranteed more to the ordinary citizen than did the whole seven articles of the original constitution.' [10] In the very first phrases, in the very first sentence, of the very First Amendment, forbade-'Congress shall make no law respecting an establishment of religion, or the free exercise thereof;'

The, leaders created a true secular document (they hoped), to the chagrin of all religions ever since. And dear to the hearts of all, it continues, 'or abridging the freedom of speech or of the press; or the right of the people peaceably to assemble, and to petition the government for a redress of grievances.' (The Constitution of the United States, Amendment, I.)

In Thatcher's enthusiasm for the absolutism of a 'new-world order,' she yearns for a 'single international democracy' (The UN.). Her religious principles would give that body theocratic power—Thatcher would have a pharaoh rule the world. [11]

We go back to the pharaoh to analyze how he ran his country and what made him successful. What can we learn about his system of governing?

The Pharaoh's control from 6,000 to 3100 BC, was in a struggle for supremacy in southern and northern Egypt by regional rulers or medicine men cults. Between 4,000 and 3,000 BC; Michael Hoffman, explains in, "Egypt Before The Pharaohs," 'Through the centuries the changes that did occur were gradual—almost imperceptible—as new ideas about wealth, power and the afterlife slowly filtered through their society.' [12] In the south and north, consolidation of mortuary cults had created two rulers and kingdoms. The south was advanced having fancier tombs and greater wealth. In 3100 BC the southern ruler Menes (sometimes referred to as Mena) marched from the south conquering the north. Thus, the first major conflict in human history was religious, between the god Horus of the south, and the god Set of the north.

In Egypt, Hoffman shows us, that it is unlikely that population pressure, competition for agricultural resources or trade would cause war. It was 'their way of death', 'their religion was tied to it . . . their system of rank and status.' Armed conflict was due to any threat to the power elite to dominate the agricultural wealth and minds of followers and, to 'bury themselves in bigger and better tombs—that ultimately brought on conflict.' 'A concomitant of power is an elite'. [13] It was a war of social values and poor ones at that. Man's intellect fell from the reasoning of a primitive, to faith, and led into slavery by superstition and savagery.

In Egypt, the deception was, 'death led into an afterlife where gods assigned to the deceased the due portion of water for the cultivation of his Elysian field.' [14] They told people that, if the body existed 'mummified,' with a wealth of funerary goods, the gods would bestow favors upon the god-king. Unity of Horus and Set caused religious wars from the first dynasty to 2700 BC when Khasekhemui consolidated his conquests by wedding a northern queen Nemathap who mothered future founders of the Third Dynasty. Dynasties were ruling royal families, by which inheritance may be matrilineal or patrilineal. It was to imply legitimacy, but in effect was to cement political alliances.

Judging from the monumental building displays, confiscation of wealth by the ruling elite, and the building of elaborate tombs illustrates clearly the success rate of force by despotic dynasty after dynasty and their noble supporters. It is said that inventions travels rapidly from culture to culture, and so did the invention of death rites and kingship. 'Thai, Balinese, and Berawan' funerary 'are analogous to death rites . . . as in Archaic Egypt.' [15] We can see the parallels in the popes, kings, queens, emperors, and in 'democratic' socialistic leaders as history repeats itself on earth in century after century, right into this millennium.

For living rulers, the burial supported their pseudo-inheritance rights to the throne. Temples and shrines were built near the tomb, so that the populace might be given time off for devotion to the despot, who, to an exhausted tomb laborer welcomed much needed rest and a festival to honor a pharaoh, said to be a god. 'For example, the tomb of Djer at Abydos was believed by later Dynastic Egyptians to be the tomb of Orisis god of the afterlife, and attracted thousands of pilgrims.' [16] This is analogous to church fathers today creating saints and celebrating them in an annual parade or festival.

The Dynasties in Egypt and Mesopotamia maintained power by the forces of the king. The key to absolute control lay in economic technique. This need to control inventories in the graineries, other foods, and their distribution, led to recording in symbols to identify economic products and quantities. These records called 'writing' began sometime before 3100 BC Nissen and Hoffman place writing on cylinder seals in the late period (3200 BC) or possibly earlier. This is empirical evidence of excessive taxation and the rise of the totalitarian state, as the following will illustrate.

The cylinder seal is similar to a wax seal, used in the past, to seal an envelope or letter. Such cylinder seals were stone cylinders with a hole bored through length wise with an engraved surface to identify the owner (an individual such as a noble), the state, or its ruling branch. Both are easily identifiable in that the 'individual' or a noble's seals were more figurative and made with extreme attention to detail. The 'collective' state seals were more abstract and in greater numbers with barely distinguishing patterns. The seal would be rolled over a pliable still soft fast drying clay that sealed a jar, rope fastening a door to a storage room, or any means to insure against tampering. [17]

In real estate, what is primary is location, location, location. With an absolute ruler it is control, control, control—the control of his elite with reward, the control of his people's minds in their death fantasies, and to control their wealth. It was through the scribes that the pharaoh maintained control over the united lands of Egypt who was its sole owner. 'As in Mesopotamia, every government transaction was recorded in writing. Scribes accompanied marching soldiers, scribes counted crops, scribes recorded monthly inspections of sacred utensils in every temple and even registered wicks made of old rags used for work inside royal tombs' [18] The higher nobles and officials 'admonishing the lower scribes to work with utmost zeal.' [19]

The soldiers were rewarded. 'They were "drunk and anointed with oil every day as at a feast in Egypt." What were the concerns for the simple peasant toilers of Egypt? 'But documents show that the bastinado and the shout of the taskmaster "The rod is in my hand, be not idle!" [20]

A ruler's motive depends on the available wealth he may control, and will bastardize any form of government for himself, his administrator's and supporter's or party's ends. This replicates to every form of government there is today. Rulers may think a government's success depends on a mix of secular and religious law. But it creates theocratic discrimination and chaos among the hundreds of religious sects in the world today. Each planning to destroy the other with *no possible political solution*, except to force all sects and cults to be territorially separate. As such, it may appear to be in keeping with the individual nature of people, but religiously, individual human nature is savaged and poverty inevitable because such people are held hostage by guilt. Yet on the other hand, for melting pots, *a just moral secular system of moral law* for theists and atheists alike, may prevent savage rulers, savage governments, savage politics, or savage citizens, and be fair for everyone. What is a right and good system of government? Can we recreate the primitive essence of the primitive Cro-Magnon's philosophy in governing?

We are a little 'free' and the wealthiest nation on earth and we are in debt far in excess than any family or corporation could mortgage in a good managed bank. If the bank saw that we could not live within our means and we borrowed every year and could only pay the interest they would foreclose, or get us on a budget. Also, if you or I had put up collateral, up front, in excess of everything borrowed, they would not foreclose until we reached the limit—the total of the collateral pledged. Our collateral is all of our future taxes and savings and our country's infrastructure, plants and equipment, homes and real estate. They have done nothing to safeguard our nation's wealth and if we go bankrupt our credit or credibility, as an economic giant will be lost for generations—Egypt never recovered and Russia may not. It is the system of governing that is wrong and immoral, and those who govern do understand economic values but have a Machiavellian 'ethical' sense of leadership. It is a world-wide condition.

There are, basically, two types of political systems 'collectivism' or 'individualism.' In *every* vote we cast we vote for one or the other. Every vote we do not cast is a vote for collectivism, i.e. slavery. I leave that for you to ponder.

Fig. 1., the COLLECTIVE is on left, and the INDIVIDUAL is on the right. Therefore, at the extreme ends of the political spectrum, the one on the left is called COMMUNISM, and the one on the right is called ANARCHY. Both lack government controls.

```
                              Fig 1.
                 COLLECTIVISM & INDIVIDUALISM

Collective                                               Individual
---------------------------------+---------------------------------
Communism                      CENTER                       Anarchy
```

All political systems fall between these two points. It is reasonable to state both above are opposites and therefore not a circle as many seem to believe. They are at the extreme ends of cultural or economic value systems. They represent the two political extremes of *no* government control. It follows then, that the *center* of the line is *total government control*, Fig. 2., i.e. equidistant from each extreme they are expressed as the *left* and *right*. The primitive nomadic clan for five million years lived in a complete state of anarchy, of individualism ("I"), or freedom (anarchy) until Cro-Magnon 40,000 years ago when they organized the first tribes of extended and/or different clans.

```
                              Fig. 2.
                       THE LEFT & THE RIGHT

                                                Cro-Magnon Tribe---
                                                    Primitive clans
LEFT                        Total Control                     RIGHT
"C"------------------------------+------------------------------"I"
Communism                      CENTER                       Anarchy
No Controls                                             No Controls
```

The ultimate 'ideal' in collectivism ("C") or communism is the citizen to have a collectively politically correct mental attitude, to create the broadest cultural synergistic behavior or ability and to each, receive an equal distribution of survival needs. That is, a person to be a true collectivist, *has no personal goals*, i.e. *no individual* hierarchy of values, but his hierarchy is the maximum effort physically or mentally in working for the group or collective. This is reaching the 'ethical ideal' or 'their moral' equivalent of complete self-sacrifice for their fellow man. From whatever is produced each may receive according to their need. Implied, in true self-sacrifice, is the *minimum* needed for existence, simply put, it is usually quoted as, "From each, according to his ability, to each, according to his need." However, as a political system it has *never* been successful. In primitive times there may have been many opportunities for communism to evolve, but for lack of humane reasons it never did. The primitive maintained his individuality in *anarchy*.

The principles of collectivism were created by the witch doctor. There was only one way the Pharaoh could tax or take the maximum amount of wealth out of the hands of the common man—that was to make sure what was left was equally distributed. The cry of the pharaoh became "share (what's left) your bounty (?) with your fellow man. If he needs help (don't ask me) extend *your* hand and heart to him, help others, as you would like to be helped." And to make sure one did not covet possessions, as the pharaoh might want, "Do not be materialistic when your fellow man is in need," i.e., materialism is evil. But, the pharaoh did not want communism, only after *his and his retainer's* cut, did he enforce communistic principles.

To be continually successful the pharaoh, or any government, must always take as much as will cause poverty, a guarantee of perpetuating altruism. Neither did Russian leaders, nor does China, or any other 'communistic,' or theocratic country, ever want wealthy poor people. They do not suffer or feel the need to sacrifice to a leader. Rulers would have no support of the wealthy poor—to create the perception of leading the poor to a death better than life, or for some Utopia for their grandchildren.

In the last 5,000 years we've heard the same cry, the same 'ethical' message to help others. Whether is it to support the king, queen, emperor, dictator, or democratic 'nation building' the same notions are present today. Those systems of government whether they are democratic, fascist, Nazi, or socialist, to guarantee the maximum in taxes or confiscation of the wealth, they must use the pharaoh's principles—'hey! They work.' If they make people feel guilty about owning material things, happiness, more sex, or anything, then it becomes a mental power tool to make people feel guilty for not paying tithe or taxes. All religious and secular governments use the same tactics as the pharaoh, so their elitism can last for their lifetime, and if possible, leave that legacy to *their* children, not yours or mine.

Two people, who thought communism possible, were Karl Marx and Frederick Engels. Although its not known, it seems they thought socialism had a shorter distance to communism than the distance to primitive individualistic anarchy. The distances from socialism, complete political and social control, to anarchy and communism are equal. In 'distance', I mean the distance man must go, from anarchy to communism, *to change his nature*. Every government has been on the right side of the centerline and that is very revealing in that it shows that the pull to change man's nature is from the right—individualism only. If he were naturally communistic it is obvious the totalitarian center would be pulling governments formed on the left to the center. The farther to the right from the center we struggle to throw off the bonds of the state assures us that we will be living in our natural state as individuals, become a success at what we choose and where we will be the happiest. And all man needs from government is justice, nothing more and nothing less.

Marx and Engels also believed that the common man would welcome communism. They perhaps believed, as 'poor innocents,' that self sacrifice was a moral ideal, or did they think it was man's nature to be collective. Or were they just creating an intellectual scam for fame or money? Obviously, in any case, they were wrong and naive on both theories. They thought that after complete control over every facet of the economy was established the culture would be free of class distinctions. '...after all production has been concentrated in the hands of a vast association of the whole nation, the public power will lose its political character,' [21] (it is usually referred to as—'the state would whither away,'—when all would be of one mind and purpose—like ants.).

Well, Karl Marx's theory got its test in Soviet Russia. They had over 70 years of opportunity. Virtually isolated from the democratic nations they had every chance to show the world the state would wither away and the poor would prosper. Most of the world was theocratic, socialistic and democratically sympathetic. Yet it became the largest most immoral killing machine of their own people the world has ever seen to *eliminate individualism*, and failing miserably. They never took one step toward communism. By all indications Lenin never meant to, by calling the new Russian union of countries, 'The Union of Soviet *Socialist* Republics' (USSR) not *Communist*. They knew they were holding people against their *will and nature*, and were paranoid in their fear that other nations would set them free. But nations would not infringe on a sovereign power, nor was there a moral necessity to do so.

```
                                Fig 3.
                        THE TOTALITARIAN STATE

                           TOTALITARIANISM
                             The Pharaoh
                               A King
                              Theocracy
                              Socialism
                            Dictatorship
                                                      Cro-Magnon Tribe---
                                                          Primitive Clans
 -------To less control                            To less control-------
"C"-----------------------------------+---------------------------------"I"
Communism                                                          Anarchy
No control                         Total                        No Control
                                  Control
```

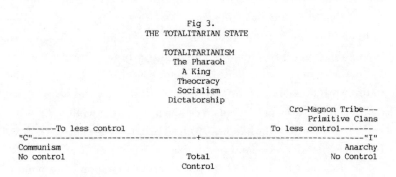

Total control of human life and wealth in political science, is a theocracy (pharaoh, monarchy), or socialism, either one may be referred to as a totalitarian state. All governments gravitate towards anarchy, for more individual freedom, and none gravitate towards communism. On the anarchy side of the center—line is where all known government systems have been created. It is the individual side, from anarchy (primitive clans) on towards the center a gradual reduction of political and socioeconomic freedom and individualism is traded for increasing state control, Fig. 3. To go towards the right reduces the size of the state and that is the last thing any totalitarian regime would permit. Therefore, coming from the left, or more likely from the right as they are pulled to the center, increasing force is required to maintain control over its citizens. To keep one in the center requires the ultimate force, usually at the point of a gun or within an Iron Curtain.

If governments were created on the collective side of the center of the line, and they proceeded from communism on towards the center, a gradual reduction of no control or collectivism, less collective freedom is traded for increasing state government control.

Human nature is just the opposite that of an ant because he is highly individuated and animated intellectually, where the ant is perhaps more physically motivated with a brain wholly functioning metaphysically, with no or low EQ, and IQ. We can not create a collective 'ant-like human,' any more than we create an individual 'human-like ant,' and if it were possible to do this to mankind it would be unnatural, inhumane, and immoral.

Reviewing pre-history, primitive man, five million years ago to 45,000 or 35,000 BP was essentially single family, or perhaps two or three related families who lead a nomadic existence. As we learned, they were by their nature, individualistic. Communistic practices may have appeared to happen in some situations but it was never complete. More likely, in some cases the family head or male was dominant or possibly, dictatorial. But with the critical need for food, new strategies every day, the best thing to do was to let all go out on their own, and see who was smart enough to bring home the bacon. If a group strategy was required, any suggestion as to how one might proceed that day was welcomed. That doesn't occur in a bureaucracy even a small one. We may assume individual anarchy was present among all clans, each with some influence, but never completely. This is the key to creating a system of government, as we shall see ahead.

Cro-Magnon after 30,000 to 15,000 BP moved the families from anarchy to control over a few more families. As the leader in control, he guaranteed the tribe family and individuals autonomy, safety, property rights, and redress for wrongs. He was the planner and *promoted* the success of the clans. This system of government was just a little to the left of anarchy. From there sometime after 10,000

BP Cro-Magnon lost control to the witch doctor and by 5100 BP the pharaoh, Menes, had unified Egypt. They were at the center with a huge totalitarian theocracy that lasted about 3,000 years, which tells us that once they have control it is improbable you will ever be free again.

The structural and administrative form of government was the pharaoh and his nobles. The nobles supported his policies to oversee the craftsmen, and scribes in the land areas they were assigned, and controlled the distribution of supplies. The military commanded the forced labor gangs to build tombs when not invading some hapless nation, or projects to irrigate and increase production for the pharaoh. Most government systems are similar whereby the structure guarantees control in tax collection and distribution of the wealth. Kings, queens, emperors, czars, dictators, republics and democracies have this basic structure.

In a democracy or republic we have a president, state governor, city mayors, and town managers not satisfied with that level of control we've added county governments/managers (middle managers) which is the most wasteful. At the head we've allowed the federal government to create bureaucracies for control of taxation, commerce, labor, health, welfare, education, medical care, social security, FDA., N.E.A., NASA, and actually, hundreds of other bureaus creating the largest government bureaucracy, ever, in the world. In our federal government alone, there are eighteen million people. Socialist countries such China, North Korea, and Mid East monarchies, are replicas in principle of the Egyptian dynastic rule. China is now becoming a fascist state, moving slightly to the right economically, to keep from going broke and to stay in power, regulating the economy and dictating cultural values.

Our trip through the centuries involved mostly complete control at the center by royalists, socialism or fascism to some degree. Religious leaders in all history lent their support to secular rulers, because that was where the wealth was controlled. As the socialist elite experimented with the limits of power tended to pull the citizen towards the center of complete control with their forms of government, in a position theocracies coveted. Here is how they stack up in a chart.

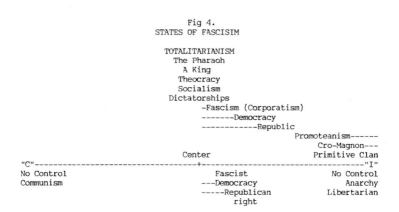

```
                                    Fig 4.
                              STATES OF FASCISIM

                                TOTALITARIANISM
                                  The Pharaoh
                                    A King
                                   Theocracy
                                   Socialism
                                 Dictatorships
                                       -Fascism (Corporatism)
                                       -------Democracy
                                       ------------Republic
                                                         Promoteanism------
                                                              Cro-Magnon---
                                  Center                 Primitive Clan
"C"---------------------------------+----------------------------------"I"
No Control                              Fascist              No Control
Communism                              ---Democracy             Anarchy
                                       -----Republican       Libertarian
                                            right
```

Fig. 4. is showing where Fascism is placed from the center of total control. Fascist Democracy is where USA is approaching that of Nazi Germany and Fascist Italy.

Fascism is the least understood, and the most covered up of all systems of government. One doesn't find it listed in many of the older dictionaries. Some define it as a dictatorship regimenting all industry and commerce fostering nationalism and racism, etc. Fascism is a socialistic form of government that allows business activity that is heavily regulated. It allows ownership of business, industry and commercial trade by the grace of law and regulation of the ruling faction called political corporatism. It is in complete control of all or social institutions to control people's lives from the cradle to the grave. Although credited to be a form of government established by Benito Mussolini in Italy, forms of it have existed for a very long time. Mussolini identified it and gave it a name, Fascism, and Hitler his, Nazism.

Mussolini, when a reporter asked, "Why not nationalize all business and industry?" To paraphrase, he replied, "Why should I when I can control the businessman by my laws and regulations." In effect, any government (not necessarily a dictatorship—even a democracy) can create a fascist state. That is why business people loudly resist price controls, market interference, export quotas, types of goods, or control of commerce.

Today, our own democracy is very close to being a Fascist state and will not give up control by resisting privatization of socialistic institutions which are government monopolies, such as education, utilities, railroads, post offices, and hundreds more. Zoning, commercial, labor, gun laws building codes, now sports stadiums, and hundreds of other laws controlling our economy create our fascist system of government. The bureaucratic drive to implement an 'industrial policy' *is* fascism. Fascism is *not* an extreme right wing government, but an extreme to the left, and only one step away from, socialism—one law away from totalitarian total control, nationalizing all business, see Fig. 4. You have to admire their strategy—the cover up—intent–it is immoral—we are not free.

Elements of Fascism were permitted and evident in early Egypt when the pharaohs allowed some craftsman or traders free to profit but under his watchful eye of law. And some rulers through history allowed or even financed some projects for merchants, maritime traders, rail transport, etc. to profit from a new idea, and subsequently take control for himself and his heirs.

In South America the *dictators* of 'Banana Republics' actually own all major business and allow few small businesses to exist by way of heavy control and taxes. Control over businesses, farm subsidies, space programs, disarming the citizenry, etc., is a sign of entrenched elements of Fascism, a sure route to a totalitarian state. A dictatorship was evident in the way Nazi Germany built its huge war machine by their 'industrial policy' imposed on their major corporations, to use state resources for social and military control that would otherwise be used for micro-managing corporations and production.

Our understanding of Fascism gives us a clue as to how we are losing our freedoms, by vote. Hitler came to power with the acquiescence of the people. We are voting ourselves social programs for the express purpose of reducing economic and social responsibility for ourselves. More recent, some liberal socialists are trying to create legislation to limit a corporation's CEO's income. What we call democratic in today's political context is very close and can be called Fascism. It is the Fascist road to socialism and in republican ideology a theocracy. Their new strategy, using Fascism for an ultimate totalitarian government, is creeping up and voters do not suspect. We are voting for Fascism a socialistic state and make no mistake they know what they are doing, but we don't. Our government wants socialism, and we think they are just being benevolent. I believe that Hitler had some admiration for Mussolini because he correctly identified and made the distinction of Fascism apparent for an interim last step to a complete a totalitarian police state.

All the above assumes that Fascism socialism/communism, theocracies, democracy's liberal left or republican religious right or any form of collectivism is a 'moral ideal' in governing. This religious collective concept is hung on to desperately, to continue elite systems of rule, not for the common man's salvation, but for theirs here on earth. There is only one overriding reason why any kind of collective is impossible, and that is because it is diametrically opposed to human nature and human values, and our opportunist nature, gets us to believe we may get something for nothing.

Thomas Jefferson, on theocracies, in a letter to a friend, "The mass of mankind has not been born with saddles on their backs, nor a favored few born booted and spurred ready to ride them legitimately by the grace of God." (Socialism, by the grace of the state)

CHAPTER 4

The Magna Carta & The Colonists

The republic or republican philosophy in a sense, was the direct result of the Magna Carta. The 'Great Charter', as it became known, and King John signed it at Runnymede in 1215. England at that time was made up of lords, barons, or earls and the king who had granted them power over the lands they controlled. The king was anointed by the church (the approval of the pope, etc.) granting him power over his lands in the Roman Empire. This was important for a king for it meant a guarantee of inheritance of his heirs (sons, etc.). His Royal Highness being included in the deity, established law, and his became the word of a god. To take any action against the king (deity) was sin or against a god. Many lords and barons by this time, either through inheritance or intermarriage to landholders on mainland Europe (barons), or Norman invaders became 'lords,' and held lands.

The barons at Runnymede in 1215, with grievances against King John for excessive taxation, misconduct, and unscrupulous dealing with lords and barons drew up the Magna Carta. In some 60 clauses it specified freedom to worship, trial by jury, ordered fish weirs (nets) on the Thames and Medway and all rivers except from seashore abolished, set standards for weights and measures, specify fair rates of compensation for military obligations, numerous inheritance rights, and freedom from excessive taxation. It was a community of lord's, or baron's list of grievances. It was their wealth and freedom, initially, in question. However, without any intention, it was felt or interpreted that the Magna Carta implied that it had included or applied as rights for all citizens in England.

The Magna Carta's implication however, split the king and the barons politically, since King John thought it could reduce his power and control considerably. John was furious. King John signed the document, but never with the intention of abiding by its principles and hastily wrote to the pope of the event that took place. The church who was building ever larger cathedrals along side ever larger castles and fortresses possibly thought they might go the way of the king, and pope Innocent may have thought (the church) would become irrelevant. Three months after the signing of Magna Carta in June of 1215 the pope condemned the Magna Carta. However, within that three month period the efficient king's chancery had penned copies of the Magna Carta, and had found their way outside John's bureaucracy, and the *idea* to guarantee the liberties of Englishmen was born. But it never happened.

Today, 'the United Kingdom, alone amongst the worlds advanced democracies, is without a written constitution.'

> 'Under certain management, Westminister, which boasts itself the mother of parliaments, is liable to extend the metaphor towards an absolute and hectoring matriarchy. But in any case while parliament is sovereign there is no appeal against parliamentary oppression. Where the barons at Runnymede devised a novel instrument to limit the power of a king and where an American theorist can trace the very concept of human rights as it is understood today back to the Magna Carta itself, Britain today has no appeal against a power more absolute than John's.' 'The crown in parliament, since 1688 supreme, combines in a single autocrat the two opposed powers which in former times acted as a counter-balance to each other. Constitutional theory provides for the vote of the people, expressed at a general election, to oust any regime, which is deemed to act against the general interest. But unfortunately, since British parliaments are habitually elected on a minority vote and since, in theory at least parliament could extend its term, there would in the last resort, be nothing—no supreme court,—no written constitution—to maintain free institutions.'(1990). [22]

The king or queen is still 'anointed' by the church and by the grace of an inherited royalty still confers parliament with an, '..Absolute sovereignty over the laws themselves (yea, over Magna Carta and all other objected acts), to repeal alter, determine and suspend where there is cause, as is undeniably its altering the very common law in many cases.' [23]

The American Colonists: What was unique and should be

everlasting about the Magna Cart was not its written content (some of which survives in U.S. and other constitutions) but its essence being, that a government was accountable, ultimately, to the people. The New World colony revolt began as to redress wrongs by the British Crown, of taxation, and resistance to grant a measure of autonomy in their colonies. The Republican Party in this country, dominated by the 'religious right,' may today side with the queen and are exchanging their 'republic' for a 'theocracy.'

In 1774 The House of Burgess (a royal body) representatives from each of the colonies, in Virginia passed a resolution of sympathy for the closing the port of Boston as 'suffering in cause.' The Royal Governor of Virginia dissolved the House of Burgess. An angry group from The House met at the Raleigh Tavern, in Williamsburg, Virginia on May 27, 1774, recommending an annual congress, to include one delegate from each of the thirteen colonies, forming the First Continental Congress.

The new Continental Congress adjourned in October 1774, again in May of 1775, and no resolution with the Crown—in April of 1775 the minute men fought the first battle of the War of the Revolution. The Congress appointed George Washington, Commander in Chief of the American Army, thereby, declaring war against Great Britain. The colonists did not see it as one for independence, but a civil war.

However, a brilliant publication 'Common Sense' by Thomas Pain, won thousands to the cause for independence and became a moving force. The time had come to act and make a declaration to be free. On June 7, 1776 Richard Henry Lee of Virginia, an advocate of independence stood before Congress and offered three resolutions. "That these United Colonies are, and of right ought to be, free and independent states, that they are absolved from all allegiance to the British Crown and that all political connections between them and the State of Great Britain is, and ought to be totally dissolved." That idea became, on July 4, 1776, a Declaration of Independence, authored by Thomas Jefferson, ' . . . that all men are created equal with certain unalienable rights that among these are Life, Liberty and the Pursuit of Happiness. That to secure these rights, Governments are instituted among men, deriving them just powers from the consent of the governed.'

'That whenever any Form of Government becomes destructive of these ends, is in the Right of the People to alter or abolish it, and to institute new Government, laying its foundation on such principles and organizing its powers in such form, as to them shall seem most likely to effect their Safety and Happiness.' [24] The Declaration continued, citing prudence in governing, and cautioning against our own despotism or abuse of powers.

The rest of the Declaration of Independence lists the grievances against the King of Great Britain. The revolution continued by the will of people who fought for the freedom from the tyranny of a ruler who thought, that he owned all the land, the citizens, and their wealth with no recourse to any grievances. In America the absolute power of kings, popes, and pharaohs was coming to an end, or was it?

The Revolution that began at Lexington and Concord on April 19, 1775, ended at Yorktown when Washington and the allied forces of sixteen thousand trapped Cornwallis's army of eight. Cornwallis surrendered on October 19, 1781. The articles of the peace treaty were signed in Paris November 30, 1782, was accepted by England and ratified by the U.S. Congress on September 3, 1783. It had taken six years of war. We were, freer than any people on earth and of those who had existed for the last 10,000 years of theocratic and socialistic governments.

With the war over, the people's government was a federation of states where all thirteen held a large measure of autonomy and many differences. It was a loose Congress of state representatives, with no real head of the government. The 55 men who met in Philadelphia in the summer of 1787, 'to make some minor changes in, The Articles of Confederation, but they quickly decided to draft a whole new document, a constitution that would establish a strong national government.' [25]

Rhode Island had refused to send delegates wary of larger states that may take away their powers. 'And of the men appointed by the other states seven felt as strongly . . . Patrick Henry, who saw in the business of the convention a threat to liberty he prized so highly.' [26] But, there were those who wanted a strong central government such as Alexander Hamilton the leading figure in calling the convention. He wanted a strong national central government modeled after the British. He thought it the best in the world. He liked the idea of a King—or a president for life and the poor would have no vote. A convention made up of two extreme views would become a compromise. Their fears of giving a national government too much power, was justified. When it was over, unknown to all, they had given the store away.

The delegate's greatest accomplishment, has been those articles that created the separations of powers, the Congress, Judicial, and Executive branches. Although they limited the time of the terms they did not limit the terms, considered a cap on political entrenchment. They had not been specific about the rights of people under the constitution and this was corrected quickly with the ratification of the Bill of Rights.

The constitution's First Amendment; The freedom of religion, and speech—the second; There was the right to bear arms, and so on, ten amendments in all. But most of the framers understood law, and knew anything that was *not* in the constitution was a right. A constitution should be a document that specifies a government's structure and its code, i.e. its limits of authority and its means to protect the rights of citizens.

States had established churches some Protestant, denominational, and Catholic. But American revolutionaries knew that established churches were a threat to freedom. 'As the Americans understood history, churches had entered into an unholy alliance with tyrannical governments to crush these ideas. Priests (and ministers) taught passive obedience and unthinking subservience to governments in order to receive in return *state-enforced tithes*. To insure freedom and the free circulation of ideas, this alliance had to be broken and establishments ended.' [27] The First Amendment prevailed, with Massachusetts the last to de-establish religion in 1833 and its tithe was no longer a part of any state's tax law.

The constitution is the people's rule of law. That all laws enacted must fall within these general or specified rules which are fundamental in guiding lawmakers. In "Understanding the Constitution" by Jack Walter Peltason, 'People create government for the purpose of securing their pre-existing natural rights. The rights come first, that government is created to protect these rights,' 'Locke argued that even in a state of nature there was a natural law to govern conduct. This natural law, comprising universal, unvarying principles of right and wrong and was known to people through the use of reason.' [28] However, in Locke's 'Law of Nature', he held, that the law rests ultimately, on Gods will. Since there are no gods who may tell us directly of a god's will, then men fantasize mythically that presence, or to imagine 'ultimate law' is where our senses and reason fail. Locke was insightful above concerning the creating of government 'pre-existing natural rights' and the morality of right and wrong and the government's role to 'protect rights' all known through reason. But, reason had failed him when he assigned the ultimate law to a god's will.

This is the dilemma that ethics presents in natural law to reconcile a value, altruism, with a moral right for autonomy, it seems like Locke and others gave up on reality to embrace mythology, and were never able to morally define *natural* law.

In Article 3 section 8 of our Constitution which gave Congress the power '..to lay taxes . . . uniform throughout the United States, . . . to regulate commerce among the several states . . . to borrow money . . . ', is where they gave the store away. The politicians act, in the interest to *provide* the 'greatest good for the greatest number', to have unselfish concern for others (altruism), and that those ends justify any means, such as unfair taxation to redistribute wealth by legislation, regulate commerce—business, labor, land, and every area of our socioeconomic lives. The Article, has been interpreted as meaning that the government goal is for some indefinable 'public good', and has been upheld by our, 'secular,' Supreme Court.

Today the trend of Republican and Democratic politics, whether it is conservatism or liberalism, is leaning to the *left*. The Republicans are embracing religious concepts, leading the electorate in the dogma of anti-abortion, would teach mythological creationism, and totally absorbed in a collective of self-sacrifice as a rule of law. Religion is gaining control of Republican ideology. The strategy is to defeat the First Amendment, the redistribution of wealth, and form a theocracy. They are headed to the *left.* (See Fig. 4.)

The Democratic progressive liberal party will fight for the same secular Marxist principles, 'from each according to his ability to each according to his need', and is nothing new for them. We came quite close to these principles in the Great Depression. Franklin Roosevelt as president, brought us very close to socialism and his principles eventually have led us to a form of fascism. It is evident by the, 'Economic Bill of Rights', he proposed that every one had; the right to be free from fear and want—his rights:

'The right to meaningful work.
The right of every farmer a profitable price for crops.
The right of business to trade in freedom.
The right to own ones home.
The right to health and medical care.
The right of protection in old age. (Social Security)
The right to an education.'

The 'rights' Roosevelt proposed, are *not* rights. What a *right* means, is to say that one has a *fair claim.* Therefore his 'rights' to meaningful work, etc., are *values*, i.e. *tangible values.* To tell people they have such fair claims or rights, with the weight of the government to promise, by means, is to take by force, tangible values from one taxpayer and give to some one else. A 'fair claim' means to the socialists and a theocracy, that people have rights to other people's values or the more they earn the more taxes they must pay, and the less one makes the more taxes (other people's money) he has a 'right' to receive. They believe in the right of a totalitarian government to 'legally,' redistribute the earnings of the successful, to those who are not, on the premise that altruism a person's success is owed to others or gods.

The only means a person can gain tangible values, is that they must be earned. The *only* means a person can gain those intangible character values, education, skill, creativity, confidence, hard work perseverance, competitiveness and have confidence in his ability to survive, is to *earn* the tangible values Roosevelt lists. Earning in the marketplace of ideas, work, business, and trading in socioeconomic interaction, is the moral earning field of fair claims. The 'rights' above have been referred to as the "gospel" of Roosevelt's theocratic socialistic politics obviously not understanding what he was immorally proposing. The following *ARE MORAL* fair claims:

Our Rights To Redistribution

We have a right to EARN meaningful work.
The farmer has a right to EARN a profitable price.
The businessman has a right to EARN in trade.
The right to EARN ones own home.
The right to EARN health and medical care.
The right to EARN protection in old age.
The right to EARN an education.

To have a right is to have a fair claim or to be fair or just in one's claims upon our society is to follow the Moral Code. It is not fair that a majority, by vote, may impose taxation on a minority who opposes paying for other people's values. No voter has a fair claim to other people's values. To propose, vote, or implement a claim on other peoples values with force of a majority, or government (at the point of a gun) is not justice, and is, absolutely immoral, an infringement on man's life and property, his survival values a moral necessity.

Elected in 1932 Roosevelt made no economic progress to end the depression of the 1930's. By 1941, the economy had no growth despite the great number of social programs, and the people were still in poverty. It has been reported he needed a reason to enter the war with England to save his administration by getting on a wartime economy. The Japanese attacked Pearl Harbor in the Hawaiian Islands, in

USS

December of 1941, he now had an excuse to declare war against the Axis Powers of Germany, Italy, and Japan.

We fought and won a moral war against Japan. We defended and befriended the USSR their immoral regime, and it's dictator 'good old Joe' Stalin of which all world leaders were aware, except Roosevelt. But the victory was hollow and Stalin used his friendship with our unwary president to create the greatest threat to human freedom for the next 45 years. The weight of a socialistic elite crushed their economy, and their system failed. However, it fell only when the citizens, millions, took to the streets and demanded their countries back. It was as simple as that–*the masses*—they tore down the East German wall (The Iron Curtain), and were free. Totalitarian rulers fled for their lives. People in every country have that power, if they are united and truly want the freedom to *earn*, in their pursuit of happiness. But those countries today are socialist democracies.

Lenin's revolution, was to give the Russians a 'New Deal', and became an economic and social disaster. But the people always had it within their power, *as a massive force,* to free themselves. That's why there never was a moral necessity to give our lives to hand them over a free country. A nation's people must control their own destiny. The finest concerns for the poor, the suffering, and struggle of the disadvantaged, breaks the heart of all, the capitalists, conservatives or liberals alike (the liberal or religious are not the only people with human feelings). Social planning or economic planning is contrary to human nature and the nature of economics (as we shall see ahead).

If we fail to understand that five million years of free autonomy and individual will cannot be changed or devolve, in the split-second time of the last ten thousand years, we will destroy our selves and our civilization. We will devolve as did the Egyptian, Mayan, Aztec, and Roman Empires, and that which covers our lost civilization will be the dust of our sacrificial human remains.

Obviously none of the known political systems work. We have gone from the right (anarchy) to the left to a socialistic democracy and/or to republicanism, their religious and/or theocratic ideals. If we are unable to stop them, it will lead to Fascism, and the next step to socialism, which some may think will save them, from the poverty that overtook them, *because* of their trip to the left. Of all the known political systems practiced since the pharaoh, none work,—'what's a citizen to do?' It is self evident, that the progress to the left, for governments to *provide* people's values, in all history, has led to socioeconomic disasters, and any correction to go to the right, to let them *earn* and keep what they value, has produced prosperity.

The colonists and our history illustrates that prosperity, is courageously tied to man accepting responsibility for himself, and when he decides others should lead him, it is to his misfortune. Cro-Magnon man had a crude morality that fit their primitive times and needs. In principle it worked for them. Many simpler pagan societies that had little or no religious influence, may have been prosperous, even very early Greek states long before Alexander the Great.

The new theocracies corrupted any moral leadership, and by design, intentionally created poverty, and the ignorance of faith that replicated into unquestionable trust in leaders. Had there been no religious influence, how would have Cro-Magnon's simple principles evolved as man gradually advanced into our modern societies? That is the proposal before us. We need a form of government that will promote, not confiscate our earnings, a state to be slightly on the left of Cro-Magnon, and to embody a natural civilized sophistication to be entirely cognizant of moral principles.

A government must be a legal instrument in action, to affect moral protection of its citizens so they may be left free to survive. In the past, Natural Law philosophy and instruments such as the Magna Carta helped create constitutions for political law. It is the matter of creating fair legal systems based on sound moral principles. Next we will review the history of Natural Law to determine what we mean by the nature of law for mankind. We must ask ourselves, 'what are the fundamental principles that will determine how and why a moral government should exist?'

CHAPTER 5

Natural Law

Natural Law is a philosophical theory to scientifically create a foundation. of principles that may be codified into practical legal codes of law for moral governance in natural existence. Natural Law as defined in a dictionary today is *confused* and has been 'ethically' defined as *'a principle or body of laws considered as derived from nature,* right reason, or religion and as ethically binding in human society.' Natural is defined correctly as, 'existing *in or formed by nature (opposed to artificial): etc..'* Another dictionary, natural is defined as, *'Fixed or determined by nature; according to nature; essential; not artificial, assumed, or acquired.* Therefore it follows that *natural* pertains to Natural Law, derived from nature by natural beings and can *not* be *artificial, assumed, or acquired,* which includes anything *outside nature such as imaginary supranatural beings that are artificial assumptions.*

Nature includes the whole universe and all that we may have a reason to speculate beyond our universe or magna-cosmos. Nature is the matter, energy and natural laws—the constituents of existence. Within the universe, in a spiral galaxy, in an orbiting solar system, and on a planet we call earth, we are human beings, unique entities of matter and energy, but it is self evident we are no more or less natural than the whole. Only a natural entity can use, create, facilitate, or to be a part of the phenomenal universe in which we exist—by laws of our nature. And it is the law that should be codified in legal terms for us to live by.

In legal philosophy, natural law is not a 'higher law,' but the law of the "down to earth" or concerns specifically human nature, survival and happiness, and the "good" life or a common citizen's expectation of justice. This law must be derived by reason, experienced as a necessity that cannot be otherwise, universally valid, and self evident for man's survival. It is the logic of a moral autonomous human being able to earn and *survive*, gain happiness, and live long, naturally and lawfully. Therefore, any law of a country must be derived by codification or directly from, The Moral Code (Natural Law), if not, it is not a moral (legal) or just (fair—moral) government. A constitution is *practical* natural law, or a codification (derivative) of natural law.

The Babylonians had many taboos such as foods especially meats. There were rules against falsely accusing a fellow man, or scorning a god or goddess and only the sacrifice of flesh to pain, wealth, or meat justified the penance. 'A whole series of over a hundred tablets records omens from public happenings, from which developed historiography. As with most religious practices, these were primarily related to the king. It is therefore not without interest that the literary form of the omen text (given that X happened, then Y will come to pass) was the basis of all recorded law.' [29] It was a king meting out pragmatic justice and punishment that usually exceeded the crime. It was where reciprocity seemed out of control.

'The Egyptians always gave prominence to the gods who were believed to help the dead.' [30] This was the psychological key to man's control. If they could make the primitive believe a god could interact with the dead then they would believe anything. A sacred ritual, burial, or gay festival to celebrate the pharaoh's harvest or death and man would give up his wealth nor question his sacrifice. Regardless of what religion or sect, the idea is psychological control, and as such, like invention, spread. With it came the rules.

The laws were hard to take but in a song or poem carved in stone made it the 'truth' or, sort of a set of commandments, such as this Sumerian text, one of the oldest, demands:

> 'Worship your god every day with sacrifice and prayer which properly go with incense offerings. Present your free will offering to your god for this is fitting for the gods.

> Offer him daily prayer, supplication and prostration and you will get your reward. Then you will have full communion with your god. Reverence begets favor. Sacrifice prolongs life, and prayer atones for guilt.' [31]

The emphasis of the above poem or set of laws of a god is to worship, sacrifice, pray, sacrifice (free will offering? give up free will follow the laws of god only), pray (humble yourself), sacrifice (again), pray some more, and your 'guilty' of something. Three times, one is commanded to sacrifice and pay homage through prayer. Note they are rules for 'you,' not for the preacher to say 'I'. It is dictatorial. It is systematic, repetitious indoctrination, a psychological-stress technique known as brainwashing that is in practice today.

Around 2200 BC, in Babylon there came a need for civic laws. Hammarabi, King of Babylon, set down some 250 civic laws or rules, perhaps taken from the experiences of people coming forth to the officials, to right alleged wrongs. He was to have received these laws from a god. He gave up no power and many of the punishments were severe. Women were reduced to property—owned by her husband. She had some chattel rights, but far worse off than she was, as a free spirit on the savanna or in a Cro-Magnon tribe.

Later, about 400 BC, another set of rules was written by Jewish priests who plagiarized Syria's Mises, calling their mythological being, Moses, and wrote their laws in ten commandments. As a code for a theocracy, the first four laws and others establish a totalitarian state. The first is discriminatory, that is cause for bias racism, prejudice, the cause of war—justifying a dictatorship; the second, art is prohibited; the third, no freedom of the press; fourth, one day off only for devotion to a god's state. The fifth is the child's unconditional duty to his parents (conditioning the child for dictatorial rule). The Ten Commandments contain only three secular natural laws and are the only three moral principles, six do not kill, eight do not steal, and nine do not lie, without any *rights for reciprocity* in the New Testament. All, except the sixth, eighth, ninth and seventh, are value issues, *not* moral. The seventh rule is included in the ninth. The tenth commandment is an ethical conglomeration of rule against materialism, and is mind control to have no desire for anything in reality. To codify the Ten Commandments would create a theocratic totalitarian government ruled by a pope, king, emperor, czar or other kind of theocrat.

When Heaclitus (d. 478 BC) said 'everything flows' describing natural change, a fundamental law of nature, and was the beginning of philosophical discourse. The spiritual world was immersed in mythology and traditions. For the religious hierarchy, this was their source of power and sanctuary from reason and truth, to foster faith, ignorance, and rule man's values. The New Greek intellectual, the philosopher, wanted to understand nature, the real environment, his being, and to find a more natural harmonious existence on earth.

The poems and stories of Greek gods were understood to be mythology, as they should be known. It was artful entertainment using fictional representations of what should be the proper behavior towards one another. The Greek's experience among their gods was only a few thousand years old. What the Greeks had only guessed, actually happened in primitive times before the agricultural discoveries. We now know the primitive had lived such a life for *five million years*, learning to create and live in harmony with nature. We can speculate that since we are here today, there were natural laws built within their nature to affect our survival for 5,000,000 million years.

There were few truly secular philosophers down through the ages. The teaching of religious myth became deeply rooted in the follower's psyche. It has been referred to as a psychological crutch, for the weak, the less ambitious, or the one who chooses not to think or reason. But maybe it was in some cases, a substitute for what possibly couldn't be known at the time. It explained, by myth, how we got here, how the world was created and that someone was behind that big spotlight in the sky. If one couldn't find an immediate answer, it was caused by gods or left to a deity's representative on earth to explain. Yet in the light of reason or new knowledge, leaders chose not to admit ignorance for very immoral greedy selfish reasons. So the 'poor innocents' believed, writing down Natural Law as a contribution to the "good' and we can not fault some of them for integrity.

Many philosophers and theologians have not produced a natural law code but have theorized some principles. The purpose of a natural law code or theory provides a moral standard or principle with which to judge conventional law, constitutional or civic law. Of all that have been produced none have been completely secular. They were trying to create a synergy in morals and values into one fundamental principle. Philosophers and theologians were struggling within societies imprinted with gods rooted in their psyche. They witnessed man's behavior in his beliefs and self-sacrifice as natural collectivism and yet were not the cause of his behavior, but only symptomatic of causes early thinkers could not fathom. They believed rulers to be rogues but could not believe they would create poverty or destroy their own species. They had faith in a leader's humanity essentially unable to believe a godly person could be despotic.

According to Paul Sigmund author of, "Natural Law in Political Thought", the Roman statesman and politician Cicero (106-43 BC) authored one of the early theories on natural law. He relied heavily on the stoic view in the writings of Zeno of Citium and Chrysippus (232-206 BC), " . . . right reason . . . was identical with Zeus, lord and ruler." [32] Zeno's ideal state, where all live together like a herd of animals, was reference to the 'collective nature of man.' Cicero believed men to have a moral duty to share the goods of nature and that self-interest was contrary to moral principles. Most natural law theories followed such theocratic reasoning, or communistic sharing, an altruistic sacrificial principle was the only way to force man, by guilt, to give up his wealth as a 'moral' duty, to create a slave state.

Ulpian, a Roman legal writer in the third century rejected 'provisions regulating slavery, it was contrary to the law of nature. "For by the laws of nature all men were born free."' 'Ulpian devoted considerable attention to the legal regulations concerning slavery, thus demonstrating that he was no more ready than Cicero to use natural law to invalidate existing societal arrangements.' [33] It was in principle, a slavery dilemma for the Roman Empire that had created Christianity. It was to counter the Jewish religion that was spreading through the Italian peninsula in the first century. The Jews did not approve of an inclusive slave mentality, as did Rome.

Christians incorporated much of the stoic natural law directly into sacred writings. What appealed to Christianity was the collective spirit as 'St., Paul's epistle to the Galatians. "There is neither Jew nor Greek, there is neither bond nor free, there is neither male nor female; for you are all one in Christ Jesus."' [34] The ideal of a god and commandments are legal references, to the collective character of religion. The communistic socialistic collective character in secular law was adopted, *in principle*, from religion, by substituting the state for gods.

Hugo Grotius (1583-1645) had advanced a modern theory of natural law. His contribution was to give some justification for reciprocity; that war was a defense to preserve a nation and that a god cannot change the laws of nature which some earlier writers had suggested.

However, Grotius used natural law concepts of religion with theological assumptions that god was the creator of nature and to him must be obedient. However, he did believe in reciprocity, material rights, *moral* necessity, and of course, 'nature's' law of god. We see many attempts to create a synergy of moral principles with values and theological commandments into natural law.

A.P. d'Entreves, "Natural Law" states, 'What Grotious had set forth as a hypothesis has become a thesis. The self-evidence of natural law has made the existence of God perfectly superfluous.' Grotius's science, 'If natural law consists in a set of rules which are absolutely valid, its treatment must be based upon an *internal coherence and necessity*. ' Grotius:

> 'In order to be a science law must not depend on experience, but on definitions, not on facts, but on logical deductions. Hence, only the principles of the law of nature can properly constitute a science. Such a science must be constructed

by leaving aside all that undergoes change and varies from place to place.'[35]

However, this theory would forever remain a theory in Grotius's time since he never questioned what was a god's law or the concept of human rights. The elite concerned itself with things of value and their positions, not the lives of their 'property.' The science to be correct in Natural Law has to guide man's behavior, with principles that conform to human nature. Unlike Grotius, they must be proven in practice depending on *experience and facts* for logical deduction, they must have internal coherence, be self evident, be invariable in time or place, and *be a necessity in human survival, to recognize human rights.* The Natural Law of, The Moral Code fully meets that criterion.

Grotius' theory remained unchallenged, influencing philosophers, and political thinkers right up to Jefferson, the American and French revolutions, and our Constitution. The word 'god' does not appear in the U.S. Constitution, but how it is interpreted, *is* religiously and socialistically motivated and that is the source of all republic and democratic problems.

Thomas Hobbes (1588-1679) split the old dichotomy of Roman law of natural right and natural law. Revolutionists saw law and right within a general system. 'Hobbes contrasts a right of nature—man's right to do anything that will preserve his life—with the laws of nature—the instrumental and hypothetical rules of reason regarding the best means to self preservation.'[36] His idea, to stem our competition to inflict death on each other, requires in Hobbes view, a sovereign power, a monarchy—a communal theocracy.

John Locke (1632-1704) believed there was a natural limit to how much a man can acquire in property because it spoiled. The invention of money removed that limit. He supported the idea of the majority's right to impose taxes for the *common good.* Locke was confident that the majority would not tax excessively but *offered no checks against it* and held that the law rests ultimately on a *god's will.* Yet Locke was a proponent of natural law rights and that man through reason can judge without a common superior. [37] He seemed to have wanted it both ways

All those that follow Locke make some reference or are vitally concerned for the common good, self sacrifice or altruism that take advantage of man's wishes to be good. Another philosopher who was most influential was Jean Jacques Rouseau (1712-1778) in his famous 'Social Contract' that he asserted as contractual. 'Each of us puts his person and all his power in common under the supreme direction of the general will, and, in our corporate capacity, we receive each other as a member as an indivisible part of the whole.' [38] This is a socialist communistic contract, meaning the same thing—collectivism—worded differently.

'At once, in place of the individual personality of each contracting party, this act of association creates a moral and collective body composed of as many members as the assembly contains voters, and receiving from their act its unity, its common identity, its life, and its will.' Rouseau called it the *'Republic or body politic.'* . . . 'It is only then when the voice of duty takes the place of physical impulses and law that of appetite, that man, who so far had considered only himself, finds himself forced to act on different principles, and to consult his reason before listening to his inclinations.' [39] Here is Rousseau's theory. "Each of us puts his person in common under the supreme direction, etc. ..' is collectivism, 'to be of one mind' 'common identity—its will.' And 'listening' to others, opposed to individualism, and to be altruistic not as a slave by force, but who does so willingly under an undefined 'supreme direction' without evidence, and no right to life.

Jeremy Bentham (1748-1832), rejecting natural law and natural rights that he called, 'subjective prejudices,' was the founder of utilitarianism. Laws were based, not on any purpose in nature but on general utility. The efficiency or usefulness of the law or legislator's aim should be to provide the greatest good or happiness (pleasure) for the greatest number. We've covered this before and it is the same message a prescription for majority rule with the idea a minority must sacrifice for the 'greater good,' to the majority. It is another altruistic collective concept.

JSS

Most natural law has been subject to multiple interpretations being very generalized without defining specifically any synergistic principle because 'ethically' one senses they never understood or were thoroughly confused as to what was *moral* or *value*.

THE MORAL CODE (Book IV) IS NATURAL LAW: It does not include principles of what may be a person's hierarchy of values, or principles of sacrifice to the majority—altruism. The Code does not designate a god as the author, nor does it leave its ultimate judgment to a deity. It is man made, lived and suffered historically in proven practical experience, and identified by this author, and the 'final judgment' of The Moral Code, will be humanity.

The Moral Code is natural and humane, based on man's nature in order to evolve metaphysically and epistemologically in his lifetime, and as a species. It is natural law, recognizing autonomously a person's self interest to survive, in pursuit of his hierarchy of values. Mankind must be free from infringement in order to succeed by his standards, by having the right to reciprocate if others infringe upon those rights. It is natural that parents raise and prepare their children for their survival. It is natural that we vote only for freedom and to respect mankind by *not* discriminating, coercively create guilt, use force, to harm, kill, and not to defraud or be ignorant of the rights of others, so they may succeed, and seek happiness is self evident. Every principle has coherence in The Moral Code and does not vary from person to person, culture to culture, place to place, or from time to time. It is a code of survival for every human in his lifetime and as a species.

The Moral Code is a deduction based on the nature of man metaphysically and epistemologically, who like all living organisms must take both mental and physical actions, in the pursuit of their individual hierarchy of values. It allows us to be free and natural, where no one need take any physical action to be moral, and this is so conferred upon all natural beings for them to be free, that *all* their mental and physical effort be towards their own survival, to guarantee their propagation. Its principles have been tested, proven, and witnessed to be true historically. The Moral Code is Natural Law, and as such is a set of coherent principles grounded in human nature that is logical, self evident, and a moral necessity, which can never be otherwise.

CHAPTER 6

Economics

Economics is the science in cultures for efficient or thrifty management of production, distribution, of commodities including food, services, and the use of wealth and income. The primitive's economy was scavenging, foraging and hunting and learning how to fish always expanding his economic opportunities. The primitive successes in agriculture, and animal husbandry created wealth for the first time in his 5,000,000 years of living in a subsistence economy. He could grow and control animals on the hoof, far more than he could consume, and that excess food is called wealth. If a robber, invader, or a government takes his wealth by force they are immoral. Surpluses create jobs and a lean moral government is instituted to *protect* a citizen's wealth. This is the issue we solve in this book. We explore how economics works in this chapter.

The whole world is engaged in economic activity. How did this great economic system, spanning the whole earth begin? What were the causes that created great civilizations, and then to fail in bankruptcy and ruin? What is in store for mankind in the future as we create more complex economies? Our culture is the economy, it means, that what we invent will change our way of living, more functional homes or better health, transportation, or services or to cosmetically affect a change in the appearances of ourselves or things around us. People are the economy, because we invent it, and we buy it *if we choose.*

The culture is the final arbiter in buying or selling. Therefore, an economy depends on its culture for creativity, risk and product success, and the result is cultural economic activity when we want to buy what a person, or company of people have invented and created. There are many people who alone provide goods and services A culture is the combined socioeconomic customs, and traditions of individuals in a culture.

Democracies or republics are multiparty, each with an ideology of what values are 'proper' to be included in people's hierarchy of values. The elitist rulers will create a bureaucratic system to equalize socioeconomic values for people. But the politician can only create the perception of equality, because between rulers and the electorate will be a great difference in reward and privilege and never equal. Alexis de Tocqueville, a Frenchman, visited the United States in the early 1800's and in 1835, published his account of "Democracy in America." He wrote that our inconsistent ideas about equality could lead us to vote ourselves into a tyranny, which was his understanding of the danger in majority rule. Was he wrong? Are we voting ourselves into a tyranny of democratic socialism or a republican theocracy?

We have allowed governments to tax, seize paychecks and property, taxing us sometimes twice, three times, etc., such as subsidies, state monopolies, capital gains and savings, thus, eliminating a large part of our spending and job creating profits businesses need to grow. Unemployment, poverty and welfare increase proportionately to the increase in taxation. Today, *over fifty percent of earned income goes towards taxes in the USA.* of which the greater amount is unseen, buried in a product's price and from wages before they add sales taxes. We may have applied the principle 'buyer beware,' but we should also take heed in 'freedom lovers beware' or 'voter beware' when voting for politicians.

By eliminating taxes means we could *double* our buying power, *jobs*, plants, equipment and *jobs as well as profits for our selves,* or for entrepreneurs who take the risks to create jobs. Governments create the poor. They have had five thousand years of rule to stamp out poverty. They have not because they confiscated wealth for themselves, and today the modern majority voter thinks he is getting something for nothing. But, we are getting ahead of the problem. To understand our economic system, is to fathom the primitive's success in agriculture and animal husbandry in the beginning. It is vital to grasp its relevance to the present.

'Love' is not the *most* important thing in the world. The only way a totalitarian state can be created is to convince people to love everyone and sacrifice themselves for their god or country. The first recipient of that love or sacrifice is the state or theocracy, i.e. the elite. But reason tells us that love cannot be the most important thing in the world, except perhaps the desire to live. Life then is dependent on our effort to survive first, because we have expectations, a need for self-esteem, and love—human happiness.

All the love in the world for us means little when facing death. Only with life fed by food may we be able to love and be loved. It is by mental and physical action that we earn our food, which feeds our physical being creating consciousness. We survive and earn a measure of our self-esteem giving us confidence. It follows then, if one wants to experience life we have to earn food to keep ourselves alive to survive so we can be loved and to love someone. For all living things *food* is the most important thing in the world. It is the natural order of values to sustain life, and reproduction of our species.

Should food disappear from the earth tomorrow the meaning of life would be clear—success—to feed oneself—would be the first priority in the hierarchy of values for every person on earth. Every material thing on earth would become valueless. Most of us have witnessed starvation through our media, and such emaciated human beings illustrate vividly, the priority of food for human life. Without food nothing follows, it is what we need to respect most of all. Only when we want to live do we find love.

In 1798 Thomas Malthus, who published his book 'An Essay on the Principles Population', wrote:

> 'I think I may fairly make two, postulata. First, that food is necessary to the existence of man. Secondly, that the

> passion between the sexes is necessary and will remain nearly in its present state. These two laws, since we have any knowledge of mankind, appear to have been fixed laws of our nature, and, as we have not hitherto seen any alteration in them, we have no right to conclude that they will ever cease to be what they now are . . . '[40]

It was on this basis that Malthus began to formulate his theories on the productivity of food and the consequences of human fertility:

> 'Darwin's principal contribution to evolution theory to explain it's mechanism—how it might occur. The germ of this idea came from reading Thomas Malthus, who had suggested for man what Darwin had observed for wild species in many parts of the world; rates of reproduction are so great that if all the offspring survived any species could soon form a solid crust of life on the earth's surface. An oyster produces millions of young each year, an oak thousands of acorns. Yet the sea does not become a solid mass of oysters or the land an unbroken stand of oak trees. These events do not come to pass because the enormous rate of reproduction is balanced by an enormous rate of mortality, especially of the young.'[41]

What Darwin may have appreciated in particular, ' . . . the best arguments for the perfectibility of man are drawn from a contemplation of the great progress that he (man) has already made from the savage state and the difficulty of saying where he is to stop.'[42] We cannot eliminate the passions between the sexes, reproducing at great speed, and populating most of world packing them in at an accelerated rate. Malthus:

> 'I say that the power of the population is indefinitely greater than the power in the earth to produce subsistence for man . . . Population, when unchecked, increases in a

> geometrical ratio. Sustenance increases only in an arithmetical ratio. A slight acquaintance with numbers will shew the immensity of the first power in comparison to the second. ..By that law of our nature which makes food necessary to the life of man, the effects of these two unequal powers must be kept equal.' [43]

Family planning is a value issue, efficiency in socioeconomic planning for living. Birth control, *early* abortion, and/or the decision to procreate are, personal choices. If all potential human life comes to pass we would cover the earth in a generation the whole world would live in poverty, and be starving. Science, our only means of survival, could not save us from the predatory chaos that would follow. But, science can, in birth prevention, aborting morally, and in food production, help create for viable life, a balance of survival values, a world of opportunity, and human happiness.

Michael Hoffman (commenting on Ester Boserup's thesis, in her book, 'The Conditions of Agricultural Growth"), 'she interpreted population growth as an independent variable which in its turn is a major factor in determining agricultural developments.' This seemed to economists to contradict Malthus' theory. But in Hoffman's 'Egypt Before the Pharaohs,' noted that, 'there is not as much conflict with Malthusian principles as meets the eye.' In time 'food supply will of course limit population growth'. However, she is correct 'in regard to early states . . . ' or new emerging countries, but, 'No technology or technological system is eternally plastic.' [44]

The defining consideration is therefore, new land areas to be farmed, and such areas are being seized for parks to keep rain forests pristine. Also, Malthus is correct if all available viable farming land is developed we may improve production, but, we cannot and have not kept up with the geometrical rate of births, such as in Africa, Asia, South and Central America.

Most of the world goes to bed hungry. The ruins of civilizations in the Mid East, Egyptian dynasties, the Aztecs, Mayan, Asian Empires, and many others have failed because the elite thought there was no limit to the land's production. Their societies went bankrupt. Many people think that, 'that was long ago we are not like that any more' but we have not changed one iota. In technology we changed, but in moral principles we have failed miserably. When a country goes bankrupt (Somalia), the leaders, government and bureaucrats disappear, and armed thieves are free to steal from poor starving food producers.

In "The Driving Force" Crawford and March postulate that, 'life is the result of plenty,' not scarcity. [45] We are aware that we can produce more, and amid this plenty proliferate, but governments and theists seem to ignore that nature is limited, plenty is finite.

Again, we go back to our roots. It has been suggested that we were forced out of the forest canopy due to over population rather than a draught. We were proliferating amid plenty, and pouring out of the trees and on to the savanna. Anthropologists calculate that the savanna could support two primitive scavengers per square mile. Our ancestors, about 500,000 to 300,000 years ago, before agriculture, even with high rates of mortality among the young, were multiplying as a result of Stone Age technology. There were about one million people on earth and spilling out of Africa into the Mid East, Asia, Europe, Australia and in to the northern regions of the world to search for food, scavenging for sustenance.

About 9,000 or 8,000 years ago there were about 5.3 million people when farming and animal husbandry began, or five times as many of 300,000 years ago. The new discoveries increased the population about 16 times to 87 million in just 4,000 years. From that time we have multiplied to about five and a half billion people, increasing 55 times and still accelerating in less than 2,000 years.

Under the strain of population increase we are attempting to boost production genetically, soil improvement, mechanization of huge farms, and herbicides, but no matter what one tries their failures and successes are met with huge environmental objections. Even with our good science we are left without a safety net and everyone will not get fed this year. We are vulnerable to the variability of natural and man made catastrophes such as locusts, draught, floods, poor yields and environmentalist's laws. But yields more likely are seized, or by taxation of the ruling elite in every country on earth, that is causing untold starvation, misery and vice of which we are witness to every day. Why then is, South and Central America, lands of poverty selling foodstuffs to the U.S. and other wealthy countries that are supporting such evil, while people go hungry? ? ?

Food Money—the 'gold' of our economy is food. The technological breakthrough in farming and herding (for this essay 'farmer' will depict farmer/ herder) gave the primitive an advantage to be able to feed his family year round. It was no longer a day to day existence of hunt and scavenge to eat, repeating it day after day, year after year. Around 7,000 to 6,000 BC, in many parts of the world, they quickly exhausted the fertility of the land (in about 10 years). They went to plant in new areas, going back sometimes to the old after as many years. Along rivers, such as the Indus, Tigris, Euphreates and the Nile flood annually, depositing new fertile silt. Nature provided automatic annual fertilization of the land near rivers.

The early farmer's grains and tubers could be stored for long periods, and small animals (goats, sheep) on the hoof, gave year round food and a stable living location. To understand the economy and food money we will create the scenario of the farmer who produces just enough food to sustain himself and a family as it occurred in the very beginning. The first priority of the farmer was to produce enough food for his family with their help. All food was gathered and processed for storage and/or penned animals alive until needed for the table. In those times he needed nothing else. He would fashion all his tools, weapons, and hunting gear. This was, as it had always been for five million years, a closed family economic system as it was on the savanna.

With his first priority to feed his clan secure, the farmer noted he could produce some surplus (*this is profit defined as wealth*) above his family needs. He was able to make life easier trading surplus food for a product or service (tools, weapons, containers, hunting gear or labor on the farm) (*he created a job with his profit*). The service or toolmaker gave farmers time to specialize in farming skills. When this happened, the closed economy of the farmer changed his society to a village economy. It was where they traded between each other, and expanded to include a whole territory. It was the pharaohs, his religious leaders and their lords who forced the farmer to produce more and more for building pyramids and their artifacts. When heavy taxes for building, artifacts and standing army to subjugate their people resulted in starvation, they invaded a neighboring nation to kill and steal their food and wealth.

Hoffman:

> 'One of the favorite arguments of historians and social evolutionists has been that such surpluses were themselves primary stimulants to the growth of states and civilization; that agriculture and animal domestication produced surpluses of food which, in turn, permitted more and more specialists in areas like crafts, religion and politics. These specialists who themselves did not produce, exchanged their services for food and gradually came to dominate society. Such a view implies that an agricultural economy is almost bound to lead to higher levels of organization—states and civilizations—and assumes that surpluses are desirable things to produce. More recent research has shown this not to be the case. Many, food-producing societies never developed into states and still lack or reject the notion that large stored surpluses are necessary. The basic impulse seems to be to follow the principle of least effort, and keep just enough seed to propagate next season's crop and provide a small margin of safety.' [46]

The above includes together, the tradesmen, and specialist of tools, with the state officials and religious orders. The tradesmen, tool maker, or helper, provides a tangible product or service of use to the farmer which benefits the farmer either in personal pleasure or material reward such as a bowl, jar, tool, wash his clothes, plow his land, baby sit his child or aging parents. He receives something *tangible*.

But it is with intangible assets that we got into economic trouble, in trading a tangible asset (such as the farmer's food) for something that is intangible. Note that legal instruments such as money, contracts, insurance policies, stocks, bonds, or promissory notes, may appear to be intangibles, but are accepted as collateral by banks, etc. as tangible assets because experience shows they are payable.

Tangible legal instruments, stocks, bonds etc., are by being of specific benefit that is promised and delivered, at a specified time. There are intangible or pseudo tangibles as a con man, legally referred to as frauds. Such contracts promises, such as voiced by psychics, the religious, boiler room sales, medical cures, organizations to help the poor may never deliver future benefits. Successful scams destroy generosity, and being imaginary fraudulent promises with intent, are immoral and illegal.

A constitution is an intangible asset and can only become tangible when secular governments honor their promises to the people. They must protect their people from infringement by criminals or invaders, and to attend to justice and freedom in people's socioeconomic society. Such a constitution can only be considered tangible or real if its benefits are legally self-evident in law and practice consistent with principles of freedom. The legal instrument obviously does not guarantee in a context of law or in practice a free economy for the people. Nor does it limit the government's infringement on the culture or our personal hierarchy of values. That is, we have no right to a free economy or a right to our own values. Freedom lacks definition in our constitution. Such freedom must be all-inclusive, consistent for every person, a realization of safety, and freedom in every aspect of their lives for all time in order for a constitution to become a real tangible asset. Anything less is morally reprehensible.

The farmer or citizen may take to heart his socialistic duty or religion shunning material gain profit, or surplus. Such societies will produce, as Hoffman has shown, no surplus, just enough 'for a small margin of safety.' We are back to a closed society that occurs in many countries who shun industry, trade, or surpluses. No effective state, socialistic or theocratic can exist, because there are no profits or surpluses, nothing of material value to confiscate, tax, or even ask for donations. They must go to work, or they may seize the farmer's food for themselves that happened in Somalia, and in every poor country in Africa causing widespread starvation we witness today.

It is obvious, if the farmer truly believes and has faith in the intangible socialistic theocratic contract, to be *non-materialistic*, he puts his government out of business—no societal economy! Note there are no leaders in an Amish society because they produce only enough for themselves and just a little more to help those in the group who may have a poor crop. So we know economically, theocrats and socialists really do not have any intention to create what they advertise as the ideal communistic society and the closed independent farming society is out of the question. They want to remain in the center of complete power to confiscate, infringe, and reap benefits of the wealth or surplus we produce.

The Constitution's Economics: We have always given governments power over the economy. The USA's constitution gives it unconditionally. Article 1; Section 8, paragraphs one, two and three, the right to lay taxes, to borrow money, and to regulate commerce. However, as Fred Rodell shows in his book "55 Men The Story of the Constitution" which was based on the day by day notes of James Madison was not their intention. The 'Articles of Confederation and Perpetual Union Between the States' drawn up by the states retained all power in the states. The convention delegates were split concerning giving power to the central government but, ' . . . both sides of the split convention still agreed that the central government should be given the power to pay back the money it had borrowed (during the revolutionary war) and to protect business and industry.' ' . . . It gave Congress the right to levy taxes to pay off federal bonds, to raise tariffs for the protection of industry, and *to regulate commerce and trade*.' [+7] They had unwittingly opened Pandora's box, referred to in economics as the 'commerce clause.'

J.W. Peltason writes in his "Corwin & Peltason's Understanding the Constitution" 1988; 'The commerce clause is another important basis on which Congress has developed a national police power.' [48] 'The power to pay debts is not restricted to the payment of the legal obligations of the national government. On the contrary, Congress may pay off its obligations that are merely moral ('ethical') or honorary, and when this power is tied to the power to spend for the general welfare, it results in the power of Congress to decide who shall receive tax dollars from the federal treasury.'

> 'A word of caution: the general welfare clause is tied to the power to tax and to spend; no general power is granted to Congress to legislate for the general welfare. But, . . . liberal construction of congressional power and the demands (voter) of our times have removed any serious constitutional limits stemming from this clause.' [49] 'The power to regulate' The 'vague words and phrases' have given congress the power over commerce, (foreign and concerns more than one state) 'is the power to govern it' 'Congress may even *prohibit* or greatly restrict commerce in order to *'promote'* the national health, safety, and welfare, or for humanitarian purposes.' [50] In this paradigm it is legal to nationalize all private business in the USA.

Our laws permit a socialist state. Our justices' definition of *promote* becomes in *all* cases to *provide* especially in social security, health, welfare, including endowments, subsidies, monopolies, schools, regulatory bureaus and on and on. The Supreme Court has given up interpretation of the commerce clause, for the 'common good' and handed its powers over the economy to Congress. We gave up our power over surplus wealth and left subsistence to ruler's discretion. *We* have created the surplus and *we have permitted* theocratic and secular politicians through inhuman taxation (legal confiscation), to provide for some undefined 'common good' 'majority,' or for the 'poor.' They have created and never intend to eliminate that clause for it is their 'cash cow,' to keep their 'poor' ideological issue alive for theocratic and socialistic wealth.

The result of a surplus economy or plenty of food has been the proliferation of our species so great it is impossible for all of us to revert to a farming subsistence. The problem is not to revert to subsistence, but for citizens to control our surplus economy and take away the power of taxation from the government, and voluntarily limit population.

Food-Money means since 'food,' per se, can not be traded indefinitely and likely to deteriorate a medium of exchange such as money, is a promissory note guaranteeing that a fixed value in food is promised upon delivery ultimately. We may be paid in money, whereby we may buy things, services or food. All money, investment, interest, profits, savings, spending, and effort is trading in food. We could call money, 'food money.' If all food disappeared from the earth, there would be no trading value in anything. All material things would be worthless and everything would become an intangible. We would cry and mate a lot. In less than 100 days almost every person would be dead. If we reverted to cannibalism it may take a little longer for us all to disappear.

Economists may not factor within an economy, food, as the stable value or backing for currency. Although there is not the space for a discourse in this book, one might believe the total nutritional value to sustain a healthy life in some increments, might be the means of adjusting the money supply or value to food production of a nation. In our high tech age of computers, future exchanges, statistic retrieval, and accumulating information, a common means of standardizing world currencies based on food production of the past year, i.e. nutrition values, not gold, or any inert material value. The economy based on paper money, is paper-thin and that strong. Our politicians have printed paper money for the last 50 years inflating the cost of goods, and when they couldn't do that, they raided social security and sold bonds, creating a very large debt saying we were only borrowing from ourselves. Leaders have proven they are incapable of handling our money, and should *never* be trusted with power over other people's wealth. Our money should be backed by a human's greatest need, that which has the highest value for mankind. The "gold" of the economy is *food.* It should somehow be tied to our medium of exchange.

Job Creation—Job Security: All "food money" or profits in a *free* society creates jobs or makes them secure regardless how it is spent, saved or invested.

The first way to create a job is to *create a new enterprise,* using one's own money from savings (which is personal profit), profits (from a business), or capital gains (from a long or short-term investment). *Profit is what* will create a product, service, or expand a company that always provides jobs. There are no other means to create jobs.

The second way to create jobs is taking one's savings, profits, or capital gains to *invest in stocks or bonds* that creates jobs or job security indirectly which may take a little longer, which actually in trading is supporting good product and confidence in corporate management.

The third way is of course one may deposit their money in a *bank savings account,* which banks use eventually as loans for cars, homes, real, chattle property, and business loans, all of which will create jobs.

Four, if the entrepreneur sells his company and takes all his capital gains, savings etc., and *spends all his money*, on services, debauchery, or in early retirement he will be supplying the economy with "job security" (explained below) with his buying power. If he dies and his family inherits the rest of the fortune, they may just spend it like him, recklessly, *creating job security* and possible profits for those creators of goods and services as they spend the fortune.

However a person with a legacy, realistically, should have the intellect to invest in the first three scenarios above. If they are not intelligent as their dead relative, they could lose it all in bad investments and many do. But they did create temporary jobs. Also, they may be successful, if so, they had the sense to learn and had the intellect to use the money wisely and create *new* jobs, thus creating buying power for more people, and he has increased his fortune.

True, the heirs have the luck of the draw in nature, but nature is also a great leveler, they must *know* how to play the hand or eventually lose it all to con men or spend it recklessly, yet still providing job security in both cases.

The above may create jobs slower or faster, but has little or no effect on spending, since spending takes place when the product or service becomes available. By buying the product or its stocks creates *job security*. The initial purchase of a new product, is the test of the viability of those newly created jobs. However, if the product or service fails for any reason, it will not be purchased again and/or others who are aware will not buy. All companies take an interest in initial orders of a new product, but must make a particular analytical evaluation on their customer's 'reorders.' Should consumers continue to demand the product or service in sufficient reorders, then employees and management may look forward to 'job security.' If there is a *great increase* in reorders more jobs may be 'created.' This 'job creation' depends on further company investment, loans, etc., to make more of the product and will create more jobs.

In a free economy, more businesses fail than succeed. All labor and skilled workers, engineers, and managers, in a new company, had to work on the job for the period of initial production—a temporary position in the economy. If successful every reorder will amount to job security requiring 'owners' to reinvest to get out the new orders and with the hope to make a profit. If the owners miscalculate or costs escalate, for some material or labor cost reason, then they may begin to lose profits or have to raise prices. If competition occurs, they must evaluate and invest in new labor savings devices and/or different or better material procurement.

Nothing said above is unknown. There is no drainage of value in a free enterprise system except in a poor product that has failed. The investment drainage occurs with the entrepreneur or those who may have invested in its stocks, i.e. taken a risk with their money. The employees and suppliers were paid (unless creditors invested with supplies) but the owners and investors lost their money to temporary wages for their employees and suppliers.

The accusations by politicians, that profits from corporations, companies, or businesses in the economy, once put in the hands of their owners, is taking money out of, or draining the economy and job creation, is completely false, and they know this.

Money in a free society will always, whether spent, saved or invested, has the overall effect of securing or creating jobs. *Money never leaves a capitalist economy.* Money never stops creating or securing jobs, except by taxation.

The only drainage that occurs on our wealth, if we are free to gain and keep our earnings, is to spend it among nations less free than we. When we do, it gives support to socialist or theocratic rulers, *prolonging* their people's misery indefinitely. We are solidifying their government and politician's power over their people and that is not treating our fellow man morally. When we approach the systematic equal of other governments we trade and we have equaled China as a Fascist state and that is why they are in favor with our leaders.

People in other countries should be autonomous or morally responsible for their own nation and freedom. Our trade cannot help them only *provide* for their continued enslavement. We 'may buy' cheap goods from foreign slave-shops but lose our jobs in the process, and waste our surplus on a dictatorship. It also, sends money to that country never to affect job creation or job security here and only a subsistence wage for the citizen and supporting a nation's despotic regime.

A government's value motives only provides a semblance of job security initially, but in a deteriorating sense. It has no entrepreneurial ability to create new products or generate a profit, only a paper pushing bureaucracy of regulations or seeking more power in the government or public affairs, or what will perpetuate their ideology, wealth and elitist positions by increased taxation. Government by using up profit of the people prevents job creation.

It should be clear from the above that those politicians who are quick to say that tax relief for the rich will cause the money they earn will be taken out of the economy and only benefit them, are lying through their teeth. Or they are terribly ignorant of economics, and in either case, do not deserve to 'serve' the people. When people begin resisting tax increases, a government then uses inflation as a means to spend money and hide 'taxation.' In effect, the only reason inflation takes place is because government *elects* to 'tax' in this respect.

A legitimate rise in material cost from the earth caused by scarcity proven probable or imagined is not inflation.

A legitimate rise in prices of goods in the economy due to limited production that is not able to keep up with demand is not inflation.

A legitimate lowering of prices due to increased production above the demand for the product is not deflation.

Prices rise or fall in a free economy that is functional in adjusting to a market that naturally varies according to the exigencies of supply and demand.

'In an economy, inflation occurs when there is a persistent substantial rise in the general level of prices related to an *increase* in the *volume of money* and resulting in the loss of value in the currency.' [51]

Governments are never honest about inflation. 'Government officials always find some excuse—greedy businessmen, grasping trade unions, spend thrift consumers, Arab sheikhs, bad weather or anything else that seems even remotely plausible.' [52] Note, how a rise in prices during an oil shortage is referred to as inflationary. They know better, and are being deliberately dishonest in order to destroy capitalism and the concept of price fluctuation related to a product's "supply and demand." in the marketplace.

Milton and Rose Friedman point out that only the government has the power of the printing press to inflate the money supply. 'Inflation occurs when the quantity of money rises appreciably more rapidly than output, and the more rapid the rise in the quantity of money per unit of output, the greater the rate of inflation.' [53] One can find the definition in a dictionary.

When the government wants to spend money on new roads or new welfare programs above tax revenues received, they simply sell bonds to the Federal Reserve Bank. The bank prints the money giving it to the government who spends it in the economy thus increasing the money supply. It has created nothing of value to earn this money and it wasn't earned tax money. The subsequent inflated economy however, is the cost (tax), to the consumer who must pay a higher price for food, clothing, shelter, etc. Plus, our children tomorrow and *we* today are liable for higher prices well into the future to pay for goods services and food, i.e. it is double taxation for reckless government spending. Since it may take months for the effect of inflation to occur few consumers ever realize what is happening and when felt, will trust their government is being honest in blaming greedy businessmen, or materialistic buyers like you, etc., etc.. But most have little knowledge of the economy in which they depend on for their livelihood.

If we give the power to the government to socialize us through public education and to run, regulate, tax and spend within the economy, we shall never be free of the specter of the pharaoh or a totalitarian government. We now live in a Fascist form of government, very close to socialism and as long as governments have legal access to the economy that danger of a totalitarian *ideology*, will always be real. We have managed for the last two hundred years to fend off theocratic intrusion but the Republicans want to revive the pharaoh and Democrats want secular socialism, both are totalitarian. Behind them, to help convince us of their benevolence, are many academics, all government bureaucrats in local, city, state, and federal agencies, their employees, bureaucratic lobbyists, politicians, schools, with their army of staffs, perpetuating huge governments to *provide* for our well being. ?

Despite our outcry lately for smaller more efficient government it will not happen, because of that huge pile of surplus food or wealth. Eighty percent (80 %) of the lobbyists in Washington are government career bureaucrats. They have a vested interest to guarantee their status and *growth*. They are free to walk the halls of congress lobbying for our tax dollars, while private citizen and business lobbyists are hassled with many regulations and limited access.

We do not need a government to *provide* for our cultural and economic well being. We are culturally competent with no need for social or economic engineering. The farmer, worker, entrepreneur, researcher, inventor, and all the craftsmen created our food surplus economy. Once the surplus appeared, like pirates, they have encroached on the real producers. Since they can not provide anything that we cannot provide for ourselves, then, the true function of a government should be *moral*, and codify The Moral Code, to promote only, *never to provide tangible values for its citizens.* First, the state's role is to *make real* those intangible or abstract moral principles as defined in The Moral Code through its judiciary, and must *provide protection of peoples freedom, their rights and values*, to be upheld by the people's Congress. Secondly, the Congress may *promote* or have 'ideas' concerning *values*, tangible or intangible principles in their deliberations, but only to inform its citizens of their recommendations. Such things may not be supported by the people, but if they reason such ideas may be a "good" in protection for their pursuit of values, a citizen may vote to act upon them only, if and when *she/he* decides.

CHAPTER 7

PROMOTEANISM

Preamble

> WE THE PEOPLE of the United States, in order to form a more perfect union, establish justice, ensure domestic tranquillity, *provide* for the common defense, *promote* the general welfare, and secure the blessings of liberty do ordain and establish this Constitution for the United States of America.

(Above: The Preamble to the Constitution, 1787, (italics mine))

A Government, should be a symbol of justice immutable in time, culture, or place. It should be changeless, static, consistent, immovable in moral purpose, and in all respects, a codification of The Moral Code. Moral freedom is a necessity in the affairs of all citizens, and the state's function in principle, is to morally protect people from infringement, and to reciprocate on a citizen's behalf. A government must never in any respect, infringe in the affairs of the socioeconomic society of its people where moral principles are not in question.

The letter of the preamble, the introduction to the principle law of the land, distinctly prescribed the nature of the law and the government's actions or inaction, where it is *providing* tangibles for the common defense, it is only *promoting* intangibles for the general welfare. It is obvious that providing for the common defense meant men, their needs, equipment, and arms to protect our nation and the freedom of its people.

Promoteanism, is a form of government where the judicial is an instrument to protect people's freedom and to reciprocate fairly for wrong behavior, i.e. infringement on the life of another. Its mandate to protect our physical being, property, contractual rights and freedom to trade; i.e. to freely seek our own values. To *promote* means or is in the context of Promotean rule, to help promotionally by communication media, meaning to publicize, inform, advertise, or to make available printed or recorded information, as a service, i.e. *to encourage–not provide*. It is a proper foundation for a *PROMOTEAN* type government, which the founders of our constitution, given their *defined words of wisdom promote and provide* in context for the law as I have set forth here. *Promotean*, and its derivatives are synonymous with the word *promote*.

PROMOTEAN Philosophy: A government's mandate, like The Moral Code, is an abstraction. It must be just, non-coercive and non-infringing in people's lives, and in their economic successes. It must be strong by upholding justice in a reciprocal value response to protecting people from those, even with good intentions, that may do them harm physically, culturally, or economically. The government's legal mandate is to prevent immoral behavior, in government, in a citizen's social life, and in his business economically. When it accomplishes these ends, militarily, judicially, and within Promotean philosophy, it will achieve a socioeconomic free state when government will no longer be theoretical, making state and The Moral Code a reality.

A Promotean government is the only form of government with a moral mandate, its law codification of The Moral Code. A government's intangible value of benevolence becomes real as its congress and executive branch attends to first, protection of the country, second, to *promote* people's autonomous nature, i.e. in their free and independent actions, to meet their own *responsibilities* without infringement in their socioeconomic pursuits.

Promoteanism, philosophically, means to protect and encourage man's will to create his own socioeconomic safety net, naturally. It leaves man free in the jungle of civilization, alone, to survive by his own values, physically and mentally, while not infringing on the social or economic lives of others. Such a government will exercise the principle, that one finds in all humans a natural survival will, that the less we provide for them the more likely they will freely do what is necessary to survive. The desire or being compelled to be free, autonomous, and responsible to succeed/survive will build those character values of independence, responsibility, confidence, creativity, ambition, courage, and perseverance. The man without such character survival values has no socioeconomic safety net, which no government can provide.

Governments have *assumed* the role of pseudo-benevolence in the cultural and economic spheres of societies. Assuming their intention to be benevolent lawmakers or rulers in a society, it is proven, beyond any reasonable doubt that, the task to satisfy and treat everyone equal in tangible values is *impossible.* The here-to-fore 'ethical' tenet to provide 'the greatest good for the greatest number' guarantees that someone's, usually many—perhaps 49%, interests in cultural or economic values will be sacrificed for the 'common good.' Therefore, it is dishonest and immoral to say the *common or public good* is being served.

Philosophy began 2585 BP, 'Thales, made an attempt to conceive nature as an intelligible order, in a cosmos. This intellectual daring in Ionia was fused with a new idea of individualism, that man does well to disagree with common opinion. A philosopher says, "I have sought out for myself" . . . '[54] Such should be the role of government to promote man's intangible values of character that they may, seek for themselves—this is what makes us human beings—men, women and children—to have morals and a personal philosophy.

To teach, philosophically, is encouraging, advising, promoting to show the way, how to be dependable, responsible, honest, persevering, ambitious, competitive, and creative, in order to succeed, find human happiness and live as long as possible. When people earn those tangible values or reach their goals free from infringement, without infringing on the lives of others, then the government has made real another abstraction, their moral benevolence. It is such a government *all* the gods, *all* the leaders, and *all* republics or democracies have failed to provide mankind in *all* of recorded history.

A PROMOTEANISTIC GOVERNMENT: Promoteanism is philosophy's answer to the question, what is the distinction between legal and moral? There is none. What is legal *must* be moral. This raises the next question to what extent may a government infringe on the lives of its citizens.—NONE—A citizen has no right to interfere in another person's pursuit of values and since a government's constitution, is a contract *between* people, the government and its citizens, it must by moral law, reflect the *ultimate* in that constraint.

Promoteanism is philosophy's answer to the question, how powerful the state? It must have no absolute power. It will derive its strength as a moral entity, *by example,* as codified in the principles of the Moral Code. A Promotian state will provide for the national defense, the judicial and law enforcement, to protect people's freedom. It may provide only services for promoting intangibly, values people seek, but to *not provide* any tangible value for its citizens, nor to have the power to take values from them. Therefore, it is a moral necessity that governments are motivated moral forces to respect, promote, and encourage the best in human values so that mankind may learn to create, and provide their "good" in success, human happiness, and long life. The government is no longer a benevolent dispersing entity of favors, but the recipient of citizen's voluntary support for moral stature.

The executive branch of government is to promote interstate and/or international affairs. The states must reflect the nature of the central government as well as cities and towns. County governments, as a middle manager is redundant, elitist, and functionally unnecessary, just another layer of costs and bureaucracy. City and town managers could accomplish what a county government takes all year to do, in a few meetings and cooperation, giving them something to do. Regulation by the federal or state governments in interstate commerce would cease. They may create promotional bureaucracies to *promote* commerce, competition, and success, on secular moral grounds without interference in the socioeconomic lives of its people.

The role of government is to protect the nation from invasion, the citizen from infringement of their person or property, to protect the right of the citizen to evolve and develop their own culture, and to protect their right to be a free socioeconomic society. It is for government to make secure man's right to be free in the pursuit of his success, happiness and long life. A government can *provide* protection, police, investigation, courts, and the whole judicial system to the Supreme Court. But, it may only *promote* the intangibles, advice, suggestions or ideas for the culture and its economy. Its role is advisory, consultative, suggestive, recommended, encouraging, an attempt to be persuasive without providing tangible values.

The government's role is to protect the country from military, social, and economic invasion by foreign people or their countries. Where others do not share our moral convictions we must hold those people in contempt of justice. Since we cannot try or imprison them, we can legally isolate ourselves from them physically, socially, and economically, perhaps, with the exception of embassy exchanges in order to promote Promoteanism and bombard them with Promotean philosophy to change their form of government.

A government's highest priority is to fund the military, to protect the country from foreign or alien invasion. Alien, is used in both contexts aliens from other countries and from outer space, The military is the only government agency justified to own means to fly in space, for military equipment research, and defense. It is for the purpose of defending our country from others and protecting us from space debris, such as asteroids, meteors, etc. We should not we be playing 'Star Trek' with billions of dollars of the *poor people's* money. The government is not defending us according to their present mandate, while children go to bed hungry, especially, since our government today takes half of its citizen's wages in taxes. Government research on earth or in space is an example of providing tangibles with no cultural or economic right morally. It is the right of its citizens to determine their own socioeconomic values, i.e. to play or not to play in space. Therefore, it must never be a function of government to spend people's wealth. Its job is forever, justice, justice, justice.

The legal system of a country is its moral reciprocal agent for the people. Within the judicial system, the police force of a community is their first line of defense. The police forces should double, triple or quadruple in patrol and investigative functions, manned by career personnel. Urban areas must use foot patrols in all neighborhoods, and within all high-density business districts, as well in towns, villages, and rural areas. This front line manpower must never feel the effects of budget constraints. A Promotean government will not endanger the people or the nation when money is tight. Every bureaucracy *must* fail before the military, police force, judiciary, and followed by the physically handicapped.

The government (Congress) shall have power to lay voluntary type taxes such as value added or sales taxes, lotteries, annual drives for donations for specific promotional purposes, and to account for all collections and expenditures. The government should not sell securities and bonds or to ever borrow money from any source except in time of war, to repel a military invasion by a foreign power, and to cease that activity when the war is over.

The government, federal, state, or local cannot inherit or own land, companies, corporations, or any real property for any reason. All property that may by default, that lack ownership will be disposed of by public lottery or other fair means, within one year. It can lease land and build facilities, or buildings, that are used in the exercise of its functions, duties and purposes in governing only. Government property, which is unused, must be like wise disposed of by public lottery or other fair means quickly. The people's land, homes or building improvements cannot be charged a tax (rent) by the government. It is a people's right to *own* their land and improvements.

The government's responsibility is to recognize, morally, that the culture and its corollary, the economy, of a nation must evolve freely. It has no moral necessity or right to reshape or maintain the customs, culture or traditions in the social and economic livelihood of the people. The state and/or its employees are hired to provide and perform moral protection for its citizens and very limited promotional *advisory* services only. It is recognized that an advisory action is a value and in Promoteanism is defined in its context to become specifically provisional, conditional or temporary *upon advisory needs only*, until no longer used by or required for the public. The measure of effective government in this respect will be the minimum need and limited duration for a bureau's existence, where nothing is better than something.

The government may not create any collective bureaucracy, or entity such as schools or colleges for the education of children and adults. Also, libraries, museums, parks, communication media, arts, entertainment, or humanitarian organizations are products of people's values. Governments by their nature, their experience and perspective *may* have good suggestions or advice in some value/economic issues, but they are not omniscient. It is best that government *promote* suggest, or advise but never to provide tangible values or immorally make them legal. It is the people's right to organize private, cultural and economic institutions in a country. Whatever ideas a government promotes by suggestion, or advises people and those that the people may reject or accept, is evidence that the public good has been served. The concern of the state is moral behavior, SETTING A MORAL EXAMPLE FOR ITS PEOPLE, to exist and follow The Moral Code, thus promoting socioeconomic morally responsible citizens.

The government is prohibited from taking part in the economy of the nation. Local, state and federal governments shall not create franchises or monopolies in commerce, industry, utility, communication media, or take part in any business venture in supplying the nation with any tangible economic, social or entertainment values. The government's function is to guarantee that no unfair competitive advantage is afforded to any enterprise and therefore, not engage in any such activity. Companies must provide a safe and a non-discriminatory environment. It must provide fair wages and benefits in health and retirement guaranteed for a lifetime, transferable (not company secured) wherever the person wishes to work. For companies it is "humane" and the role of the government, without delay to prosecute for immoral actions by businesses that do not follow The Moral Code. The state's role, to *promote* social and economic values, to advise or be able to distinguish between good and bad, and *provide* the moral foundation, for right or wrong.

Survival is a citizen's first priority and his responsibility. That begins with having a perspective on human life, the history, roots, economics, government's role, or the state of technology, to understand our nature, and who we are. It all helps us to make good choices as we evolve in our lifetime. The role of a Promotean government is not to infringe upon the evolution of an individual's life or our specie to gain their values, and be independent. We are naturally endowed with unalienable rights to be free of a government's oppressive taxation of earned property. We must be free to learn, free to choose a way to success, free to be ourselves, free to try and fail, free to risk and succeed. Then free to love and marry, free to raise family, free to struggle, free to laugh and cry, free to change one's values, free to volunteer, free to give and help others—for we were born free, as such, for five million years, and became a unique success. Freedom, for the primitive was to be entirely responsible for his own life and family. Responsibility was the foundation for survival then and a role model to be updated in a new millennium, for a moral Promoteanistic government—now.

The above, and the following proposals may change technically, but not in principle, and it is inevitable, that the future will have to embrace Promoteanism as a viable role for government on earth. There never has been in the last 10,000 years, nor is there any regulatory or legal moral form of government in the world today. It is an incalculable tragedy of human misery caused by lazy greedy elitists who have created theocratic, socialistic and democratic states throughout history and none have been *moral*, in any sense. The only real freedom man has ever wanted was to be responsible for his own life, and family, supported by government to help protect those rights. He is now cognizant of true freedom, and has the opportunity to achieve the moral right to his own life, if he is brave enough to votes for morals–his responsibilities.

CHAPTER 8

The Promotean System of Government

The following structure or system of the Promotean government, its Constitution, articles and amendments, and all its laws and regulations must be in principle codified derivatives of The Moral Code. There is no doubt that the government will provide systems and/or bureaus that may provide value temporarily with justification by people's vote annually. The only legal bureau that may provide values is in the area of the physically handicapped only, *may* being the operative word, as explained below. The danger of losing a

Promotean state is in believing that by giving something of value may be promoting the general welfare, which is erroneous. When giving or providing any tangible value there is *no guarantee* that the general welfare will be served, or improved, or cause an economic or cultural disaster. A value may never accomplish, do precisely, exactly, correctly, or be a good thing as given or as received. To give is not a government function but a personal one.

The first responsibility of government is to honor The Moral Code and create or change its Constitution, to outline and specify its articles. Our Declaration of Independence and the Constitution were scientifically created, as a result of the Renaissance period of Enlightenment. They saw a social connection to science by following the thinking of such notables as Newton, who found a natural order to the physical universe through reason. The reasoning that *individuals had natural rights* was derived from such thought, it follows that *in the physical universe a sentient being through reason may derive scientifically A Moral Code, a natural order in his behavior to guarantee survival for the individual and our species.*

Charles de Secondat Montesquieu (1689-1775) a philosopher and social essayist a noble Baron of La Brede in France who in his work "The Spirit of the Laws" 1748 was politically influenced by Locke, created the theory of three or four divisions of power within a free republic. The separation of powers was to be a safeguard against the despotism within the structure of the government. His book was translated to English in 1750 and influenced political thought in America. In the summer of 1787 the framers of the Constitution were fully cognizant of this practical political science. Their emphasis was to be the protection of property rights, not democracy.

Under the early government, a state's right to legislate may have been necessary since they all had a sense of autonomy as a nation in themselves. They were in actuality thirteen separate states or countries. Distance was a factor, as was their cultures, and environment, in making them feel as separate entities. Such an attitude no longer exists. In a Promotean federal government the states are well represented to live by the laws that are made to be morally *uniform* throughout the nation.

There will be no regulating of any one in the nation because of place, person, or time. Any regulation, under the present system is a law, such regulations (laws) to prevent immoral behavior are means to control behavior that has not occurred. The law must be designed to punish infringement of people's rights, not on the odds that it may occur. Morally, if an immoral action takes place, courts are to reciprocate to full extent of the law, but regulating behavior on the basis it *may lead* to immoral infringement is not just.

The Constitution may be amended and the following are some of the amendments that a Promotean government may need to create a moral state. They do not affect the foundation upon which our Constitution was created, and will change little with relatively few amendments leaving intact this great document we have treasured, for it holds the *promise* of true liberty. What will change drastically is the size and power of the present government over all our lives. The huge change will come from the courageousness of 'we the people' to forgo political party ideology in order to create our own utopia.

Article I, of our Constitution is the first of three separate powers in our government. Congress, will essentially remain the same with the exception of the ages of *electability* to conform to actuarial age probability at the time the Constitution was written and now, which would increase the age requirements for congressmen and senators. (We live longer, have an extended childhood and their age requirements were mature for that time.)

Also in Article I, Section 8., has come to be known as the 'Commerce Clause,' which has been interpreted so as to give great power and size to the federal government. The Constitution would be amended to morally legalize:

Section 8. First paragraph, to be repealed. Amended for, voluntary taxes only—sales or value added tax on items sold, by lotteries, promos, fund drives, and others, uniform for every states. There would be no value-added taxes on food, clothing or shelter.

Second paragraph, "To borrow money on the credit of the United

States:" is subject to repeal to prevent borrowing from outside the country.

Third paragraph, "To regulate commerce with foreign nations, and among the several states, and with the Indian tribes." This is what came to be known as the "Commerce Clause" and repealed to read, "To regulate commerce with foreign nations." eliminating by repeal, 'and among the several states, and with Indian tribes.'

The "Commerce Clause" along with the last paragraph of Section 8, "To make all laws which shall be necessary and proper for carrying into execution. . . ." is called the "Elastic Clause," together they are permitting unchecked federal expansion and this to be repealed and defined for Promotean legal/moral correctness.

Paragraph five, would not change. An amendment would require the government to base the value of money, each year, on the nutritional value of all food grown in the country the previous year, estimated for the next.

Paragraph six, to remain unchanged.

Paragraph seven, "To establish post offices and post roads:" would be repealed. (Mail and packaging business to be sold as separate companies and all mail delivery secure in continued service and integrity, as such, for not less than fifty years.) All roads to be sold for toll access or free.

All the following paragraphs eight to seventeen remain. The eighteenth paragraph, its 'elastic clause' may be repealed and amended for Promotean correctness. Section nine and ten may remain the same.

Article II, of our Constitution is the second separate power in our government, vested in the President and Vice President and how they are elected. It grants legal powers and responsibilities to the executive branch. This article and its sections will remain the same with the exception of the ages of *electability* to conform to actuarial age probability at the time the Constitution was written, and now, which would increase the age requirements for the President and Vice President. (We live longer, have an extended childhood and their age requirements were mature for that time.)

USS

Article III, of our Constitution is the third separate power in our form of government where the judicial power of the United States, shall be vested in one Supreme Court, and in inferior courts. No changes required.

We have the finest legal system in the world, but it is burdened with cultural issues. It must begin to distinguish between what is moral and what is value, which will simplify its 'legal' mandate. That which is legal can only be moral and shall be its original jurisdiction, a codification of natural law, The Moral Code. The legal system can not protect people from themselves. We are regulating behavior that has not infringed on anyone, but may hurt him self. If a person volunteers to act irresponsible towards his own person he does not deserve protection. Only those socially involved with such a person *may* help to protect him from himself. Society, as a whole has no socioeconomic mandate to control its members, but others may_help, by volunteering their time and funds if they find *value* in such acts.

If giving, helping, volunteering, i.e. any sacrifice was moral it would have to be the law and a government would have a legal right to force its citizens to sacrifice, help or give as the moral thing to do. The meaning of moral then would be whatever the collective needs you must give, that is, to sacrifice, and individual desires would be defined as immoral. Yet our government has through forced taxation, with their 'legal' right give its citizen's earned income to welfare, thousands of grants, endowments, etc., etc., etc., which in reality, is immoral for a government to do. It is this state of confusion in 'ethics' as to what is *moral* and a *value* in the courts and in the governing of the United States—and the rest of the world.

No one, any person, group or society is morally bound to help another. Under Promotean law it is not the mandate of the government to be involved in the hierarchy of people's values. For what it does for one it must do for all and all it can do for its people is to be just and treat them morally equal by its laws. It should be what their Constitution means—legal freedom, the relationship of Promotean government to individual liberty.

The Judicial in a Promotean government would exercise its role as a separate power especially in the making of new law by the Congress. There is no just reason why the constitutionality of a law cannot be reviewed by the supreme court *before* it becomes law, *after* passage by the president, so as not to waste the court's time on bills that may be vetoed. An amendment would be added to the Constitution to repeal and correct the sequence after passage of a law in the Congress in Article I, Section 7.. The purpose is moral, the public does not deserve to be infringed upon to suffer the existence of an unconstitutional law, or the infringement to suffer the time and expense to bring it to the Supreme Court's attention. Yet the people will still reserve the right to bring any law into question before the Supreme Court when practical application proves it is immoral.

Article, III, would remain essentially the same.

Article, IV, Section 3., paragraph two may be amended to limit the power over all territory in the United States and of any particular state which belongs to its citizens. Washington DC, its governing facilities, land and property may have immunity and own such territory and not infringe on private property therein.

Articles, V, and VI, to remain the same

Article, VII. second paragraph repeal phrase,' in the year of our Lord.'

Amendments, I, to XV, shall remain the same.

Amendment, XVI, shall be repealed.

Amendments, XVII, and all others shall remain as prescribed by law.

There may be other amendments, unforeseen at this time and experts in constitutional law will have to include amendments to codify The Moral Code to create the legal framework for a Promotean government.

The Bureaucracy: the present 'cabinet' of the presidency consists of about eighteen members who control the bureaucracies of the government, that have hundreds of agencies under their control. This is wholly unlike a board of directors who are primarily advisory to a company. The cabinet is in charge of bureaus in the government and is responsible for budgets, operation, and following the policies of the president and the laws they must honor. It is where the money is collected and spent. Yet they meet infrequently and usually only when some crisis occurs. Crisis management is *not* how a country as large and wealthy as ours should be governed. It is also not businesslike to have so many people reporting to the president. He cannot properly supervise so many responsible people effectively.

Cabinet members should not be on their own for long periods of time and the president should be meeting with them regularly almost daily, as any good CEO knows. To make it work is to have fewer people reporting to him. Ideal would be four or five, but conceivably, six or seven, which may include:

The Vice President; would report on matters in Congress and his/her other duties.

The Secretary of Defense; who would have reporting to him/her the Army, Navy, Air Force and Space Guardians, Coast Guard, Immigration, and Veteran's Affairs,

The Director of the Central Intelligence Agency: who would report to the President separately daily on foreign intelligence.

The Secretary of State; would have reporting to him/her all embassies. Its work is to teach and encourage Pomoteanism in all nations.

The Attorney General; who would have reporting to him/her the National Bureau of Investigation (FBI), the U.S. Marshalls, the Secret Service, and the Drug, Alcohol, and Firearms Division.

The Secretary of Commerce: who would have reporting to him/her the Department of Agriculture, Industry, Transportation, Securities and Exchange, Energy, and HUD phase out.

The Secretary of Labor; who would have reporting to him/her Job Services—Employment and Unemployment, Occupation Safety, Health and Human Services, and The National Education Advisory Board.

The Secretary of the Treasury; who would have reporting to him/her the Voluntary Tax Collecting and Reporting Bureau, the U.S. Mint, and the Banking Advisory Board.

It would be a simple matter for a president to change

responsibilities of his people, or by his request have a particular head of a department be present at a meeting. But his cabinet would be manageable and frequent meetings would be productive to keep him deeply involved in the business of the nation and a chance to be apprised of possible problems ahead. He would be truly a ruler and felt throughout his government and nation.

Some of the following would be written into an amended constitution to guarantee the citizen's right to a moral government. If we believe that a government is our savior or a secular social experiment, then the choice is very simple, we either want one, a totalitarian collective theocratic or socialistic state, or two, we want freedom and a Promotean moral government.

The government has no moral authority, to ask for the citizen's vote for programs to provide tangible values, nor does the citizen have the right to vote forcing others to give up something of value, and to live according to the values of a voting majority, or by force.

The government shall not standardize values. It can only *promote*, advise, strongly suggest, or advertise what it 'believes' or may have found or statistically shows to be a good standard, procedure, product, value, etc., but it shall never become law.

The government has no moral authority to adopt into law, theological tenets, commandments or totalitarian socialistic police state law that will infringe on the tangible or intangible hierarchy of values, of any citizen.

People are free to volunteer or willingly join a collective that has informed them of the true nature of its ideology, religion or purpose as a group, and to give warning with honest and proper disclaimers, not to, is fraudulent.

The government has no moral authority to make laws that taxes any citizen against their will. But it may levy taxes that are voluntary, such as, but not limited to sales or value-added tax, lotteries, donations, specific fund drives, and may heavily tax imports, of nations that do not reflect our moral law and form of government. Such duties must increase the costs to levels greater than similar products made here. A Promotean country will not tax its imports from, or exports to another Promotean nation. Fees for services of government are taxes and illegal.

To *provide* by voluntary donation assistance to the physically handicapped (physiological or neural physical damage only) with the highest priority in promoting their general welfare. The state will not recognize any psychiatric mental or psychological dysfunction—only physical damage to the brain neurally that is obvious to physicians. Chemical imbalances will not qualify for assistance, since they may be self-inflicted or by parents, doctors, etc..

The government's role is promotional in every respect and to promote moral thinking and will, it is to provide protection and justice. It may promote value—by whatever means available, but to never provide real tangible values for its citizens or others.

A government is a success, only when it provides for the protection of its citizens and makes real for people those intangible values of autonomy, dependability, ambition, success, happiness, and long life. To those who would call Promotianism a valueless form of government, they are right, it is not just something of value, but a moral necessity to *protect not provide* the values of its society. A moral government will create a grateful public and they will be very generous.

I would predict that a country who embraced a Promotean government, unfettered by theocratic or socialistic rhetoric and resistance may in a generation, accumulate a sufficient private endowments that may eliminate value added taxes. The government would exist off of private investments functioning far more efficient with law and order a reality. Only right and good can come from a moral government, anywhere, anyplace, for everyone. The idea that a government must infringe on its citizens for the greater good, we know is a contradiction and immoral.

Equality: We are not born equal, socially or economically. No one has nor will anyone ever be born equal in any cultural economic society. This false issue of achieving equality creates for politicians, lawmakers and rulers, their 'ideologies.' The citizen in choosing such value oriented groups have only one motivation in the voting booth, to vote for their own hierarchy of values with little concern for the minority, or for a concept that eludes them, *freedom.*

The voter becomes part of a partisan group to gain unearned value(s) and when their group wins, they claim it as their right, regardless who must provide. Thus, inequality is the result—not equality. It becomes more and more unequal with every such vote.

In philosophy we are born equal *metaphysically*. We can all experience reality consciously in a world that, through our effort, can sustain us. Nature is *material* and *materialism* is our means to survival. Every material good, bought and sold, in our economic life is of great value. For every thing we buy or sell *means, someone has earned their food.* Our society and government must be such that we have an equal opportunity to join the economy to *earn* a living. To be born *genetically, physically* unique, healthy, whole, and functioning normally, is to be born *equal metaphysically in society.*

We are born equal *epistemologically*, if our *brain and senses* survive birth and childhood *intact physically*. They are the engine and tools of the mind, awareness, memory, reason, and learn how to extract from nature materials for our survival. We should learn how to survive in our youth, and by the time we're young adults have goals, be mentally prepared to work, and achieve happiness. If we waste those years, we still have a brain, and can achieve anything later in life. That may be a social inequality of which no one has any control over except, the parents and the child. All parents rich or poor must be held accountable for molding ignorant or immoral children.

When our parents fail, we do the best we can, do not give up, and we can achieve a measure of success and happiness. We still have our senses to see or read, hear, feel, taste, and smell to experience things and gain knowledge. It is in our power to learn, study, reason, and create no matter what our age or place in society, with perseverance and will. The only equalizer we have is our brain, and we have to use it. Our great advantage is, most people do not want to think.

We are always epistemologically equal with the potential to create our own values, and/or seek our own goals, if we use our brains.

Millions discover in their own successes, that they can learn anything as they take one step at a time. Only if the brain is physically and/or genetically impaired, we may be mentally retarded—unequal epistemologically. We must be vigilant that the medical and psychiatric practitioners do not relate psychological dysfunction to genetics. It has become the dumping ground for the lack of scientific proof, as was instinct in the early 1900s. There may be history of mental dysfunction in a clan, and since we learn everything, we can only deduce they are learned behaviors and tastes from their families, or a lack of thereof.

The particular success we seek is only a matter of will it has to be *wanted* very badly. If we attempt to provide others with any measure of their goals then we eliminate, proportionately, a measure of need and will. This is a natural human law to seek an opportunity, to survive with the least effort. But the law of need (food) is nature's incentive for will, to cause, to risk, have ambition, creativity, and take responsibility to make life easier and better. We are equally endowed with the faculty of will but may not be equally motivated as others.

Human beings *had to be forced* out onto the savanna[7] for our species to evolve through individual effort. We live in nature where every organism in the universe is different, and forced to survive. Nothing in nature is the same (EQUAL) especially humans. All other sentient creatures are like us, metaphysically individual, unequal. We likewise, are eventually forced out in society (nature) and have to survive to exist.

However, all sentient beings other than ourselves, have very small brains (compared to we humans), with limited memory or differentiation epistemologically, causing the same behaviors to a considerable degree over millions of years which is an equality of sorts. Yet, man's mental capacity is far beyond that of any natural being, in behavior or motivation mentally. Individualism is inequality, a fact of nature, but with the same brain, but only when we *have* to think for ourselves to decide what things we value are we individual.

The success of any science comes from man's respect for the laws of nature, to live within the boundaries of complex natural phenomena and to bring about change that will serve his nature. Socialism's (Soviet) attempts to socially engineer the individual, to be of one mind, ended by destroying their people's spirit and their economy. There was no equality they had a two-class system, an elite class with great wealth, and one huge poor low class. It was simple economics, the worker would produce and the elite confiscated the workers wealth—just like royalty and priests have done since the first pharaoh. Russia may never catch up to the west because they retain most of the old laws and have few property rights. They are still without equal opportunity to be human, and without a moral government.

Promoting the General Welfare: We need a Promotean government that is efficient, where there is freedom in choices of the family and reproduction, (based on scientific and technical knowledge of birthing and birth control). With choice in all aspects of our lives we will find that economic market forces, if entirely morally free, would create slower, safer and a measured population growth. The job of a Promotean government is to provide a moral foundation on which to promote jobs for its children's future.

A moral Promotean state would place a *high priority* on replacing present immigration policy *to protect employment opportunities for its citizens.* Immigration (temporary quotas) would be considered only when unemployment rates are operating say, at five to ten points *less than zero percent.* Only acceptable educated immigrants in numbers kept under zero percent, and if unemployment increases by say, one-percent, immigration would automatically cease.

The number of emigres permitted in a country should be according job availability. Guaranteed sponsorship is a must, and job availability, the law. If legal immigrants work, etc., present law would apply. Alien invasion of illegal immigrants, on all borders, would be defended by the military. The immigration service would be a department in the military, and the role of congress and by public referendum to authorize the amount of entries for citizenship only. It would be against the law to hire illegal and legal visiting immigrants with stiff penalties for domestic employers. All illegal immigrants would be tried in military courts and deported. The age of cheap labor in this country would be over. We are presently importing poverty and they will join our poor population. The increase in poverty requires greater taxation.

A Promotean state can, which is technically possible, keep a month by month, or year by year rate of population increase (births), and decrease (deaths under retirement age) to correctly project the employee population. Unemployment, job openings and reductions should likewise be monitored and published. Exports would be unrestricted, except for nuclear technology and those with military necessities. Imports are to have tariffs in proportion to how closely the exporting countries reflect our moral Promotean laws and maintaining a *balance* in exports and imports.

Also, a Promotean moral state would not provide any tangible values but promote the general welfare of its people. The increase in income from a system of non-coercive taxation (except voluntary) would give the citizen more money to spend (guarantee jobs), to save (create jobs), to invest (to create jobs), and as fact, that in such an economic healthy American culture, philanthropy would explode. True, there are cheapskates among the rich, the middle class, and the poor who may have reason. But it is fact that we Americans, who are richer than the rest of the world, have always been generous and not pernicious as many would have us believe of someone with wealth. To promote the general welfare would become unnecessary.

A Promotean socioeconomic government agency would be cognizant of where to go for help in time of need, primarily, for jobs. Such bureaus would help people find work, for free food, clothing, and shelter, for scholarships, for voluntary tutors, a good school, the best rehabilitation clinics, for anything a person needs when in trouble through no fault of their own. This agency would find help in the private sector. It would be their job to help promote a worker's success through private means. They would know how to advise and point him/her in the right direction, that is all.

There would be a new 'social worker,' not one that is trying to socially engineer a culture, but one who helps promote the culture that free people create for themselves. And finally we may create any kind of philanthropic organizations that citizens may donate. Private funds given to a state agency a portion of their fund's earnings to be set aside for extreme emergencies, that they would specify, to help. Such funds would not be for the expenses for the agency but privately managed endowments and its income only for needy victims of natural disasters, or other unfortunate catastrophes and kept in privately managed funds.

For the new social worker in a Promotean state it is evident according to Aristotle, such giving, would be the most difficult thing in the world to do, to give to the right person, at the right time, for the right reason, etc.. If such agencies do their jobs properly, private philanthropy will prevail with government participation and the 'social worker' may become almost irrelevant.

In a Promotean society, people responsible for their own welfare, free to regulate their families and businesses, with government to help them, help themselves, will adjust itself to dictate it's own population growth. As socioeconomic market forces take over, sharp recessions or depressions and growth swings will level off. The birth rate with choice will adjust according to success.

A Promotean president with a nation of responsible citizens will be quick to bring the good news of newly created companies, job opportunities, or new nations that have embraced Promoteanism, etc.. He will also be quick to bring the bad news of problems in the economy, of impending doom from space or some other threat, and never to be kept secret from the people. Citizens will be responsible people of reason, and not a herd to be managed, because they are thought to be emotional basket cases.

Today, at the beginning of the third millennium, countries all over the world are breaking up, seeking independence from larger theocratic or socialistic governments which is a good thing. The real problem they have is that they will find themselves likewise in smaller theocratic or socialistic regimes and not at all free because they have not defined *freedom.* Only a Promotean form of government can achieve their dreams, if they have the will.

USS

In principle, the most important things to protect are life, liberty and property. It is evident we must give people control of their lives, and let them secure their means to exist, because it is natural and moral.

CHAPTER 9

The United Nations

The label, 'The United Nations" states specifically, the intended goal and purpose of that organization—to *unite* all nations. It is building a world government, for absolute central control of all nations, people, and their wealth. It is building a bureaucracy heavily laden with people who believe in world central power, and is pushing in the political direction towards world socialism. Its latest scary move in this direction is their own 'war on poverty' to feed the hungry of the *world.* Where did we hear that before? However, this move is a way to establish the 'benevolent big father', image with the people on earth. It is to shame the countries for money. They are using the same old theocratic and socialistic tactics to cause guilt, to sacrifice our wealth to solve indigence. We know such a government will be self-perpetuating, and must create more poverty, because their source of power and wealth is control of man's conscience, to capture 'poor innocents.'

The UN will spawn huge bureaucracies of international centralized agencies to 'serve' the people. There will be thousands of U.N. delegations and fact-finding missions to each country studying, analyzing and infringing on their processes, each country could and should do for itself. The agencies with their bureaucrats, officials, analysts, statisticians, and the list is getting long, will entrench themselves, whereby, the solution will never manifest itself, since that would in effect eliminate their power and their elitism. They wish to usurp the autonomy of nations. We will create a great force, 'the more ultimate the power, the greater its corruption, ultimately.'

If some form of Promoteanistic rule does not take hold we will face the pharaoh or dictator in a world government, whose concern or law will not recognize the individual or the little family in 'world' deliberations. In such a large collective, guilt and sacrifice is for the undefined 'common good' and will be replicated to, "world good." the world politicians are inventing another layer of bureaucracy where the individual or autonomous nations can never be recognized as a "common denominator."

The more U.N. bureaucracy, the greater and the more centralized, they become. The U.N. 'peace keeper's' global strategy is to use force. Their military force is strategically weak, to try the patience of those who wonder "why can't they keep peace or stop this war?" When we are psychologically stressed or brainwashed, we will be fed the perception that the U.N. needs more power, greater mandate, the freedom to go in, occupy, and force a system of rule, achieving the central power the U.N. is now planning.

To stem this tide of world power is to withhold funding and concentrate our efforts with other nations in summits much like our present day economic summits. There would be more all over the world between say, the central African nations, the northern nations, or groups of nations to discuss the economic problems of their continents or regions. Worldwide continental summits could be held with representatives from African states, Mid East, North American States, etc. The more often all meet and talk the greater stability in international relationships. It is not what will be decided, but that there is regional personal communication between nations and/or territories, giving national leaders wide perspectives in their Promotean responsibilities. All summits should be scheduled as often as possible, and perhaps recreate the present 'World Court' with Promotean principles to verify international laws that may be in dispute as we do now. It would magnify the irrelevance of 'world government' as a concept.

CHAPTER 10

The Party is Over

The party is over in more ways than one. Political party 'ideology' in a Promoteanal government could not exist. Issues, values or promises to create a culture by some group's standards would find no constituents or need. Individuals would be creating their own hierarchy of values. The party would have nothing to promise. There will be nothing in tangible values to wheel and deal for, i.e. *no pork*, and the 'party' is over.

Every political party's 'ideology', includes a body of doctrine, myth, or belief with reference to some political socioeconomic plan, as that of a theocratic kingdom, socialism or fascism along with its bureaucratic devices for putting it into operation. Its what the politician sells, and for us to buy. Buyer-beware of the politician with an 'ideology' for a vote to give your mind and wealth to a political party. Promotean governance is without an ideology, which may exist in individual values and cannot be construed as a moral issue, but in the context of present political schemes, political ideology is selling values of which we in effect lose control, and is now responsibility of the government. Such a political ideology is culturally a hierarchy of specific values of which government has no moral mandate to *provide* people, which was the original intent of the 55men who created the Constitution in Philadelphia.

A Promotean government eliminates a party politician and his bureaucrats who would have to go home, to run a business (really create jobs), go back to his law firm (chase ambulances), or (woe is me!) go find a job. Career politicians and their 'experience' in wheeling and dealing with other people's money would end. No one would be able to select a profession because of their charisma, power, 'romantic' elitism, or skilled in the art of sophism (baloney), who are selling control over people's tax dollars. We will be searching and voting for a morally responsible executive (a president or congressman) that had experience in job creation and *knew* how to promote diplomatically, international trade in every part of the world, while protecting his domestic jobs.

All people will be subject to the same law, and every citizen will receive equal justice. There will not be plush jails for the elite, the legislator and the private powerful. All government and economic sector criminals will be incarcerated in the same jail facility and suffer equally for crimes regardless of *their* high or low class, and this is called justice.

A Promotean government and its electorate will not be immune from fraudulent politics, since all people may be subject to evil thoughts and a few will become criminals. That may never end, because we have free will to choose good or bad in values, and may decide right or wrong in morals. Therefore, there may be political fraud. They may falsely claim expertise in a profession, or in their personal moral qualifications for an elected, appointed, or hired Promoteanal government position. But that is why the people must learn and be educated in moral principles (of right and wrong) of their government, its history, and what "good" values are worthy of effort in their socioeconomic lives. We need not fear the criminal. Our only fear will be the fear of freedom.

The danger of fraud can occur in campaigns by candidates who may propose by some twisted convoluted semantic theory of collective concepts, which are actually contrary to the Moral Code, or Promotean government philosophy. Only an electorate, that fully understands the principles of the Moral Code and is educated in the philosophy of a Promotional form of government, will reason and may vote to

USS

preserve their freedoms, because they would know what was politically collectivism or individualism.

The 'idea' prevalent today, that people's politics or theistic beliefs are not proper subjects for discussion, is an effort on the part of those institutions in these matters, to prevent us from seeing the light of reasonable discussion. To never discuss and/or argue their merits is to deny meaningful discourse concerning our cultural heritage and the cultures we will create in the future. Are they above the First Amendment? It is a dereliction of intellect, to conceal, neglect, or deceive our selves in accepting any ideology of an elitist theocracy or democracy as above reproach, is there no free press? At stake are two great issues we face today. Do we want theocratic or socialistic state ideologies, or Promotean freedom? What kind of government will protect our personal autonomy and make us free, collectivism or individualism? Or is freedom too frightening and we would rather be ruled from the cradle to the grave?

Today we have many political parties and each has a collective ideology. There are many with ideas on how we should live under their cultural rule of law. They are, in effect, asking us to vote for, which will dictate how our American socialistic or theocratic culture should be managed? It begins with the complete education of our children, day care, dressing them all alike, (an affront to our individual nature) feeding them breakfast, their mental and health care, universal control of the medical profession, colleges, Fascist industrial regulation, and hundreds of infringements on our freedoms. The people who would control our minds and wealth under Promotean rule would have no issues to argue, and no agendas—only freedom with moral rules.

In a Promotean government, there will be no 'to the victor go the spoils,' only their pay, if not voluntary, and thoughtful creative service *for* the people is where they will find their just rewards. With no great elitist promises or schemes for ideologies an electorate, the absence of pork, political payoffs for contracts, campaign workers, friends and relatives, or special interests, who could not create large campaign contributions or the subsequent high taxation for their campaigns.

Only moral issues, job creation, and the protection of people's wealth and freedom would be left for campaigning. There would be little room for corrupt elections or governments.

A Promotean nation would attract people who are morally bound and interested in working *for* an informed electorate. Also, people who understood the changing values of a society would be running for election, *and there would be many*. Fraudulent promises and the 'party' of politics would be over.

The only problems the citizen would have are that he will have are, the responsibility for creating his hierarchy of values, and managing his own wealth.

CHAPTER 11

Privatization

Privatization is the process of creating private companies, corporations or institutions from government bureaus, agencies or departments in the federal, state or local governments. To change radically and tear down present bureaucratic functions may cause hardship among the people. Any proposed privatization as a Promotean necessity will call for the replacement of the function, equal or better and is available such as Social Security and they are free to join or not. They need not change, but at some proper future time new people may not be admitted into a government program. Government workers will have available private jobs before being dropped from government payroll. The transition to a Promotean government would have to be sensitive and humane.

How do we create a Promoteanal government? We privatize. The people who have a vested interest in our bureaucracies are resisting privatization vehemently. We have all witnessed how socialism, with complete control, in socialist countries failed. The walls came down to expose their societies, totally bankrupt without capital, outdated industries, infrastructure destroyed and an economy of no value to themselves or the rest of the world. Their socialistic ideology led to cultural socioeconomic immoral behavior towards their citizens and the rest of the world they came in contact. Socio-economically they are a half a century behind us. Any technology they enjoy, they stole. Our bureaucrats are oblivious to the cause—total infringement within the culture and economy of its people. Left wing socialistic democrats and theocratic republicans, (their poor innocents), still believe their collectivism can work. But the real players for power want more of that power, because they believe altruism is 'ethically' moral and it doesn't matter whether it works or not, or who gets hurt.

The pope-kings of the Middle Ages maintained an iron-fisted rule, by creating god-king despots, helping them set up serfdoms and keeping people poor and ignorant, for over a thousand years. We still have a huge poor class due to a fifty-percent tax rate, and yet, quite don't know why poverty occurs. The rest of the world is worse off, and they don't have a clue.

Our cities are dying. We can witness that decay in our cities as politicians strive to revitalize and recreate their confiscating tax base back into the city. When taxes have been spent, they borrow from any source, even from the state or federal government to build stadiums sports centers, art centers theaters, etc.—all the trappings of the elite. Our children and their grandchildren will pay for the ruling elite's bills. And you will note the poor white and black so called trash, yes, the human trash-heap the elite has created that can not afford to attend these 'fine' art palaces—by design. These are cultural values that only free people should create—not governments. So perverse is taxation by governments they have created a huge poor class in every city on earth.

A peaceful revolution is preferred to preserve our nation and give the control of people's wealth back to them. There are countless books, suggestions, and theories on how we might privatize and gain control of our wealth. The first serious suggestion to that end and beyond was Murray N. Rothband's "For a New Liberty" 'The Libertarian Manifesto' published in 1973. It has many good suggestions and reasons for privatization. His thesis or theory of anarchy, however, cannot work in the long run or the short-run either. The problems of behavior, moral law and order, defense of our country, and the need for a moral spokesman among nations, is crucial to our living in the real world, since free will, could be moral stability in a Promotean nation or an immoral liability for societies without government.

The people must *protect* their values, specifically their cultures, to assure their society is evolving morally free. The need for laws to control immoral behavior, and limit government intrusion on people's socioeconomic values, eliminating regulation, subsidies, or economic actions that are not moral issues. Emanuel S. Savas author of "Privatization" is a help to better government, a step in the right direction. Where Rothbard goes too far, Savas may not go far enough, but could be an interim condition. He does not quite get the government out of socioeconomic control of the culture. When one controls the economy the control of culture is the result and vice versa, the control of culture controls the economy.

The problem of present governments engaged in value encroachment on society is that there is no clear-cut idea of where to stop. The boundaries set today will always be argued as unfair to someone now or tomorrow, and where we make law in response, the regulation will be challenged for providing more values, never less. Examples, are school budgets, which are insisting that sports along with entrenched art and music be included in the curriculum and social programs take precedence over science related courses. Some states are seeking to prohibit voter debate on sports issues in their budget. It is obvious that the state now understands the electorate is oblivious of immoral implications in the majority vote, even in a frivolous issue. Also a republican theocracy wants to teach religious myth as part of school curriculum and post the Ten Commandments in public buildings.

We witness creeping socialization at work today, also, in social security, minimum wages, and war on poverty, Medicare, universal health care, and welfare. They say they are changing welfare, as we know it—we shall soon see. Why kick the poor they create when they are down? Why not use space funds for welfare to the states? Do we let the government take over insurance companies, drug companies, or guarantee the home mortgage, if we default? In effect, we are asking to be relieved of responsibilities, to be taken care of from the cradle to the grave, i.e. socialism, but not for the poor. But, the school is the quintessential tool to build a socialist state, and for this reason it will become our greatest struggle to wrest it from their greedy hands. Religions, who teach all over the world, understand that a child, properly brainwashed at a young age, will accept any fantasy as true by simple repetitive indoctrination. Lenin, Mussolini, and Hitler, understood, and socialistic educators here and abroad today understand and use such means to control people's minds.

Our salvation is to privatize and we will be reminded of the evils that it may incur. However, if such evils did happen in the past it was with the acquiescence of the state. A Promotional government to be a moral force in peoples lives, will prevent, protect, and punish infringement using principles of The Moral Code. It is their mandate, their *only* job, and the right of the people to expect that they carry out that assignment. Therefore, if the nation is to survive, it is well to expect the present government and its people must be humane in the transference of wealth, and the *power*, from the state to the people, and keep it that way by enforcing moral behavior.

Privatization must begin with the voter. There is a vested interest for those in power—all elected and non-elected bureaucrats to maintain a status quo. Their whole career hangs in the balance of power, but we have the real power, the creators of wealth, a moral sense of justice, and the vote. However, there are tremendous problems. The voter is convinced that because he has voted in a majority, it makes his argument moral or right—albeit, to the victor go the spoils. Its no longer the gun but the physical force of the majority that rules. The vote they site, created the greatest good for the greatest number, and therefore morally justified. With that pseudo morality, the minority must knuckle under the power of the majority.

To initiate privatization, begin in the local school systems, and lobby for, or get elected to school boards, and push for voucher systems from the town, city, and in your state. Where resistance stops progress, voters, en mass, should withhold, school taxes and tax returns. Support your effort with moral reasons in literature, speeches, local newspapers, and with everyone you meet or know.

As a taxpayer write, then be very vocal, vehemently insistent, confront them, in their face, constantly, be moral consistently and specific.

The argument that will be the most bothersome is, they will cite the reason 'poor children' will not get an equally good education:

First, the poor rate the lowest in all test scores, throughout the country– it is not equal now. What is their excuse? They teach—?

Second, the poor have time on their hands and are ideal for home or private schooling with a voucher to compensate for, materials etc..

The third step is to eliminate all taxation for families earning under, say, $100,000 per year if they are, in home or private schooling, an interim solution until all income tax is repealed.

Four, if the middle class receives voucher money for private schooling there would be more than sufficient taxes from parents who no longer have children in the system, the childless, single, retirees, and businesses contributing to the poor. The working poor pay taxes too. We should also remember Hong Kong enjoyed the highest average wage in the world before China's takeover. And to be truthful there was a poor, but working culture there, but we have free will, and there are people all over the world who will not apply themselves, under ideal educational and job creating systems, even among many spoiled rich. Using the poor is the poorest argument, because they cannot continue to take people's wealth and eliminate jobs the poor man needs.

The problem of change, the Promoteanal voter must join in a grass roots peaceful revolution, to tear down the tax base, and take children out of public schools. We can never hope to change government until we remove ourselves from the influence of *state* run schools. They are the learning centers for theocratic and socialistic ideology. Taking control of the schools is the hard part, the rest of privatization will be a cup cake. However, for the present, as it has been through all time, it is still our decision. A society engulfed in immoral behavior, expecting something for nothing, will end up in an evil empire—from evil comes evil, which we will deserve.

What we expect from government, whether we are rich or poor, is the example it will set for families, and for society as a whole to live by, The Moral Code. We all must have a conscious appreciation for fairness (justice) or moral behavior, to know what is right and wrong in dealing with others, and to know for ourselves and our children what is good and bad. When parents give up responsibility for their children to someone else they help destroy their child's heritage for an ant-like state. Only when we really care enough to be there to teach, and care, in every way possible, do they become *ours*, and we begin to earn a measure of immortality we truly deserve. For what other reason do we have children? If we can get that right, we just might make it through the 21st century, the whole earth living in moral Promotean societies. Privatization is the key to a Promotean government.

CHAPTER 12

The Promotean Vision

Career bureaucrats who constantly lobby our lawmakers, for

funding or increased budgets year after year man the great regulatory bureaucracies we fund today. Eighty percent of the lobbyists in Washington are bureaucrats seeking to increase their share of our money. They are not interested in reducing spending, but seem to be increasing the socialistic trend of government. They work in bureaucracies creating regulations, hiring more people to busy themselves in regulatory paper work procedures. They *promote nor provide* anything valuable in expertise or advise to *help* the people in a free economy. As socialists they may actually hinder the economy purposely, to destroy capitalism a threat to their bureaucratic system of government.

To *promote* does *not* mean to *provide*. To promote is to encourage and further a free economy for its citizens. A promotional bureaucracy is one whose only function is to gather information and publish 'How To' and general updates on the conditions, problems, and how each could be solved by the people themselves. They would not be large bureaus, in *federal, state or_local* governments. Within each bureau would be people who would help advise and guide people who came in for general information and specific advise. Others would handle mail inquires, etc.. On another level there would be people who would research the economy for updating and creating new ways to advise and guide people in a changing economy.

The federal or state bureau would advise large interstate companies in the international market import, export, and how foreign bureaus operate, as well as the information they may use to help their businesses. There would be no interstate or regional regulations, only vehicular, registration, and safety laws. There would not be the profusion of bureaus we see today, since their only concern would be to promote the economy, not regulate or social engineer the people in their towns, cities, states or the nation.

Bureau heads, directors, managers, and their employees would qualify on education, experience and character values. However, the most important requirement would be that *every* person have considerable experience in that sector of the economy, say, over twenty five years, the more experience, the better. If a man lost his job, for reasons other than dishonesty, violence, stealing, etc., nearly retired or over fifty years of age, would legally make the best candidates for experience and sound advise.

There will be no 'career' bureaucrats only people with expertise, ideas from the field and with a nut and bolt understanding in the agency's sector of responsibilities. There will be more changes in personnel, no one lasting more than ten or fifteen years. Bureaucratic management would serve less than ten years. It is primarily to prevent entrenchment of old ideas, or having people without field experience, and to make way for a fast changing economy, or new ideas such people can bring to a bureau directly. The only people who may not need that experience may be janitors, laborers, etc., but even they will be hired by the same age and character requirements of fifty five or older in need.

Our unemployment bureau, say, would consist of people from personnel or human resource departments in companies or from private employment agencies. All will have considerable experience, over fifty five, and of good character. Those manning the office would be advisory to help find work not unlike their present organization. However, there would be no unemployment check. They would be guided to the many private, voluntary philanthropic organizations that provided specialized help. They would be advised which ones provided money, and job search and the bureau would make the necessary contacts and arrange appointments. It is more likely that unemployment insurance companies would surely sprout in such a vibrant economy, that employers would recommend for payroll deductions. Unions would retain their present status under moral law that they would welcome.

A Promotean nation will not be taxed excessively even though they will have a free reign in applying a one time (the end product, not all its parts are taxed) sales tax. If the government raises the sales tax too high, then people will not buy the product and job security will be affected quickly. Hidden taxes, those included in the product not at the point of sale, such as fees, licenses, material, labor, investment, savings, profits, real estate and a host of other taxes that are not visible at the point of sale would be eliminated. At present the politician is able to blame the greedy business community, manufacturers, wholesalers and retailers of greed and ripping off the public. But present hidden taxes have the same affect as one excessive sales tax to make a product unaffordable and to eliminate jobs. Taxation causes unemployment and poverty. A Promotean government voluntary tax system would be providing empirical evidence for the public, of job loss in the economy if the tax is too high.

The end product or sales tax excludes materials to be sold to make an end product. All mining and artificially man made materials, parts, and products not used in an end product would be not taxable unless exported. Any end product such as machinery for manufacturing products (other than food farming and animal raising and processing which would be exempt) for production or office such as computers, etc., would be taxed as an end product. What ever end product is sold to a dealer or wholesaler should be labeled as to display *all* taxes incurred in the manufacturing capital equipment, etc., much like the present nutrition labels, and material content in present labeling, by the Commerce Bureau and socioeconomic commercial or industrial associations.

The tax law would prohibit the lack of tax labeling and dishonesty in dollar or percentage amounts. A family or businessman will keep all that they earn, and though they spend it unwisely or in sound purchases and investments would make no difference. The end result will be job security or job creation. No one entity person, organization or government can hope to plan the cultural or economic needs of the citizen except they themselves. Understanding that, people must be assured that what he or she earns belongs to them and to volunteer taxes if that is their desire. People have a right to know what the tax bill is before, purchase. In that way government and the economy both earn their needs by performance.

A Promotean government with its nearly self regulating voluntary tax base will not have access to huge sums of money to create very large bureaucracies. Money restrictions will keep them small and lean. Wages may not measure up to what bureaucrats and their underlings get today, but, it will be employing the older people that have the experience and may enjoy that work. Those who want to help people and volunteer will be in the bureaucracies dedicated to do just that. "But where will the young in the government be represented?" it may be asked—it will be *their mothers and fathers helping* in government, who will promote their best interests. They will be the new 'social worker' or ombudsman/person to handle job search, or legal problems. We cannot do any better than that.

The people in a Promoteanal bureaucracy will be helping the society help them selves when they are in trouble. If the government is an effective moral force, all the people will respond to their requests in kind. The government will be promoting responsibility, individualism and autonomy for each and every person in the society. People will be promoting the *human safety net* of those intangible values that no state has ever, or can ever provide, such as, morals, autonomy, individualism, independence, responsibility *scholarship*, ambition, creativity, and risk to be an entrepreneur. It will be noted that in earning their success, in their endeavors, they will have made all those intangible values real. *Only*, when a person earns by learning and succeeding in some endeavor, or by gaining tangible values, can a citizen be identified as owning those intangible character values of scholarship, ambition, responsibility, independence, etc., etc..

The role of Congress would continue to operate as it does today. However, any law must pass the Supreme Court test *before* it may receive the president's signature. Once a law is enacted and in practice, the citizens, or congress may challenge its constitutionality. Our congress would take on the nature of an immense jury for the country upholding law, not 'creating' new ideological socioeconomic regulating entities. It would be our jury, concerned with the right and wrong aspects of moral law. 'Does it interfere in our free socioeconomic or expression of the individual citizen or not?' 'Does this bill support our businesses or how will jobs be affected?' 'Can we do this and reduce taxes?' or 'Why do we keep that bureau?' Our congress originates all money bills but never passes one to save taxes—only to increase taxes and their power. The congress would be responsible for approving bureaucratic appointments from the executive branch. House members will approve of bureaucratic workers and/or review resumes of elders applying from their districts for national and state government. Legislators would do the same for their state governments. City and town governments may have a citizen's watch dog group. No relative or campaign worker of a representative would be eligible for work in government—the *end* of 'To the victor go spoils.'

The government will cease all scientific research, and businesses with more of their profits can resume exploration. Pure research in colleges and universities would decide the future of our technology, not government. We have many private organizations that ask for donations for 'research' to eliminate symptoms but not immunizations that prevent such diseases. We should create for researchers private lotteries a type that from our huge donations each year will reward substantial immunization prizes out of such a fund for a laboratory's successful discovery. Then we may see results.

Promotional government that will protect our freedoms socially and culturally without coercive taxation will create on earth, the greatest job zone the world has ever seen. With jobs, exceeding people, the competition for labor would increase tax-free wages, for spending, and securing more jobs, creating a vibrant economy. Businesses would have more for research, creativity, the science of manufacture, more for plants and equipment to create more jobs. Investments by entrepreneurs and small business would increase and there would be *more* jobs for all. Unemployment would disappear and with a wise immigration law, protect high paying jobs and increase opportunities for our citizens. The government would be *promoting* jobs and the people would be *providing* jobs. The poor will disappear.

Social Security will survive and be grandfathered until private sources have prevailed and make it irrelevant. The same would happen to present Medicare and Medicaid. Actually, these may be taken over by private investors who may as insurers increase benefits substantially since these government bureaus have grossly mismanaged our funds. That is why the medical professions have

USS

raised costs, because there is no organized accountability in governments.

Promoteanism will create the greatest tax-free investment zone in the world. Foreign Investors and corporations from heavily taxed countries would invade our shores with dollars to invest, to cash in on untaxed profits and savings to reinvest over and over, creating more jobs and opportunities of unimaginable proportions. Companies large and small would compete for employees and contribute more to benefits, providing all the goodies such as medical care, retirement, insurance's, vacations and leaves for all kinds of reasons. Not only would foreign countries suffer a 'brain drain', but a 'money drain' as well. The world would *have* to follow suit and become tax-free governments.

Those countries that fail to become truly Promotean nations would be isolated economically. We do not need their slave labor business nor will we do business with them to further their regimes and keep their status quo with our dollars and goods. When we do business with such nations we only prolong their rule over their people, we sustain their misery. We have never needed the rest of the world to create our wealth. And as a moral society, to trade in supporting such despotic governments is immoral.

This is only a brief sketch (perhaps the subject of another book), but, with a little will and the creative genius of the American people as well as people all over the world, *all of it is possible.* The structure here will change somewhat with legal and moral minds that will eliminate transitional problems, in constitutional think tanks dedicated to the principles of Promotean Philosophy and The Moral Code.

There will be a loud outcry that 'IT CAN NOT WORK!' This will be an insult to the integrity of mankind. Some will yell 'ISOLATIONISM!' but we were isolated and our success the envy of the world, and they came to us. American citizens, I believe will pay little attention to those outcries, and just *make* it work. Note that 'It can not work' and 'Isolationism' will come from socialistic and theocratic statists who are only greedily concerned with controlling our minds, and how to confiscate our wealth. When we come to realize that all governments, before this book was written, had only such purposes, then with a vengeance, we *must and can* take that control upon ourselves.

Once again we may get the chance to lead the world towards real freedom, this time we should not bungle it.

GLOSSARY—DEFINITIONS

From Book IV, Morals:

moral (mor'al, mor'), adj. 1. of, pertaining to, or concerned with principles or rules of right mental conduct or the distinction between right and wrong; The Moral Code: moral necessities, 2. expressing or conveying truths or counsel as to right conduct, as a speaker or a literary work; moralizing: a novel.

3. founded on the fundamental principles of right conduct and legalities codified from

The Moral Code: a moral obligation to follow its principles.

4. OK

5. conforming to the rules of right conduct (opposed to wrong or immoral): a moral man.

6. is a value issue OUT, replace with: Opposed to ethics' synergism of morals and values.

7. OK

8. OK

9. OK

10. The embodiment or *nature of behavior*. (italics—correction)

11. OK

12. The moral mental acts of censorship of immoral mental/physical act Syn. 5. right, righteousness, rightness, rightly, honest, honorable, non-infringement, integrity, principles of survival in human behavior. (All references to ethics or the ethical should be eliminated.)

Definition example above from: 1987 2nd edition: The Random House Dictionary

New words below:

Promo'tean: n, cap. 1. a moral state in which all its laws are a codification of The Moral Code; where the government is a judicial and military moral force, only, and holds elected offices. It will encourage to help further its people's right to exist and flourish autonomously, by not providing tangible values, but may, by Promotean means, to suggest, encourage, to promote with encouraging information only—limited to intangible values. Or in the context to 'promote' value, to encourage only.

2. a government in which the supreme power rests in the body of citizens entitled to volunteer or to be paid for public service and their representatives elected directly or indirectly by them to provide protection for their freedom and earned values exercise the vote.

3. any body of persons viewed as autonomous individuals.

4. a state in which the head of government is elected—not a monarch or other hereditary head of state.

5. to promote or encourage intangible values as may be found in a person's hierarchy of values, and to provide no tangible socioeconomic values for its citizens.

6. a person or the people who favor a Promotean form of government.

7. a member of a Promotean organization.

—plural—Promotean—Promoteanal, adj.—cap.

Promo'teanism: n, 1. the Promotean theory of governance.

2. procedure or practice in accordance with form of government.

1. Promotean moral principles, policy or adherence to them as codified according to The Moral Code.
4. the philosophical science of Promotean principles and its form of government.
5. A natural government stage following theocratic, socialistic, republican and democratic political systems.
—Promoteanism—cap.
Promo'teanistic: adj. 1. of or pertaining to Promotean or Promoteanism.
2. in accordance with Promotean or Promoteanism.
3. advocating or supporting Promoteanism.
—Promoteanistical—ly adv.—cap.

Promo'teanize:-ized,-izing: v. 1. to make Promotean.
—Promoteanization n.—Promoteanizer n.—cap.

NOTE:

The nature of the term, promote, and its derivatives may inadvertently, through speech in contexts, political and societal, and will be synonymous with Promotean definitions that have been derived from the verb promote as follows.

promote: v. 1.—per dictionary definitions (Random House).
X. phil. v. to help to encourage to exist or flourish; in government, (in philosophy as defined in a theory of a moral government, may promote intangible values only, but does *not* provide *any* tangible values.).
promotional: will perhaps be colloquially used in the context of describing a
Promotean form of government.
It is synonymous with Promotean n.—Promotionalism n.-
Promotionalistic adj.—cap.

Promo'tionalism: n. (slang), 1. referring to the Promotean form of government Synonymous with Promoteanism.

2. procedure and practice in accordance with this theory.

3. Promotean moral principles, policy or adherence to as codified according to The Moral Code.

4. The philosophical science of the Promotean principles and its theory of government.

5. A natural moral government stage, following immoral theocratic, socialistic, republican,

democratic political systems and their variations.

—Promotionalism n.—cap.

Promotionalistic: adj. (slang) 1. referring to Promotean or Promoteanism.

2. may be used in accordance with Promotean or Promoteanism.

3. may be used in advocating or supporting Promotean principles, or Promoteanism.

-Promotionalistical—ly = Promoteanistical—ly adv.—cap.

BIBLIOGRAPHY: GOVERNMENT

Ref.
No.
Chapter 1

-0-

Chapter 2

1. Lowie, Robert Ph. D.: "Primitive Society," Pub. by, Liveright Publishing Corporation, 1947: P. 205-6.

2. IBID, P. 235.
3. Nissen, Hans J.: "The Early History of the Near East, 9,000 BC. to 2000 BC.," The University of Chicago Press, Chicago, Ill. 1988: Chap. 2., 'The Time of the Settlements,' P.35.
4. Lowie, Robert Ph. D.: "Primitive Religion," New York: Boni & Liveright Publishers , 1924: P. XV.

Chapter 3

5. Peikoff, Leonard: "Ominous Parallels," Briarcliff Manor, New York; Stein & Day, Publishers; 1982: P. 49.
6. Raushing, Herman: "The Voice of Destruction," New York: The Putnam Berkley Group, Inc., 1940: P. 239-40
7. Peikoff, Leonard: "Ominous Parallels," Briarcliff Manor, Pub., by, Stein & Day/Publishers, 1982: P. 51.
8. Machiavelli, Niccolo, Introduction by Max Lerner: "The Prince and the Discourses," Pub. by, Random House, New York, 1950: P. 64-65
9. Thatcher, Margaret: "The Moral Foundations of Society," Pub. By, Imprimis, Hillsdale, Michigan: 'Reprinted by permission from IMPRIMIS, the monthly journal of Hillsdale College', March 1995: Vol. 24, No. 3, P. 1.
10. Rodell, Fred: "55 Men The Story of the Constitution," Harrisburg, Pennsylvania; Stackpole Books, 1986: P. 206.
11. Thatcher, Margaret: "The Moral Foundations of Society," Pub. By, Imprimis, Hillsdale Michigan; 'Reprinted by permission from IMPRIMIS, their monthly journal of Hillsdale College', March, 1995: Vol. 24—No. 3, P. 1.
12. Hoffman, Michael: "Egypt Before the Pharaohs", New York: Dorset Press, (Copyright Holder, Alfred A. Knopf, NY.) 1990: P. 200.
13. IBID. P. 343, 345.
14. Garrity, John A., & Peter Gay, Eds.: "The Columbia History of the World," Pub. By, Harper & Row, Publishers Inc., New York, 1988: P. 69.

.USS

15. Hoffman, Michael: "Egypt Before the Pharaohs," Pub.by, Dorset Press, (Copyright Holder, Alfred A. Knopf, NY.), 1990: P. 328-29.
16. IBID, P. 331.
17. Nissen, Hans J.: "The Early History Of the Near East, 9,000 BC. to 2,000 BC., Pub. By, University of Chicago Press, Chicago Ill., 1988: P. 74 80.
18. Garrity, John A., & Peter Gay, Eds.: The Columbia History of the World," Pub. By, Harper & Row, Publishers, Inc., New York, 1988: P. 77.
19. IBID, P. 77.
20. IBID, P. 79-80.
21. Marx, Karl, & Frederick Engels: "The Communist Manifesto," Pub. By, International Publishers Co., Inc., New York, 1968: P. 31

Chapter 4

22. Hindley, Geoffery: "The Book of the Magna Carta," Pub. By, Constable & Company Limited, London, UK, 1990: P. x.
23. IBID, P. x, xi, Great Britain has so acted in the past, and may do so at any time–Hindley gives examples.
24. Jefferson, Thomas: "The Declaration of Independence", July 4, 1776.
25. Rodell, Fred: "55 Men The Story of the Constitution," Harrisburg, PA, Stackpole Books, 1986: P. 4.
26. IBID, P. 14.
27. Bushman, Richard: E. Foner & J. Garraty eds.: "The Oxford Reader's Companion to American History," Boston: Houghton Mifflin Co., 1991: Essay, 'Revolution,' P. 943-4, parenthesis and emphasis mine.
28. Peltason, Jack Walter: "Understanding the Constitution," Orlando Florida: Holt, Rinehart and Winston, Inc., 1988: P. 4.

Chapter 5

29. Wiseman, Donald J., Author: Parrinder, Geoffery, Ed: "World Religions," New York: Facts On File Publication, 1981 permissions granted by Octopus Publishing Group, Ltd. for their div. Hamlyn Books; London: Mesopotamia, P. 130.
30. IBID, Griffiths, J. Gwyn, Author: Ancient Egypt, P. 140.
31. IBID, Wiseman, Donald J., Author: Mesopotamia, P. 125-6. (Counsels of Wisdom,)
32. Sigmund, Paul E.: "Natural Law In Political Thought," Cambridge, Massachusetts: Winthrop Publishers, Inc., 1971: P. 20, to 24.
33. IBID, P. 27.
34. IBID, P. 27.
35. d'Entreves, AP.: "Natural Law," London: Hutchinson University Library, 1970: P. 55.
36. IBID, P. 55.
37. Sigmund, Paul E.: "Natural Law In Political Thought," Cambridge, Massachusetts: Winthrop Publishers, Inc., 1971: P. 77.
38. Beardsley, Monroe C., Ed: "The European Philosophers from Descartes to Nietzsche," New York: The Modern Library by Random House, 1960: P. 330.
39. Sigmund, Paul E.: "Natural Law In Political Thought," Cambridge, Massachusetts: Winthrop Publishers, Inc., 1971: P. 138

Chapter 6

40. Malthus, Thomas R.: "An Essay on the Principles of Population," New York: W. W. Norton & Company, (text 1798) 1976: P. 19.
41. Garraty, John A. & Peter Gay, Eds: "The Columbia History of the World," Harper & Row Publishers, New York, 1988: P. 29-30.

42. Malthus, Thomas R.: "An Essay on the Principles of Population," New York, W. W. Norton & Company, (text 1798) 1976: P. 19.
43. IBID, P. 20.
44. Hoffman, Michael: "Egypt Before the Pharaohs," New York: Dorset Press, (Copyright holder Alfred A. Knopf, A Div. of Random House Inc.), 1990: P. 309-10.
45. Crawford, Michael, & David Marsh: "The Driving Force," New York: Harper and Row, Publishers, 1989: paraphrased.
46. Hoffman, Michael: "Egypt Before the Pharaohs," New York: Dorset Press, (Copyright holder Alfred A. Knopf, Inc.), 1990: P. 318.
47. Rodell, Fred: "55 Men The Story of the Constitution," Harrisburg, Pennsylvania: Stackpole Books, 1986: P. 57.
48. Peltason, Jack Walter: "Corwin & Peltason's Understanding the Constitution," Orlando Fla. Holt, Rinehart and Winston, Inc., 1988: P. 57.
49. IBID, P. 57, (parenthesis (2) mine).
50. IBID, P. 60, (emphasis mine).
51. Flexner, Stuart B. Ed.: "The Random House Dictionary of the English Language," New York: Random House, 1987: Def. *inflation.*
52. Friedman, Milton S. & Rose: "Free To Choose," New York: Avon Books, 1981: P. 242.
53. IBID, P. 243

Chapter 7

-0-

Chapter 8

-0-

Chapter 9

-0-

Chapter 10

-0-

Chapter 11

-0-

Chapter 12

Suggested Reading: Rothbard, Murray N.: "For a New Liberty," Revised Edition, Pub.by, Fox & Wilkes; San Francisco, CA, 1973, 1994.

Savas, E.S.: "The Key to Better Government," Pub. By, Chatham House Publishers, Inc., Chatham, NJ 1987.

Chapter 13

-0-

BOOK VII

AESTHETICS

CONTENTS

AESTHETICS

Illustrations:
Chapter 7. Art Forms Fig. 1. Sense and Art Form
Fig. 2. Apolaustic Characteristics
Fig. 3. Aesthetic Characteristics
Chapter 9. The Sport Fig. 4. Rating Aesthetic Sports

Chapter:
1. Defining Art & Aesthetics 505
2. Art and History 509
3. The Greeks and Romans 516
4. Philosophers on Art and Aesthetics 519
5. Perception, Cognition, and Emotion 524
6. The Apolaustical & the Aesthetical 530
7. Art Forms 533
8. The State of Art 537
9. The Sport 546
Bibliography 557

CHAPTER 1

Defining Art & Aesthetics

Aesthetics is that branch or science of philosophy that deals with what is beautiful, in more ways than one. The essence or sense of what is pleasing in aesthetics has two components, first, that which is pleasing visually, to the ear, etc., i.e. to our senses. Second, to our sensual, emotional and cognitive response or those feelings we have concerning reality, human nature, morals, values, happiness and living a full life, or its meaning to us personally in a socioeconomic sense, is *aesthetics.* We have sensed, "What is it?" and mentally, "what does it mean to me or others?" They are the two representations an aesthetic artist attempts to portray in his work. These are the two questions most viewers ask of an aesthetic work perceptively/ emotionally, and reflecting consciously to understand. 'How do I feel?' and, 'Why do I feel that way? The philosophical terminology is art perception, a value judgment, and may become an identity of one's philosophy, or learns something new.

Art is a form of representation or imagery, i.e. to produce something that we find emotionally beautiful. It is the science, technique or skill of the artist to produce an image of something that is beautiful, pretty, appealing to the senses, or *a design of beauty.* Art does *contribute* to the concept of aesthetics, but is incomplete except in its idea of unique design only—or as an instruction to artisans—those who create and deal in such art in design, advertising and commerce.

Most philosophers, critical writers and artists today and in history used the terms 'aesthetics' and 'art' interchangeably. In ancient times, art was the word associated with producing things of beauty, body adornments, artifacts, drawings and paintings, sculptures, vases, plays, acting and architecture. In literature, art is associated with poetics, novels, plays, documentaries, or what is written. In the performing arts, there is the dance, staging of plays, music, filming of literary works, Olympics, and live games. Television may be an art but only in the sense of its choice of art to be displayed and its scheduling to effectively reach the public. All craft endeavors were thought of as an art form, such as the art of doing one's job, bringing entertainment or creating hand made products or artifacts for the public.

Almost all other art skills are employed in those things that have a utility value. They are things that are made by hand or manufactured, such as shoes, clothing, vases, dinnerware, furniture, kitchen utensils, etc.—useful things. They were, at one time, were produced by artisans or craftsmen with hand techniques that were and still are to some degree much admired. The sophisticated elite has usually looked down at this sort of artisan since he worked with his hands, but the artisan who created artifacts and jewelry had more prestige.

However, the visual works of the artist in painting, sculpture and some architecture has been considered as the 'fine arts.' The visual arts affect our sense of sight in painting and both our sense of seeing and touch in sculpture. If our emotional reaction, is to sense only that which is beautiful, i.e. gives sensual joy as opposed to the ugly, then it is 'art'.

In the act of seeing a beautiful work of art, all our sensations form into percepts and perceptively we apprehend the reality of the work of art. It is this awareness of the work that implicitly gives us a feeling it is beautiful—i.e. visual joy. Our first mental reaction is emotional—joyous—which in actuality is a lightening glimpse and scanning our memory of anything relevant we might have concerning the image being viewed. There is an emotional immediate value judgment response in a second, like a computer. The same process is evident in every sense, hearing beautiful music, the scent of ones lover or the smelling of good food, there is a whole range of tastes from sweet to sour and there is those feelings of being touched and touching a feeling of the heart in love. Our next mental action as a human being, is to identify what was witnessed and what it means. It is to sense only, *or*, to sense *and* find meaning, which is the 'fine art' conflict.

When we begin to identify what was joyous and why, one school of thought is that we identify what the artist did to make it beautiful. One should look for definition in design, color, contrasts and the like as well as balance, unity, and harmony. The image or what is represented is not as important as the expression (impressionist, etc.) and the organism of all its components (how well every thing goes together), that is to attend only to the constructive features of art, i.e. their forms, etc.. Even if all the elements of the artist's skill is not evident, this is not criterion for rejecting it as art since all artists are individuals of special skills, ingenuity, imagination, and creativity. Excellence in one area makes it art. The extreme of this thought is when we see a large framed canvas perfectly painted in a kind of pink color. Art here is to be a visual experience only and any attempt to imply meaning to the work, they say is meaningless. But the meaning is in the color and how that makes one feel.

The conflict is; is art or aesthetics only about the art itself with meaning in its execution to attract attention only, with no meaning in moral and values. Or is art and aesthetics a science of creating art that has meaning in morals and values, as well as its artistic execution. We will explore the history and the conflict of art and aesthetics.

The other school of aesthetic thought began millenniums ago in

Paleolithic Art about 30,000 to 25,000 BC. A small figurine, dated about that time, was found in Lower Austria near Willendorf and is one of the earliest works of art. The 'Venus of Willendorf' figure, four and one half inches high, made of limestone, was of a very voluptuous woman standing with her arms across her huge breasts. She had great buttocks, belly and genitals, which prompted artists and many people to assume the figurine had meaning, i.e. 'as a fertility symbol.' [1] Since man had no concept of fertility, at that time, that assumption is highly erroneous. Other 'Venus' figurines, dated around 22,000 BC, were carved in stone and ivory, with one holding a horn of an animal and voluptuous, is likewise mistakenly interpreted as a 'fertility' goddess. Having no knowledge of how pregnancy occurred, there was no thought of prevention, and having babies, for any woman was an uneventful normal function except for its gender surprise.

The discovery of the 'Venus' statues gave us the evidence of the earliest art, but its meaning to Cro-Magnon man was actually, other than fertility and certainly not religiously motivated. It is not surprising that the very first carvings were of women, obviously carved or sculpted representations of a male's most prized possession. Though men joined a Cro-Magnon tribe to take part in big game hunting, it was by an agreement that he and his family be autonomous. Big game hunting was his means to supplement his own hunting or the other way around. In any case, he was good at both and his family was well fed. His mate was fat, not having to run and participate in chases or scavenging for meat. She may have been a sign of health, and empirical evidence of his prowess as a hunter and provider a sign of wealth, being sexually attractive to him, soft, comforting, or perhaps they were humorous exaggerations.

Many men today are likewise attracted to voluptuous females. Also, it is difficult to tell whether such a voluptuous woman is pregnant until she gives birth. 'Venus' may also be a representation of man's greatest mystery, her ability to give birth—create life. As such, Venus is also empirical evidence of man's, early attempt to create an aesthetic work of art. It was the next step for a toolmaker, in a Stone Age reasoning mind, to be challenged and sculpt something all could recognize and admit was skillful and meant something. He did just fine, he gave us art, and a message of his skills, to hunt, and carve what he felt, by trying to tell everyone what his woman meant to him about twenty five thousand years ago.

CHAPTER 2

Art and History

The 'Venus' sculptures, mentioned in the last chapter, as a first in their time, perhaps did more to motivate the 'artist' in others. They were all experienced craftsmen, and we can imagine the indignant mate who may say 'Look what he made for her!' or the vixen ask, 'Can you carve one for me?' Many such figurines were found in Europe and in "Arctic Anthropology" (1967) 'Paleolithic Art in the USSR,' Z.A. Abramova reports of hundreds in Sibera, Crimea, Caucasus and sites in the Altai and Ural Mountains. [2] By the late or upper Paleolithic times (16,500 to 12,000 BP), not only women but also animals were also favorite art objects. Stone Age people experienced in flaking tools for hunting, fishing, and trapping, their inclination may have been, at times to apply those skills to make things of beauty for body ornaments, gifts to loved ones, and carvings of their quarry in the hunt. It was intimately tied to their economy, their family and social life or to their clan mother.

Man, having no concept of fertility, the primitive looked upon himself as the head of his clan and loving his son or daughter was completely devoid of any concept of 'blood' relation. It was purely a value issue of loving his mate, a psychological, epistemological, and metaphysical bonding to his woman. He was naturally tied to her, and the children, nurturing their well being, and to defend her and her child as *his*. Later, he would carve pendants, beads, headpieces, and other body ornaments for his woman whom he revered above anything else. We may have overlooked the possibility, that women may have created some of this art.

For millions of years the primitive saw the colors and shapes in nature, such as flowers, or looking at the earth from high on a hill, and they were in awe, even by a cowrie shell. But if the first artist carved something they could not identify in nature they might identify it as another stone. There is little psychological motivation—to identify the perception such art may cause. However, they have carved such a stone, because it was what they *valued* and kept that we have found because it was *meaningful* to them—"Venus."

Carvings of some animals, which were of different species not found in that particular region, suggest the artist may have immigrated. There are carvings of animals that were plentiful in that area which were tied to their survival. Did they carve it to teach hunters of their quarry or as a representation for others to learn from, or as a learning toy for the children? Were they cognizant of teaching methods that the real experience or its representation could help teach? There can be no doubt that from time onward there would be a challenge to improve those skills for pride in craftsmanship and artistic reasons. Was there competition among toolmakers to make something better, unusual or something only he saw at one time?

The paintings and carvings on stone walls and in caves had practical motivation, and in most respects, not just a learning tool to identify for those who never saw the animals, but also for strategy or to devise the best way to entrap, employ weapons, and chase the wounded. Like all skills, the drawings were improved in succeeding generations by painting over or adding significant details to help teach. And much later, one could suggest that paintings on the walls for art's sake, may have been a motivation to make something better or more realistic. Scientists find *no* evidence of spiritual or mystical motivation in early artistic development.

As human progress in the tending period led man into agricultural and animal husbandry technology, so too, did the tools of the economy change. In the very Old Stone Age, there was a variety of tools for scavenging animals such as flaked stones for cutting, striking clubs of bone, large stones, with one sharp edge called cleavers. They fashioned anvils, hammers, stones, and hand axes to attack smaller animals. Their design, shapes, and workmanship improved for two million years.

About 50,000 to 30,000 years ago when Cro-Magnon began big game hunting, we begin to find spear points, evidence of the bow and arrow, fish hooks all fashioned from stone but also bone, antler and ivory. The agricultural period (as early as 7,000 BP) saw the development of the new stone tools for turning or pick axing the earth. As farming became more successful in the Mid East and Egypt, the Old Stone Age materials were increasingly becoming obsolete as man began smelting metals with the better control of fire.

By 18,000 BP, Cro-Magnon's success in big game hunting decimated the large herds. Cave paintings after that date ceased and much later the few that have been found were perhaps for artistic reasons—copycats, or to illustrate bygone days—history. We also begin to see sculpting approaching full three dimensional forms as in the two Bison in a cave at Le Tuc d'Audoubert, France. In the Neolithic period, (12,000 to 7,000 BP), we have discovered human figures (no longer stick figures) of full human shapes in a cave at Addaura near Palermo in Sicily. Its meaning has been interpreted as a dance or possibly depicting torture. However, it appears by the failures to complete many of the figures and some distinctly being carved over others, it may be that the artist was practicing or perfecting his technique. Perhaps they were the precursors to hieroglyphics in story telling, or just to practice carving in stone. [3]

The New Stone Age from 10,000 BP, to 5,000 BP, was the beginning of Neolithic Art. New materials were being sought in Sumaria and by 6,000 BP; they were experimenting with, metallurgy and entered the Bronze Age. The Sumerians had by this time harnessed the horse to the plow and used horse drawn wheeled carts. Vegetation, grains and other agricultural foods could be kept for long periods if stored where insects, rats, etc., could not get at them. First, they made bowls or containers. Then the art of ceramics, the fashioning of bowls or jars and the potters' wheel was invented. The clan mother drew a design, colored with dyes on her jars, etc., to place a mark of ownership on *her* property. Usually, by unique markings which *no one* dared copy, it was her signature. The result was, it became more complex or with pride in workmanship, ever more beautiful. What we unearth from such times, we now think artful perhaps was just practical.

The Egyptians were scientifically far behind the Suzerains; Egypt's pharaoh's, priests and scribes controlled food and technical arts. It wouldn't be until 3750 BP, when they were invaded by the barbarian Hyksos before they began using bronze or wheel drawn vehicles. In Sumeria the witch doctor or priests, dating about 5,000 BP, were in control and moving produce into the temples to be portioned out. But in Egypt, burial cults and building of pyramids became their technology. Artifacts or 'Powerfacts' became a mark of prestige for the Pharaohs and their priests, retainers or scribes who employed the artisans.

There would be for every religious cult to follow, only that which is of immediate value to the power of the theocracy could be valid. It was the beginning of the conflict between science and religion. Each new discovery would have problems of control or may conflict with their god's theology of existence. It was their paranoid fear to be wrong or in error and destroy religious credibility, *knowing* they had very little in the light of reason.

The pharaoh controlled Egyptian art in the Archaic Period and the Old Kingdom, 5200-4200 BP, and the artist was fed and depended entirely for his existence by the state. His motivation, creativity and competitiveness were to serve and please the pharaohs, and the state's elite. For that he was rewarded at that time with the privilege that when the pharaoh died, he took much of his art and probably the artists were buried alive with him. Did they all go happily? Evidence shows in the African Sudan that some favorite wives of kings were placed on tables in the burial vaults and had their arms and legs broken. Ironically, we see the artist today begging the state for employment (in art endowments) and obviously, because he lacks skill to make an honorable living in his art. Such people help create the poor so that he may be rewarded grants to be frivolous.

In Egypt, hieroglyphics, pictorial representations usually recorded the pharaoh's life. The artisans depicted the glorious life and events in the reign of the pharaoh, no doubt authored and scrutinized under the direction of the pharaoh or his successors. For successors, to guarantee their inheritance of a throne paid particular attention to glorification and being buried with vast amounts of wealth to be taken with him to his grave (to deliver to the gods). It also perpetuated the belief in an after-life for the poor innocents. Guaranteed was that his heirs would have to do likewise during his life and he would complete much of his tomb according to his taste, giving an account of his god-like reign. As for meaning or truth in the hieroglyphics, sculpted reliefs (raised carvings on slabs), friezes (in architecture sculpted cornices or decorative bands on walls) and statues, one would be extremely naive to believe the stated or implied historical accounts of a pharaoh, and their scriptural representations.

It is evident that artisans in Egypt were talented but were also limited creatively. They were adept at making a frieze or relief but not of large freestanding statues of people. Most large statues of pharaohs and kings in Mesopotamia were almost three dimensional but carved with the back still attached to part of the larger stone (similar to a large relief). They were unable to extend arms out from the body and had the ability to only bring one foot slightly forward to denote action. Facial detail was good but their expression up to 4700 BP, were expressionless—vacant. Most were carved from limestone, diorite or sandstone, grainy porous stones, easier to carve than harder stone, granite or marble. Small tiny sculptures about 25 inches high or less had far more detail.

The only free standing statute is of the Fifth Dynasty of Kaaper from Saqqara, 4400 BP, made of wood. It was however, the most realistic work of a pharaoh with one foot slightly forward as if in the act of walking, one arm down the side attached to the lower hip with his left forearm extended, holding a staff. He had a potbelly and a smug expression. [4] Artists solved the problems of facial expression from 4500 BP, and beyond, but most were limited, most likely by the pharaoh, to show stern faces of authoritarian leadership and the seriousness of the gods. There were no pleasant, smiling, or happy pharaoh faces.

By 4000 BP, there is evidence of more sandstone and granite increased in use. The granite statue 1950 BC, of Princess Sennuwy at Kerma Sudan over five and one half feet high is represented as sitting with her back and feet placed on a huge block, her upper torso is three dimensional sculpted all around from her buttocks to the top of her head. The arms are straight without anatomical detail of shape, close to the body and extending over her upper thighs. Her face however, is appealing with the hint of a smile. [5]

The Egyptians never did solve the three dimensional, free standing, arms extended or legs to show action. The Famous bust of king Akhenaten's queen Nefertiti (3360 BP) made of limestone is painted expertly and shows an anatomically long graceful neck and facial features exceptionally well sculpted. Her facial expression is also smug. [6] Later (3360 BP), king Tuthankhamen ('king Tut'), probably a half brother of Akhenaten, died a young teenager between 18 and 20 years old. His tomb was found in 1922. King Tut's tomb has been the *only* one ever found intact. The excavation revealed a fabulous array of beautiful art objects. The coffin was of solid gold weighing 2448 pounds, the cover of which was a carved a polished portrait of the young king. [7] If this king who reigned only a few years being of little significance in history, who was buried in such splendor, then the amount of wealth that was buried with the greater and more revered pharaohs, can only be imagined. The regret one feels about the 'find' of king Tut's tomb intact is that the grave robbers missed that one.

Egyptian architecture of funerary temples and colonnades were huge and imposing, made of sandstone. The columns were carved or fluted to imitate the bark of palms that supported huge stone beams and roofed over with stone. The pyramids were colossal, symbolic of great power, pointing high as if into the heavens where the pharaoh would ascend to the afterlife. Today's extraordinary high churches, temples, and structures with spires in order to influence one emotionally that the soul will rise to the heavens. The Sphinx at Giza was built about 4530 BP, of sandstone, a huge body of a lion with the head of a pharaoh, measuring 65 X 240 feet. The Sphinx implies power of the body and head of a lion, like the king of all animals, a simple representation of the pharaoh's reign of power ruling over his land and subjects, a lion king.

Another huge pillar statue of the pharaoh Athenaten, at Karnak, is sculpted with accusing or suspicious half-closed eyelids, narrow face, with large Nubian lips closed and drawn slightly down at the ends seems to be looking sternly into the evil souls of his subjects. [8] All artifacts and luxury were the domain of the pharaoh and his elite, a symbolic meaning of wealth and power. All architecture was designed to overwhelm and humble the innocent into believing that the god-king was bigger than life and more powerful than any one in his kingdom and only *he* knew the gods, something mere man could never know, but only believe or have faith in his pharaoh's word.

Mesopotamia was a hybrid of Egyptian deity and diggings have unearthed a similar society. Their architecture and burials were not as imposing as in Egypt, but the kings ruled with similar pomp and authority. Mid-East deities ruled with the same attention to the arts, and confiscation of the people's food production. The same scenario took place with Christian popes, the pharaohs of their time for a thousand years, held people in poverty, and art was forever to be dominated by religious rulers.

CHAPTER 3

The Greeks and Romans

By 3000 BP, Egypt was in decline and Greece was awakening. The Greek gods were not omniscient, more like humans with problems of love, infidelity, conflicts, and deception. For the Greeks, no man ruled the earth, nor did Zeus, king of gods, nor did they think of an afterlife. Greek artists sculpted from limestone but soon, between 2800 and 2700 BP, they turned to marble. Although some of the early Greek sculpture did not match Egyptian art of 2000 years before, by 2600 BP, we find full standing sculptures, ten feet tall, such as that of Kovros of Sounion. They were of *marble*, with space between the arms and body, but with hands still attached to the upper leg flanks. [9] Figures were stiff looking, much like Egyptian sculpture, but anatomically (a lot naked!) strikingly superior. The Greek artisan was obviously free-lance, not under religious or state control, and this is reflected in the fast pace at which Greek sculpture developed in about 700 years. It was in far less time than in Egypt where little progress had been made in 3000 years.

Greek artisans soon solved the problem of extended arms showing natural action, muscles, or pleasant smiling expressions, depicted in a work like the Oriental Archer of Aphaia (2510 BP), made of marble. Bronze statues of the magnificent nude god Zeus and the famous Discus Thrower show their success in studying anatomy, fully extended arms, action and the materials to create beautiful works of art. [10] Greek architecture far surpassed anything that Egypt or Mesopotamia had ever created.

Greek paintings of people showed the same realism of anatomy not found in Egypt. The Greek saw the human body as something beautiful, where the Egyptians and Sumaria looked upon it as ugly—

to be draped without form. By 2228 BP, Roman ambassadors went to Athens and Corinth and began their exodus into history, and by 2140 BP, the Roman Empire consisted of Sicily, Sardinna, Corsica, the two Spains, Gallia Transalpina, Africa, Greece and Macedonia. Classical Greek art and architecture had influenced the known world when Alexander the Great built the city of Alexandria, then Rome came and learned from the masters.

After 1999 BP, Rome struggled to maintain its power and Christianity was invented by the empire to counter the Jew's religion on the Italian peninsula. In 1932 BP, Linus became the first Bishop of Rome. By 1540 BP, much of the art was architectural, with construction of huge basilicas, cathedrals, and palaces for popes, kings and emperors. The church controlled all art forms as was literature and scientific works. There was a profusion of 'Madonnas' and religious subjects all clothed, except for the mythical Jesus in a loincloth. It was just another pharaoh's fairy tale.

The 1400's mark the beginning of the Renaissance and a beginning in humanizing of the arts. Michaelangelo, DaVinci, and Cellini were still dominated by church commissions. By the 1500's, the High Renaissance period, Luther lodged his protest in 1517 against the sale of indulgences—he believed in the church and only wanted to reform the Roman Catholic Church. He was summoned before Cardinal Cajetan in Rome, where he refused to recant his objections. In 1519, he questioned the infallibility of papal decisions. Luther was cross-examined by the church, banned from the holy Roman empire and was imprisoned in the Wrotburg, where he began his German translation of the Bible.

When Luther returned to Wittenberg, he condemned the iconoclasts and fanatics, and completed the translations of the old and new testaments. Hans Lufft, over the next 40 years, produced over 100,000 thousand copies of the Bible—it was the first time in their 1500 years history that people could read the word of a mythical god. The Egyptians saw their gods and writing in hieroglyphics that were carved in stone–*if it was carved-in-stone they believed that it must be true* that same *mentality* transferred such belief to the *printed words* on papyrus or paper, i.e. a bible. The Polyglot Bible, in Latin, Greek and Hebrew, was published in 1522. It was the *art* of painting, sculpture and literature in mythology that for thousands of years their fantasies has become imprinted upon the minds of most as being real. Art was form of entertainment, to see picture or sculpture show of mythical beings or people and places they never saw, just imagined, and art was meaningful to the Egyptians, Greeks and Romans. In 1525 however, Luther married the former nun, Katherine VonBora—which obviously has nothing to do with art.

The Renaissance was the rebirth of invention and art. Although it was still dominated by the church, the hold on tradition was broken with new techniques, inventions, and subject matter. The High Renaissance was a period of creativity in music, composition, and astronomy (Copernicus in 1512 calculated mathematically, that planets turn around the sun). There was the discovery of the Americas in 1492, and the 1500's were marked by scientific excitement over the New World when Magellan circumnavigated the globe. In 1615 Galileo faced the Inquisition that Pope Paul III established in Rome to discover, try and judge heretics. It halted the march of reformation, which was now called Protestantism, but only in Italy. The genie was out of the Christian holy grail and progress in science, culture, economy, and the arts exploded.

We won't belabor the progress during this time, but it is a matter of record. The church only suffered a reformation of some sort, but its tenets imprinted in man from birth had a hold over the minds and wealth of millions. What the Renaissance did was to begin to free man from a pharaoh's absolute power over man's mind and wealth. It was the beginning of the age of reason. What was being questioned and resisted was church insistence that art, all painting, sculpture, etc. must represent, ultimately, religious dogma, and conviction. However, the result was the artist would discard the religious, and all other convictions as well.

Johann Joachim Winclelmann (1717-1768), in 1755 wrote, 'The stories of the saints, the legends and metamorphoses (mythological tales etc.), have for several centuries been almost the only objects of painters. They have been varied and contrived in a thousand ways until finally the connoisseur of art is bored and disgusted.' [11]

Gradually art would be for art's sake and from that time up to the present, they would struggle with the idea that art was not a product of strict or fixed firm beliefs—something that had meaning but only for its own sake. They would attack and reject their traditions of religion, per se, and like 'throwing out the baby with the bath water' throw out any convictions about life—morals and values. Art would take the 'moral high ground' and be for *nothing*. Here is where reasoning may have gone wrong in the arts. To review the conflict, which is rather ridiculous, we will go back to learn what the philosophers had to say about art and what it should mean to mankind.

CHAPTER 4

Philosophers on Art and Aesthetics

Most philosophers had something to add to art in insight or as critics. Plato had problems with representation, citing that an artist's rendition of an actual object was true and untrue at the same time. It was true, being an image of an actual object, but untrue since it was not the actual thing. In some way it always falls short of the actual image. Therefore, he saw all art as imitations. As for knowledge or any group of the eternal forms (innate or arch type knowledge) from art, to the writers of Plato, they would be imitations of imitations. However, art, as a good was placed high in his sense of beauty, so they wrote of him.

It is difficult to give credence to the image of Plato's thought being written some 1800 years after his death. Ancient historians such as Lacteris mention Plato as a philosopher, but with no reference to his 'writings' or details of his life by Florentine authors. They portrayed Plato as 'all knowing' of art in that he supposedly at one time took up art and was an accomplished one, therefore speaking with authority on the subject. We can discount all this, it obviously being a fabrication, and we may assume any argument he puts forth was perhaps credible in Florence about 1500. The innate, intuition, or even given by a god was believed to be sources of knowledge in 1500 and throughout our recorded history. Artfully, the Florentine writers produced a glorious fictional myth surrounding a historical figure briefly mentioned in history. 'Plato's' insight that art is both untrue and true or imitations of the actual thing, is moot. It is a universal obvious expectation of any one being shown art in any form, even children.

Aristotle composed the Poetics in 347-342 BC, which concerned the written art of literature, particularly poems. He understood the image or imitation as naturally pleasing if it is recognized as such. Imitation was to Aristotle, if recognizable of any object, is learning, i.e. *a pleasant way of learning*. Therefore, the basic aesthetic experience is cognitive, not of the construction itself, but of what the observer may learn. The *motivation* for the observer, reader, audience or listener *is that humans find learning pleasant*. To be entertained (beautiful artistic expression) at the same time, a *most* pleasant meaning. The skill of the artist or the teacher is to create interest and teach. If the artist wants to create interest only and his message is, 'how to create interest,' for the viewer to ask, "How did he get my attention?" Then that is up to the artist. In theater, the artist may only display acting technique, or the dancers only their methodology. The movie should be of no story or impart any meaning in morals or values, but a demonstration of acting skills or it cannot be called art. What is a poem without a meaning in morals or values?

Aristotle took the most difficult of arts, the poems and the *tragedies* of his time, to analyze and critique. He understood that art could promote pleasure or enjoyment by coherence, concentration, plot, and that it was in accordance with nature. The author or artist must know human nature or something of the nature of his subject that it is a probability or a necessity. A poetic tragedy is an unpleasant expression and there is a catharsis or by tragically emotional events of the characters, we purge or purify ourselves of what is impure or undesirable. In this sense we learn what is impure, the inevitability of irrational thought and actions which means, we may learn by unpleasant and pleasant experiences. It seems that a tragic poem, or theater there is a kind of poetical whipping, to teach us a lesson, in morals or in meaningful life values.

The Stoic Philosophers Zeno, Cleanthes, and Chrysippus also dealt with poetics. Stoic Diogenes of Babylon and Cicero were concerned with beauty. They held a delight in beauty is a rational uplift, of our soul, and is an 'ethical' advantage or poetry's primary justification.

Epicurus thought art did not affect the soul 'ethically.' The pleasure of the arts in the very early centuries in the Epicureasn and Roman period, thought, technique, and form transform the soul to investigate style and form, i.e. art, an emotional motivation. Plotinus, however, saw beauty in what is seen or heard, and in good character behavior or what gave comeliness to art. He also felt the artist to be able to imitate nature to add to where nature lacks, in art called natural idealism.

Christian art during the Middle Ages was a copy of a pharaoh's use of artistic expression as giving meaning to scriptures literally, 'ethically', spiritually or mystically. Much of art was symbolic—or metaphoric (something representing something else, in visual art—or literal figure of speech, to mean something else), to denote logical justification much in manner of pharaohs. Christian art depicted Christ and his family in the apostles, the birth, Mary, and the death, many in halos, where all art was to be motivated by the bible.

The Renaissance was more humanistic with an end to live ethically, successful, and happily here on earth. Humanists sought to civilize themselves and in art, according to Leonardi da Vinci (1452-1519) "The good painter must paint principally two things: man and the ideas in man's mind." The Renaissance philosophy was in the fourteenth century, the dignity of man, a reformation of a simpler deity and the exhilaration of conscious reality. "What a piece of work is a man! in form and moving how express and admirable! in action how like an angel! in apprehension how like a god! the beauty of the world! the paragon of animals!" [12]

Renaissance art was consciously created to give meaning, to be read, to teach, illustrate events, people, morals, and values. Cro-Magnon man drew illustrations to identify animals and strategy in big game hunting for practical utility, the artist followed to create realistic representations of reality. And the signature on a woman's bowl the artist followed to create decor for man's surroundings and utensils of life. So art seemingly took two roads, one practical in his morals and values, the other with some frivolity in decor. But it was a time of some awakening from the oppression of medieval mythical theology, to grasp the goodness of a successful life, instead of suffering the 'virtues' of poverty. Free men with wealth could better serve charity or good will than churches, cathedrals, palaces or inquisitions. There were no atheists, but gods far simpler and kinder with respect to man. Alberti's excellent work on the family, in the Renaissance heart, was man's ambition to benefit from his work, to be moral, and seek happiness in his family values. 'True happiness consists in the possession of both capital and virtue.' [13]

Up to this time, art was essentially meaningful in virtue, and ideas to judge the medium only, rather than any secondary meaning had been argued among artists and philosophers long before the Renaissance. Aristotle's concept of the poetical as an imitation of human action was criticized as rigid or too inflexible. Theorists saw the rules as conforming by including reason for an artful experience. But rather than expand or improve the rules they eliminated them. Anything was art, provided it had color, lines, balance, unity, form, or just throw paint at a canvas. Artists reduced their craft to the concept of design art, for the immediate response or perception only. 'But we must remember that the worth of any great work of art is not something that can be grasped in a moment.' [14]

Alexander Gottlieb Baumgarten in his "Aesthetica" (1750-58) a philosopher of great intellect fully identified, and defined aesthetic art. He coined the term 'aesthetics' as "criticism to taste," setting down the theory of aesthetics aimed at poetry and to implicate all art forms with levels of "sensory cognition." The levels were from obscure ideas to the higher levels of clarity, or the distinct to the confused, but where there is clear confused ideas combined, they could be judged. It was an elaboration of Descartes and Leibniz distinctions. A science of 'extensive clarity' was established as aesthetical. [15]

Baumgarten had reasoned that art and the clarity to cognitively imply social values, and the aesthetical was theoretical, a *science* to be studied and evaluated as a branch of philosophy. He was cognizant of the technical skill in evaluating art, but he was concerned to include what artists had for centuries created in their art, a cognitive awareness of social morals and values. His definition of the science of aesthetics and taste is a self-evident concept, which clarifies both art and implying social morals and values to teach is aesthetical.

Kant, upon learning of Baumgarten's coining of, "aesthetics" as a concept promptly set out to steal it as his own, by redefining the concept aesthetical as the 'science of perception' only. Artists, art lovers, and a host of 'aesthetical' philosophers have been attempting to rob the concept (see Rand's 'Stolen Concept') of aesthetics, as a descriptive definition exclusively of design skill only, is, by any measure, intellectually dishonest, and a gross infringement on Baumgarten's incorporeal property rights. But they cannot steal aesthetics, for its definition is exclusively Baumgarten's or they shall have to kill him posthumously or burn all his books. He created the term and conceptually defined "Aesthetica," and justly, it is eternally Baumgarten's. [16]

If art is to be created only for the sake of art, we are creating something without any purpose. It's like building a kaleidoscope that is unusual, just to look good, or is an oddity even children may lose interest quickly. A work of art that has no relation to reality *is* design and at first glance may be beautiful. However, it is a real creation not seen before, it may hold our attention temporarily and if there is *no* personal cognitive value, one may lose interest with some degree of speed. Only another artist or artisan may appreciate its design and skill more. But its technical effort is of little interest to the general public.

The *artist* it follows then, from art's thesis for art's sake may more appropriately be defined as, "Art for Artist's Sake." It is an idea where the rest of society is isolated. Whereby, those not included in the arts are excluded from their technology like any technician. It is apparent that they have no philosophical message, but may be compiling an instruction manual, for would-be artists. It will be a great help to students, artists, aestheticians, and commercial artistic craftsmen. It is a narrow technical science with little chance for public popularity.

The *aesthete* is one who professes to understand and have special appreciation for what is beautiful, and endeavors, with skill, to construct his ideas in painting, sculpturing, poetics, literature, etc., into practical or meaningful manifestations cognitively, that is, to create an aesthetical work. Both these functions can be measured, evaluated or judged on their merits. Therefore, aesthetes may create poor aesthetical works, in others, exceptional clarity of beauty, a clear cognitive message in concepts of morality or values. It is the aesthete who creates artistic and social synergism in fine art—the art of sensual *beauty*, with some *humanitarian* meaning, being a moral or social implication for mankind *is* the *aesthetical*. The aesthete creates interest resulting in various emotions and reflection. Rader aptly terms the *artist* as an *'isolationist,'* and the *aesthete* a *'contexturalist.'* [17]

CHAPTER 5

Perception, Cognition, and Emotion

Perception is cognition and emotion, they are functions of

consciousness or awareness. We cannot make any judgment perceptively, cognitively or emotionally/intuitively, unconsciously. Any immediate evaluation is accelerated reasoning, not entirely reliable but may be useful in threatening emergencies. But their prime function is to serve as motivation to explore, what was perceived, emotionally, and intuitively, that might be of self-interest, and to identify those (theoretical) perceptions. We usually go to an art museum with the expectation of becoming emotionally surprised, then to find out why.

In Kant's "Critique of Judgment"—'The Judgment of Taste is Aesthetical', his opening statements, 'In order to decide whether anything is beautiful or not, we refer the representation, not by the understanding (knowledge from experience) to the object for cognition but, by the imagination (perhaps in conjunction with the understanding) to the subject, and its feeling of pleasure or pain. The judgment of taste is therefore not a judgment of cognition,..' [18] The judgment of taste is an emotional response to a work of art. It is this perception that his followers may have embraced, the idea that emotion is not cognitive.

The act of perceiving is cognition. Our brain is turned on by our senses (cognition!) (like ignition!), and when we are unconscious or we go to sleep, they are turned off. Whatever emotion is created is a function of memory and will affect our motivation, with or without reasoning first. We cannot imagine something without having a memory bank to draw on. Therefore, the judgment of taste *is* a judgment of *cognition*. Without cognition there is no pain or pleasure. Kant's attempt is to obfuscate the issue.

The 'judgment of *taste*' which Baumgarten was referring to, at that time, was the mental perception of *quality*, *judgment*, or the *faculty* of being *discriminate*. It is in the context (ex. "To get a taste of having to live frugally."), or the quality of having good taste by *experience*. To note Kant's conclusion, "The judgment of taste is therefore not a judgment of cognition." does not make sense—even in his time. Whether it is a fast emotional or slow reasoned judgment both are cognitive, only *time* is the difference.

Imagination is the faculty of imagining or recalling in one's mind, something perceived in the past and identifying concepts of such images. In creating a concept or solving a theory, imagination is a reasoning function to assemble memories to logically make a judgment upon the truth of *what* we have perceived (theorized). Without ever perceiving anything in reality, we would have no imagination. In art or aesthetics imagination is a cognitive reasoning process the artist or aesthete must use in his work by shuffling together specific pieces of memory images to create something no one ever saw before. He can only do this with 'the understanding' meaning it is acquired knowledge from experience. The artist and aesthete's works *are* the result of cognitive judgments and so will it be of those who witness and analyze art. Images in the mind are all from memory. Our perceptive emotive intuitive moment of cognition, is an immediate lightening-like value judgment of our experiences.

A child is born tabula rasa. If at birth or perhaps one month old, one showed the child the most beautiful painting in the world, there would be no emotional response of pleasure or pain (except to drool all over it)—so we know what he thinks of it! There is very little memory experience within the child's subconscious to create an affective state of consciousness of pleasure, beauty, pain, sorrow, fear, courage, hate, love or the like, perhaps only hunger pains. He has only his sense of sight or hearing something (?), and perhaps desperately trying to understand or gain more experience with his mother's nipple.

Amnesia or comatose victims are good examples of the mind's memories and experiences being unconscious. The patient will not recognize nor have any emotional reaction to spouse, children, friends or previous tastes in things. Doctors and nurses look for any reaction emotionally, because it is an indication of memory recognition. Only then, if he should sense something, can he react consciously in any way experientially, with any emotion. An emotional response, *is* a cognitive response, an immediate mental estimate of his experience that sends neural messages from the mind to the body causing various physical reactions. The emotional reaction is a physical reflex to a cognitive value judgment. It is initially, in the beginning but thereafter it should be, 'mind over matter.'

For the artist to believe he is appealing to an emotional sense only is to separate emotional reflex from all experience, i.e. from cognitive and volitional processes, is a natural impossibility. The artist to appeal emotionally must take into account the *experiences* of some *individuals*, the *society* as a whole, or *his own*. To take into account some people's experiences, the best the artist can do is to appeal to individuals with a common interest say in art design, advertising, illustrating, architecture, connoisseur, or to specific people.

To appeal to society as a whole one may understand that many people like curves or the square, men like blue, girls like pink, young boys geometric design, and young girls like—whatever. The point being it is difficult to make design art appeal to a wide group since their experiences are diverse, but may take interest in it as odd, different, or beautiful.

The artist may ignore all, and create designs relevant to *his own* life and just splash on paint, or erect sculpture, perhaps in iron or junk, whatever moves him on a given day he creates his view of reality. Many may never understand or share his emotional responses. We may guess what others think about, but we can not experience some one's sense of life, perhaps a mate may have some idea.

What we call our emotional state are those physical feelings we experience which follow sudden perceptual encounters. Emotions are in a continual mode of change. We feel good about some experiences, and bad about others through out the day. We shift, most of the time we seem to be in neutral. This happens whether we are at home, work or play. We have many 'moods' when conscious, an indication of a consistent vigilant mind poised to make value judgments concerning all events, things, and people we encounter throughout our waking hours. A conscious state is a variable emotional mental roller coaster ride interrupted at the median by periods of reasoning, or sharp spikes of sudden emergencies all requiring reflection, pauses of rest and quick analysis to protect our beings. Being conscious emotionally is mentally, man's first line of defense in his battle for survival.

The mind may receive stimulation unexpectedly, but when seeking knowledge which is evaluated or to transmit judgment as we work there is cause for emotional reaction in success, of being pleased, raising one's self esteem or in failure, evasive actions, or self disappointment. Sudden environmental stimulation, perceptively, may leave little time to make careful decisions or judgments yet the emotional, may be trusted or relied upon when one has had repetitive experience, the basis for gaining skills with an object, technique and/ or our expectations emotionally.

In art, to witness a thing of beauty may initially be judged beautiful, but until we *identify* by imagining and reasoning to understand why it is beautiful, or what it means we cannot make a sound judgment. It is primarily how normal metaphysical epistemological human beings function. This is true in art for artist's sake, and the aesthetical.

In the present state of art many believe, that if there is any cognitive evaluation of a work of art, the only relevance it should have is in its beauty and how it was constructed. Whatever form, shape, balance, unity, color coordination, space utilization, organism, order, definition, etc., i.e. to produce a work relegates and makes art relevant to those who wish to understand the elements of *design* and the artist's *skill or technique* to affect emotional responses. There are few that go to an art museum for that reason and may never use or appreciate such knowledge.

We see designs of beauty everywhere in society from complex logos to background moving designs, as when television stations introduce themselves. In these cases it means our favorite television show will be on. They have designs on cereal boxes to influence buying that turn out to be 'tasty' and which the children identify rapidly. Geometric designs, the round, the smooth elliptical, the deep colors and pastels, the collage, logos, and all the artifacts of pleasing artful creations in all the things we buy and use, make our life pleasant. We like beauty and there is a place in a museum for art for artist's sake, and/or design, but they are *not* aesthetical.

Artists create artifacts such as design art, jars, vases, utility items, furniture, televisions, and our automobiles, are artifactual in nature, and is apolaustical art, being scientific or technical in practice.

Aesthetics regardless of their abstractions, with the intent to create a representation or an expression of something recognizable in natural reality, suggesting implications for human character is aesthetical

In time, art may become irrelevant since it is not in the interest of taste psychologically, morally, and socially for the general public, except in pots and pans, cereal box graphics, and the automobile.

Artistic strategy today seems to reduce the *fine arts* to Kant's idea of an emotional high of something without *any* cognitive interest beyond the thing in it self. It is not unlike creating an emotional high of a hallucinogen, to feel good only, and nothing beyond except suffer a let down, once out of sight with nothing to contemplate. For the technician who must learn how to attract one's attention for some other purpose, this is fine. However, for the general public and a teaching or verification of the moral and good life values, it may give the wrong message. That is, if all that art has to teach is to get an emotional high, then we may *feel good* without mental effort, without searching for reasons of the cause, without ever contemplating what morals or life values are right or good.

When people are happy or feel good, there are reasons and they are usually easy to discover. Just as we contemplate pain, or the reasons for pleasure makes them justified or real. Where unidentified pain causes worry, pleasure without reason may cause us *not* to think, i.e. *not* to search for a justification of why one is frightened or pleased is not identifying one's perceptions, it lacks the simple lesson to think, "what am I happy or sad about?" Or on the savanna, our ancestors asked, 'What's that noise?'

Many families drag their children to the museum with the idea they will become more cultural and learn something good. If there is nothing but an emotional high without meaning we have taught the young that a sensually induced sensation without a meaningful cause is good. It is a simple psychological message that may cause one to translate that to a life of emotional highs, created by whatever means for no reason at all. One doesn't have to think to be happy, no effort, just go to the museum, shoot up the arm and hallucinate, or go find a prostitute to have an orgasm without intercourse. That may not be the intent of artists, but it could be the result, and obviously, not the purpose of the aesthete.

CHAPTER 6

The Apolaustical & the Aesthetical

The Oxford Dictionary of the English Language defines 'aesthetic,' in both meanings in some contexts, from pertaining to sensuous perception, received by the senses, to the philosophy of taste honoring Baumgarten's philosophy. At the same time they outline the popular arguments on both sides and it seems they concede that the two sciences are evident. Oxford quotes M. Pattison (1868) in the 'Academic Organ' recommending 'Two professors of the science of (art) and aesthetic, dealing with painting, sculpture, etc..', and Bain, (1864) 'Senses & Intelligence, 'The first object of an artist is to gratify the feeling of taste or the proper aesthetical emotions.' The statement implies a second object of taste. [19]

The frustration and struggle for both schools of thought is first illustrated by Sully, 'Sensation & Intuition' (1874), 'Aestheticism in their love of simplicity, have persisted in forcing all forms of art under this one conception.' And because all art was dominated by the Christian Church for 1300 years, it had absolute control over art and its representations and whatever meanings they were to imply. The momentum of the church's influence was still evident in 1876. H. Spencer in "Psychology," (1868) would say strongly 'to deal fully with the psychology of the aesthetics is out of the question.' [19a] He qualified the statement with 'fully' to imply both are legitimate. The church would only accept art based on its religious themes to glorify the message of its deity. They took the narrow view that the aesthetical was legitimate art, and art for arts sake not in keeping with seriously joyless devotion to a man suffering on the cross.

Art for artist's sake creates a work that has form, balance, harmony, unity, structure, contrast, etc.. No one may really care how the artist created it or if it is a figment of his imagination, any more than we care how someone built the car or toaster. The artist got our attention with color, lines, etc., the design. Our concern is (now that you got our attention with a beautifully designed car) what are its features, how will it function, how comfortable, how safe or how many miles to the gallon? A piece of art, yes,—now 'what does it do for *me*?' or 'What does it mean?'

It is conceded that the representation must be beautiful and now that it got our attention, what is the artist saying? A person may be in a perceptual emotional high but no one can maintain such a state for five, ten minutes, or one half hour. A perception triggers the cognitive immediately—why do I feel this way and what does it mean? How well the aesthete creates the inference between the art metaphysically, and theme, epistemologically, by making them both expressively clear, is coherence. Baumgarten thought the aesthete unifies the whole, making the representatives of the theme the focus. One may also apply the correspondence theory to further understand and evaluate how a unified whole corresponds to reality.

Baumgarten reasoned quite skillfully, what theologians had always inadvertently applied, and perhaps understood, that in creating metaphysical representation, a means of empirical psychology, was another application to the *theory of knowledge* which he called "*gnoseology*." It is conceded that there is a simpler science that treats only the conditions of sensuous perception. Much of the art world would eliminate all other art contexts from its meaning of art for arts sake. However, *a science or theory of one aspect in field of study or creative endeavor, does not invalidate all others.*

All knowledge is the result of sensual perception cognitively creating emotions, to identify, quantify, and create greater complex abstractions, which have primitively evolved and has been refined into our present sciences. We still want to discover universal truth, certainty, the self-evident and we still possess a good sense of reality—empiricism. We live in the real world, where our survival, success, happiness and long life depends *entirely* on learning a wide range of options.

If art and artists wish to focus their attention in singular perceptual and sensory study and creativity which may be merely design for people in advertising to catch one's attention it is a valid science. Besides, art is free to create whatever will give someone an emotional high, which by the way, lasts about as long as an orgasm. However, a museum or artists showings may lose would be viewers to the aesthetics, of a baseball game. Talk about getting excited and orgasmic over something real, lasting a lot longer, and learn much about fair play, physical fitness, honesty, and why lead a moral life with good values, all at the same time.

The simplistic idea, art for artist's sake, is where one may create a work out of pieces of metals, plastics, and fabrics in round and geometric shapes, form, color, etc.. However, to make it 'fly' from an abstraction into a cognitive experience of simple cultural values relative to human existence, is not unlike creating an aircraft to take to the air. It requires complex mental skill and knowledge of human nature to create a metaphysical representation to teach or verify man's estimation of himself, his cultural legacy, a moral, or the future of mankind. If not, then we reduce art to perceptive ecstasy of which Sir William Hamilton in 1859 suggested, although obviously incorrectly, 'the term "apolaustic" may be a designation for aesthetics?' But this was either facetious or a defining error on his part as art being only an emotional high. It becomes far more appropriate and correct by definition when describing or defining design art and is unquestionably synonymous with 'art for artist's sake' or sensual or frivolous art only. Apolaustic meaning, 'concerned with or wholly devoted to seeking enjoyment; self indulgent,' is the much more synonymous with art for art's sake and a proper name for science of design art or 'art perception.' Apolaustics is a legitimate science in the study of perceptive emotional sensual responses only.

We may here hence-forth found establish the science in philosophy known as, (cap.) "Apolaustic" meaning—1. n. concerned with or wholly with or wholly devoted to seeking enjoyment sensually; self-indulgence. 2. the science in philosophy, of art for the sake of art. 3. the metaphysical creation of a work of art for arts sake only, thereby not includes any epistemological inference in morals or values. 4. the science of design art creation, its techniques, technology, materials, and form, style, color, etc., as a means to please the senses only, or art for artist's sake.

There is ample room in the hearts of mankind to hold respect for all forms of art, art for art's sake, aesthetics, the humorous, sensual, funny, the serious, and the rational or irrational.

CHAPTER 7

Art Forms

Hopefully we've settled the question—there are *two* sciences in that branch of philosophy known as 'art', one science is 'Apolaustic' and the other 'Aesthetic.' As mentioned before, our natural means to survival is to sense, perceive, which is theoretical, and to identify or analyze to create a new concept of what was originally sensed and perceived. That which we imagined as theoretical was emotional or intuitive, and how humans identify or analyze each emotion is through a mental process of reasoning. Art forms appeal to the senses or our perceptions as the following illustrates.

Fig. 1.
SENSE & ART FORM

Sense	Art Form
Visual and touch	Painting, Sculpture
	Utility
Visual	Architecture
	Language
Visual Sound	Literature, Novels, Poems, Story telling, Stand up comedy. Reading, Poets & Authors
	Performance
Sound	Music, Song (music w/words)
Visual and Sound	Dance, Theater-plays, Opera, Movies Singers, Sports, Parades
	Food & Drink
Taste & Smell	Chef, Vintner

Sports?!—Parades?!—While some people were arguing over theories of what art should represent, other activities became artistic vehicles for entertainment and learning, inheriting their bored audience. Parades usually accompanied by a festival are meaningful in that they celebrate and honor people, events in our history, people, or our community. Sports have become the most *meaningful* art form in the twentieth century—a recreation of Grecian Olympic games that were buried under medieval religious art forms for hundreds of years. We will cover 'The Sport' ahead. The problem we face is in the definition of an art.

If we define attributes of art, how do they lead us to their sciences? How do we measure and define sensual response? Where is the science? If we list, and we will below, all that is required to make art forms beautiful, what are the standards or the defining attributes for Apolaustics or Aesthetics?

Winckelmann in his 'Reflections . . .' began a defining process in essays for such attributes as 'Natural Beauty,' 'Contour,' 'Drapery,' 'noble simplicity and quiet grandeur.' There was also 'Working Methods' for the Apolaustic of 'expression,' 'perspective,' 'composition,' or 'coloring,' plus what has been identified since that time. [20] A work of art may have some, all, but obviously not limited to those attributes or characteristics listed below:

Fig. 2.
APOLAUSTIC CHARACTERISTICS

Individuality	= uniqueness - style.
Representation	= of the imagination only.
Non-Representational	= nothing in reality.
Instrumental	= a prop or means to produce sound.
Harmony	= symmetry, unison, accompaniment.
Unity	= uniform, integration.
Composition	= composed, formation, combination.
Balance	= equilibrium, stabilized.
Order	= methodical, organized.
Definition	= in line - color or explicit, etc..
Contrast	= differentiate, distinguish, emphasis, unlikeness.
Variety	= more than one focus, major, minor, etc..
Form	= structure, shape, outline, design, arrangement or idea.
Organicism	= all parts function together, organized.
Symmetry	= beauty itself or of harmony & balance, etc.
Perspective	= three dimensional draftsmanship.
Color	= (un)coordinated, contrasted, complimentary.

There are others such as textures, light, shades and shadows.

All, many, few or any one of the above may serve to teach the apolaustite to create a vehicle to enhance a sensual perception of beauty or any image for the spectator. The aesthete who wishes to touch people's persona must not only create a beautiful image of sensual perception as above, but one that implies the essence of man's morals and/or values. In that respect, he is faced in addition to Fig. 2., with the following, but not limited to:

Fig. 3.
AESTHETIC CHARACTERISTICS

Representation	= something in reality or an implicated entity.
Allegory	= simile - parable.
Coherence	= logical interconnection, concretion.
Correspondence	= all elements in accord with the intended.
Theme	= message, moral, or main idea.
Expression	= the art, shading, color, creativity, uniqueness.
Relevance	= pertinence, fitting, germane, appropriate.
Consequence	= end, result, significance.
Simplicity	= classic, clear, homeliness, elegance.
Myth	= imaginary, phantasy, fiction.
Context	= setting, situation, position.

The synonyms of those above lead to definitions, theory and solution. But if you could carry the above two charts with you to a museum it may be fun trying to make your own evaluation, which may not be that, difficult.

The aesthete has the most difficult task that may also lead him to innovate within the science of Apoulaustics to illustrate new ideas in morals and values. Therefore, the esthete is involved in both sciences, of which each which may be extremely complex to create a representation for a particular theme.

Many philosophers and artisans dealing in art are aware that in the application of such attributes as form, balance, theme, relevance, etc., to art, there is a danger of being ambiguous. Ambiguity, unless intentional, may be a problem and a clearer or more adequate expression may be the aesthete's primary goal and challenge—because otherwise—'Thus painting is deprived of that which is its greatest fortune—the representation of invisible, past, and future things.' What

Johann Winckelmann in his wisdom was saying, in terms of the theory of values in this book, is that the *intangible may be made real through art.* ' . . . he will attain this goal if he has learned to use allegory not to conceal his ideas but to clothe them.' ' . . . his art will inspire him and kindle in him the flame which Prometheus took from the gods.' Therefore, 'The connoisseur will have food for thought and the mere admirer of art will learn to think.' [21]

CHAPTER 8

The State of Art

We may now ignore all those who argue about the meaning of art. The Apolaustic philosophers may work on their theories of sensuous perception, the theories of harmony, balance, color, etc.. The Aesthetic philosophers may work on theories of correspondence, relevance, inference, coherence, etc.. Each should be setting standards in their particular disciplines *and standards of behavior* under the auspices of art, and let the show begin.

Art has always played a great part in our lives. It is displayed, written, spoken, played, perform-ed in all the media, and in our daily lives. The Pharaoh and his art were for the glorification of him and his deity. He convinced the primitive that he was earth's representative of the gods and the most powerful, omniscient, ruler of all. This was the meaning that was implied in sculptures, paintings, and most important, the immense pyramids were built to humble and overwhelm people into submission. There was song and dance in festivals (they loved a day away from the whip) to celebrate the successes of the pharaoh, to show appreciation to their deity for his benevolence. The people were to be both happy and in awe to see even a likeness of their pharaoh in a sculpture or painting. Art was the means that served this ruling elite. That was the state of their media, architecture, sculpture, painting, and festivals of the gods. It was their only *entertainment* for 4000 years.

The state of the arts today is alive and well and those that think social aesthetics has run its course are not living in or not observing the real world. All art, to be art, has a sense of perception which may well include a morale or value representation, If not, then all actors, singers, sportsmen and their plays, movies or games can't be called artists or art—then what? Art and meaningful cognitive learning is everywhere around us for those who use their senses and minds. The artist takes reality and artfully wraps it around our body and senses, as proof that our existence is meaningful, and only then is the ecstasy of our perception justified.

The dancer, the actor, the singer and the musician are performers just like the sportsman con-trolling their mind and aspects of their body to create a representation that transcends the act, dance, song or movie. Therefore, they project from their activities, very powerful and meaningful mental images culminating in exciting emotional pleasure to confirm morals and verify or discover new human values. They are all aesthetic, a beautiful vision, beautiful attitude, beautiful behavior, beautiful skill, beautiful muscle coordination or the consummate inspirational human.

Architecture creates home and work living spaces within our nature. The skylines for our cities, evidenced in many countries of the spirit of free men risking their fortunes in economics that provides our means of survival. We live in homes great and small and though it may not be an architectural wonder, when one drives in the yard it is 'home' and what it contained has meaning in our lives. If it's an apartment, behind that door lies comfort, safety, and the privacy to be naked in mind and spirit, or in 'old sweats' just to relax. Many couples who brought up their families in unpretentious homes would never give them up, except when they can no longer care for it themselves—it holds so many memories, so much meaning.

Literature, beginning with Homer and the classics, to the novels and poems of today, commands a huge market. To be sure, many have the same themes and lessons of life, but there is aesthetic variety in penning new literature for the culture of the times, in a new media or by creating new representations. The oldest forms of entertainment for people, whether it is a classic, detective, love or humorous story, give us some moral or value meaning. The magazines, periodicals, and those that help us in our work or play are saved for when we can relax, pay attention to it exclusively–to be entertained and learn. The newspaper we carry under the arm or in a briefcase, we look for a place to have coffee, light up, and read the news. We read the columnist's views, local news of people we know marriages, births, and the death notices where if our name is not there, we know we have to go to work.

We read the sports and yes, on Sunday, the ads. Its all done aesthetically and cleverly, even the funnies, which some of us save for last or read first—you know. The printed word is alive and well. Even the bad news helps verify and remind us, to reaffirm what is right and good.

Music and song is an influential art form that graces our lives. Songs (music with words), or poetry sung with music, has always been popular which outlives our lives as they become classical. Each generation not only has its own songs but a different kind of music or beat or instrumentation. Each generation grasps the meaning of their time with their songs and style of jazz, the blues, rock, western, and rap. Rap is a modern primitive kind of beat, tone and poetics that originated thousands of years ago.

If we can, in our nostalgia, bring back the symphonies and baroque from hundreds of years ago, then bringing back the primitive nostalgia is also appropriate. If its message is of morals, love, sex, and values, it is valid aesthetics. If it demands or encourages immoral behavior or bad values they will destroy lives, their rap and music. However, much music in hard rock, and rap is good, and rap poetics, very clever.

There was a popular song you may not remember, or heard, "My Happiness." It was very appealing musically, driving everyone wild, radio stations played it over and over and over, until it made us crazy, but it's personal impact (the words of basic human need *'my happiness'*). It was an artful implication representing one of our greatest values in the meaning of life, Human Happiness, it was true art and aesthetics.

Music (without poetics) has been argued to be direct emotional ecstasy with no apparent pre-cognitive analysis. There is no pre-cognitive analysis. However,—*the very first time we hear* (perceive) *a new piece of music* we may be unable to cognitively (identify) or create meaningful images, ideas, events, people, or lovers, because there is no memory of the tune. Nor do we know the mental images, memories or emotions that motivated the musical score. In Mozart's "Requiem," a funeral mass, we may sense his mood emotionally. Therefore, we make an immediate value judgment of emotionally liking or disliking the music based on music we were exposed to as a child and young adult or the music we have come to appreciate as we grow older.

The tones, beat and instrumentation of a piece of music, which may or may not be pleasing to our sense of hearing, but is a new sound perception by which we scan our memory bank. In this emotional construction we recognize the style, beat, even some series of notes, etc., but otherwise never heard score before. That is of course if we grew up hearing such sounds (the style of the times)—if not we may suffer some distress, such as an American who may hear his first piece of Chinese twanging music. If we enjoyed a piece of music, the next time we hear it, in the context of events, people, times, and style, we enjoyed or loved, it may conjure up those memories via emotions. Only then is a clearer cognitive connection made with the music thereafter—"It reminds me of us, when," they were the good times and it had meaning—happiness. The art or style of music, certain instruments, timing, beat, melody, or harmony is learned by the listener and is very personal in preference which, with or without poetics, is established at an early age. However one may *learn* to have an appreciation for other styles of music and differing instrumental arrangements.

Music is sound and a sense that works just like all other sense perceptions. We cannot have a value judgment emotionally without a memory. You may never witness a child, under a year old, tap their foot to music. Its like acquired taste, only in sounds for the ear, tone, beats, in note combinations, or in soft to loud sounds that sets our mood, like a good recipe for the palate—good taste. We learn everything.

The dance is a real live perceptive representation creating in a choreographer's imagination to suggest, imply or enhance morals and human values. The dancer's aesthetic ability to perform makes the choreographer's idea real and meaningful. So it is to the director of a singer in our MTV performance or a play as well as a movie. Movies have been enjoyed for a century and are still alive and well. Films may have some trouble with meaningful story lines—movie making however, has made great strides in directing, technical photography, musical scores, and performers creating credible situations in lifelike representations. When we compare the campy stage acting of one hundred years ago, and fifty years ago in movies, to today's performances, great skill is evident in representing emotions, action and in building characters, yet the quality may vary.

Television is an art form that choreographs programming of news, movies, sports, etc., selected and timed, for audience impact. Television program aestheticians have been creating meaningful news hours of good and bad news, children's programs, sitcoms, talk and game shows, documentaries, comedy, etc. etc.. The arrangers of programs *must* understand the culture, habits, human nature, motivation, and in timing when most people may be in front of a television. It is the culture they sell to. Any attempt to change that culture and the television owners find themselves on the bottom of ratings. We still control our culture, i.e. what pleases and informs us.

However, given all the above, television can influence people who rely on it for all their information, entertainment, news, social correctness, political and moral behavior. Television can control any agenda of those people who watch and believe everything they see and hear on the tube. They have such a captive audience, over fifty, percent, and may have a measure of control of morals, values and political views in the USA.

Movies and television sell sex and violence and although not knowing quite why, it sells—people watch, and hopefully learn. Many people cringe at sex and violence, but if we understand the book on 'Values,' sex and love must be learned early in a child's life, by experience, hearing sex talk and learning about love, marriage and its responsibilities. Television and theater offers an ideal opportunity for them to see a representation, and learn the complexities of relationships. It is a time for parents to be with them to help them through this delicate period, while they are young and curious instead of waiting for them to grow up unsupervised, exposed to homosexuality, or, after many divorces, to finally learn what should have been early lessons without consequences.

Television, i.e. movie violence *is justified* if it is a representation of guaranteeing successful reciprocity. When primitive man had only a club to fight with—that was the means of fighting—someone was an aggressor and the other a defender. The aggressor, who was wrong and immoral for attempting to steal or kill for the primitive's food, women or children, the defender was moral to enact the principle of reciprocity—fight back in a vengeful defense. Today, we are civilized and reciprocate in courts to punish an aggressor to defend our selves or to exonerate the innocent.

The primitive in his time defended himself, fighting the aggressor with all his skill, weapons in hand, with righteousness on his side, and won. *IF* he had a 'TV' and saw this representation on his set, he would cheer, feel good and would understand that it takes skill, preparation, the intellect to understand right from wrong, and to act—otherwise the good guy would be dead or without food. In this case, as most in primitive times, the aggressor received a good blow to shoulder or head and ran away. He might die if he was wounded which may easily become infected, living in such unsanitary conditions.

Millions of year's later, man had bows and arrows, and in the same scenario, the aggressor got an arrow in him—with a greater chance of dying. If Cro-Magnon man were watching it in a 'movie,' he would cheer and feel good about reciprocity. Still later, when men were on horses with shield and sword, the aggressor came with the force of hundreds and hundreds died. Both the vanquished and the victor suffered. Much later, after gunpowder came into use, the robber could shoot from a distance or unseen could ambush the good guy. Later, as *we* watched the movies of the Wild West, the posse caught up with the robber by expertly reading the trail. They cleverly snack up to surrounded him, and when he wouldn't surrender, trying to shoot his way out, and they put a hundred bullets in him. As he died a slow agonizing death, we were happily relieved he was dead, and no longer a danger to the good cowboy and his family.

Today criminals may still have the same weapons as we do. So we must be smarter, stronger with more power, prepared, and knows right from wrong. The bad guy now has machine guns, long distance missiles, bombs, atom bombs, ships and planes. The violence and destruction has escalated to unimaginable proportions from when our little primitive existed on the savanna. What can happen to us is far more violent and destructive in defending our lives and property.

What the *child* may see on television is the aggressor attacking *him or her (they have apathy for the victim)*, with all that weaponry at their disposal shooting, bombing, and firing hand held missiles at them, killing and maiming the good people. In turn, they, fight back to kill the evil men with those same weapons, only more skillfully, better prepared, more fit, and knowing right from wrong. The child is glad to see the evil people running down the street on fire, dying horrible deaths, glad knowing that's what happens if you are evil. It is how we teach morals and the consequences of evil, the best representation in 'show and tell.'

Throughout history the child was told these stories, fables and myths of the good vanquishing the bad. Later, the children could read these stories and they still can, but, but we saw them in movies and heard them on the radio. Today they can read about them, see them in movies, and on television. The child can even be the good guy in a video game to kill or defeat the bad guy.

If a writer or producer creates a violent film and by some

psychological reasoning or twisted sequence of events, the bad guy gets away with stealing from or hurting others, then the story has no moral content for children or even for some adults to watch. If the show of violence represents that violence is going to be met with violence, then the child begins to understand that the bad and evil will not get away with aggression and the good guys always win. If not the child grows up *not experiencing* these truths, without any concept of potential violence or its consequences, by not teaching him the reality and nature of good and evil, his nature has been spoiled. And *he* may just turn out to be an aggressor, because he does not know any better.

We also create unwitting victims who have no concept of the nature of evil and the philosophy of fighting for what is good and right. It is ignorance that causes conflict. We should worry more about the story and its outcome. However, if an immoral person wins or is not punished, it is a theocratic society that will say 'turn they cheek,' and that is bad and immoral aesthetics. But, if the *bad* guy died a horrible death, or got locked up in jail, and then they threw the key away, now that's good aesthetics.

What we have left in the list of entertainment, or pleasant way of learning, includes sculpture, painting, plays, the sports and parades. Sculpture is a limited form of representation or imitation rather confined to human or animal form taking years to sculpt. It has become an antique art form that was challenging and done skillfully which filled a void in people's lives. In early Egypt people wanted to see what their pharaohs looked like and in Greece the beauty of man's body. It all culminated in Michaelangelo's 'David,' from that time onward, much was copied except for a profusion of warriors on horses and gargoyles on churches. Today, sculpture is meaningless taking erratic forms of junk, sticks, plaster and plastic. When a local sculptor was asked what his carrot like form was, he said, "I don't know. I may find out what it means someday."??? By his own admission, he did not know what he was doing. Sculpture has run its course—become irrelevant, except for gravestones.

Painting may also become irrelevant for the same reasons as

sculpture. People have found other means to be entertained and learn. In the past, a portrait or the presentation of a battle was interesting. Today the pictures, illustrations, come to them live or they can take photos of scenes that mean much more to them. They no longer need to commission an artist to paint Grandpa or Grandma they can take them to a portrait studio and get a framed *realistic* picture for posterity. Abstract or design art leaves most people without anything to say or think about. They have to go to a porn shop to see a nude, since nudity, love and sex has been driven underground, or take his children to a ball game to learn and be entertained.

There is a need for artistic experimentation to make beautiful non-representations for artists and designers, also for the elitist, connoisseur, or hobbyist interested in the technique of art. But one suspects that the elite needs only a *symbol* of an elite—the fact that it is meaningful or not, is not critical—only to give the perception of being *the* power elite. Painting, then, is being relegated somewhat to antiquity where only the old, and little of the new is of any value at auctions except to those with elitist 'tastes.' Art museums are virtually empty every day of the week, whereas the science museums, libraries, bookstores, movies, rock concerts and television are doing very well.

The state of the arts is alive and well and the good art seems to be that which is aesthetical, or, we should say the most attended to by the masses. Art as taught in schools, as part of the curriculum, sounds the death knell for the fine arts, everyone is going to be an artist and the competition will keep them broke except for those who receive government grants. Theaters, i.e. live plays, are dead, except for musicals which still has a very special niche in the hearts of spectators. But those arts that may live through the next millennium will be music, the novel, home and public viewing for entertainment, news or information, as well as theme parks and/or vacations and *sports*.

CHAPTER 9

The Sport

There were art and artifacts in Mesopotamia and in Egypt, but in Greece about 1,000 BC, their gods being more human, with little concern for the afterlife, artists were freelancing unfettered by governments. The Greeks improved the arts beyond what a pharaoh could ever imagine. They wrote poems, myths, of people and gods and they were read to in the temples or gymnasiums. To hear or read is to imagine the places or what the people looked like. The sculptures and paintings of Zeus and the gods and of brave warriors in their wars gave them an image, credence, or understanding of the moral and value principles in poems and myths. Their art was meaningful.

Grecians had festivals to honor gods who were only of the imagination (in the mythical sense) and more *equal* to themselves in nature. They had other events as well where every male in Greece was expected to defend his city or state, and military preparedness was of great importance. It meant each man must be physically fit. The young were to train and hone their bodies to withstand the great rigors of war that was paramount for victory.

Military training included exercises or games of combat and every young man was hailed as a defender and honored. Thereafter, and not only for military purposes, per se, but individual pride in ones physical fitness became of great value. The gymnasium became the focus not only for physical fitness, but a center for social and political discourse, and also in events to *compete* for physical endurance.

Games of competition became a sport. The games required great strength, agility, endurance with grace, and an intellectual understanding of the limits and versatility of human action. The Olympic games were first organized in 776 BC, as a Panhellenic contest every four years. Sports are aesthetical by their nature and therefore a valid art form, because we can and must witness its actual performance, affecting our senses of morals and values.

Victory in the games was of the highest honor that glorified man and his ability. Sculptures of athletes such as Myron's 'Discus Thrower' (2450 BP), the 'Spear-Bearer (2440 BP) and a host of others became a representations of the beauty in physical fitness. At the same the game required mental ability to control strength, agility, coordination, the mental acumen of strategy, creative display, and with all the psychological pressure of being in competition with the best for the whole Greek world to see, and judge.

For the spectator, the sportsman is a representation of the spectator's estimation or theory of *the ideal*, in physical fitness, mental ability or *mind over body*, instead of 'mind over matter' as in science that includes the universe. What makes that distinction important is that man may not be able to control *all* matter, but can be master over his own mind and body. And each spectator feels in himself the possibility of that accomplishment because he has witnessed in his own kind.

The sportsmen or women are real metaphysical entities, with the motivation to represent the best in mind and body. And, that in order to make real those imagined virtuous values, he/she must compete *in reality*, an actual performance that demonstrates such qualities in complete control. We know an actor in a play or movie cannot actually perform as the real person he depicts. The real actor can fake it, the sportsman cannot. When a real player wins (given honest empires, judging or scoring), then the spectator (fan) is emotionally ecstatic to know and to have witnessed an actual perfect representation, in real control, of mind over body.

Sports teaches earned values, replicating psychologically that man can succeed, it is possible to be physically able, have complete control over his mind and body, the grace and self confidence to accept loss, and to have perseverance, to try, try again. *Sports teaches morals*—to follow abstract rules—to know right from wrong—in competition, to be fair (just) *always*. In the child's mind, only the *whole* person who is physically able, morally right, with good values, deserves to win in the game of life and especially in his favorite sport.

Sports takes its place among the contemporary art forms, they are aesthetic, and their players as representations—aesthetes. First, we must eliminate as aesthetic or apolaustic as artful, any sport that includes animals. These are *not* sports; cock fighting, bull fighting, kangaroo boxing, horse racing, dog racing, hunting, or rodeos. Training animals to suffer in order to perform for our entertainment is bad art, nor is it immoral, but one of *poor values* for society.

We cannot have a Moral Code or covenant with an animal. It has no concept of its abstract principles nor can it honor or be trained to respect the code. It can only perceive our instructions, and usually by mistake, but cannot identify its concepts. As a pet, it need only learn a few behaviors—where to go to the toilet, eat, and sleep. Whether it is a pet or assisting us in our work we treat them equally physically in a humane way because of their value to us. A Seeing Eye dog is of good value for both the blind and dog.

When an animal behaves properly habitually, it becomes of great value to us and we depend on its presence as a living thing that 'appears' to be 'loyal' and grateful for our generosity. If it is brought up in the family from a kitten or a pup, it learns its few basic habits and becomes attached to us much like Lorenzo's ducks. It welcomes us to hold and pet it, bringing us great joy and love. A pet knows no other treatment and we owe it that kindness, consistently, as one of great value. This holds for all other animals that we employ, to treat them in a humane manner. It is a question of kindness and sympathy, for we all feel pain, including the innocent, and the more concerned we should be of their suffering, especially those we pet, work and value as food. We must put them to sleep humanely so they may not suffer death in terror and pain.

To rate a sport for aesthetic value is to show what sport where more of us are able to compete, see rating chart Fig. 4., ahead. The greater the opportunity for people to perform the higher its aesthetic value. The *individual performer* being the highest as opposed to a team. The single athlete, with the greatest amount of competition that is possible, is the runner. He has more competition because it is the least expensive and any fan may feel it is entirely within his ability to possibly perform. All they have to do is take off their clothes and run in their underwear. The fan feels personally involved for that reason and for friends or relatives who perform. What makes a fan or spectator find meaning in sports is that, given his situation, it *was* possible for him to be the hero, the fastest runner, the best cyclist or the greatest jumper. No matter how old the fan is, he cheers his hero on, for they feel it is possible. However, a sports child taking part in a sport, his whole future is at stake and may sense failure, it is emotional terror.

Therefore, a child must have some emotional maturity and/or experience in losing in normal childhood, before taking on serious competition. We see this in children, crying, in defeat, when perceiving they disappointed their parents or peers. It is evident in a lack of maturity in players, and coaches who lose their tempers on calls by officials or in player errors. It is also evident in fans that riot after suffering their favorite team's loss.

The next evaluation are those with great expense, like downhill skiing and skydiving, figure skating, golf, tennis, diving, swimming, and gymnasts, require not only equipment, but facilities, fees, and trainers. Expense may limit access to the sport and unless they are wealthy or get a sponsor, it is not possible to participate. What becomes apparent, the more accessible in expense and facilities the more popular the sport, such as soccer in Europe and baseball in the USA, and runners all over the world. The greater the risk to life and limb are justly the least popular. Some high expense, high-risk sports may create a great interest in special events such as boxing championships, Indianapolis 500, motorcycle, boat racing, and bungee jumping.

When human beings are physically competing against one another and there is a great *risk of injury or to one's life*, those sports are at the lowest point of the aesthetic scale. The lowest in aesthetic values is *physical contact competition.* In that category we may place *boxing* as the lowest with the highest risk to injury. *Hockey* seems to be next, and *football* follows. Football's higher position seems to be that there is a perception that the quarterback with great skill and agility can overcome the great forces in the defense of the goal, by running or passing accurately to a receiver. Much has been done to protect them—what is left may be to put them in a suit of armor.

Fig 4.
RATING AESTHETIC SPORTS

Aesthete	Least Expensive	Facility Equipment Expense	High Risk
Single performer	Runner	Swimmer	Boxing
	Walker	Diver	
	Wrestler	Surfing	
	Jumper	Tennis	
	Discus Thrower	Golf	
	Javelin Thrower	Gymnast	
	Pole Vaulter	Ice skater	
	Marksman	Skier	
	Weight Lifting	Bungee Jumping	Bungee Jumping
	Fencing	Sky Diving	Sky Diving
	Archery	Marshal Arts	
	Sledding	Bob-sleding	
	Fishing	Hunting	
Team Performer	Soccer	Football	Football
	Baseball	Hockey	Hockey
	Softball	Ice Dancing	
	Basketball		
	Relay Running		
	La Cross		
	Cricket		
	Boccie		
Vehicle Extension	Bicycle Racing	Motorcycle Racing	
Sportsmen	Skate boarding	Auto Racing	Auto Racing
		Bob-sledding	
		Sail Boat Racing	
		Motor Boat racing	
		Ballooning	
		Air Plane Racing	
Animal Sports	(No Aesthetical Redeeming Value)		

High-risk activities above may be more accurately listed, with an analysis of statistics using studies of sports insuring corporations.

Team sports, where a group of players are in competition with low physical risk, the most readily available facilities, or the least expense is higher in popularity than the others mentioned in aesthetic values. People with special abilities are placed in team positions to be the most effective in the team effort, their performance being choreographed by coaches or trainers. The most popular are baseball football basketball and soccer in that order, ascending in aesthetic value to fans. In some countries soccer is the national game of choice. All team sports are very colorful events from cheerleaders, to the music, pomp and circumstance and the field of play is a beautiful sight to behold. Even the uniforms have been designed with great thought as to their artistic value.

A night baseball game is very exciting, fun, and breathtaking to see—the carpet of green,—straight white lines,—the diamond,–the suited players,—the ads around the perimeter,—the scoreboard illustrated,—the bright lights,—the sounds of human voices in a din and an uproar. Then, as the organ raises the pitch to celebrate a run and the crowd goes wild, with the whole full vibrating stadium under a canopy of darkness. The team is a group effort, in control of mind over body, in a cooperative effort, competing to win and provide entertainment representing human values of skill, physical control, agility, reasoning, and psychological stability.

Lo, behold! The athletic aesthete who cheats, gambles, takes drugs, steroids, is not a good sport when losing, or is not an exemplary citizen, they are no longer held in high esteem. Parents have a hard time explaining to the child why an admired player went wrong. But they have to condemn such athletes, hoping they never see him on the field again. If not, and allowed to play or perform is obviously the wrong message to the child who must have an ideal, to be convinced of the credibility of what he sees on the field is a real man or woman.

Not too long ago Pete Rose was caught placing bets and barred from the sport, and although he was one of the ablest players, was not allowed to play or to be admitted to its 'Hall of Fame." It was the finest lesson the children could learn. The commissioners, owners and sportsmen alike *understood and acted* to enforce the highest standards of integrity among its performers, something unheard of in most of the artistic community. Mike Tyson should be banned from sports, because he is a poor example for as boxer for fans. The boxing commissions and promoters know he is, but are shamefully greedy for the money he will draw to the fights. They are destroying their sport since it no longer has standards of morality or values, to measure an ideal for fans especially the young they influence, and many are losing interest.

To answer those who seem extremely envious, objecting to movie actors, sportsmen, and CEO's, in sports or industry, because of their high earnings is that we find, and must remember, they negotiate by contract—they are all contractors, and they are *not* employees. Actors or sportsmen are the *product that is being bought* and the CEO is a *contract executive* to be responsible for managing the profitability of a corporation. It is they, that sell the public to belly up and buy tickets or invest. The fans buy tickets—to see the *real* player—in person—their ideal in a club's stadium—that sells food, drink and souvenirs at outrageous prices—which never seems to upset the fan too much—"There he is!"—"Look at that sucker run!" Families turn on their televisions for the team with the sportsmen they admire and respect, their ideal. That is why television and advertising rights are worth millions. There are no moral principles or law to govern sportsmen, actors, or CEO's choice of contract, share of profits of the team or company he wishes to negotiate with—unless we want a fascist or socialistic state. Whatever amount of money he may successfully contract for, he has a moral right to, and which he deserves, no matter how *envious* we may be of their success, or the money and stock options he negotiated for.

However, the contractor must be cautious and not hold out too long or bid too high. But if the company or club pays, then they obviously think they know the product, player, employee, or manager will perform. To their obvious dismay, the sports person or CEO may not perform and loses fans or doesn't bring in a profit. Whatever the contract agreed to give them in such an event, they are morally entitled. A deal is a deal no matter who makes it. It is such deals that have given this country its economic successes. They are all enterprising free individuals striving to succeed. It is a lesson for children—and adults. One may lose the game *and fans too!*

To make basketball more popular, the league people may take note of our evolution. Players are taller than 50 years ago when the tallest was six feet. With almost seven footers as the rule, the basket should be raised somewhat. Also, no hand should touch any part of the basket hoop or net. Such changes are usually mentioned by those who have lost interest in the game, and think the 'SLAM DUNK!' ridiculous. With changes, scores may be lower, and the level of skill in competition raised for *taller* players who seem to be the only ones who qualify to play.

The next sport with some aesthetic value are *vehicle extension performers*, usually racing in planes, boats (motor), auto, motorcycle, sailing, and bicycle performers, where the sportsman involves his machine in an extension of himself, against others. It is low aesthetically because it is expensive and some with risk. The bicycle has the least risk and expense, with more personal physical endurance relative to the others, and therefore, outperforms the others in popularity and aesthetic value.

We may learn things such as morals and values in all the arts even though they may not be in a 'Fine Arts museum.' Although sports may never overtake literature, movies, or television in popularity, aesthetically it has a realism that surpasses all art forms. We are not all sports fan, but to a degree cognizant of the big games being played such as the Rose Bowls, Super Bowls, the World Series, the Indy 500, and others, especially the Olympics, We like the supernatural effort and the sportsmanship of games.

Today the sand lot is organized by the state, allowing moms or dads to coach and school teachers officially to supervise and the child seems to be a mere pawn in a grownup's ego trip and a ward of the state. The schools command or rule the free enterprise of the community to organize and control every aspect of a child's social activity including art, music, and sports. There is nothing left for the child to do but follow. They are being socially indoctrinated that the state is the final arbitrator in his values, since that is what they are being taught. The convenience of not being responsible to organize these events justifies letting others do it—the state *wants* the responsibility and lucrative government jobs and taxes. And that is how we build a socialist state.

There should be a sandlot and parents may buy soccer balls, bats and gloves and Let them play creating the world of great sports figures, as they experiment with others how it feels to be their hero. It will be their motivation and burning desire to organize want to achieve in some way what they witness. And it is at time of play that parents *come to watch*, to understand what they do, right or wrong, good or bad, and to tell them *at home* of errors in organization and in play. That is when the parent teaches and helps the child, to overcome disability in skill and how to think in a team effort or in an individual sport such as running, etc.. Parents may give them the equipment they can afford with encouragement, the rest is up to them.

The highest in aesthetic value is the *individual competitor*, in regional and World Olympic competitions. It is where a single sportsman competes with all others in his special sport—*for he or she stands alone* to face all others, as in life, but with the eyes of the world upon him. So too the artist, who must make his display for all to judge. In all the beauty and pageantry of the Olympics, it is the young aesthete who is a true representation of an evolving human, beautiful in form and fitness, with the mental ability to control their strength, agility, and maintain psychological stability (to be cool and calculating).

The young come every four years to perform greater, better, faster, and higher feats than those in the past. With confidence they overcome the huge psychological pressures of the world watching and judging to become what they represent the best in human morals and values. That is why the world watches. The problem for the future of the Olympic Games will be standards being set for entry. For the Olympics to be authentically true to the original games, and gain the widest possible audience, should they perform naked? EH? Recent site scandals involving payoffs to Olympic officials is betrayal and greed, and when all of top management should resign in shame.

Plays, opera, and symphony or philharmonic orchestras are the antiques of entertainment and seem to have a small elite following. Many lament the lack of interest or support for the 'art' industry as though painting, sculpture, plays, operas and philharmonic orchestras contribute to culture's aesthetic health, which is not true. From this writing table, it seems they have been in the service of the elite all along, out of reach financially for the general public. Many say that society is losing its 'soul' but it's the old arts that may have never had it in the first place. People have found their 'soul' in other arts. The arts of radio, television, movies, computer graphics, and sports are affordable and meaningful to our culture. They are edging out the old and bringing in the *new*. The old 'souls' still embrace the ruling elite riding on the backs of the poor with tax dollars.

Television, movies, sports, and art in general, have their work cut out for them in providing meaningful entertainment for the future. The task is, to define and represent what is right morally and good in values, not in a ghost but in reality. Glorify the human spirit, do not humble and sacrifice mankind on the altar of gods. People need the lessons of the real world.

Codify, The Moral Code in the art of teaching principles through all forms of artistic expression. Show the human struggle to be autonomous and responsible for him self and all self-imposed obligations. Create the morally selfish human being striving for the best in ambition, and in his pursuit of values, before he can be generous. It is a new reality to explore—its values unlimited for the truly moral.

Build up the individual, creating a society of one, where man is not a slave to his community, but to those he values most. He does not owe allegiance to all people, to a deity, or the politician, but to his ideal, a *moral* society he can respect. Seek to govern yourselves within the morals or ideals of a Promotional state where the people's struggle to survive is an *opportunity* protected by the moral force of human decency. Tear down the 'Lion Kings,' the 'princes,' 'political foxes' and their immoral 'ethic'—altruism. Teach, the savagery of 'we,' in a theocratic or socialistic ruling elitism, that is bound to create a sacrificial collective culture, immorally ignoring in 'we', that *we* are all an "*I*." Show the result of altruism, the destruction of individual freedom. Do not keep man ignorant—teach what is wrong or bad, right and good—give people back their mind and bodies. It is what moral aesthetic responsibility is all about—if the *naked truth* hurts, or makes them happy—you have their attention and can teach another fact of reality.

There is a whole new universe of right or wrong, good or bad in morals and values, to artfully explore that we felt was there all along. Represent all those morals and values that are an example for the young to learn. Illustrate our philosophy, the "meaning of life", moral success, human happiness, and a productive long life. Show how to gain those intangible values in people, by being *really human*. Find those values that create traditions, customs, and cultures in the *home* and not in the halls of institutions or government bureaucracies. Repeal all laws that provide or control values. Repeal theocratic dogma of sacrifice, their socialistic control of man's mind and wealth. But we are looking to the sky or an imaginary utopia to solve our problems, when we should be keeping our eyes and minds on earth, and our pocketbooks.

Much has been done in the last fifty years to take the mystery out of love and sex, by defining it as a value issue but certainly not in most of the world. We will continue to *build* the nuclear family hopefully in freedom. As artists, apolaustic or aesthetic, they should take the lead away from social planners. Continue to entertain and teach moral necessity and show everyone the way to live, and succeed. Artists must take their rightful place as a guiding force for society, and then let them follow art's bare butts through the twenty-first century. As for the children, don't forget to turn around and egg them on to play, but also to learn every day of their lives and try to be ideal human beings. Teach them, to uphold The Moral Code and to pursue success, human happiness and long life, whilst leaving others to seek their values.

BIBLIOGRAPHY: AESTHETICS

Ref.
No.
Chapter 1

1. Hartt, Frederick; "Art: a History of Painting, Sculpture, and Architecture," Pub. by, Prentice Hall, Inc., Englewood Cliffs, N.J. and Harry N. Abrams, Inc., New York, 1976; Vol., 1., P. 26, Fig. 1. P., 27.

Chapter 2

2. Abramova, Z. A.: "Arctic Anthropology," 'Palaeolithic Art in the USSR,' Madison, Wisconsin, The University of Wisconsin Press, 1967: Pages 87,88,89,90 (paraphrased).
3. Hartt, Frederick; "Art: a History of Painting, Sculpture, and Architecture," Prentice Hall, Inc., Englewood Cliffs, NJ. and Harry Abrams, Inc., New York, 1976: Vol.1. P. 30, 31, (paraphrased) and Fig. 8. Two Bison, and Fig. 11. Ritual Dance.
4. IBID, Pages 64,65, (paraphrased) and Fig. 66, Kaaper.
5. IBID, Pages 67,68, (paraphrased), and Fig. 73, Sennuwy.
6. IBID, Page 137, Colorplate 9. Nefertiti.
7. IBID, Pages 72,73,-138 (paraphrased) and Fig. 85., Colorplate 10. Tuthankamen.
8. IBID, Pages 71,72, (paraphrased) and Fig. 83., King Akhenaten.

Chapter 3.

9. IBID, Pages 107, (paraphrased) and 108, Fig. 145 Kouros of Sounion.
10. IBID, Pages 115, (paraphrased) and 116, Fig. 161 Oriental Archer. Page 120, 121, (paraphrased) and Fig. 173. Zeus. Page 121, (paraphrased) and Fig. 174. Discus Thrower.

11. Winkelmann, Johann Joachim: "Reflections on the Imitation of Greek Works," Pub. by, Open Court Classics, L aSalle, Illinois, 1989: 'VII Allegory' Page 61.

Chapter 4

12. Garraty, John A. and Peter Gay, Editors; "The Columbia History of the World," Pub. by, Harper and Row Publishers, with Dorset Press, Div. Marboro Books Corp., New York 1988: P. 504.
13. IBID, Page 506.
14. Reese, William L. "Dictionary of Philosophy and Religion," Humanities Press, New Jersey, 1991: Page 108, Pierre Corneille (1606-1684), ref. Page 583, and Tragedy (2)
15. Baumgarten, Alexander Gottlieb, "Aesthetica," 1750 to 1758 "Reflections on Poetry," by Karl Aschenbrenner and William B. Holther; 1954 Berkeley Press: Page 78.
16. "The Compact Edition of the Oxford Dictionary," New York, Oxford University Press, 1971: Aesthetics.
17. Rader, Melvin: "A Modern Book on Aesthetics," Pub. By, Henry Holt and Company New York, 1952: P. xxix.

Chapter 5

18. Kant, Immmanuel (1724-1804); "The Critique of Judgment," 'The Judgment of Taste is Aesthetical'

Chapter 6

19. "The Compact Edition of the Oxford Dictionary," New York, Oxford University Press, 1971: Aesthetics.

Chapter 7

20. Winckelmann, Johann Joachim; 1989, Open Court Publishing Company, LaSalle, Illinois: P. 3, 25,33, and 43
21. IBID., Pages 67 and 69.